Crossing
Cultures

Crossing Cultures

*Creating Identity in
Chinese and Jewish
American Literature*

Judith Oster

University of Missouri Press
Columbia and London

Library of Congress Cataloging-in-Publication Data

Oster, Judith.
  Crossing cultures : creating identity in Chinese and Jewish
American literature / Judith Oster.
     p.   cm.
Includes bibliographical references and index.
  ISBN 0-8262-1486-X (alk. paper)
1. American literature—Chinese American authors—History and
criticism. 2. American literature—Jewish authors—History and
criticism. 3. Jews—United States—Intellectual life. 4. Chinese
Americans—Intellectual life. 5. Identity (Psychology) in
literature. 6. Chinese Americans in literature. 7. Culture
in literature. 8. Jews in literature. I. Title.
PS153.C45 O75 2003
810.9'8924—dc22

2003014540

Text design: Stephanie Foley
Jacket design: Susan Ferber
Typesetter: Crane Composition, Inc.
Printer and binder: Integrated Book Technology, Inc.
Typeface: ITC Garamond

For permissions, see page 283.

With love to

My mom—Betty Link
Who got me writing as soon as I could read and still cheers me on

My children—Sondra, Debbie, Naomi, and Howie—
Their wonderful spouses and children
Bilinguals and biculturals all

and—as always—
Joe

Contents

Acknowledgments

Saying "thank you" requires looking back just at the time one is looking forward to a completed project. Writing acknowledgments is, for me, the pleasure of remembering those who helped and inspired me not only as I worked on this book, but also in some cases before there was even such a book in my mind. I refer first of all to my students, especially those in the first course I taught on the immigrant experience in American literature at Case Western Reserve University. From their responses, discussions, and enthusiastic support, ideas became sprouts which subsequent students and classes strengthened and helped to grow. Their writing inspired mine. They—as well as the many international and immigrant students I worked with before and since—are all in some way here. They are far too many to name, and yet a few stand out for their dedication, which went on after the end of the course: Lisa Chiu, Carlinne DiGeronimo, Peggy Johns, Ray Killian, James Lin, and Mina Tabrizi read through reams of their classmates' writing, and helped select, edit, and produce what became a privately printed book, *The Immigrant Experience: Voices and Visions*.

My greatest help came from graduate teaching assistant Donna Gessell (now Professor Gessell), who shared with me the designing of the course as well as its teaching. All this was made possible by an Eli Lilly Foundation Teaching Fellowship, administered at Case Western Reserve by Professor (then Associate Provost) Sandra Russ, who encouraged us "fellows" and has continued to take an interest in our publications and careers ever since. I would also like to acknowledge help at a very early stage from Sau-ling Cynthia Wong, who generously advised me regarding texts she had found effective, and also sent me material.

I was extremely gratified by the interest that then President Agnar Pytte took in the course and the publication. It is most unusual for a university president to give attention to an individual undergraduate course, and to express his appreciation so graciously. I am also very grateful to the university for a sabbatical which gave me time to immerse myself in these literatures and theories in preparation for undertaking a book. I appreciate as well the W. P. Jones Faculty Development Grant which helped to fund my giving papers in Malaysia, and the support of my department and dean for doing the same in China. These were experiences that widened my intercultural horizons, not to mention allowing me the opportunity to get together with many former students on their home turf.

Not many colleagues are friend enough to offer to read a whole book manuscript. Thank you, Suzanne Ferguson—erstwhile dean and chair, always and still good friend, colleague, and cheering section—for your careful reading, your comments, your encouragement, and your friendship. Thanks as well to Joseph Skerrett Jr. for important feedback and encouragement. I also want to express my appreciation to Jay Parini for enthusiastic help and support—especially as he is a writer and scholar I have long admired. Many thanks as well to Andrew Furman for strong and helpful support and for excellent suggestions I have gratefully incorporated.

Footnotes acknowledge those who allowed me to interview them or quote from their papers, but footnotes cannot express my appreciation for their time and their willingness to share their experiences and feelings with me and my readers. I say a profound thank you to them now. I am grateful to the several young bilinguals I interviewed, for their time, for their efforts to answer my questions fully and honestly, and for their permission to quote them.

Much appreciation to the editors at the University of Missouri Press: Beverly Jarrett, director and editor-in-chief, and Clair Willcox, acquisitions editor, who encouraged me to send them the manuscript and saw it through to acceptance; Jane Lago, managing editor, who patiently and promptly answered all my questions and continued to advise me through the editing and publication process; and my editor, Gary Kass—meticulous, thorough, considerate, and an excellent reader—whose cooperative and helpful spirit lightened the whole process.

Carrie Shanafelt, graduate assistant par excellence, has my profound gratitude for getting the final manuscript and documentation in order. Whatever her own pressures, she pushed on with unfailing good cheer, patience, and a smile. Thanks too to Frederica Ward, department administrator, for always being there when I needed a quick and friendly help-ing hand.

Finally, my family—to them I won't say "thank you." Rather, I have dedicated this book to them with love. They have all made me proud of them—given me much "naches." What's more, they always willingly shared me with my work, none more than my husband, Joe—life partner, best friend.

Crossing Cultures

Introduction

This book began as so many begin, before articles or papers or discussions with colleagues: in the company of students. In this case, the discussions began in a course titled The Immigrant Experience in American Literature, which focused on narrative texts written either by those who had left another country, thus crossing national boundaries and cultures, or by their children. While these children may have been born in this country, they were nevertheless living in two different cultures and speaking two different languages. The protagonists of their texts, and, one suspects, their authors, are often engaged in a struggle to negotiate conflicting pulls and expectations. The complicated process of constructing an individual identity is even more difficult for them than for those living in the country where they were born, raised by parents who grew up in the same country, speaking the same language (the differences in "culture" and assumptions from one generation to the next notwithstanding). *Who* one is cannot easily be separated from *where* one is, where one can feel "at home"— ideally, both in the world one seeks to inhabit and in the world one has come from. Such difficulty can also apply to subsequent generations, whose cultures and ethnic roots remain strong and influential.

As we know, facts alone never move us as much as individualized narratives do. George Steiner put it so well:

> It is one of the responsibilities of the novel [and I would include much autobiographical narrative] to chronicle small desolations. These are sold short in that harsh artifice of selective recall we set down as history. Whose birthday party was cancelled by the fires that leaped over Troy? Who, on the Friday after Robespierre's execution, paid the laundress who had kept the great man's linens starched? . . . In the troves and vestiges of Pompeii, it is the form of a dog, wide-eyed with terror,

1

still chained to his post, that numbs the spirit. The skein of experience is
woven of these threads, of the immemorial weight of the particular. . . .
Of all remembrancers, the novelist is most entirely pledged to the mystery of private being.[1]

And what my students were reading, talking, and writing about were all
stories of the particular, of triumphs and "desolations" large and small—
narratives already in the "canon" or at least in the more specialized canons
(such as Asian American, Jewish American, women's literature) that are
every day making it into the more inclusive American Literature Canon. In
many cases, experiences of their own immigrations or their own life in two
cultures affected their responses to the texts. When shared, their responses,
in turn, enlivened the class—not only in the sense of making discussions
more lively, but also of making the *texts* more alive.

What became apparent was that this was a body of literature that resonated—from text to reader, from one reader to another, and beyond
books and classes to the larger community outside our walls.[2] But there
was an almost predictable pattern of intensity of response, ranging from
an immediate, almost visceral response to what seemed one's own story,
to the less immediate response of the reader who was able to identify with
a character or narrator and thus was drawn into the text, but as if playing
a role, sometimes as a participant, sometimes as an interested spectator.[3]
In the first category were those who saw themselves almost directly in the
mirror of another's story. Gina Kopeliovich, a Russian immigrant, for example, wrote of Eva Hoffman's *Lost in Translation:*

> I have never read anything like this before in my life. This book
> makes my hair stand up on end. I feel as though I am reading about

1. George Steiner, "Unsentimental Education," 85.
2. The piloting of this course was funded by an Eli Lilly Foundation Teaching
Fellowship, which made it possible to produce a small book of representative student
writing—critical, autobiographical, informal. While the course was well received (and
has since become institutionalized), nothing prepared me for the response the course
and the "book" generated: the president of the university sent the book to the trustees,
and twice invited my students and me to make presentations at Friends of the University weekends. The *Cleveland Plain Dealer* ran a feature in which two of my students were interviewed. The course was highlighted in the university's annual report,
and six years later was reported on in the alumni magazine. I have received appreciative letters from people I have never met.
3. I use the terms *participant* and *spectator* as they are used by D. W. Harding in
"Psychological Processes in the Reading of Fiction" and by Geoffrey Summerfield and
Judith Summerfield in *Texts and Contexts: A Contribution to the Theory and Practice of
Teaching Composition.*

my childhood, my psyche, and myself. It is scary in a way, that at one point and time another human being felt the same way. There were some passages that were so touching I had to call my mother and read them to her. She will be reading the book soon. Often people ask me: well, did you hate Russia, were they awful to you and your family? I answer that no, I loved my childhood, Kharkov, the park where we went every day, the ice cream parlor next door (when there was ice cream), our summer home, my childhood friends and the fact that my parents did not work so hard. . . . When Hoffman talks about their small apartment that never felt small, I remember my grandfather's 50th birthday party when over 60 people were eating dinner in our living room. No American could imagine that.[4]

When Gina arrived in the United States she was only a few years younger than was the thirteen-year-old Hoffman; she too came from Eastern Europe; she too was a Jew, escaping the anti-Semitism of a country where she otherwise felt at home; and she too had to cope with the loss of friends and place, the strangeness of language and school and classmates. It could have been her story. And of course, her saying just that to her born-in-the-USA classmates made the book more real to them as well.

Where the experience of immigration, or of ethnicity, is the same for the reader as for the writer of the book, the connection (whether positive or negative, sympathetic or hostile) is naturally most immediate: This is my story; this is my family whether I like them or not, whether I'm comfortable with them or trying to get away from them, whether I am pleased with this portrayal of them or embarrassed, or angry at the author for misrepresenting them. Then too, there is the protective stance, rightly concerned that a highly individual authorial voice might be taken as representative of the group (so often, writers are rebels rather than representatives), that "outsiders" might too easily generalize from one situation to an entire culture. In any or all of these cases, the book is related to a reader who cannot pretend to be neutral and objective.

At the next remove are those who are also "other" in some way to the majority culture. They may belong to a racial or religious minority. Their parents may speak a different language or have expectations and experiences very different from those of the mainstream, which might make these parents different as well from those forces influencing their children. "Others" thus are able to share more experiences with the narrators and characters of these

4. Gina Kopeliovich, unpublished student paper, Case Western Reserve University, Cleveland, Ohio, 1991.

texts, and with one another, than with even the most empathetic readers and peers who have never experienced these issues firsthand.[5]

And then there are those who are not of a minority: the "majority," the "mainstream." I have found that there is something in all these books—perhaps only one issue—that anyone could identify with, be it conflicts with parents (the much-touted generation gap), misunderstanding of another's "language" or meaning, religious questioning, or entering the culture of the academy, often so very different from home, hometown, or previous school. The very process of growing up, of becoming, is a continual working within, or against, the cultures of our childhood. The forces that have shaped us and the ways in which we want to shape ourselves are sometimes in concert but often in conflict, and the shaping never really ends. To these issues in us all, these texts speak loudly and clearly, for in these narratives such conflicts are overt, foregrounded, more extreme and dramatic, but nevertheless not so very different from what we all have experienced in one form at one time or another. To be sure, there were students who remained alienated from some texts—interested and sympathetic, but alienated—yet they were intensely involved in other texts. One student (who described himself as "pure Indiana white bread") pointed out that difference can, paradoxically, highlight similarity: "[The book] does not come from a culture with which I am familiar, or even one that I hear very much about. Consequently the parts of the stories that are alien to me seem all the more alien. However, this surface difference serves to make the underlying similarities between my experience and [the author's] more striking." Maxine Hong Kingston, responding to an interviewer's comment that a student who was the daughter of Irish immigrants felt that Kingston's parents in *The Woman Warrior* "could have been her parents," said:

> I get lots of letters from women and from people of different ethnicities. They come from all over—Finland, and *a lot of Jewish people*—so I know that I am telling a very human story. Even though it is very

5. On the importance of discussing common denominators among minority cultures, Abdul R. JanMohamed and David Lloyd write: "Cultures designated as minorities have certain shared experiences by virtue of their similar antagonistic relationship to the dominant culture which seeks to marginalize them all" (*The Nature and Context of Minority Discourse,* 1). I would modify that statement in the context of this study, in that I do not find these minorities "antagonistic" so much as skeptical, hurt, even resentful at having been discriminated against, but nevertheless desirous of acceptance and willing to make amends. I do agree, though, that shared experiences of marginalization link minorities, and that articulating common denominators is an important endeavor.

specifically Chinese American, it is also everyone. . . . Some people resist feeling by trying to understand my book as a Chinese book: the
Chinese people are like that. And they understand it intellectually that
way, but I see that as a sign of a person who's denying their own identity and their own feelings.[6] [emphasis mine]

While I would agree that "it is also everyone" in some ways, and that everyone's identity formation has much in common with Kingston's as portrayed in her book, in equating readers' experiences with those in the
book I would have to say that some readers' experiences are more equal
than others. Other children of immigrants, other ethnic "others," and, closer
yet, other Chinese Americans will more readily find themselves "in" the book.

I emphasized "a lot of Jewish people" above because I have found that
somewhere between the "in-group" response and that of other ethnic minorities there is a mutual recognition between Jewish Americans and Chinese Americans, different as their cultures are, different as they look from
one another, removed in history and geography as they have been from
one another. I have noticed this in the responses of ethnic Chinese students to Jewish texts, and in the responses of Jewish students to writers
such as Kingston and Amy Tan. For one thing, they all seem to have—or
at least to joke about—very similar stereotypical mothers.[7] But the similarities don't stop there, and it is the affinities between these cultures that I
hope will become apparent in this study. When I tell people I am working
on Chinese and Jewish American literatures, I often see a puzzled expression: You see them as similar? You are making some sort of comparison?
Others reward me by concurring that there are indeed interesting commonalities.

One graphic example is the cover of Gish Jen's *Mona in the Promised
Land*—an Asian eye peering through a bagel, which is in turn set on a
plate of lo mein. Jen gives us another example *in* the book—the conversation between Mona and her mother at a moment when her mother
seems to be reconciled to Mona's conversion to Judaism: "And how similar the Chinese are to the Jews, all of a sudden! What with their cultures so
ancient, and so much value placed on education. How are classes at the

6. Pete Brown, unpublished student paper, Case Western Reserve University, May 5,
1993; Maxine Hong Kingston, interview in *Conversations with Maxine Hong Kingston*,
ed. Paul Skenazy and Tera Martin, 178.
7. A Chinese American student shared with me an in-group list of Chinese mother
characteristics, surely because she was confident I would understand it and share the
joke. While not many items on the list described my own mother, I recognized them
from some Jewish mothers I know, and from Jewish American literature.

temple? she asks Mona for a change. What is she studying there? . . . and is it true that Jewish mothers are just like Chinese mothers, they know how to make their children eat?" We cannot miss the tongue-in-cheek way Jen cites all the usual stereotypes of both groups; in an interview she speaks of her "desire to play with stereotypes, . . . my kind of humor." Perhaps in a more serious vein, though, she tells her mother: "we are a minority, like it or not, and if you want to know how to be a minority, there's nobody better at it than the Jews."[8]

My most encouraging justification, though, came from China: Professor Xu Xin of Nanjing University, a pioneer in introducing Judaic studies to China, had edited (and translated most of) a one-volume version of the *Encyclopedia Judaica* in Chinese, and wrote in his English-language introduction:

> Without either Chinese or Jewish cultures, world civilization as we know it today would be diminished. These two major existing, living societies developed into highly civilized forms in ancient times and kept continuous recorded histories of their origins which impacted upon world civilization. Those who have been exposed to both cultures (in some depth) are often struck by the realization that—while the historical evolution is quite dissimilar—they nevertheless contain many commonalities in terms of basic values and world outlooks: Both are based on traditions of wisdom, learning . . . Both share strong family traditions with respect for elders. . . . Both value education. No matter how poor and how difficult the lives, Jewish and Chinese parents want their children to learn . . . As a result, teachers and scholars are highly respected. Both cultures survived in spite of severe setbacks and evolved and flourished while other civilizations rose, fell, or even disappeared into oblivion. . . . Unfortunately, these two great, rich civilizations seldom met historically. . . . As we enter the 21st century, Chinese are facing a challenge to move toward a more active world role. To understand Jewish culture is an essential step in preparation for the challenge before us because the whole world has been stirred by Jewish thought.[9]

Evidently, this strange mirror I had been peering into was two-sided, and here was someone looking into it from the other side. When we met,

---

8. Gish Jen, *Mona in the Promised Land,* 119; Gish Jen, interview in *Words Matter: Conversations with Asian American Writers,* ed. King-Kok Cheung, 227; Jen, *Mona,* 53 (hereinafter cited in the text as *Mona*).

9. Xu Xin et al., eds., *Encyclopedia Judaica, Chinese Edition,* 1–3.

Professor Xu encouraged my work, and invited me to give a paper in Nanjing at an international conference he was organizing on Judaic studies. He gave me a copy of his book (in English) on the Jews of Kaifeng, who made a vibrant community that existed from the days when Kaifeng was the capital of a number of dynasties until the nineteenth century—approximately eight hundred years of living in harmony and sharing leadership roles. He has also written in Chinese on anti-Semitism (a phenomenon foreign to the Chinese) and on the history of Jews in China (we shared our knowledge of the Jewish community that Shanghai hosted and saved from destruction by Hitler), and he has translated Jewish American and Israeli writers into Chinese. (Incidentally, Professor Xu is not Jewish.) At the conference, I met other Chinese scholars who had moved into Judaic studies through history, literature, philosophy, or studies of ancient sacred texts. When I asked Professor Xu what in American Jewish literature would most interest his audience, he replied that what really interested him and his colleagues, in the face of such large numbers of overseas Chinese, was how the Jews managed in the diaspora (a word they incorporated as a loan word, there being no such term in Chinese)—how had they become so successful, and how, over so many centuries and such wide geographical dispersion, were they able to maintain community? Similarly, Xiao-huang Yin writes that "Jewish Americans are important to Chinese immigrants not merely as exemplars of an economically and politically successful group, but also because they represent a commitment to affirming ethnic identity within assimilation." Community, family, antiquity that still lives, the importance of the word and of ancient texts in their original language, of customs and traditions, of success (not only financial but academic)—are these not the stereotypes of "model minorities," in part mythical, in part true? Still, they are positive models, goals as well as stereotypes, and many a Jewish or Chinese child has felt both enabled and oppressed by these expectations; many a mother has swelled with pride when they are realized. My paper, incidentally, was entitled "The Lure and the Cost of Success in American Jewish Literature," wherein I argued that one's definition of "success" says everything about one's value system, and then showed the high price that was paid for their definitions by a David Levinsky and a Willy Loman.[10]

10. Xiao-huang Yin, *Chinese American Literature since the 1850s,* 193. In preparing my paper, I read Arthur Miller's book *Salesman in Beijing,* which, among other valuable insights, demonstrated how and why his Chinese actors and audiences were able to identify with Willy and Biff. I also had the pleasure of meeting with a group of English majors who were preparing to stage *Salesman,* and their comments and interpretations also bore this out.

It seemed as if not only Xu Xin but also some Chinese American writers were looking at American Jewish literature of an earlier time, and seeing, albeit in their particular and postmodern way, similar themes—themes that these more recently empowered voices, looking at families more recently arrived, have in common with Jewish writing in the earlier part of this century. My sense of this was confirmed when I learned from Yin's *Chinese American Literature since the 1850s* that an important theme in recent *Chinese-language* literature is Chinese views of Jewish Americans: "Chinese-language writers tend to use the Jewish experience as a mirror image against which to redefine and compare their own."[11] Perhaps it is only that what they are looking at and experiencing is similar to what the earlier wave of immigrants went through. But I believe there is more in common than just immigrant struggle to survive and adapt: there are the "commonalities" alluded to by Xu Xin as well, as evidenced by the weight given to such issues as language, tradition, family, and education in both bodies of literature. Both groups position their characters and their situations along these axes of greatest conflict, but also of potentially greatest creative achievement—those issues most integral to their forming identities (elusive and multivalent though those identities—any identities—may be): facing a fragmented self, struggling with language or bilingualism, navigating between the combined forces of family and tradition and the pulls of the mainstream, recognizing the shaping power of education. And finally, in a writer, shaping and integrating one's life into text, integrating, if not the lived life, at least the text of a life. It is these issues around which this study is organized: each will be the focus of a chapter designed to expand upon it, bringing to bear theory related to the issue at hand, as well as relevant literary texts.

I will be exploring these issues in and through literature in hopes that the literature *and* the issues as they exist outside it, in real individuals, families, and cultures, will illuminate one another. In the same spirit, it is my hope that by placing two cultures face to face they too will illuminate one another. It is important to see similarities between groups, but not at the expense of their uniqueness and differences. Nor do I attempt to force complex individual voices and rich cultures into neat comparisons that would be reductive and overgeneralized. But there *is* more likeness than many realize.

There have been many excellent studies of Asian American literature, such as those by Elaine Kim, Sau-ling Cynthia Wong, Amy Ling, King-Kok

11. Yin, *Chinese American Literature,* 189–90.

Cheung, Bonnie TuSmith, and Shirley Geok-lin Lim, and of Jewish American literature, such as those by Irving Howe, Robert Alter, Mark Schechner, Hana Wirth-Nesher, Louis Harap, Daniel Walden, and Sanford Pinsker. There have been critics, such as Thomas Ferraro and Amritjit Singh and his coeditors, who have treated works by authors from various ethnicities in a single volume. But I know of no book to date that has featured two groups, specifically Chinese and Jewish Americans. In putting two complex, admittedly heterogeneous groups between the covers of a single book, I hope to avoid parochialism, even as I also hope to avoid facile, stereotypical comparisons. Ethnographer Michael Fischer advocates a sort of triangulation: a third case to add to the observer/observed in order to avoid simplistic better/worse judgments, to check against assimilating the other to the self or producing a dualistic contrast.[12] In reading two cultures that differ from the mainstream, my work provides that "third," whose triangulation will keep shifting depending on the stance of the reader. I have chosen Chinese American and Jewish American literatures not because they are similar in all respects, nor because the similarities I find exclude other groups—marginal or mainstream, minority or majority. I am putting together two cultures whose affinities I see despite their great differences. Bound as they are within a single book, the texts are positioned to reflect one another. Readers who notice the reflective possibilities may begin to see their own reflections, albeit vaguely, with features, or color, or gender, or age, or backgrounds that do not quite match.

What I hope my readers will see is not just the *overt* dramas within the narratives under discussion, but the *implicit* drama of one culture encountering another as texts are discussed in tandem, paralleled and placed with one another in shared contexts. To notice this is to acknowledge as well the possibility of seeing oneself through the lens of another, gaining a clearer view of the self through the experience of reading another.[13] With the reading process often comes a move toward greater affinity with characters or narrators and with their cultures—certainly not in order to assume a like identity, but rather the sort of identification that comes with entanglement in a text (a term I borrow from Wolfgang Iser, whose reader-response theories, along with others', are important to what follows and

12. Michael Fischer, "Ethnicity and the Post-modern Arts of Memory," 199.
13. What I do not intend is a facile and reductive analogizing of histories (the dangers of which Emily Budick has shown). Rather than comparative history, I see the process as more similar to the experience of an ethnographer or linguist (such as Edward T. Hall) who finds that in studying other cultures, and seeing them as an outside observer, one achieves a clearer view from that perspective of oneself and one's own culture.

will be further discussed in subsequent chapters). My students' reading stances as I have outlined them (immediate to distant), radiating outward from those who are "insiders" to those who are "others," to those who have never considered themselves as having any ethnicity at all—just American (whatever that actually is)—do not necessarily remain fixed categories. While no one who was not already a Chinese or a Jew or a Hispanic or an Indian has become one, distance from text tends to decrease as the term goes on. Those progressive "removes" from the text can just as well be facing inward, drawing readers closer in. When the focus is on only one culture, a reader who is not a "member" might well feel excluded, or at best an interested but neutral observer. Seeing one culture's affinity to another, however, invites any reader to see affinities, whether between cultures or between the reading self and the text. It is my hope that, in recognizing affinities among these texts, constructing parallels and intersections, and drawing conclusions of their own, *my* readers will be drawn into that process, drawn in at least close enough to see its possibilities. That intermediate remove—one "other" seen parallel to another "other"— can serve as a link to those whose experiences have the least in common with the people they are reading about. By both identifying directly with the narrative and entering into the process of discovering connections, the reader can be drawn in closer to those others, finding and feeling connections even among differences.

Ultimately, if what I learned in school—what happens in my classes, and what has happened to me and to other readers of these books—can be shared more fully, more closely, by readers of *this* book, I will have made some contribution to our meeting and *seeing* one another.

One Other Looks at Another Other

I am white, of European extraction. I am Jewish, but as I was told by a black student, still "meltable" because I look like everyone else. True enough. But . . .

I went to school in a neighborhood that was at least 50 percent Jewish, so I shouldn't have felt "other." I can't say I suffered because I was Jewish; I wasn't called names. The boys who delighted in calling me Link the Stink (my last name was Link) were also Jewish, but they weren't the popular ones anyway, so who cared? I had enough friends, boys as well as girls, that I certainly wasn't threatened by their rhyming games. I was too naive to recognize the only real anti-Semitic comment I heard in elementary school: I was in first grade, and my best friend, Jean, asked me what I was doing that afternoon after school—could I come to her house to play. I told her I was sorry, but that night was to be a Jewish holiday, and I had to get ready for it—set out my new clothes, take a bath, go to services. Oh, she exclaimed (as naive in her way as I was), I didn't know Jews took baths! I had trouble understanding why my mother was so furious when I told her about my friend's dumbness. I had not yet heard the term "dirty Jew." All I knew was that suddenly I was removed from that class. Only later did I realize how often Jean must have heard the words "dirty Jews" at her house, which, innocent six-year-old that she was, she took literally. By the time I understood, Jean and I lived in the different worlds of other classes, other friends.

When I was in my teens my family went for a vacation to Florida. My father had had his mail forwarded. Among his letters were some from Jewish organizations. As soon as we arrived at the resort where we had booked a cottage, we were told we would have to leave ("I'm terribly embarrassed.

11

I couldn't tell from your name. I would have written you. Um, you can stay until you find another place," on and on and on. "But we don't have Jews staying here. I'm so sorry. Rules. It's not my place, blahblahblah"). I was not traumatized. I knew of "restricted" places and neighborhoods, even one beginning on the next block (Jean's block!) from where we lived. I knew the South was bigoted. There were plenty of people there who had it much, much worse—at least we could find another town nearby, another resort. I knew about Jim Crow laws, and was glad the South had lost the Civil War. But it was another place—I didn't live there. Even the sign that read "No Jews or Dogs Allowed" didn't throw me. This was the South, after all. What should I expect? What Hitler had done to my family: grandmother, aunts, uncles, cousins, including my cousin Leah, just my age— what would have happened to me had we not left Europe exactly when we did—I knew all that, so how upset could I be at a stupid resort manager carrying out orders in a place where I no longer wanted to spend five minutes. We found a much nicer place in the next town, a mile farther down the beach. I didn't live in that other bigoted town. Where I lived, in Cleveland Heights—the part of Cleveland Heights where I lived—such things didn't happen. It hadn't hurt me where I lived.

I was different, though, from the others, including the other Jews, because my family was observant—orthodox. That meant that after school every day I went to Hebrew school (not just once or twice a week, the way the other Jewish kids did.) I couldn't eat very much of the food in the cafeteria, because it wasn't kosher. Friday night dances, Saturday football games were off-limits to me because this was our Sabbath. Everyone had heard of the Jewish New Year, even the seder nights at Passover, but when I claimed I had to be absent for the holiday called Sukkot (Tabernacles) or for the last two days, religiously observed, of Passover, or for Shevuot (Pentecost), my teachers had trouble believing me: the other Jewish children were there, why not me? Christmastime didn't mean "Jingle Bells" and a bit of Hanukkah in those days. Hanukkah didn't seem to exist.

In Grace Paley's delightful story "The Loudest Voice," a Jewish girl wins the leading role in her school Christmas pageant. Our Christmas production was a nativity play, and I was an angel hovering over the Christ child's manger. Being culturally different wasn't "in," so none of us Jewish kids voiced any objection to religious drama and song. Except for Joe Levine. He refused to sing the Christmas carols, refused to be in the play. (And he wasn't even orthodox! He went to Saturday football games.) And how did I feel about Joe's courageous stand? I confess it, I was embarrassed. Had I been less shy, had the teacher realized I could have sung a good solo and given me "Oh Holy Night" to sing, or "Little Star of Bethlehem" (in *my* loudest voice), I would have jumped at the chance, uncomfortable though it would have made me, guilty as I would have felt singing out loud the words I wasn't supposed to say, proclaiming a belief that was not mine. (Even when I was in the high school glee club and sang church music in the context of classical music, not religious observance, I felt more comfortable singing in Latin. Though I had studied Latin, and knew very well what "Dominus" meant, it came out of my throat more easily than "Christ the Lord.") In that nativity play I would have sung out "Fall on your knees! . . . Oh ni-ight divine, oh night when Christ was born" rather than stand out, rather than feel any more different than I already did, rather than offend or make waves in a class where I was the Other and glad that I was accepted. Yes, I was proud to be Jewish, but uncomfortable with being different, unwilling to call attention to difference, happy that I wasn't tormented or called names, as I knew by then other kids in other places were. I was also happy that I had Christian friends as well as Jewish ones, that my teachers liked me. It was my loss that I missed a few games and dances. I had as good a life as anyone else. A little discomfort or embarrassment seemed a small price to pay. Especially in the light of history past and in the making. I was in America. I was safe. I had a future.

But when I read about kids who hide their ethnic foods, I understand.[1] I wouldn't let my mother give me sandwiches on delicious challah, because it didn't look like Wonder Bread. Nowadays bagels, pita, tacos, Chinese food are all the rage. Then such food tucked into our lunch boxes made us want to run and hide, throw it away, eat it where no one could see. My British mother's first attempt at a birthday party menu for me consisted of tiny, thin cucumber sandwiches for tea, as ethnically "other," Anglo though it was, as blintzes or tortillas or dim sum, and just as far removed from peanut butter and jelly, from hot dogs and fries.

I was helping an Iranian graduate student with his English writing. This was just after the revolution in Iran and the installation of Khomeini and his new policies. The student, who had come here with his wife and young daughter, had been very well educated—his spoken English was impeccable—and he said that what Khomeini was doing to education in his country made it imperative to leave everything behind, to flee, to bring his child here to be educated and to be free. During one of our conversations, he

1. Elaine Kim, *Asian American Literature: An Introduction to the Writings and Their Social Context,* 226.

exclaimed, with tears in his eyes, "And I was one of those who helped him—we have been betrayed, betrayed!" Then he wondered at the fact that he was telling me such things, entrusting to me feelings, conflicts, bitterness that he had been so careful to keep inside at home. "There is something about you, something—" I laughed and said that English professors have to have read a great deal of literature, and literature gives us many privileged views of character and situation; insight is our stock in trade. But he wasn't satisfied. "No, that can't be all, reading can't be all. There has to be something else." He was right.

He wasn't the only international student to confide in me, to feel more free to express feelings of cultural dislocation, homesickness, fear, and anxiety, to talk about difficulties in interacting with Americans. When I reminded one Middle Eastern student that I was one of those Americans, he replied, "But you're not *like* an American." It was meant as a compliment, of course. But I thought, What? Me not an American? I always put out the flag on the Fourth of July; I go to my mother's every Thanksgiving for turkey and the works. I grew up proudly pledging allegiance to the flag of the United States of America, and got a lump in my throat when I saw the flag wave to the tune of "The Star-Spangled Banner." Even in this disenchanted post-Vietnam, post-Watergate era, I cannot help the feeling I get whenever I return from overseas and follow the arrows to the line for holders of U.S. passports. Even though I now know how many of my people America could have saved—and didn't—in World War II, I feel a gratitude that no one born here could possibly feel. I never take this country for granted. But nothing in my accent or manner could have given that away. How, then, am I "not like an American?" Perhaps there *is* "something about" me.

When I taught the Immigrant Experience in American Literature course—to a class that was about one-third immigrant students, the rest similar to the student who dubbed himself "pure Indiana white bread"—we had two grand debates: one when I disclosed that Danny Santiago, author of *Famous All Over Town,* was really an Anglo named Daniel James; the other when we discussed Maxine Hong Kingston's *Woman Warrior.* James/Santiago upset the real immigrants who were doing their own autobiographical writing and who felt co-opted and cheated by an "impostor" writing as if he was an insider. They were answered by American-born English majors citing Mary Ann Evans/George Eliot and the whole issue of assumed voices in narration, reminding the objectors that James's book was a novel and not an autobiography, even though it was written to seem like one. They added that Samuel Clemens/Mark Twain was not a fourteen-year-old boy like Huck Finn, that Holden Caulfield was not the author of

Catcher in the Rye. No matter, the "real" ethnic "others" felt that some kind of pact, some integrity they expected, had been undermined.

The next debate centered on the way Chinese were portrayed by Kingston. While Kingston's power as a writer was acknowledged by everyone, one Chinese American male was very angry. Another Chinese American student, an English major, worried in my office about Americans who might take Kingston's book as a "textbook of Chinese culture and family life," but she stood up for Kingston in the class discussion, defending Kingston's need to write it as she felt it, as well as her "right" to make use of the Fa Mu Lan legend, which she had changed to suit her own purposes. This student agreed with the other English majors that traditional myths and tales are often used, altered, remade by new writers, genres, and times. I commented that in her two very different reactions—one in my office, the other in class—I sensed a conflict between her English major self and her Good Chinese Daughter self. She agreed. (Was this Joe Levine and me all over again?) What was most interesting to me was the way the "Indiana white breads" reacted to the debate: What is the problem? You're overreacting, oversensitive. This is the way it is in literature; everyone knows that we mustn't judge a culture by one book or character; we understand stereotyping, etc., etc. They just couldn't understand the conflict, the anger and embarrassment of the Chinese students. But I could. I told the class about the furor Philip Roth raised in every Jewish community with *Goodbye, Columbus* and *Portnoy's Complaint,* and I told them about his article defending his work, "Writing about Jews." I went further in answering my noncomprehending students: If you have never had the experience of being in a group that has been discriminated against or persecuted, you cannot possibly understand how sensitive those groups can be, how protective, how afraid of being seen in a bad light, of hanging out dirty laundry for "the goyim" to see, of giving them ammunition for their already dangerous anti-otherism.[2]

---

2. The question of how "responsible" authors should feel to the sensitivities of and threats—real or perceived—to their ethnic groups has been the subject of much debate. Roth's case is not only well known, but he has incorporated it into several of his novels and discussed it in *The Facts: A Novelist's Autobiography*. (Roth originally published "Writing about Jews" in *Commentary* 36 [December 1963]: 446–52, and later collected it in *Reading Myself and Others*.) Among Asian American writers and critics, the most famous debate on this subject has been between Frank Chin and Maxine Hong Kingston, but it is not exclusive to them. Xiao-huang Yin sees the issue in terms of a dichotomy between a socioideological approach and an aesthetic-individual approach, and notes that since the eighties the distinction has blurred, owing to the younger generation's experiencing more diversity and less poverty and segregation (*Chinese American Literature,* 241–43). Helen Zia shows how fear of airing "dirty laundry" has covered up domestic and other violence (*Asian American Dreams: The Emergence of an American People,* 237).

After class my angry Chinese student came to my office to thank me. He no longer minded that we were reading the book. He could go back to it now, appreciate its good points, and write a paper on it—which he did, critically but beautifully, including a discussion of his own difficult processes of reading it and coming to terms with it.

In such a context I was less uncomfortable presenting the ugliness as well as the beauty, the conflicts and betrayals as well as the loyalties, the traditions and their subversions, in the Jewish literature we read. It was not surprising that some of the most sensitive reactions came from my Asian students, as well as from the other immigrants. Not that the mainstream Americans weren't wonderfully sensitive. They had, after all, elected this course, and were an ideally self-selected group of nonstereotypers. But the Asian students, and the Muslim woman from Iran, could identify strongly with the conflicts common to them all, involving language, religious traditions, parents who wanted their children to remain loyal to their traditions and children who wanted to be "American," difficulties in school and on the street.

But perhaps most important of all, and until then unarticulated, was the great task of deciding who and what they each were. They realized that they were straddling two worlds, navigating two cultures and languages. More than one student expressed what Susan Ervin-Tripp's research on Japanese American war brides had shown: that they did not feel quite the same person in one language as in the other, even if they were fully bilingual (an issue to be discussed more fully in Chapter 3). Out of their various identities, out of their conflicts, languages, and self-perceptions, they had to create a new hybrid one, something neither typical of where they had come from, nor typically American (whatever that is, but they think it does exist). If they were not to fall in between, vacillate back and forth, or teeter on the brink, they would have to weave, knit, and fashion a textured, richer whole out of the threads of their existences. And they found that their reading and their writing helped them to do this.

That reading—what did it do? What happened when the Asian student read *The Rise of David Levinsky?* Or "Eli the Fanatic," or *Call It Sleep?* What draws me to Amy Tan?

Who Is It I Am Seeing in the Mirror?

I look into a mirror and I don't see Chinese features. My mother's table is not the image I see when I look at a Chinese dinner; incense burned at family altars doesn't look like or smell like or mean the same thing as my Sabbath candles. And yet, as if in a distorted mirror, I recognize something of myself, even as the difference, the novelty of what I see, fascinates me, draws me to look, makes me look again—more closely—to discern what I can, finally, recognize. Perhaps a common "otherness." Perhaps, for example, chicken soup.

The mirror stage, Lacan tells us, is essential to the baby: Who is that "other" that imitates me, smiles when I smile, whose hand meets mine when I bang against that hardness, comes forward to meet me but hasn't the softness of other hands, whose face is hard to my kiss? It is a crucial moment when the baby realizes that play "other" is "me," because it's the first real object lesson in "me" as "other"—as separate even while same. Something outside my body is "me" but also *not* me. It is the beginning of individuation—me as other to something other, connected by my actions to this mirror, connected in nurturance to other human beings. It is also the first experience of "discontinuity between inner experience and the presented self," a vision of unity and harmony that is, as Ellie Ragland-Sullivan puts it, "asymmetrical, fictional, and artificial."[3] But that very discontinuity, that fiction, helps me to define myself by recognizing an identification that is nevertheless separate: differentiation in the midst of identification. Paradoxically, out of this "twinning" emerges a sense, maybe not yet of "this I am," but of "am-ness"—out of affinity, integrity; out of fascination with reflection, an ultimate boredom with sameness, a reaching out to other similars whose responses are individual to them and warm—not mere cold imitations of myself. If I am not to be stuck in narcissistic self-parody, cold kisses, and pats of palm on reflected palm, I must seek out *other* others, less predictable, less within my control, but more interesting. They, in turn, respond out of *their* desire for the similarity plus differences that makes them understand their own uniqueness, just as the encounter (and here I would include a reader's encounter with a text) helps me to understand mine.

Charlotte Linde relates this mirror stage to the emergence of the reflexive self—the self that can see itself among others once it has developed "the ability to relate to oneself as an object or an other." She seems to be saying that being able to see the self as other is requisite for community (which I see as applicable both to an individual in a family or in-group and to our ever more diverse American community), presumably because

3. Charlotte Linde, *Life Stories: The Creation of Coherence,* 121; Ragland-Sullivan quoted, 122.

only in this way can we imagine ourselves in another's place, see another as a "self." She goes further, quoting Margaret Mead: "one has to be a member of a community to be a self." Linde posits that we learn to see the self as other by narrating, a process that separates the person who tells from the protagonist of the narration, the inchoate from the formed, edited version. At the same time, Linde makes important points about why we need self-narration for our *own* benefit. Linde's insights connect to the cross-cultural mirroring and "reading" under discussion here. She writes:

> Although narrative allows speakers to present themselves as being one actor among others, there is in fact a radical difference between the experience of the self and the experience of others. First, at a conscious level, everyone believes that he or she has privileged access to his or her own plans, motivations, and intentions, whereas these can only be inferred for others. At a much deeper level there is a more radical difference. . . . We experience flashes, textures, smells, pressures, and ghosts of emotion that cannot be languaged. This kind of experience is extremely unlike what we seem to see others experiencing, since that experience is already packaged. Our own internal experience . . . is of a self without armor—perhaps without boundaries as definite as we would like—walking around in a world of others who appear to have proper boundaries and effective armor. Hence we may perceive ourselves in an alarmingly vulnerable position. . . . And the remedy is to narrate, to create a self as other, replicating our experience of actual others we seem to experience.[4]

It is true that the "unlanguaged," unlanguageable experiences of our fellows is not within our power to see; even if it were in their power to express or show it, how much would they be willing to show? We see others edited and packaged. But sometimes that packaged form allows us as listeners and readers a nevertheless intimate view of a narrator (to use Linde's wonderful metaphor) unarmed. What we, as readers, are privileged to share is text whose form may be packaged, but whose contents focus on the struggle to form—whether self or text, or texts whose forms reflect that

4. Ibid., 122, 120, 106, 122, 121. According to Paul Smith, Lacan, in speaking of the subject's separating from its construction in the field of the other, and simultaneously erecting itself in the garb of coherent subject, manipulates the French verb *séparer* (to separate) by exploiting etymological puns: *se parer* (to deck oneself out, to adorn oneself), as well as the Latin *separare*, so like *se parere* (to be engendered). Smith goes on to say that in the act of enunciation, "I" is both the mark of an alienation and also the garb or disguise that disavows alienation (*Discerning the Subject*, 75, 76).

struggle. In the act of reading—perceiving *and* constructing—we less-than-fully-armed individuals feel less alone, helped to construct our own armor as we construct the text before us and enter into whatever relationship the text privileges us, invites us, to share. In a bicultural situation, fragmentation and identity confusion are often more obvious, more dramatic than in the monocultural. They may be our situations writ large, or, if we share such bicultural issues, they may seem like our own stories, suits of armor to borrow, or to serve as models for creating our own.

Asian American writers and critics bristle at "exoticism"—the gawking, pointing, and picture-taking of tourists in Chinatown. We remember Amy Tan's Waverly Jong "shrieking with laughter" as she recommends "Guts and duck's feet and octopus gizzards" to a Caucasian tourist who has just photographed her outside a Chinese restaurant, her humor and glee fed by resentment at having been made an object, a curio just like all the junk in the shops on Grant Avenue.[5] To what extent is reading Tan and Kingston a politer version of that gawking? When does it become something else? What if the text draws, attracts by virtue of its "otherness," another face, with each holding the gaze long enough to say: there's something here I recognize, that in its similarity *and* differences helps me to carve out this being that I am; that helps me *and* you as we look at one another, connect, separate, and thereby individuate; that helps us create images that are not mere reflections or imitations, nor wholly curios to point at from afar. For to point at from afar is not at all the same as to bring the curio closer, to notice its reflective properties. What do I see when Waverly's mother polishes her daughter's chess trophies? What does Tan see when David Levinsky cuts off his sidelocks? Perhaps we both recognize mothers of our own, recognize too that in shedding old appearances we might also be cutting ourselves off from our past and our traditions. It is when we see ourselves through the actions of others that the distances narrow.

Just as important, though, is the question of what "they"—the majority, the mainstream—see when they look at us, and why they find us so interesting. The flowering of ethnic literatures could not take place without a marketplace of majority shoppers. Is this phenomenon merely Chinatown gawking revisited? Politically correct guilt? While these may very well be factors, I see other possible explanations, with none of these theories mutually exclusive. Difference does engender curiosity; boredom with the same old plots and locales and conflicts does engender a search for the

5. Amy Tan, *The Joy Luck Club,* 91 (hereinafter cited in the text as *Joy*).

"different," hence the "exotic."[6] But here, as with the mutual mirroring of "others," what is seen, what perhaps is being sought, is also connection. Sander L. Gilman and others speak of the covert side of anti-Semitism, anti-blackness (Gilman relates the association, in some cultures, at some times, of Jews *with* blackness—the Jew as black), which is a projection of what an individual or society most fears in itself, its "dark" and secret underside externalized, exorcized, alienated, repudiated, vilified, segregated into ghettos, deported, and, in the Nazi era, exterminated to a degree limited only by time and available technology.[7] I would like to suggest that at the same time there is attraction both by what is different and by what is similar.

The term *philosemitism* has its parallels in what Sau-ling Cynthia Wong calls "exoticization"—it's not necessarily so great to be loved stereotypically because it's still being stereotyped and "othered." Asians are not always pleased to be called the "model minority," as if it's not the case that plenty of Asians flunk out and take to the streets.[8] Don't stereotype us, please. Furthermore, some of us are not so great in math; some of us write novels and poems. Jews of past generations "suffered" the same sort of "admiration." No one spoke, though, of either models or minorities: we were Jews, period. We were stereotyped as smart—not on our way to becoming engineers, though, but doctors. Yet that view had its price: Jews were greasy grinds, grubbing for As, unlike the stereotypical WASP who settled for "gentleman Cs" because it was uncouth to compete, to study harder than one socialized; besides, for many, the Old Boy network provided assurances of the future that immigrants had to struggle for. Clean-cut gentry had no need to prove themselves. Of course quotas had to be established to keep the majority of interlopers out, to keep things from getting too rough and competitive, to keep those "others" from taking over. Yellow peril, Jewish takeover—it's all the same. I can't help but imagine members of "model minority" Asian groups scanning the list of Nobel

6. Werner Sollors writes that many native-born American writers have complained that "the uniformity and homogeneity of American life . . . militated against good fiction," while immigrants and European travelers "were fascinated by the imaginative possibilities of the ethnic variety of America" (*Beyond Ethnicity: Consent and Descent in American Culture*, 142).

7. Sander L. Gilman, *Jewish Self-Hatred: Anti-Semitism and the Hidden Language of the Jews*, 5–7.

8. Sau-ling Cynthia Wong, *Reading Asian American Literature: From Necessity to Extravagance*, 9. For discussions of model minorities, see Bonnie TuSmith, *All My Relatives: Community in Contemporary Ethnic American Literatures*, 33; Phoebe Eng, *Warrior Lessons: An Asian American Woman's Journey into Power*, 188–90; and Zia, *Asian American Dreams*, 207.

laureates with a mixture of pride in all those familiar-sounding names but also with latent nervousness: Is all this attention good for us? Will we be envied? Envy can be dangerous. To be held up for emulation, as any bright, well-behaved sibling knows, is also to be resented; to advance too quickly is potentially to be held—or pushed—back.

Let us assume now a different climate, a welcoming one. In what ways do modeling, mirroring, and fascination with difference apply? We cannot underestimate what inspiration the so-called American Dream gave to Americans and immigrants alike: the myths of limitless possibility for the deserving; that anyone (born here) can be president; that, Lincoln-like, one can grow from log cabin to the White House—mainly by means of long, hard study and integrity—from being a member of the poor underclass to being the Great Emancipator. Horatio Alger's Ragged Dick and Abraham Cahan's David Levinsky were both models of rags to riches, even if materialism won out over ideals; for every decision has its price, every dream its potential for nightmare. To value success, whether material, intellectual, or artistic, to see it as attainable for anyone and everyone in a supposedly classless society, is also to fear failure; for if the brass ring is there for anyone, what excuse is there for failing to grasp it? And if parents have sacrificed a past, a place, a heritage to bring their children to the Land of Brass Rings, what responsibility must be felt by those children to their parents and those dreams? Is it a coincidence that *Death of a Salesman* was written by the child of an immigrant?

In this sense the immigrant is not simply a mirror of the hopes and fears, difficulties and successes of the American ideal, the American majority, but of those issues magnified. The mainstream (for want of a better term) can look at the difficulty the immigrant experiences, look with the greatest sympathy, and breathe a great sigh of relief—thank God we are not "them"—coupled with even greater appreciation of what they have heretofore taken for granted. In a journal entry responding to his classmates' entries, James Lin, my "angry" Chinese student, wrote:

> In the journal some foreign students wrote of feeling . . . encouraged by reading the stories. Some admired the author . . . most people related the stories to themselves. I was surprised that no one mentioned: "God, I never realized how fortunate I am as a native English-speaking American—how fortunate to be able to do whatever everybody else is able to do, and to speak whatever everybody else is able to speak." One has to imagine the language handicap along with the problems of culture shock, homesickness, confusion, frustration, and hatred. You also have to hope 24 hours a day, 7 days per week, 365 days per year

for ten years in order to get out of that narrow, self-isolated world of your own loneliness. . . . I clearly remember each morning having to recite for myself "This is the United States not Taiwan. This is the United States not Taiwan." Then when I came back from school I recited "These are the restaurant people not school people." [James worked at his family's hotel/restaurant.] I woke up in the middle of the night because I dreamed that I was sent back to that period of time again. I am terrified just thinking about it.[9]

One mainstream response could very well be: Whew! My worries, my difficulties, pale in comparison with these. Yet James's fears and difficulties *are* of the same order, only magnified. The goals the immigrant has come seeking, striving for, are those we all share: upward mobility, education, esteem. When we see stories of successes over even greater odds, more and greater obstacles, we can feel inspired; we may ask, What is your secret? Tell us how you managed. And so we have Horatio Alger and the immigrant novel.

Then there are the struggles we all have to undergo to become adult individuals, to become—or flee from, or mold in our own way—what our parents so earnestly wanted us to be, each of us protagonist of our own bildungsroman. Emerging from the cocoon of family; feeling alienated from parents and friends; needing to rebel against the previous generation, to leave it behind and learn our own ways to express what no other person, no previous generation, has needed to express; forging our own identity out of all we have experienced and learned at home and at school—is this not what we see in cross-cultural literature, literature written in the throes of immigration or of living in an immigrant family? Kingston's narrator asks: "Chinese Americans, when you try to understand what things in you are Chinese, how do you separate what is peculiar to childhood, to poverty, insanities, one family, your mother who marked your growing with stories, from what is Chinese? What is Chinese tradition and what is the movies?"[10] The question is not simply a Chinese American one. It mirrors any cross-cultural attempt at self-definition. And it shows the mainstream individual in a magnifying mirror—distorted, perhaps, but recognizable.

In *Ethnic Passages,* Thomas J. Ferraro issues a strong call for critics to attend to the literariness of novels in immigrant genres. He finds troubling

9. James Lin, untitled essay in *The Immigrant Experience: Voices and Visions,* ed. Lisa Chiu, Judith Oster, et al., 16–17.

10. Maxine Hong Kingston, *The Woman Warrior: Memoirs of a Girlhood ·among Ghosts,* 5–6 (hereinafter cited in the text as *Warrior*).

"the antithesis between parochial concerns and aesthetic accomplishment," when "what is most ethnically specific and what is most aesthetically compelling will be found at the same narrative sites . . . in allied, mutually interrogative, and cross-fertilizing ways," and of course he is right.[11] He speaks, for example, of Henry Roth's *Call It Sleep* and Kingston's *Woman Warrior*. But there have been Jewish writers before these culturally aware times who "made it" into university classes and fiction anthologies—Philip Roth, Saul Bellow, J. D. Salinger, for example. The fifties and sixties Jew who wrote not of ethnic passages but of alienation and angst was "in," probably because alienation and angst were "in." The postholocaust, bomb-scared generation may have gravitated to writers from a historically dislocated, wandering group of "aliens" who might express for the previously complacent mainstream what alienation feels like. Jewish writers (some of whom were themselves already assimilated, comfortable and secure until Hitler) held up mirrors, asked the questions so many of us were asking, serio-comically satirized easy answers and outworn pieties. Tell us what it feels like to be alienated and afraid and disillusioned, readers seemed to be asking of these writers. Questioning, whether out of respectful curiosity or a sudden jolt of recognition in a hazy, distorting mirror, mitigates the intrusive gaze. It asks for recognition in return; it merits, if not answers, at least a dialogue on the questions, if only because there has been enough interest to *ask*.

Such a dialogue did not seem to take place when Sara Horowitz's immigrant father looked into the "universalist mirror" and found it to have been deceiving. Horowitz writes: "Peering into the universalist mirror held up at the university, my father thought he could discern his own features. But outside the walls . . . he realized he had been staring at nothing. Many years later his daughter squints into that same mirror. . . . Peering back is an image only vaguely like herself. Already she sees that the magic mirror does not reflect back woman, does not reflect back Jew." Perhaps there can be no universalist mirror reflecting our identical likeness. Perhaps an image vaguely like ourselves is the most we can expect. But what I am suggesting here is that the "universalist" who peers into an ethnic mirror might *also* see a vague reflection of herself, and that an "ethnic" peering into the mirror of another ethnic might find an even less vague, even greater likeness. What can two very different ethnicities, for example, Jewish and Chinese, see mirrored in one another? Obviously, their common

---

11. Thomas J. Ferraro, *Ethnic Passages: Literary Immigrants in Twentieth-Century America*, 4, 3.

marginality in America, for starters. While Chinese festivals have little in common with Jewish ones, the festivals of both groups have names, occasions, and practices that are very different from those of the mainstream; the times of their occurrence are dictated by the group's own calendar, and they are important to members of the group—as individuals, as families, as occasions for coming together to feast or celebrate, to exchange gifts with family and friends from the same culture. As noted by the Chinese scholar Xu Xin, both groups represent "ancient cultures which have survived thousands of years, retaining language and texts from ancient times which can still be understood. Both are rooted in a strong family tradition which emphasizes education of children, caring for the elderly, and independence." Xiao-huang Yin discusses the Chinese-language novel *The Ordeal,* by Yu Lihua, as one example of many wherein both Chinese American and Jewish American themes figure strongly and positively. According to Yin, "Chinese interest in Jewish Americans . . . in part reflects Chinese curiosity about Jewish American culture, which seems to resemble that of the Chinese."[12]

To illustrate this tendency to find affinities, there is no better example than Gish Jen's *Mona in the Promised Land,* whose protagonist, Mona Chang, actually becomes Jewish. (There were readers who assumed that Jen was Jewish.)[13] The cover design, which I've discussed in my introduction, symbolizes Mona's Chinese/Jewish identities, but it also provokes the question: why *Jewish?* Why not Protestant? Why not just plain assimilated "American" if she's only rebelling against her Chinese family? In the first place, she'd never be able to "pass" the first three letters of WASP. While she seems comfortable being a Jewish convert, she is fully aware of her anomalous identity(ies)—"what it's like to be not Wasp, and not black, and not as Jewish as Jewish can be; and not from Chinatown either" (*Mona,* 231). In fact, she is continually contrasting what her mother says, buys, and would never buy with what is said and done in the Gugelstein home, and yet Barbara Gugelstein becomes her best friend—they understand one another. Barbara's rabbi becomes Mona's advisor on matters cultural and familial as well as religious, and it is clear that Mona feels more comfortable with the Jewish crowd than with any other, which is what brings her

12. Sara Horowitz, "Jewish Studies as Oppositional? Gettin' Mighty Lonely Out Here," 153 (see also Sollors, *Beyond Ethnicity,* 163, and the quotation from JanMohamed and Lloyd in note 5, p. 4, of this book); Xu Xin, interview by Jordan Lubetkin, *Cleveland Jewish News,* December 1, 1995, p. 10; Yin, *Chinese American Literature,* 190.
13. Jen, interview, 229. Jen went on to say: "In a way, I've tried to contribute to the process of boundary crossing."

to all those bar mitzvahs and welfare projects in the first place. What does she have in common with them? Parents pushing Harvard, for one thing; also being a minority very recently discriminated against and excluded, and yet *here,* in late sixties Scarshill—her family living comfortably, aiming high, struggling to meet all that is expected of them, whether materially or intellectually.[14] "And where does it come from, the will to make yourself into something more than your endowment?" Mona wonders as she listens to a lecture in developmental biology. "Is that just inherited too? There are Jews in China, Mona knows. Will she one day discover them to be her long-lost relatives? Auntie Leah! Uncle Irwin!" (*Mona,* 267).

Mona's visit to the posh summer resort where her sister and her sister's black roommate work as waitresses (only Harvard/Radcliffe and Yale students need apply) crystallizes the subtle and not-so-subtle attitudes of guests such as the Ingle family, and the differences between them and even the wealthy "white" Gugelsteins. Mona is amused by their "Protestant play ethic"—their aggressive push for the tennis courts before they even check in, for example. Mr. Ingle's daughter, Eloise, who has only recently discovered that her deceased mother was Jewish, and thus that she is Jewish too, has been in Mona's classes at the temple, and acts as a sort of cultural translator, all the while deprecating her genteel stepmother. Mona, invited to eat dinner with the family (Mrs. Ingle is interested in China, about which Mona knows nothing), enacts a scene that could be a Jackie Mason routine: She orders two of each course (after all, it costs the same no matter what she orders) and wishes she could hide it all when Mrs. Ingle has only a bowl of clear broth, a piece of swordfish, and steamed broccoli. Then there is Mr. Ingle, a higher-up in Mr. Gugelstein's firm, earlier seen wearing a hat

> that would make Mona's dad look like a boob. So flinty a type is Mr.
> Ingle, however, what with his thin straight mouth and thin straight

14. Xiao-huang Yin seems to corroborate Mona's greater comfort with Jews: "The Jews have altered the rule of Americanization and given it new meaning. It no longer equates with assimilation into the WASP culture; rather it means integration into a diversified society while maintaining one's own roots" (*Chinese American Literature,* 193). Philip Roth's Coleman Silk, in *The Human Stain,* seems to have drawn a similar conclusion. Andrew Furman reminds us that Mona's sister Callie is studying Chinese in college, which is also incomprehensible to their parents, who have worked so hard to "de-Chinese" their daughters and become "American." Furman points out that this situation is characteristic of much recent Jewish American fiction as well ("Immigrant Dreams and Civic Promises: Identity in Early Jewish American Literature and Gish Jen's *Mona in the Promised Land,*" 214–15). See also my discussion on pp. 152–56 of the younger generation reacting against their parents' assimilationist ideals.

nose and thin straight eyebrows, that even thus attired he looks to be
throwing care to the wind in a philanthropic manner. He is clearly the
sort of man who does not raise his voice. He is clearly the sort of man
who uses phrases like *The evidence notwithstanding* and *Make no
mistake,* and without having to rehearse them first. (*Mona,* 172)

But of course he has since "dressed for dinner." Only later do we find that
during that same dinner, when he was called out to the telephone, he quietly arranged the sacrifice of Mr. Gugelstein "for the good of the firm" and
its reputation, "the evidence notwithstanding" of Gugelstein's innocence in
a stock scandal. Such experiences, even in comfortable, upwardly mobile
Scarshill, are common to the Changs and the Gugelsteins, and give them
common cause against such as the Ingles despite their socioeconomic similarities.

At the positive pole, it is a desire to repair the world, so much the zeitgeist of those years, that draws Mona to her Jewish friends and to the
Hebrew term *tikkun olam,* or repairing the world, as her friend's rabbi explains it. Given the nature of the rabbi's Reform temple, Mona can be
Jewish without the strictures of dietary laws or Sabbath observance; it is
Jewish philosophy that attracts her. Already schooled by her Chinese family to think beyond herself to the whole family, to her responsibility within
and for the family, it is only one more step to feel responsible for the
larger group, and even beyond it. At bottom, Mona and her friends are
suburban teenagers of their era, their friendships cutting across color lines.
Both of these groups have been, and in many ways still are, marginalized, but it is neither class nor economics that have set them apart from
the majority.

In the essay quoted above, Sara Horowitz too makes a comparison between Jews and Asian Americans. She writes: "The geographic and intellectual history of Jews in the world addresses the way the outsider coexists and
often struggles with the insider in order to maintain both physical and cultural survival," and that for these reasons, as well as for previous exclusion
from canons and classrooms, Jewish studies would seem to have as compa-
triots programs such as minority studies and women's studies. In fact,
though, multicultural studies do not include Jewish studies at Horowitz's
university nor in most others, an issue—and challenge—Andrew Furman has
since taken up in his *Contemporary Jewish American Writers and the Multicultural Dilemma.* Horowitz sees Jews and Asians joined in this common
"dilemma": "[T]he multicultural agenda fails to see Jewish studies as representative of a marginalized culture because the generous presence of Jews

in the academy contrasts with the under-representation of women and other racial and ethnic minorities. Like Asian-Americans, Jews are victimized by their own positive stereotypes."[15]

What resonates here for me is the affinity I feel between the Chinese father in Kingston's *China Men,* who attaches his pigtail to a hook in the ceiling the night before his imperial examination so that he will be forced to stay awake while he studies, and the many legends of scholars staying awake over their Talmud—legends Jewish children are raised on. And here is my own family legend, repeated in jest to my children, but originating in dead earnest: When I cried to my father about how much studying I had to do, how many papers to write, he answered: "What do you do between four and six in the morning? When I was your age, and I had to go to work, that's when I studied Schiller and Goethe, Torah—learned English." And of course there is Abraham Lincoln and his candlelit study mirrored as well for all who perpetuate the tale.

I want such affinities to resonate between cultures, among us all. Therefore I do not want to focus here on a single culture—neither my own Jewish culture, nor any other. I agree with Bonnie TuSmith's statement in *All My Relatives: Community in Contemporary Ethnic American Literatures* that "how ethnic cultures relate to one another" needs to be made more clear, that "if we continue to overlook the relationships and connections among American cultures and persist in separatism, we scholars are guilty of perpetuating misunderstandings."[16] At the same time, there is such an abundance of riches in "ethnic" literature that I feel the need to narrow my scope to two major groups, even as I realize how vast each is, and even though I draw in passing on other literatures. In enclosing two cultures within the binding of a single book, I hope to position the texts to reflect one another and, paradoxically, to invite all readers to notice those reflective possibilities, even though they may merely suggest, or resonate, or distort the felt similarities. While TuSmith is right to include more than one ethnicity in the "community" of her book, I notice that only ethnicities of

15. Horowitz, "Jewish Studies," 155. In discussing the exclusion of Jewish studies from "minority" canons and classrooms, Horowitz posits as one of the reasons the "mistaken apprehension that 'Judeo-Christian' is a shared culture, a hybrid product, responsible for the colonialist project rather than in itself an instance of colonization. . . . The 'New' Testament retroactively interprets—and rewrites—the 'Old,' first by renaming, then by renarrativizing. It effectively negates, rather than retains, the Hebrew (Jewish) Bible, effacing its Jewish meanings," and this, as is well known, is done in the service of Christian typology, which seeks possibly predictive references to Christ in the Hebrew Bible (ibid., 157).

16. TuSmith, *All My Relatives,* ix.

color are there. It is my intention, rather, to study literature cross-culturally in a manner that deliberately includes those who are "white" and those who are "of color," those who live in poverty and those in the middle class, for race, class, income bracket, level of education, and gender are not synonymous, nor are they always the point; these are not the only obstacles to comfort and achievement. I hope in my selections to transcend these delimiting categories: The Chinese laundryman may have been a scholar in China, where there are no Chinese laundries. The Jewish peddler on Delancey Street may have been a Talmudic scholar. Jewish immigrants came to America with vast differences among them in culture, class, economic status, education, and geographical origin. The same was true of the Chinese, some of whom came as permitted scholars, others to work on the railroad. In today's immigrants, too, there are vast differences.

In other words, it is possible to be white and poor, educated and oppressed, of color and wealthy, female and any of the above. To come from a third-world country is not necessarily to come out of poverty: these countries also have people of immense privilege, whose children are taken to private schools in chauffeured cars, who never pick up their own dirty socks. But issues of marginality, of moving between languages and cultures, of family and way of life uprooted, of how much or how little to assimilate, of how to educate one's children and oneself—these issues deserve attention and understanding. While they are certainly exacerbated by economics, even obscured by more pressing material needs, one must tease out factors that are not always necessarily, nor permanently, related. Refugees may have had to leave great wealth behind and learn a whole new way of life economically as well as culturally and linguistically; doctors and engineers become orderlies and technicians when credentials and native language are of no use in beginning their professional lives here. Some make it, some don't. Some do not even try, or haven't the money or leisure to do so. The Asian family that runs a mom-and-pop grocery store, everyone helping fourteen hours a day, children taking turns going to school and doing homework, might find much in common with the Bober family in Bernard Malamud's novel *The Assistant,* could they but read and speak the same language. The thoughtful reader can see how one reflects the other, and how both reflect a grandparent or a neighbor.

Only mirrors—literal mirrors—return perfect images, two-dimensional illusions of identity that are, in reality, silver-backed glass, not faces at all. At best, the image conveys an illusion of depth. And the illusion seems to imitate every expression of the person facing it, peering into it. Figurative mirrors, on the other hand, render only partial, or approximate and selective, likenesses—attempts at mimesis—and are much more dependent on the viewer's inclination to notice figures and reflections, on a viewer who "reflects" carefully enough to see.

Reflection—Imitation—Mimesis

Art, Aristotle tells us in the *Poetics,* is imitation—of actions, of men in action, of sounds, of objects. He writes of the human instinct to imitate, to learn from imitation, and to take pleasure in things imitated: "Objects which in themselves we view with pain, we delight to contemplate when reproduced with minute fidelity. . . . Thus the reason why men enjoy seeing a likeness is that in contemplating it they find themselves learning or inferring, and saying perhaps, 'Ah, that is he.' For if you happen not to have seen the original, the pleasure will be due not to the imitation as such, but to the execution." Aristotle points to three sorts of "pleasure in things imitated": learning ("to learn gives the liveliest pleasure"), recognition ("Ah, that is he"), and what we might term aesthetic—appreciation of the craft ("the execution, the coloring, or some other cause").[17] We admire the manner in which the artist or writer has been able to create the illusion of reality—the imitation, mimesis.

Of course we now know that exact referentiality is impossible, that neither art, nor drama, nor words are ever truly representational, ever merely mimetic. Still, there *is* the pleasure of learning, there *is* recognition, there *is* appreciation of the way a text renders or creates a world we can recognize sufficiently to make sense of, and further, to identify with, even to recognize ourselves in it. Inge Crosman Wimmers points out that personal identification is an important factor in reading, that interpretation includes both text interpretation and self-interpretation, with self-understanding as a way of giving a text its significance and veracity. To the pleasure of recognition (which includes the pleasure of feeling "smart") we might add the pleasure of realizing significance, which is set in motion when we recognize something we can identify with. A heightened response and closer connection occurs when we can say not only "Ah, that is he," but also, even in a very small, very partial way, "Is that myself I see?" Antecedent to our apprehending the mimetic work, however, is the work in its inception, springing from what Aristotle sees as "lying deep in our nature. . . . [T]he instinct of imitation is implanted in man from childhood . . . the most

17. Aristotle, *Poetics,* trans. S. H. Butcher, part 4.

imitative of living creatures." And so to Aristotle's list of pleasures in imitation we might add the pleasure—the need, in fact—of performing as well
as apprehending the imitation, an act that must of necessity always be
frustrating in its failures. But it is in the struggle to render, in the failure of
mimesis, that images become enriched, and thus create not only illusions
of reality, but also new realities. This failure to close completely, to mean
or reproduce exactly, is the source of what (in literature) Wolfgang Iser
terms "gaps" in a text. And it is these gaps that invite readers in, to fill them
in as we can, thereby creating our own readings and, in the process,
newly creating ourselves. Language itself—as creative, as structuring, as a
system of movable parts capable of infinite arrangements—can also be
seen as material out of which we build, creating the "speculative instruments" with which we see.[18] At the same time, as language "imitates" reality or attempts to, so do its discrete units, words, imitate and reflect. The
reflective property of each tiny mirror is capable of entering into countless
kaleidoscopic structures and designs, available to the one who first arranges
them, and also to the one who looks, turns and rearranges them, and looks
again.

Ambitiously, stubbornly, language attempts mimesis—and fails gloriously.
The images that language creates, even the illusion that it *is* mimetic, are
rich because, being only approximate, they are also more elastic. Language and "mirrors" as imagemakers are therefore not simply reflective
agents, but much more. To the classical notion of art as mirror of nature,
the Romantics added the concept of light—the colored light of feelings.[19]
In this context, the language that not only reflects but also illuminates can
shed light outward, illuminate for the reader a version of "reality" that renders feeling and experience; it can invite the reader's empathy, and possibly
even illuminate the reader's likeness in that mirror. Even more important,
the attempt to render in language can shed light inward for the writer,
helping to create a reality out of what is inchoate and only felt; to reconcile what is familiar with what is strange, the new face in the mirror with
the one that will not go away; and thereby to forge a new, always evolving
image that is neither one nor the other, but created out of both. "Attempt"

18. Inge Crosman Wimmers, *Poetics of Reading: Approaches to the Novel,* 8; Aristotle,
Poetics, part 4; Wolfgang Iser, *The Act of Reading: A Theory of Aesthetic Response,* 22.
Wimmers's theories, as well as those of other reader-response theorists, will be discussed in more detail in Chapter 8. "Speculative instruments" is I. A. Richards's term,
cited by Ann E. Berthoff in *The Making of Meaning: Metaphors, Models, and Maxims
for Writing Teachers,* 113.
19. See M. H. Abrams, *The Mirror and the Lamp: Romantic Theory and the Critical
Tradition,* 52–55, for a discussion of these metaphors.

implies that such illumination and such creation require conscious effort, and implies as well the ever-present possibility of failure.

The most radical lesson in mimetic failure occurs when one is plunged into a foreign-language environment; even a young child in this situation learns quickly how dismally mimesis fails, how the word no longer represents the thing. It may do so for the speaker, but not for the listener. Even once the listener learns the word for that object or that feeling, will the new word express the same reality or alter it? Can faith in language ever again be what it was when it seemed so simple to find and express meaning in familiar words, when one could be confident of being understood?

The most accomplished learner of the new language, the bilingual language artist—the writer between languages—perhaps understands best how mimesis fails, and how, out of that failure, richer, more evocative meaning can be created. Usually that same creator-out-of-language has had to struggle with the language of culture as well. The works I will examine contain moments when protagonists search for meaning in language, and search for themselves in their new language. When language fractures, they seek their own images, past or present, literal or figurative, and are compelled to ask: Is this still me? At times it is the mirror that seems fractured, and language becomes the way to negotiate the fractures. This metaphor became literal for me quite by chance one day when I caught sight of myself in a cracked mirror; my face looked like a Picasso, its planes distorted and out of place, fragmented, comical, barely recognizable as me. If it had been a Picasso it would have called out for interpretation, for restructuring in language to give it meaning. Fractured language necessitates the mirror; a fractured mirror necessitates language to interpret the fragmented image to the self and to the reader, who may find in that text a "fractured mirror" or reflection of herself.

Georges Gusdorf refers to autobiography as "the mirror in which the individual reflects his own image." He writes of how the invention of silver-backed mirrors in Venice at the end of the Middle Ages made possible the self-portraits of Rembrandt and Van Gogh, and of artists' fascination with them. True, Christian self-examination preceded this invention, witness Augustine's *Confessions,* but the "theological mirror," according to Gusdorf, is a "deforming mirror that plays up without pity the slightest faults of the moral personality. . . . The Venetian mirror provides . . . Rembrandt with an image of himself that is neither twisted nor flattering." We have here three types of self-image: the one seen in the silver-backed mirror, the self-portrait, and the autobiography. They all require some sort of self-examination, with the latter two involving the subject in creating a likeness, not simply observing it, and producing, whether in paint or in words, versions of the self that imply psychological depth and the possibility of varying point of view and perspective. In addition, the autobiography, unlike the portrait, presents a life developing in time, attempting reconstitution of the self (or a version of it) in a "special unity and identity across time."[20] While we may contest the possibility of ever really achieving that unity, we assume the existence of a person who subsumes various subject positions, or attempts to do so, to represent, if not *the* life, at least *a* life of the subject. In the works of fiction under discussion, protagonists share the bicultural and bilingual situations of their authors, and seem to share their need to answer the question "Who and what am I?"—the need to look in the mirror, to fashion an identity that has depth and history, and to do so in language.

The texts I will examine dramatize the instability of subjectivity, as well as the urgency to create it. While deconstructionists undermine our notions of identity, personhood, and subjectivity, the writers of these texts, who already know about fragmentation of life and language—its instability and unreliability—attempt the reverse process: to shore up the fragments, to create, however tentatively and inadequately, wholeness out of those fragments. One could even say that the very act of structuring words and fictions, of creating characters, of binding language and situations into artistic wholes, is itself mimetic—an imitation, as in magic—of what is desired. The work of these writers, like their daily lives, whatever else it may be is also an attempt at a "temporary stitching together of a series of often contradictory subject positions."[21] As we read their successes, which are always partially failed attempts, we admire the mimesis that shows us so familiar a condition. Their need to shore up the fragments mirrors us, the readers, in the act of reading and in the acts of our own attempts at resolution, at creating our own "subjectivities." Foucault's term *author function* cannot possibly describe what these authors actually feel in the process of writing, in the exigency to fashion momentary stays against confusion and fragmentation. The urgent question "Who and what am I?" cannot be satisfactorily resolved by definitions based on fluidity, or assumptions of being always already constituted.[22] These authors have already experienced that fluidity, and feel themselves constituted out of differences that often conflict and confuse and destabilize. They want now to pick up the pieces and knit them together somehow, in texts, in life. Surely they have read

20. Georges Gusdorf, "Conditions and Limits of Autobiography," 33, 34–35.
21. Lester Faigley, *Fragments of Rationality: Postmodernity and the Subject of Composition*, 9.
22. Michel Foucault, "What Is an Author?"

the theories, but what these "immigrant" authors are feeling and writing from, what comes through in the characters they create, is theory on the pulses.

Language, then, creates new "mirrors" in which the writer sees herself anew and which reflect her new (perhaps hybrid) identity. Examples in the chapters to come will show such identities set off intertextually against several such "reflectors": mirrors, language(s), and narrative acts, whether of traditions and legends or lives. The face that peers into the mirror asking "Who am I?" or "Who are you, and why do I see you when I look for my own familiar reflection?" may find an answer, a richer and more complicated likeness, in language: for the writer, a newly formed and gradually forming identity, and, on the page, a new home.

2

See(k)ing the Self

Mirrors and Mirroring in Bicultural Texts

When David Levinsky puts on his new clothes and has the barber cut off his sidelocks, his mentor remarks: "Quite an American, isn't he?" as he brings him to a mirror. To quote Levinsky: "When I took a look in the mirror I was bewildered. I scarcely recognized myself. . . . It was as though the hair-cut and the American clothes had changed my identity."[1]

It seems to me no coincidence that mirrors and mirroring occur so often in texts written by bilingual, bicultural authors; that in work after work either the mirror surprises the one who looks into it, or an "other" in some fashion mirrors the protagonist. Typically there is some discrepancy between the actual, surface, external mirror image that any onlooker could see and the interior, mental self—whether wished-for, or felt, or despised—which prompts the questions "Who and what am I?" and "Which is the real me?" Admittedly, this phenomenon is not exclusive to bicultural texts any more than are the issues of identity formation and conflict at the heart of this imagery. One remembers the "stranger" in Jane Eyre's mirror at those junctures where (like the bicultural protagonists) she embarks on a new life and perceives herself in a new light or new role—for example when, in her wedding gown, she looks in the mirror and sees "a robed and veiled figure so unlike [her] usual self that it seemed almost the image of a stranger."[2]

---

1. Abraham Cahan, *The Rise of David Levinsky,* 101.
2. Charlotte Brontë, *Jane Eyre,* 362. See also William R. Siebenschuh, "The Image of the Child and the Plot of *Jane Eyre,*" 309, 313. To speak of "mirroring" (and not simply mirrors) is to recognize the relationship between mirror image and mirroring double. This of course calls to mind the pivotal role played by *The Picture of Dorian Gray.* Doubles "mirroring" what one does not want to face in the self are discussed later in

Kathleen Woodward writes of the preponderance of mirror images in literary representations of the aged body, and the horror at the recognition they force on those looking into the mirror. In a way, this is the reverse of the baby's "mirror stage" experience as Lacan analyzes it; there the mirror image is whole, an image of a unified "self," creating an illusion of harmony belied by the discord of images, sounds, and sensory responses the baby actually experiences. The aged person, on the other hand, carries around a youthful self-image, one of a body still "whole" and strong, of a face unlined. Woodward cites an example from a footnote Freud appended to his essay on the uncanny. While Freud was sitting in a train compartment, the lavatory door swung open "and an elderly gentleman in a dressing gown and a traveling cap came in." Freud jumped up to redirect the stranger, assuming he had come into the compartment by mistake. He writes: "I at once realized to my dismay that the intruder was nothing but my own reflection in the looking-glass of the open door. I . . . thoroughly disliked his appearance."[3]

What these examples have in common with each other, and with the examples I find in bicultural texts, is that they dramatize the difference between a mental self-image and an "external" mirror image. Coincidental though it may be, the context of the journey is an appropriate "frame" for the mirror incident. Whether it is a literal journey, such as Freud's train trip or the immigrant's crossing, or a metaphorical one, such as Freud's arriving at a new awareness of how far along in age he has come, Jane's arriving at a new "station" in life, or the immigrant's becoming more like an American, the mirror can suddenly force the "traveler" to see how different he or she is from the "others" who seem so much at home. But more complicated is the strangeness one can feel when, looking in the mirror, one sees no discernible difference from those around one, but rather a difference from one's former image and from the people at mother's dinner table—a difference more complex and more conflicted than the first.

For this reason, the look into the mirror—indeed, the very need to look into the mirror, to seek one's image—assumes greater urgency in bicultural

---

this chapter, as are societal and identity conflicts. Wilde fits into this category by dint of his "marginalizing" homosexuality. It is telling that the writing of *Dorian Gray* coincides with the period of his newly surfacing sexual identity (Mel Gussow, "Displaying All Wilde's Many Sides: A London Show Moves to the Morgan Library, Continuing the Rise in the Assessment of His Multiple Talents," *New York Times*, September 12, 2001, sec. E, p. 1). It is conceivable that Wilde was at this time experiencing an identity crisis that parallels the bicultural protagonists under discussion here.

3. Kathleen Woodward, "The Mirror Stage of Old Age," 104; Sigmund Freud, "The 'Uncanny,'" 106.

texts, where change and difference is more obvious or more sudden and therefore more clearly dramatized, than in the conventional bildungsroman or metaphoric journey of progress through the stages of life, maturation, and self-realization. Whether sought or come upon accidentally, a view in a mirror is instantaneous, not a gradual process over time; the unexpected difference reflected in the mirror is a trope (as well as a crucial incident) expressing identity disruption or formation. Levinsky's image is suddenly and radically different, and that difference is but the physical manifestation of a suddenly, radically changed environment and way of life. He has crossed to an unfamiliar place, become surrounded by an incomprehensible language, is stripped of all former intimates and even nodding acquaintances. This new life, and this mirror image, seem to have no connection with the young man he had been only yesterday, or with the way he had looked a mere fifteen minutes earlier. In bicultural families, differences in languages, customs, and assumptions can loom as conflicts or require identity decisions daily.

What postmodern theorists have been undermining—stable ego, personhood, identity—bicultural writers feel on their pulses. Phillip Brian Harper makes the point that in works of the "socially marginalized" such issues have always been of concern, and have predated postmodernism; he goes on to say that "marginalized groups' experience of decenteredness is itself a largely unacknowledged factor in the 'general' postmodern condition." These writers, and their protagonists, are always acutely conscious of a nonunitary self. Postmodernists, in their theories of subjectivity, contest classical concepts which assume a unity and continuity over time, such as Emile Benveniste's or Georges Gusdorf's. Like postmodernists, characters in the works under discussion (whether overtly autobiographical or sharing only biculturality with their authors) confront their own fragmented subjectivities and are only too well aware of the various, often conflicting, elements that destabilize, even as they construct, identity.[4]

The persistent need to construct that identity, though, to attempt some

---

4. Phillip Brian Harper, *Framing the Margins: The Social Logic of Postmodern Culture,* 3–4; Barry N. Olshen, "Subject, Persona, and Self in the Theory of Autobiography," 9. bell hooks writes eloquently about the pain of fragmentation and the need to put the broken pieces back together, but her "fragmentation" seems to have a different source (*Talking Back: Thinking Feminist, Thinking Black*). While pain and hurt are in evidence in bicultural texts, one feels less "brokenness" and abuse than dislocation: the "break" between a past of seeming stability and the not-yet-reached, possibly illusory stability that attracts even as it excludes or provokes guilt over one's desire for it. Between these lies an unstable, shifting space, often the source of "fragmentation," whether of place or identity.

sort of unity and continuity over time, does not go away. It is as though a force for wholeness and integration asserts itself against the forces of fragmentation. The living, breathing person living a fragmented life, or the character who seems to, needs no theory to point out abstractly the destabilization which he so acutely, even viscerally, feels. Rather, he seeks out images and creates forms that integrate, or at the very least appear to have a unity, in an attempt to give the lie to divisiveness and incongruity. Of course, that attempt may fail—fail, that is, in conquering fragmentation and achieving harmonious reconciliation. But other kinds of success can result, driven by that very failure: a satisfying expression of one's feelings; a hard-won coming to terms with what must always be negotiated; an enlarged, stereoscopic vision of oneself and others, to mention a few. It is as if the greater the fragmentation, the greater the force for wholeness and integration. The result, as we shall see, can be creative—even saving. A character seeks a confirming image in the mirror (no matter that its "wholeness" is as illusory as the neatness of an incident in the "telling"); a writer pieces the fragments, the differences and conflicts, into the wholeness of a piece of writing, orders and structures the narrative, and achieves at the very least the unity that comes of enclosure between two covers—achieves, thus, a binding.[5]

Of course, any sense we have of coherence must be both momentary and general. Even if we have never left our home culture or language environment, our view of ourselves is constantly disrupted: a newly capped tooth, a new hairstyle, a new book, an unflattering photograph, an unfamiliar situation all shake our previous notion of who and what we are, our sense of "coherence," and there are enough of these disruptions that we cannot possibly think of ourselves as unitary. We see ourselves anew every hour; we play various roles in quick succession, at times simultaneously, every day, every hour. With each new stage in life, we become what we have never been before: a schoolchild, a lover, a parent, an in-law, a widower. Such jolts, whether joyful or traumatic or both, can seem to confer new identities. Even when a role has been gradually prepared for, as with a career, our new title—doctor, lieutenant, professor—takes time to assimilate

5. In relating marginal or ethnic writers to innovation in literary forms, Werner Sollors writes of their "acute sense of doubleness," the "double consciousness" discussed by Emerson and Du Bois. He goes on to say: "Double-consciousness characters may be attracted to mirrors, reflecting windows, or smooth-surfaced ponds" (*Beyond Ethnicity,* 249). See also Harper, *Framing the Margins,* on modernist writing; Norman N. Holland, *The Brain of Robert Frost: A Cognitive Approach to Literature;* and Oster, *Toward Robert Frost: The Reader and Poet,* on Frost's discussions of (and need of) form as a saving sanity.

to our names and our "I." There is, for quite a while, a tendency to look behind us to see who is really being addressed, the temptation to ask: "Why do you dress me in these borrowed robes?"

Surely these phenomena are magnified and multiplied when we move into another culture and language, or exist (and must therefore constantly navigate) between two separate ones. But even in these situations, as with the monolingual nonmigrant, we still answer to our names, "mean" the same "person" when we say "I," even where names have been changed or "I" doesn't come easily. We still feel unique, and need to be reminded that we are unique, whatever our logically, theoretically, intellectually constructed denials of such possibilities.[6]

What happens in bicultural texts when characters face their mirrors? In or out of texts, a mirror reflects the one who looks into it; in all cases that reflection is an illusion—perhaps an illusion of wholeness, perhaps a "prepared" face that conceals who and what a person really is, protecting the "inner" self by maintaining an image a mirror can faithfully reflect, the same "face" that satisfies others. At times the illusions in front of these characters interact with what they imagine, feel, desire—or wish to deny. Or the face in the mirror looks strangely unfamiliar, and that very "newness" engenders a new view of the self—perhaps new power: Jing-mei crying at the sight of her ordinary, "ugly" face in Amy Tan's *Joy Luck Club,* "trying to scratch out the face in the mirror," then seeing a face she has never seen before—her prodigy side: "I looked at my reflection, blinking so I could see more clearly. The girl staring back at me was angry, powerful. This girl and I were the same. I had new thoughts, willful thoughts" (*Joy,* 134). In this example, the character's inner anger is actually reflected in the mirror, but what had looked simply "ugly" becomes power when fueled by anger—power newly felt and newly seen, or rather, newly felt because it is newly seen. It isn't that the mirror reflects an image different from the anger Jing-mei feels, but that it makes such feelings manifest for the first time. *This* image of herself is unfamiliar, and the shock of recognition at her "new" face, her prodigy side, leads her to feel a new inner power that allows her to defy her mother. As she matures, though, she exhibits less power than the mirror promises.

6. Certainly, one must tread gingerly over that slippery terrain of the language of identity, self, and subjectivity, recognizing how unstable are these concepts and our uses of these terms. For more detail on these terms, see Olshen, "Subject, Persona, and Self"; George Levine's collection of essays *Constructions of the Self,* including his own introduction; Paul Smith's *Discerning the Subject;* and, not to be forgotten, Erik H. Erikson's *Identity: Youth and Crisis.* On subjectivity in "minor" texts, see Harper, *Framing the Margins,* and hooks, *Talking Back.*

The mirror of another character in the book, Lindo Jong, shows an image whose beauty and bridal purity serves, on the one hand, to conceal her thoughts, and on the other hand, to symbolize them. She says of look-ing into a mirror on her wedding day:

> I was surprised at what I saw. I had on a beautiful red dress, but what I saw was even more valuable. I was strong. I was pure. I had genuine thoughts inside that no one could see, that no one could ever take away from me. I was like the wind. I threw my head back and smiled proudly to myself. And then I draped the . . . red scarf over my face and covered these thoughts up. But underneath the scarf I still knew who I was. (*Joy*, 58)

It is as if the bridal image (typically an image more regal and beautiful than the one a young woman sees every day when she washes her face) inspires her, the external image raising her self-esteem to the point where she feels a new inner strength. In addition, Lindo's now-draped face parallels her resolve to cover but preserve (and even further de-velop) who she is. And it dramatizes clearly the discrepancies between outer and inner views—the mirror image anyone can see as opposed to the unseen that is more genuine, more pure, and more strong. In both of these examples, the one who looks into the mirror is inspired by a view of herself as different, unfamiliar, and recognizes as well that inner power or sense of self can be very different from what is seen or has heretofore been seen.

Mirrors can surprise, they can reveal, and they can deceive by showing only masks and smooth surfaces, but always, what they show is illusory or incomplete at best. They can reflect only what is put in front of them: a bride; an angry, tearful face; a newly shorn Eastern European Jewish im-migrant. The heart of the mirror scenes in these texts, though, lies in what *else* these faces bring to the mirror, what depths beneath the shallow sur-faces, what needs, what expectations. More important, how do these char-acters reflect on what they see? To what extent are they torn by the discrepancies between the merely visual and what is felt to be "real"? Very different from Lindo, and closer to Jing-mei's initial reaction to her reflec-tion, is the disappointment experienced by Jook-Liang in Wayson Choy's *Jade Peony*: Dancing before a mirror, she performs all the Shirley Temple motions and thinks: "*I'm not ugly . . . I'm not useless.*' . . . My heart almost burst with expectation. I looked again into the hall mirror, seeking Shirley Temple with her dimpled smile and perfect white-skin features. Bluntly reflected back at me was a broad sallow moon with slit dark eyes, topped by a helmet of black hair."[7]

In a very different example, David Schearl in Henry Roth's *Call It Sleep* uses "mirrors" as the vehicle for wish fulfillment, in this case the wish to not be, or at least to not be who he is. David needs to deceive himself about his present existence, and mirrors help him to do so, to split himself into being and not-being as long as he identifies totally with what the glass of the shopwindows show him, as long as he can convince himself that his being is identical with the image he sees. As he slows down on his walk home, conflicted between needing the safety of home and fearing what might await him there, as he makes a futile attempt to separate himself from his guilt and his present from his actions of a few hours before, he keeps catching sight of himself and then losing his reflection between the windows. He tries to change his unbearable reality by pretending that when he is between the "mirrors," thus invisible to himself, he is no more.[8] This image-obliterating has its parallels in the times he desperately imagines himself elsewhere: "Be two Davids." This need to split himself into two people, or to occupy two places at once, or to go back to an irrevocable past, occurs at moments of great fear, or guilt, or inability to find his way home.

In the autobiographic *Lost in Translation,* Eva Hoffman's imagined image seems more authentic to her than the one she would actually see in her friend Penny's mirror were she to step in front of it. She has difficulty fitting in with her American teenage friends, who are primping before a party. They rely on the accuracy of mirror reflections to create equally shallow surfaces. Their mirrors help them to construct not identities but "images"—in Eva's view, "slightly garish bonbons." Rather than showing the boys who they really are, they will "show them what they want"—in effect, reflections of the boys' fantasies as the girls imagine them.[9]

Still struggling with her Polish American identity, Eva tries to picture the self she would see if she were still in Poland:

> If you had stayed there, your hair would have been straight, and you
> would have worn a barrette on one side. But maybe by now you
> would have grown it into a ponytail? Like the ones you saw on those
> sexy faces in the magazine you used to read? I don't know. You would

7. Wayson Choy, *The Jade Peony,* 43.

8. Henry Roth, *Call It Sleep,* 377–79 (hereinafter cited in the text as *Sleep*).

9. Eva Hoffman, *Lost in Translation: A Life in a New Language,* 129 (hereinafter cited in the text as *Lost*).

have been fifteen by now. Different from thirteen. You would be
going to the movies with Zbyszek and maybe to a café after, where
you would meet a group of friends and talk late into the night.

She contrasts those friends with "these churlish boys who play spin the
bottle," and concludes that it is the Cracow Ewa who is "more real" (*Lost,*
119–20).

In this "dialogue" Eva/Ewa is not in front of a mirror, but rather trying
to imagine her reflection as a Polish teenager. She is combining her past
place with her present *time* and thus constructing a "self" that cannot
possibly exist, at least not anywhere but in her imagination. The image
and the scenario she constructs are fabricated partly from memory, partly
from imagination, and that fabrication is presented as an incident in her
teenage-American past by the present Eva telling her memory of her
teenage identity struggle. Robert Folkenflik speaks of the "doublement" in
autobiography between the "I" who is talking or narrating and the figure in
the past, the past self as "other."[10] In the Hoffman example, this is *double-*
doublement: the present-day mature writer, Eva Hoffman, narrates the
teenage Eva's contemplation of what her Polish teenage self might have
been. Within Hoffman's memory is another doublement: the teenage Eva
in Canada contemplating the imagined teenage Ewa in Poland. Within the
"othering" that is inherent to any autobiography, then, there is an othering
created by this teenage dialogue, wherein the Polish Ewa is addressed as
"you." Thus Eva/Ewa is having the sort of conversation one imagines taking place in front of a mirror—an "I" addresses a view of herself as "you."
In doing so she is further separating and distancing herself from the Polish
version of herself, a distancing which is especially poignant in that the
"you" is the self she prefers to the "I." In this case the othering is not one
of time (the dialogue is between two versions of Eva at the same age) but
of place, with the "I" Eva located in the cultural milieu that is Canada, the
place of spin-the-bottle and primping for the boys in Penny's mirror. But
the imaging of a teenage Polish Ewa has a temporal dimension as well, for
it is neither simply a "reflection" on Eva's possible teenage-present counter-
part nor a memory of her past in Poland: rather it is imagination projected
on memory, the memory of how teenagers looked and acted when she

10. Robert Folkenflik, "The Self as Other," 234. Charlotte Linde makes the point that
the narrator stands apart from the protagonist of autobiographical narrative (*Life
Stories,* 123). Agnes Heller writes that modern autobiography has a dual author: the author of the text is at the same time the author of his or her own life ("Death of the
Subject?" 277).

observed them in her Polish childhood—an educated guess necessarily qualified by changing times and conventions and by her ever-present nostalgia. We realize as well that to the past Ewa whom Eva can actually remember, this teenage Ewa would have been in the future. The mirror may flash a static, imagined image, but it also depends on memory; the contrast of two places in the present time cannot be separated from longing for the place and milieu that exist only in the narrator's past.

The key to such fusion is the narrative act, with the imagination not only filling in gaps in knowledge and experience, but also collapsing the distinctions between space and time in order to "create" contrasting images. Narrative, unlike a mirror image or a painting, spans time (as does Freud's "mirror" on a moving train, and as a journey spans both time and space). Folkenflik, in fact, sees autobiography as a kind of mirror, "as a mirror stage in life, an extended moment that enables one to reflect on oneself by presenting an image of the self for contemplation."[11] In Hoffman's case, the "image of the self for contemplation" is *also* contemplating: looking backward in space and in time, and, from the past, constructing a hypothetical future that would bring it to the teenage present, an unrealizable, unrealized hybrid present—which is, of course, the past to the author of the autobiography. The book brilliantly shifts back and forth among narrative modes from a timeless hypothetical subjunctive (the imaging of Ewa), to a "present" in the writer's past (as a teenager in Canada), and ultimately to the present writer engaging in the autobiographical act, gazing at "an image of the self for contemplation." Another example illustrates how such manipulation of time, mode, and tense is accomplished: Eva is asked by a Polish friend whether she regrets having left Poland. "How can I possibly answer? I no longer know who would have lived the life I might have lived here." What follows is a hypothetical history of *ifs* and *would haves*, and then, this blending of modes:

> Where would I have gone? Israel, America, West Germany, Sweden? Here the speculations become more attenuated, for I don't know the person who would have made that decision: I don't know how her daily life felt until then, how successful or frustrated she was, how adventurous or timid. I don't know the quality of her sensations, or what her yearnings were, or how she satisfied them. I don't know the accidents that left little scars on her skin, or the accretions of sorrow and

11. Folkenflik, "Self as Other," 234.

> pleasure on her soul. No, one can't create a real out of a conditional
> history; in light of the simple declarative statement of actual existence,
> "would have been" or "as if" loses its ontological status. (*Lost*, 240–41)

In fashioning a text, though, Hoffman puts it together for the reader, but
more important, she seems at last to have put it together for herself. The final
words of the book—"I am here now"—can, indeed should, be read and
reread so that in each reading the stress falls on a different word. In these
four words, and their formation into a declarative sentence, everything in
the book is contained: identity, existence, and the time *and* the place which
contain them both. The narrative has not left us with the teenage Eva, or
even the college student or married woman, but with the "free" adult, recently returned from a visit to her former world, to those Polish friends of
her past in the present-day adulthood they actually inhabit.

The "I" has become confident in its right to speak as a subject—going
further, as the subject of a sentence, one in which the "I" asserts as well as
locates itself. It assumes an integrity that is hard-won, achieved by an act
of articulation. In *Sources of the Self: The Making of Modern Identity*, the
philosopher Charles Taylor manages to reconcile fragmentation and de-
centering with inwardness, the quest for meaning and sense in life with
expressiveness and articulation. He writes that the unique way he experiences activity, thought, and feeling makes him "a being that can speak of
itself in the first person." Yet Eva Hoffman and Maxine Hong Kingston
both write that for a long time this is precisely what they were unable to
do—they could not say or write "I."[12] Their first-person books stand as tri-
umphant testimony not only to their arriving at that stance, but also to
their need to do so; we can see how their books have both mapped and
enabled their torturous journeys. Identity and (in the immigrant novel especially) a sense of place require construction. Heidegger points out that
Ich bin (I am) has as the root of its verb *bin* the verb *bauen* (to build, to
inhabit).[13] All three meanings—be, build, inhabit—and especially their
conflation are immensely relevant to people between cultures, languages,
and/or places in their need to construct both identity and home-as-place.

12. Charles Taylor, *Sources of the Self: The Making of Modern Identity*, 18, 22, 131. It
could be said of Kingston, though not of Hoffman, that the conventions of her culture
may have prevented her from asserting herself as "I"; however, I do not think this is the
primary factor here. Emile Benveniste writes of such conventions in *Problems in
General Linguistics*, 226.
13. Heidegger quoted in William Boelhower, *Through a Glass Darkly: Ethnic Semiosis in American Literature*, 43.

To return to the *subject* of that verb is to return to *Ich*—the self, the subject that requires construction and that also constructs. Emile Benveniste points out that, unlike nouns which have objective referents or the third-person pronouns that refer to them, "each *I* has its own reference and corresponds each time to a unique being who is set up as such. . . . It is solely a 'reality of discourse.' . . . *I* signifies 'the person who is uttering the present instance of discourse containing *I*.' " The "I" then is always active, constructing, immediate. As both referent and referee in the discourse it constructs, it is always already "double," even as is the mirror image and its "referent"—the one seen, or sought, or differentiated from in the mirror, that *I* see(k)ing that me.[14] Benveniste goes on to say, "Ego is he who *says* Ego," which demonstrates that "it is in and through language that man constitutes himself as a *subject*." Benveniste emphasizes "says" (language), but we must not forget the "he" (or she)—the person doing the languaging. Benveniste also writes: "It is by identifying himself as a unique person pronouncing *I* that each speaker sets himself up . . . as the 'subject.' "[15]

Erik H. Erikson's relating of language, philosophy, and psychology as he discusses sense of identity is both useful and moving:

> In order to clarify and even quantify man's attitude toward himself, philosophers and psychologists have created such nouns as the "I" or the "Self," making imaginary entities out of a manner of speaking. Habits of syntax . . . say much about this obscure subject. No one who has worked with autistic children will ever forget the horror of observing how desperately they struggle to grasp the meaning of saying "I" and "You" and how impossible it is for them, for language presupposes the experience of a coherent "I."

14. Benveniste, *Problems,* 218. I realize that I have used *me* instinctively (rather than writing "that *I* see[k]ing myself"), but in analyzing my choice, I arrive at its logic: I assume a greater distance, a greater sense of "otherness" in *me* than in *myself,* incorporating as it does the notion of "self," that "structure maintaining the subject's conscious and unconscious, psychological and somatic sense of his or her own identity" (Olshen, "Subject, Persona, and Self," 6) that persuasion of "something utterly mine" (Irving Howe, "The Self in Literature," 249–50). This seems consistent with the history of *self* as a reflexive pronoun: it enters usage at about the same time that *self* became a noun— an "entity." The OED shows first uses of *my self*—*my* modifying *self*—as early as the fifteenth century, but for the one-word *myself* the first entry is Samuel Johnson, 1759. *Myself* had been used as an intensifier, while reflexivity was expressed by means of the direct object pronoun: for example, the archaic-sounding "Now I lay me down to sleep" or "I hie me"; note too Milton's use of the intensifying form to replace "I" (or possibly to intensify a deleted "I") but not as a reflexive direct object: "Which way I fly is Hell / Myself am Hell."

15. Benveniste, *Problems,* 224, 220.

Taylor, while recognizing "the modernist multileveled consciousness" as "frequently decentered," nevertheless insists on what he terms "radical [in the sense of root, essence, at center] reflexivity"—the stance that adopts the first-person standpoint, which attends not to my wounded hand, to take Taylor's example, but to myself as the agent of experience and making this—my experience and my agency in it—my object.[16]

Agency, the I/myself connection—this is the grammar of reflexivity even as it is self-reflection, whether in the sense of thinking about (reflecting on) the self or of seeing oneself *as* self. In the latter case, self is the seen object, as with the self reflected, and it is the grammatical object as well. Where but in a first-person narration of one's own story (either by an author or a character) do we find that the grammatical subject of the discourse is also the topical subject of the discourse, and at the same time the object being viewed—hence reflexive, as grammar shows us, and as Taylor terms the first-person (radical reflexive) stance. To continue unpacking "reflexivity": the reflection I see in the mirror results from the reflexive act of looking in the mirror. When the image I see is not the one I have been carrying around in my mind, or when I feel a disjunction between different versions of "me," I am forced to ask which one is the real me, or, more troublesome: "Is this also me?" or "Is this even me at all?" How do I reconcile these "me"s? This launches acts of construction. It also makes me very much aware that rather than being "always already" constructed, I am always still in process.[17]

I notice that in assuming the first person, I am eliding the "I" that Taylor discusses, the "I" in the texts under discussion, and the "I" writing this chapter, who, in examining these texts, find myself, and my own multileveled identity, at least partially mirrored—an apt illustration of a point made by Betty Bergland, who writes: "For contemporary readers who wish to understand the multiplicity of subject positions that constitute a single agent, ethnic autobiographies provide a site for developing the perspective; they enable us to see the concrete effects of multiple discourses in the

16. Erikson, *Identity,* 217; Taylor, *Sources of the Self,* 481, 130–31. Erikson reminds us that asking "Who am I?" is not equivalent to identity formation, that no one asks himself this question with the exception of one in a "transient morbid state" or engaged in creative self-confrontation (*Identity,* 314). The issues and texts discussed in this book certainly fulfill the latter requirement, and in milder or more severe forms might even apply to the former. See, for example, the study of immigration as pathology by Leon Grinberg and Rebeca Grinberg in *Psychoanalytic Perspectives on Migration and Exile.*

17. See Jan Welsh Hokenson, "Intercultural Autobiography."

culture, and thus permit a better understanding of cultural construction of difference."[18] I would go further: in presenting such overt multiplicity, these texts bring us face to face with it—aspects of ourselves in a magnifying mirror.

Within texts, too, we have all seen such "facing" occur: characters come face to face with aspects of themselves, one character confronting another who "mirrors" her. And the encounter can be profoundly unsettling. The very real little girl whom Maxine tortures in the school bathroom in *The Woman Warrior* is such a mirror image, representing as she does the very problem that Maxine has been working so hard to conquer; in the girl's mirroring silence, fear, and lack of personality, she must be conquered again, no matter how cruelly (*Warrior,* 175–81). Similarly, in Philip Roth's story "Eli, the Fanatic," the Hasidic "greenie" mirrors all that Americanized, suburban Eli Peck has so successfully been denying. Both texts are examples of the "disowning" that Sau-ling Cynthia Wong finds central to all doubles, and of the more particular minority dynamic where self-definition is shaped by more powerful others who define us. Hence her perception that "to become acceptable to a racist society, one must first reject an integral part of oneself," to disown precisely those characteristics by which one has been defined. As Wong expresses it with regard to Asian Americans, "One of the bitterest necessities . . . is having to contend with total devaluation of their Asian ethnicity." Often Asian Americans internalize white judgments, and live, as Jeffery Paul Chan and Frank Chin put it, "in a state of euphemized self-contempt." They must also contend with the consequences of definition by the mainstream: "However scrupulously [Maxine] insists on her difference [from the quiet girl], the larger society will not bother to distinguish between the two . . . she will never be accepted into the dominant group."[19]

The similarities between some of Wong's points and those of Sander L. Gilman in *Jewish Self-Hatred: Anti-Semitism and the Hidden Language of the Jews* are striking. According to Gilman, "Self-hatred results from outsiders' acceptance of the mirage of themselves generated by their reference group—that group in society which they see as defining them—as reality." He goes on to analyze the way this "illusionary definition" of the self

18. Betty Bergland, "Postmodernism and the Autobiographical Subject: Reconstructing the 'Other,'" 157.

19. Sau-ling Cynthia Wong, *Reading Asian American Literature,* 85, 89, 77; Chan and Chin quoted, 77.

is contaminated by the protean variables existing within what seems to the outsider to be the homogeneous group in power. This illusion contains an inherent, polar opposition. On the one hand is the liberal fantasy that anyone is welcome to share in the power of the reference group *if* he abides by the rules that define that group. But these rules are the very definition of the Other. The Other comprises precisely those who are not permitted to share power within the society. Thus outsiders hear an answer from their fantasy: Become like us—abandon your difference—and you may be one with us. On the other hand is the hidden qualification of the internalized reference group, the conservative curse: The more you are like me, the more I know the true value of my power, which you wish to share, and the more I am aware that you are but a shoddy counterfeit, an outsider. All of this plays itself out within the fantasy of the outsider.[20]

Jewish comedian Groucho Marx managed to capture all this in a single line when he said that he wouldn't want to join any club that would accept him as a member!

Gilman discusses the "double bind" this situation creates, which causes the person faced with such contradictory signs to repress the conflict and to assume the contradiction to be within him or herself, and not within the desired ideal. In another context, he quotes Bruno Bettelheim on the subject of the debilitating and destructive loss of identity that occurred when the Jews, who defined themselves based on the values of the society in power—rank, position, status—were stripped of these values by the very society to which they aspired. In other words, there is danger inherent in giving in too readily to what the outsider thinks the "insider" wants, or will accept.[21]

The desire for acceptance, then, and the concomitant willingness to mold identity to what "they" might accept, surely exacerbates the fragmenting of identity experienced by those whom Phillip Brian Harper calls the "socially marginalized."[22] I would separate, even more than he does, the condition of political disfranchisement from this social condition, where

20. Gilman, *Jewish Self-Hatred*, 2.
21. Ibid., 2; Bettelheim quoted, 305.
22. Elaine Kim points out another form of marginalization: "The Asian American writer exists on the margins of his or her own marginal community, wedged between the hegemonic culture and the non-English-speaking communities largely unconcerned with self-definition" ("Defining Asian American Realities through Literature," 147). This phenomenon is shared by non-Asians as well, those writing in a language—or schooled by a culture—different from the one at home.

marginalization is not necessarily felt only as an up-down, powerful-to-subordinate relationship, but more painfully as an inside-outside one; where the desire for inclusion (especially on the part of individuals, in or out of literature) is more deeply felt than a desire for power, and gives rise to the forms of self-rejection discussed here.

The disowning that is common to doubles in literature is generally thought to be a disowning of something in the self that has been repressed or denied by the protagonist. The appearance of the double attests to the fact that whatever that "something" is, it is very much alive and will not permanently go away. In the person of the double, it is usually menacing, sometimes fatal, and at the very least, extremely disturbing. As a psychological phenomenon it has been correlated with previous or attendant emotional disturbance (according to some theorists, in the character, in the author, or both). At the sociohistorical level, its occurrence in literature is associated with German romanticism and subjective idealism ("the struggle of the 'I' to extend itself beyond its mortal limits [where] the will of the 'I' is infinite and . . . is bound to conflict with the fact of its finite limitations"), with psychology (including Mesmer's theory of magnetism), with the general self-division experienced by nineteenth-century writers (for example, divisions between rationality and irrationality, intellect and imagination, morality and art, action and imitation, the lawful and the unlawful), with the industrial revolution and its machinery, and with colonialism.[23]

We may ask why such a literary technique is resurfacing now, and in bicultural texts. It is not difficult to find analogies between these larger historical and sociological phenomena—and the upheavals, dislocations, and anxious questioning which accompanied them—and the deep-seated questioning of identity and place (in society, in the family) on the part of individuals whose identity seems sometimes bisected by, sometimes a fusion of two different languages and cultures: in other words, the socio-psycho-historical development and milieu of bicultural individuals. Their dislocation can only be exacerbated by their having to carry the baggage of others' opinions, by the ways those in power see them or talk about them, especially if they have been made to feel that their "other" self is an inferior one, that what they *are* should, in fact, be repudiated. The doubles

23. C. F. Keppler, *The Literature of the Second Self,* 186–89; see also Paul Coates, *The Double and the Other: Identity as Ideology in Post-romantic Fiction,* 2. For an excellent survey of doubles theories and examples, I recommend Sau-ling Cynthia Wong, "Encounters with the Racial Shadow," chap. 2 of *Reading Asian American Literature,* and gratefully acknowledge its having pointed me toward some of the books I have found helpful.

that Wong finds abounding in Asian American texts are surely related to all the examples of mirroring which I find in bicultural texts, and which I have claimed cannot be coincidental. Paul Coates goes so far as to claim that stories dealing "explicitly with the Double seem in the main to be written by authors who are suspended between languages and cultures."[24] Doubling thus serves to dramatize the tensions and contrasts inherent in the bicultural situation, or, further, the need to be rid of that which the "other self" represents. What seems to account for the violence of Maxine's reaction to the quiet girl is her need to deny what she sees as disempowering Chineseness. She cannot bear it in the other girl; she cannot bear the reminder—or remainder—of it in herself.

There are elements of this scene that suggest scapegoating—the quiet girl tortured and made to suffer so that Maxine can be rid of her own silence and passivity and fear, cleansed in that bathroom. But, as C. F. Keppler reminds us in *The Literature of the Second Self,* the double is not a scapegoat, even though the elements of fear and suffering can make them seem similar. The quiet girl remains strong in her silence. Nothing can make her give in. Furthermore, it is not Maxine who chases her into the bathroom; the girl *follows her in.* As Keppler says doubles must, she has a profound effect on Maxine, both during the episode and afterwards. "The inflicter of the suffering and the sufferer are one," says Schopenhauer.[25] That Maxine is suffering as well is made very clear—she begs, she cries; that their mutual suffering may make them "one" further supports their "doubleness."

What, though, is the influence of the girl on Maxine? What "light" has she introduced, as Keppler might ask. Is there anything positive she represents, or effects? She is made to suffer, but she is not destroyed. She is allowed to remain silent and withdrawn, cared for by her family, we are reminded, as she might have been as a girl in China, never having to leave the shelter of home. Perhaps a Chinese girl in America needs to be reminded of such an option. But more significant, surely, is the effect of the incident on Maxine:

> The world is sometimes just, and I spent the next eighteen months sick
> in bed with a mysterious illness. There was no pain and no symptoms,
> though the middle line in my left palm broke in two. Instead of starting
> junior high school, *I lived like the Victorian recluses I read about. . . . I*

24. Sau-ling Cynthia Wong, *Reading Asian American Literature,* 78; Coates, *The Double and the Other,* 2.

25. Keppler, *Second Self,* 210; Schopenhauer quoted, 209.

saw no one but my family, who took good care of me. I could have no
other visitors, no other relatives, no villagers. My bed was against the
west window, and I watched the seasons change the peach tree. I had
a bell to ring for help. I used a bedpan. It was the best year of my life.
Nothing happened. (*Warrior,* 181–82; emphasis mine)

We find here the emotional disturbance so often associated with a "double" experience. We remember that in grade school, too, Maxine's teachers
worried about her mental health; she is obviously suffering from guilt and
exhibits the symptoms of severe depression. But far more intriguing is the
way she, like the quiet girl, retreats into the cocoon of family, the way she
becomes, for a time, a more extreme version of the quiet girl. Robert Rogers
writes: "Both death and birth are associated with doubles."[26] Maxine tells
us that the middle line of her palm broke—in other words, her life line.
There is a way in which the Maxine in the bathroom "dies" into the other
girl, and then, at her mother's pronouncement of her readiness eighteen
months later, suddenly gets up. We are left to question whether it is the
same Maxine who gets up, or a changed one. Do the eighteen months
represent depression, or stasis—the chrysalis stage from which she emerges
ready to fly? Is the bathroom incident and its aftermath the prerequisite?
We may also question what "nothing happened" means. Was her mind
working? Was she beginning, mentally, to write? Did she arise from her
shell as the writer-to-be of the book we are reading? Does she go out into
the street with a new attitude toward the girl who remains at home? We are
not told, but the possibilities are there.

To ask such questions and to admit such possibilities is to focus, as
Keppler ends up doing, on what can be positive and "light"-bringing, even
redemptive, in the confrontation with the double. Wong is right to point
out that "the universalistic theories that have informed readings of Western
classics of double literature . . . must be modified" in order to be of use to
students of Asian American literature—and, I would add, of other bicultural literature.[27] So much "double" literature and discussion of it pits good
against evil; its moralistic overtones imply associations between the second self (or the double, or the other) and the devil (or the id, or one's
baser instincts or dangerous uncontrolled desires). One modification, clearly,
must be that the other is not necessarily an evil or destructive other, but
that other Wong and Gilman speak of—the other whose characteristics
have been internalized as inferior. But this is still to polarize the two selves

26. Robert Rogers, *A Psychoanalytic Study of the Double in Literature,* 9.
27. Sau-ling Cynthia Wong, *Reading Asian American Literature,* 78.

along a hierarchy of better and worse. Confronting both Maxine and Eli are "others" who represent *difference.* To be accepted is to conform to what society considers acceptable. To move *up,* one must try to move *in;* to make it in a society where making it is the ideal, one must become "one of us." But more to the point in this context: being considered "one of us" *is* making it. These doubles, then, represent that which keeps Maxine and Eli back from being "real" Americans, from being accepted, reminding them that there are ways they can never be the "real thing" no matter how much they want to be, no matter how hard they try.

The question is: is that so bad? Is the second self, in fact, inferior, much less evil? One of Keppler's categories of second selves is the Savior, who, though he may *seem* to be the dark or destructive other, is in fact a force for good and for healing. Even Keppler's destructive or evil categories, such as the Tempter or the Vision of Horror, can be "instrument[s] of self-exploration, self-realization, of expanded rather than contracted being."[28]

Keppler does not discuss "Eli, the Fanatic," but to see it in the light of his categories and their complex interweaving of dark and light, the destructive and the redemptive, is to better understand the haunting power of Roth's story.[29] Eli Peck, a lawyer, is charged by his fellow Jews of suburban Woodenton to confront Leo Tzuref, head of a Jewish school, with the town's zoning laws and force his compliance. ("'Eli, in Woodenton, a Yeshivah! If I want to live in Brownsville, Eli, I'll live in Brownsville' . . . 'Eli, when I left the city, Eli, I didn't plan the city should come to me.'")[30] Complicating Eli's mission is the fact that Tzuref's students are orphaned survivors of World War II, that Tzuref and his young assistant (the "greenie") are also DPs (displaced persons) recently arrived from the horrors of the Holocaust, and that Tzuref, a Talmudic scholar, is a formidable opponent

28. Keppler, *Second Self,* 208.

29. Seeing the story in this light also helps to differentiate it from Roth's other fiction about "doubles," of which *Operation Shylock: A Confession*—wherein the protagonist, Philip Roth, is plagued by another Philip Roth who looks like him—presents the greatest challenge. To analyze *Operation*'s doubling and identities would carry this discussion beyond its scope; certainly the book deserves treatment in its own right. Still, a distinction needs to be made. A major difference is that *Operation* takes doubling and identity confusion as a subject. Freud quotes Ernst Jentsch on the principle of uncertainty that operates in the uncanny, the necessity of leaving the reader in uncertainty "and to do it *in such a way that his attention is not directly focused upon his uncertainty,* so that he may not be urged to go into the matter and clear it up immediately, since that . . . would quickly dissipate the peculiar emotional effect of the thing" ("The 'Uncanny,' " 132; emphasis mine). Roth *does* focus our attention directly upon our uncertainty, and, yes, the emotional effect of the mysterious double is dissipated.

30. Philip Roth, "Eli, the Fanatic," in *Goodbye, Columbus, and Five Short Stories,* 184 (hereinafter cited in the text as "Eli").

when it comes to disputing laws and analyzing legal language. He counters Eli's "You can't have a boarding school in a residential area" with: "Residence means home . . . it is [the children's] residence." When Eli says, "We didn't make the laws," Tzuref concedes, "The law is the law," but then goes on: "When is the law that is the law not the law? . . . And vice versa." But Eli already knows this: "sometimes Eli found being a lawyer surrounded him like quicksand. . . . The trouble was that sometimes the law didn't seem to be the answer, *law* didn't seem to have anything to do with what was aggravating everybody" ("Eli," 181–83).

Eli's friends remind him that Woodenton is a modern community; as Eli writes to Tzuref: "Woodenton, as you may not know, has long been the home of well-to-do Protestants. It is only since the war that Jews have been able to buy property here, and for Jews and Gentiles to live beside each other in amity. For this adjustment to be made, both . . . have had to give up some of their more extreme practices" ("Eli," 189). From this premise, Eli suggests the compromise that religious activities be confined to the school and that "Yeshivah personnel are welcomed in the streets and stores of Woodenton provided that they are attired in clothing usually associated with American life in the twentieth century." In this he alludes to the greenie's habitual costume, "the black coat that fell down below the man's knees" and "the round-topped, wide-brimmed Talmudic hat" ("Eli," 183).

Tzuref's reply: "The suit the gentleman wears is all he's got" ("Eli," 190).

At first the solution seems simple: the Jews of Woodenton will just provide the greenie with a new suit—a small price to pay for "invisibility," community harmony, and peace of mind. But Tzuref keeps repeating, "That's all he's got. . . . to take away the one thing a man's got? . . . I tell you he has nothing. *Nothing*. You have that word in English? *Nicht? Gornisht?* . . . A wife? No. A baby? . . . No. . . . And a medical experiment they performed on him yet! That leaves nothing, Mr. Peck. Absolutely nothing!" ("Eli," 191).

While this story is rich in other elements common to doubles literature—shadows, darkness, dusk, hints of previous emotional disturbance, inordinate preoccupation with the other—it is through suits of clothing that the doubling between Eli and the greenie is made unmistakable. Over his wife's protest—"I love you in that suit. . . . It's my favorite suit. Whenever I think of you, Eli, it's in that suit" ("Eli," 197)—Eli puts his green tweed Brooks Brothers suit in a box, together with another suit, shirts, underwear, socks, and hat, and delivers them to the school with a firm note and a generous offer of more clothes as needed.

The next day the greenie is seen in town, walking, albeit with his own "shlumpy gait," in Eli's clothes. At his door Eli finds his own designer box has been delivered back to him, and inside, the greenie's clothes: "The shock . . . of having daylight turned off all at once . . . black soon sorted from black . . . the glassy black of lining, the coarse black of trousers, the dead black of fraying threads . . . the mountain of black: the hat . . . he *smelled* the color of blackness." Soon after, standing in front of the mirror, wearing the Hasid's black garments, "he was momentarily uncertain as to who was tempting who into what. . . . He felt those black clothes as if they were the skin of his skin" ("Eli," 206, 212). Wong points out the irreducibility of racial difference; the Hasid, too, is defined, rendered undesirable, by *physical markers*.[31] Of course, in reality, one cannot take off one's skin as one can take off a suit—in that Wong is correct. But in this story, this situation, the greenie's black clothing is made to seem equally inseparable from his being. "It's all he has," Tzuref impresses upon Eli. For the greenie, to remove his suit is to peel off what identity is left him out of his shattered world, to separate him from that which marks him as who and what he is—which is precisely the marker that the Woodenton Jews cannot abide. They do not want to be reminded of what their generation has left far behind; it is no longer *their* identity. And identity is precisely what is at stake when Eli puts that black suit on. His neighbors mistake him for the Hasidic Jew, but Eli replies, "That's me." When Eli sees the greenie in town wearing the tweed suit he has given him, he has "the strange notion that he was two people. Or that he was one person wearing two suits." In the Hasidic garb, he stands in front of another glass, the one separating visitors from the hospital nursery, and introduces "himself" to his new baby ("Eli," 208, 209, 215). We could say we have come full circle—Eli in the clothes David Levinsky had cast off, the clothes in which Levinsky *would* have recognized himself.

Although Eli's friends assume he is having a breakdown and have him sedated, Eli, through his conflicts and his disturbing "double," seems to have achieved at least a momentary integration with a history and an identity he has so carefully submerged beneath his modern, suburban self.[32]

31. Sau-ling Cynthia Wong, *Reading Asian American Literature*, 89.
32. Clifford Hallam finds Jung's doctrine of the shadow to be a significant contribution to the discussion of the double in literature. Relevant here is Hallam's finding that the shadow is not necessarily evil; it may appear neutral, representing the unlived portion of the personality. Further, his point that "the more repressed the more 'alien' the shadow will appear when projected into the world" allows us to apply this phenomenon not only to Eli (the personal), but to the community (the collective), and leaves room for varying perceptions of the degree of the greenie's strangeness and his potential to harm the life of the assimilated Jews in Woodenton ("The Double as Incomplete Self: Toward a Definition of Doppelganger," 17). See also Freud's discussion of the hold on us of old beliefs while we are still insecure about new ones ("The 'Uncanny,'" 156).

Earlier in the story, Tzuref senses that Eli is capable of responding to his appeal, but Eli, strengthened by his role as representative of the community, states: "I am them, they are me, Mr. Tzuref." To which Tzuref replies: "Aach! You are us, we are you!" ("Eli," 192).[33] But this knowledge does not come home to Eli until he puts on the greenie's clothes, and sees *this* self in the mirror. What sort of second-self experience is this—the greenie who looks like Eli, Eli in Hasidic garb? It certainly is disturbing, as all such experiences are: a stranger comes to exert control over Eli's first self; his second self forcing the first to come to terms with that in his self-conception which he has left unrealized, left behind, excluded.

Of all Keppler's categories, the most obvious in this story is the Savior, the one who, even in his darkness, strangeness, and possibly destructive aspects, nevertheless is a force for good, potentially healing and beneficial, though this may not actually be the outcome. More interesting, though, is the way the greenie might be a version of Keppler's Vision of Horror, a second self whose weapon is not what he does but what he is.[34] However, it is not the horror of Eli's own interior he forces him to confront, but the horror of his history, his experience, an experience Eli begins to see he can no longer separate from himself. "You are us," Tzuref tells him, and the mirror shows him.

The greenie also falls into Keppler's category of the Second Self in Time, a then-self. We might see the then-self as going beyond the single life of Eli Peck and back into the history of who and what Eli is, his ignorance or denial of the past that has formed him, what he has been spared but also what he has been cut off from—alienation that goes back in time and deeper than his recent alienation from the Protestants of Woodenton. Another way of seeing the Second Self in Time is as a now-self, as opposed to the self Eli might have been, which is more closely related to both the self in history and the self as Vision of Horror than any other examples in Keppler.

More powerful than the question "Who am I?" is "What am I?" This other who exists in the present—the greenie-in-the-flesh—is also a carrier of history, both recent and ancient, its horror and its richness, both the blackness that has reached down to his soul ("Eli," 216) and the "light" he

33. The name Tzuref sounds suspiciously like *tzuris,* the Yiddish word for troubles, problems, suffering. But even more telling is the meaning and etymology of the name in Hebrew: A *tzoref* is a silversmith, derived from the Semitic root verb *tzoref,* whose various meanings are related to refining, smelting, purifying, soldering, removing base metal, and creating jewelry. The verb is also related to burning, hence purification by purging, and to testing (Keppler, *Second Self,* 11).

34. Keppler, *Second Self,* 78.

has never been shown. And so we find that it is not only customs, parental expectations, beliefs, clothing, and physical features that enter into an identity or identity conflict, but also the question "What baggage am I (or should I be) carrying?" Or have I left it behind at a previous station? If so, should I go back and retrieve it? Is there something precious tucked in among the unfashionable, old, worn clothes I was so glad to leave behind? And are these old garments merely worn or totally worn out, fit only to be discarded? What if I have mistakenly discarded precious antiques or still-usable treasures? If I go back and retrieve the baggage, will it be possible to sort and choose, or must it be all or nothing—take the whole trunk or leave it?

The Hasid in the mirror, who is really only a reflection of Eli Peck dressed up in a Hasid's clothing, raises questions such as these, questions we find endemic to much bicultural literature. Maxine and Eli, confronting their doubles, share a revulsion at the other. They have in common what Wong says of Maxine: "She is seeking confirmation that her own meager, fragile achievements in assimilation would guarantee a hopeful future. A recent and insecure convert to Americanization, she cannot tolerate counter examples." One major difference is in the violence of Maxine's reaction, attributable to her need to deny what she sees as disempowering Chinese-ness, whereas "white" suburban Eli seems to be taking on the self he has *previously* denied—or has been denied.[35]

The paradox here, and in the other conflicted mirrors, is that difference and multiplicity result in newfound integration, if only momentary; the disturbing "other" in the mirror not only creates the need to define oneself, but also enables the process. Lacanians point out that although the mirror stage in the evolution of the infant's body image signals the beginning of a sense of identity and wholeness, it is still found outside the body. Our early experience is dependent on our relationship to others, our maturation and sense of wholeness on the continuing recognition and reflection of others.[36] This is not so different from Benveniste's point that the "you" is necessary to the use of "I," dependent as both pronouns are on the

35. Sau-ling Cynthia Wong, *Reading Asian American Literature,* 90. Alan Cooper finds real resolution of Eli's Jewish American identity question impossible. Eli will never become a Hasid, a prediction I agree with, as I do with Cooper's assertion that Eli is "a vacuum of personal Jewish identity" (*Philip Roth and the Jews,* 39). But I feel that Eli has had a profound experience, the kind that results, as Keppler puts it, in "self-exploration, self-realization, of expanded rather than contracted being" (*Second Self,* 208). His social life and practices may not change, but I submit that his attitude and system of values can never be quite the same.

36. Ellie Ragland-Sullivan, *Jacques Lacan and the Philosophy of Psychoanalysis,* 49.

immediacy of discourse. Since each speaker in turn fills both (empty) positions—"I" and "you"—the two speakers must meet in face-to-face dialogue; in letters the absent reader is evoked as "you," made to feel
"present" to the writer and vice versa. Likewise, in a narrative addressed to
a "you," the reader is brought closer "into" the narrative, into the circle of
conversation with the speaker. Charles Taylor makes the point that agents
are constituted by exchange and consensus won through argument, and
Mary G. Mason (whose theories of women's autobiography could apply to
marginalized voices of either gender) that writing or speaking in relation
to an enabling other is endemic to female self-writing.[37] Eva Hoffman's words
of arrival, "I am here now," are enabled by an other: she is speaking neither to a mirror nor a memory of Eva or Ewa but to an*other* person, her
American friend Miriam, who has just taught her the English names for the
flowers blooming in Cambridge, Massachusetts. She has the good fortune
to have found an enabling, languaging other, and to have written a book
whose last words integrate time, place, and sense of self.

If an other can be enabling, if even a threatening double can be saving,
an "instrument of . . . expanded . . . being," in Keppler's words, then perhaps that other culture that constructs me, that other "me" in dialogue or
conflict with me, not only urges me to define myself, but enables me to do
so. Further, that "other" in the mirror who does not seem to be me, or who
does not please me, who I keep hoping will improve or become reconciled to my mental image—that troubling image may very well be what
rescues me, even in alienation, from the dangers of solipsism and narcis-
sism, the dangers inherent in seeing so static, so undeniable, a likeness
that I need ask no questions. This is to be trapped in the infantile mirror
stage, or the narcissistic one of total and narrow self- or group-absorption.
It starved Narcissus to death; in groups, it kills others.

According to Taylor, the recognition that we live on many different levels has to be won against the presumptions of the unified self, and this
means a reflexive turn, something which intensifies our sense of inwardness and depth. The turn inward, contrary to what we might assume, may
take us beyond the self as usually understood, to a fragmentation of experience which calls our ordinary notions of identity into question, or beyond that, to a new kind of unity.[38] If this is so, might not the view
outward of fragmentation re-turn us to a newly (if temporary) coherent
"self" even as that self remains open to still further disruptions and inte-

37. Taylor, *Sources of the Self,* 509; Mary G. Mason, "The Other Voice: Autobiographies of Women Writers," 210.
38. Taylor, *Sources of the Self,* 480, 462.

grations, always still in process? To take this a step further: is not the conflict, or pain, or doubt, or confusion caused by that fragmenting image not an affirmation of existence, of being an experiencing self? We could say that difference reifies and forms, that it works toward constructing wholeness.

Perhaps what most distinguishes the authors and protagonists I have discussed from postmodern theorists is their seeking, despite conflict and doubt, integration—their unwillingness to accept fragmentation philosophically as a postmodern fact of life. The actual experience of fragmentation is what seems to drive them to their mirrors—not a narcissistic desire to gaze at the perfection of the image, but rather a need to find an image more to their liking, one more "whole" than the inner conflicts and the outer differences they experience would have them feel. At times they experience success; Amy Tan's mirrors, for example, show binding and bonding as well as difference. It takes the hairstylist looking at both Waverly and Lindo in the mirror to remark how alike they are, and Waverly ultimately sees their double image with pleasure. Jing-mei finds that her twin sisters mirror not only one another, but, as she looks at their faces and hers in a Polaroid image, she sees in the combination of three faces the image of their dead mother, and also the connection among the four of them and with China (*Joy*, 288). In these examples the protagonist discovers her place in a composite; in others, we have seen the reactions when one's own face is unfamiliar, or the face of another only too familiar. But even when the quest for a unified self or a desired reconciliation fails, the expanded, stereoscopic vision remains both for the protagonists and the writers. All these examples, while offering painful reminders that identity is without unity, that it is multiple and vulnerably "other," also offer occasions wherein the need to construct versions of the self is felt or recognized— recognition scenes with a difference. While solutions may not be finally satisfying, and resolution never easily or completely won, one senses the ceaseless effort to bind up the fragments, to reconcile, form wholes, if not *in* the work, then, I submit, by creating it.

3

Language and the Self

Being Bilingual

To Shakespeare's Mowbray, being banished from England has no consequence more devastating than being separated from his native language. It
is a sentence, in effect, to "speechless death / which robs [his] tongue from
breathing native breath," and likens him, at forty, to one who must "fawn
upon a nurse." He compares his tongue to a "viol or a harp" "unstringed"
or "cased up," its music silenced. His own tongue, "enjailed . . . doubly
portcullised with . . . teeth and lips," is held prisoner by the jailor "dull, un-
feeling, barren ignorance"—ignorance, that is, of the foreign tongue that
he will now need to speak (*Richard II,* I.iii.159–73). Who and what he is
or thinks or sounds like—all this will remain trapped ("cased up") within
him, or emerge, to his shame, as "tuneless," broken, infantile—a frustrating
phenomenon that immigrants unfamiliar with the language of their new
home understand only too well. What Mowbray does *not* touch upon is
the extent to which a different language environment might change even
what remains within, how it might affect not only what he is able to say,
but also what he has to say—change the way he thinks, and even the way
he conceives of himself. Who and what he is might well change, whether
this remains trapped within or allowed exit and expression once he is no
longer imprisoned by ignorance of another language, once he opens his
mouth to raise the portcullis and free his tongue. Language, then, as well
as image, is an aspect of our sense of who we are.

Researchers in bilingualism are divided on the issue of the extent to
which identity is bound up with language, even assuming fluency and
confidence in one's second language: Are we "someone else" in another
language, or is it that the social context in which we are speaking or the

topic we are discussing makes us feel different in another language? To what extent can the "untranslatability" of a term or idea be attributed to the lack of a similar term in the other language, the constraints of syntactic structures, or the limitations of the translator, and to what extent may the difficulty lie, rather, in the untranslatability of the culture carried by the language, the untranslatability of the person herself? In what ways are language and culture analogous, in what ways inseparable? (If these are valid questions when we assume equal fluency, it is not difficult to imagine how much more intense they become when speaking the second language is still a struggle at the level of vocabulary and syntax, when the "prison" of ignorance lets very little of oneself out, when self-esteem in the new language is low and fear of failure, ridicule, and appearing infantile or stupid are high.)

The bilingual writers I will be discussing are obvious masters of English, but somewhere in their pasts or in their homes they have experienced or witnessed these struggles. Some of what follows may apply less to authors and their protagonists than to their parents, which shifts the site of struggle from struggle *with* the language to struggle *over* language, through and between languages, and, more profoundly, struggle with what different languages symbolize, with what they communicate or fail to communicate. At least as significant is what the *choice* of language communicates, as well as the perceived valuation communicated *to* the speakers of two languages about either of their languages, or about their bilingualism.

Of course, language is never just a means of representing or conveying information, never just an instrument of communication, but, as François G. Grosjean points out in *Life with Two Languages,* a symbol of social or group identity, an emblem of group membership and solidarity, and, quoting Einar Haugen, "at once a social institution, like the laws, the religion or the economy of the community, and a social instrument which accompanies and makes possible all other institutions. As an institution it may become a symbol of the community group." The question becomes: *which* group, *which* community, and what does the choice symbolize? Further, is a choice to develop greater solidarity with the "new" group seen as defection or disloyalty toward the "home" group, or is it valued and encouraged? Or, in another scenario, what might it signify that one chooses to remain more identified with one's native language group and culture? It might seem an obvious solution, once language permits interaction with a second culture, to live in both worlds, to take the best of each, enjoy each in its context, or somehow combine both, and thus to consider oneself bicultural. (Grosjean characterizes the bicultural person as living in two or more cultures, adapting, at least in part, to both, and blending aspects of the two.) But even where one culture is permissible to the other (and this is not always the case), for a person to accept a bicultural identity, to be able to say, "I am bicultural, a member of two cultures," he or she often has to go through a long and trying process.[1] Since one's language is so bound up with one's identity, and culture so connected to language, language facility and language choice loom large in bicultural identity. Therefore, I will preface my discussions of language/culture/identity in bi-. cultural texts with some insights from theory and research on bilingualism. I will include, in this chapter and the next, information from sources other than Chinese American and Jewish American literatures that illuminate— even validate—the issues under discussion in these literatures, and that show once again the commonalities of experience beyond any one or two cultures.

Language and culture—bilingualism and biculturalism—are not identical, although in writing this I notice how difficult it is *not* to speak of them in the same breath. It must be remembered that not all bilinguals are bicultural, nor all biculturals bilingual. Grosjean's definition of a bilingual is useful: one who speaks more than one language regularly in everyday life. (Note that this definition is not restricted to perfect, accent-free speakers, nor does it necessarily include literacy.) Bilinguals do not automatically belong to two cultures; one can speak a second language in specific contexts or places, quite unrelated to one's cultural identity.[2] On the other hand, one can identify with a second culture and still be monolingual—for example, an American Jew who does not speak Yiddish. In the texts I will examine, though, as with most immigrants we come into contact with, language and culture are, if not interdependent, at least so strongly associated that they "go together," despite their being different systems. Cross-cultural conflicts—and cross-generational conflicts, which are surely cultural—come encased in, carried by, associated with languages, especially where the cultures are represented by speakers of different languages. Children of a home culture different from the mainstream will associate the home culture with the language of their parents or grandparents whether or not those children are bilingual.

1. François G. Grosjean in *Life with Two Languages: An Introduction to Bilingualism,* 117; Haugen quoted, ibid., 87; François G. Grosjean, "Living with Two Languages and Two Cultures," 29.
2. Grosjean, *Life with Two Languages,* 157–58. It may be useful at this point to quote Grosjean's definition of culture: "Culture is the way of life of a people or society, including its rules of behavior; its economic, social, and political systems; its language; its religious beliefs; its laws; and so on" (ibid., 157).

One need not go to such emotionally charged, potentially conflicted situations to find it difficult to draw the line between language and culture. Grosjean gives an example of an English-French bilingual's faux pas in using *tu* with a peer—one who had been introduced as a friend of her host's. She understood the grammar of *tu* and *vous*, understood as well the etiquette of *tu* which confines its use to the familiar. She analyzed her error as follows: "I realized that the relationships covered by their term 'amie' and my unconscious translation 'friend' were not equivalent."[3] Where, in this situation, does language leave off and culture begin?

A very different sort of example is the well-known study conducted by R. C. Gardner and W. E. Lambert on the role that motivation plays in language learning. While *instrumental* motivation (the need for the language—its potential usefulness to one's career, for example) certainly aided in learning, the far more decisive motivation (and learning factor) was *integrative*—the desire to participate in the culture, or at least to share in its riches.[4]

In another famous study, Susan M. Ervin-Tripp arranged for a Japanese/English bilingual to interview Japanese war brides in California. Each woman was interviewed twice—once in Japanese and once in English. The questions were the same, as was the interviewer; the only variable was language. When the questions were asked in English the responses were quite different from what they were when the questions were asked in Japanese. For example, one woman completed these sentences as follows:

"When my wishes conflict with my family's, . . .
[Japanese] . . . it is a time of great unhappiness."
[English] . . . I do what I want."

"Real friends should . . .
[Japanese] . . . help each other."
[English] . . . be very frank."

One could argue that the women were indeed different people in each language, or that, conversely, the associations triggered by each language

3. Ibid., 157–58. It is telling that when Grosjean asked about the inconveniences of being bilingual, some of his interviewees answered using the terms *biculturalism* or *cultural group* (ibid., 269).

4. R. C. Gardner and W. E. Lambert, *Attitudes and Motivation in Second Language Learning*.

elicited different culturally appropriate responses. We cannot resolve this question here, but what does emerge is that no matter how we explain the influence of language, it is undeniable that it made a difference.[5]

This makes sense to Lydia, a Ukrainian American university student I interviewed. Lydia commented: "In English I say what I think; in Ukrainian, what I should!" and attributed the difference to the conservatism of Ukrainian society, its association in her mind with the church, and its public image of righteousness and morality. English is the language she associates with openness and open-mindedness. This ties in with her comment that there is greater formality in Ukrainian; unlike English, Ukrainian has no slang. It must be noted, though, that even where two languages come perfectly naturally and there is no issue of self-consciousness or fear of error, individual personality is an important variable. For example, Yehoshua, a thirteen-year-old American Israeli who had lived in Israel since infancy, thought about school subjects in Hebrew and had good friends who were Hebrew-speaking, but still tended to do his private thinking in English. In our discussion we concluded that though he was sociable and played sports a lot with his friends, their conversations were superficial. His more intimate conversations were those he had with his family, and the language of his family was English. His older brother, Donny, on the other hand, had made a conscious decision to be "the real Donny" in both languages, to create a "Donny blend" of his Hebrew and English selves.[6]

Donny offered an example of the language/behavior/culture interaction as he observed it among his fellow bilinguals: He had noticed that his friends acted "more babyish" when they spoke English. When speaking Hebrew they acted more Israeli—more mature, "cool." He posited as a possible explanation that they spoke English at home; it was the language of their early childhood and remained associated with childhood. Their Hebrew was learned later in their development and was spoken with friends their age as they were coming to greater maturity. In like manner, the Ethiopian boys in his school acted "wilder" when they were speaking Amharic. Lydia, the university student, felt her Ukrainian-language self was more "her" during her early childhood and that her English-language self was more "her" during her middle and high school years, but that they came

5. Susan M. Ervin-Tripp, "Interaction of Language, Topic, and Listener." Laura Uba writes that in bilingual therapy situations there are variations in what clients say in different languages (*Asian Americans: Personality Patterns, Identity, and Mental Health*, 241).

6. Lydia Kosc, interview by author, Case Western Reserve University, fall 1997; Yehoshua and Dan (Donny) Baras, interview by author, Israel, July 1997. Lydia, Yehoshua, and Donny are among several young bilinguals I interviewed and whom I quote in this chapter and the next.

together during the year she spent in high school in Ukraine. Again, it is difficult to draw the line between what is cultural—a function of a social group—and what is purely linguistic.

Another way to look at the relationship between language and culture is to see them as analogous: learning a new culture and feeling comfortable with it, identifying with it, might be likened to learning a new language, gaining ease and fluency in it. (In *The Silent Language,* Edward T. Hall called culture a language.) In any case, it will be helpful to become familiar with some concepts in second-language acquisition and bilingualism, and with such terminology as can facilitate this discussion.

Living at the entryway or on the margins of a new cultural and linguistic environment, moving further toward it or deeper within it, or navigating back and forth, creates a "between-ness" that might be likened to what language researchers call *interlanguage.* This is a stage in language learning that is no longer simply a cataloging of errors in the new language, but a language system in its own right that seems legitimate to the learners: "a structured set of rules which for the time being provide order to the linguistic chaos that confronts them. . . . This is neither the system of the native language nor . . . the target language, but instead falls between the two; it is a system based upon the best attempt of learners to provide order and structure to the linguistic stimuli around them."[7] We might coin a term—*interculture*—to express the analogous between-ness that so often accompanies and parallels language learning.

Clearly, such a system continues to evolve and must be characterized as in a state of flux, permeable to the penetration of new rules. The rate at which the learner approaches nativelike ability in the new language is affected by such factors as opportunity to learn and interact with native speakers (receiving feedback that prompts and reinforces continuing correction and change) and motivation or need to learn the new language. Interacting with native speakers; learning, questioning, and informing others; taking pleasure in and imagining in the language; and becoming a "well-mannered" member of the new group are language functions and stages that require continued permeability and flux, change and mobility in the interlanguage as it approaches native speaking.[8]

---

7. H. Douglas Brown, *Principles of Language Learning and Teaching,* 168–69. "Falls between" is a metaphor that emphasizes between-ness more than ordering or structuring. It introduces an element of danger or anxiety, which is perhaps what Brown wants to convey.

8. Ibid., 139, 97–98. It is to be expected, though, that rules will be distorted and overgeneralized into quite logical errors or gaffes (Larry Selinker and John T. Lamen-

In tension with such flexibility is the tendency to *fossilize*—that is, to cease further systematic development in the interlanguage, to lose permeability. This usually occurs at the point where one's perceived needs are being met. Obviously, those who want or need to communicate sophisticated conceptual or abstract messages, to interact socially in nonformulaic or emotionally charged situations, will not be so easily satisfied. While some consider fossilization inevitable, others, such as John H. Schumann, see it as a plateau surmountable by higher degrees of social motivation, as well as by a decrease in psychological distance from the target culture. In his attention to psychosocial factors in second-language learning, Schumann stresses the importance of such factors as the extent to which the two groups share professions, workplaces, churches, schools, and clubs as points of contact; conversely, he sees the cohesiveness and size of the second-language group, as well as intended length of stay in the new place, as factors which affect learning—or nonlearning—of the new language.[9]

If fossilization can be seen as the absence of a pro-learning force, can it also be seen as a positive process which acts to halt further development of the interlanguage? Might it in some cases be evidence of resistance to further assimilation—either into language or culture; might it indicate fear of losing one's original language, or losing that self-in-language that is so bound up with one's identity? If there is any truth to the Czech proverb "To learn a new language is to get a new soul," there is much more at stake than forgetting words in one's native language. Alexander Z. Guiora theorizes that there is such a thing as a *language ego,* the identity a person develops in reference to the language spoken:

> For any monolingual person the language ego involves the interaction
> of the native language and ego development. Your self identity is

---

della, "Fossilization in Second Language Learning," 134). The initial stages will be characterized by narrowly communicative functions, with emphasis on content words expressed in a sort of simplified, reduced pidgin (Jack C. Richards, "Models of Language Use and Language Learning," 97).

9. Selinker and Lamendella, "Fossilization," 132, 137, 139, 134; S. P. Corder, "Language Learner Language," 83; John H. Schumann, "Social and Psychological Factors in Second Language Acquisition," 165–66. Brighton Beach in Brooklyn illustrates this well: its boardwalk on a summer evening seems to be a "little Russia." The talking, joking, laughing, and singing create a supportive community in an alien land, with communal homesickness almost palpable beneath the music and laughter. On the other hand, I have had Russian students who spoke of Brighton Beach with disdain. Natasha Lvovich writes of it as a place where her family "landed" but now goes to only for food shopping. She writes of the fossilization of those who remain in Brighton Beach forever, "in the frozen lethargy, in a strange nonexistent world, a product of collective imagination" (*The Multilingual Self: An Inquiry into Language Learning,* 93, 97).

inextricably bound up with your language, for it is in the communicative process—the process of sending out messages and having them "bounced" back—that such identities are confirmed, shaped, and reshaped. . . . [T]he language ego may account for the difficulty adults have in learning a second language. The child's ego is dynamic and growing and flexible through the age of puberty, and thus a new language . . . does not pose a "threat" or inhibition to the ego and adaptation is made relatively easily as long as there are not undue sociocultural factors such as . . . a damaging attitude toward a language or language group.[10]

Still, as noted above, even the child or maturing young adult will associate different situations, or aspects of the self, or stages of maturation, with their different languages. Rafael, a university student majoring in English who immigrated to the United States from the Philippines at the age of thirteen, has come to think more deeply and abstractly in English, the language of his more sophisticated education and socializing. He tends to talk to his brother in Waray, their native dialect, but once the conversation starts "getting deep," he switches to English. Back in the Philippines for the summer, he made a conscious decision to avoid English. Initially, his relatives laughed at him for his awkwardness in the local dialect, but he was determined to remaster it; he also wanted to know how people in his hometown felt and thought, and for this he had to stop speaking and feeling "like a foreigner." But this came at some cost, even, surprisingly, to his painting: he realized that when he painted he was thinking in English, and for this reason he found himself unable to paint. He had been writing poetry and journals in English, and wondered how he would write about his childhood, for that was his Philippine-language self.[11]

Far more than learning a new set of words and rules, then, acquiring a new language is, as H. Douglas Brown points out, an enormous undertaking for an adult or young adult; the leap to a new or second identity is no simple matter, and requires sufficient strength to overcome both inhibitions and fears of losing the self. As one might imagine, adults will more inevitably fossilize at some point than will children, whether that point is pronunciation (mainly a muscular problem), sentence structure, vocabulary, idiom—or culture. Obviously, the different stages at which adults and children, or older and younger siblings, might fossilize in language or

10. Selinker and Lamendella, "Fossilization," 138; Grosjean, *Life with Two Languages,* 282; Guiora quoted in Brown, *Principles of Language Learning and Teaching,* 50.
11. Rafael Brown, interview by author, Case Western Reserve University, fall 1997.

culture—the very different needs and attitudes they might bring to the process of language learning or cultural assimilation—can create chasms that are difficult to cross. In the case of adolescents, their more fragile egos will seek protection in the security of the language ego; in addition, peer pressure on adolescents to conform among those who have less tolerance for differences, to be "like the other kids," provides greater motivation to overcome resistance and inhibitions and begin to sound, look, and act like their peers. This pressure, however, can cut both ways: on the way to being "like the other kids," the adolescent is painfully aware, acutely self-conscious, of the ways in which he or she is still different, still sounding "wrong" in the face of that very intolerance and pressure to be like the others. Rachel, an adolescent bilingual who had immigrated from the United States to Israel at age nine, confessed that the first year she was there no one heard her speak: she waited until she felt she could speak without needing to be corrected, until she could speak like the rest of the crowd rather than "sounding like an American."[12] English is a prestige language in Israel, but what we see here is the greater importance to a schoolgirl of "fitting in."

It is through individualized, particularized voices such as Rachel's that we are best made to feel and understand what theorists so carefully research and explain. It would come as no surprise to lovers of literature that Michael Fischer found the autobiographies and novels of immigrants to hold great potential for social scientists in their work, nor did it come as a surprise to me as I researched the phenomena and psychology of bilingualism when I found it most powerfully and graphically articulated by bilingual writers in their literary texts.[13] And it should come as no surprise to teachers of nonnative speakers that their students' experiences can stimulate poignant writing that can move and teach us all. For example, on the pain felt by an adolescent between languages and cultures, a Korean immigrant freshman wrote:

> As I watched my American friends, I became envious of their lives. So I tried to become one of them: I talked, dressed and behaved like any one of them. To me, I was part of the whole, but this was to be only an illusion. Even though by every other aspect I was an American, because of a small physical difference, the people saw me only as an ori-

12. Brown, *Principles of Language Learning and Teaching,* 50–52; Rachel Stein, interview by author, Israel, July 1997.
13. Fischer, "Ethnicity and the Post-modern Arts of Memory," 195.

ental. To my parents I was an American: I spoke mostly English and behaved like an American. I was in a world of my own, a world without a culture, a world without history, a world without people. . . . There was no one in school that I could talk to that would understand what I felt. So I drifted even farther into isolation. As my learning grew, I could no longer accept the ways of my parents. . . . I am a person without a world, a culture that is a mixture of two, lonely . . .

And this, from a foreign student, describing his return to his Middle Eastern country, where his former friends either could see no problems or were unwilling to discuss them:

A heavy Western wind blew the dust that had accumulated over my head throughout the years. By reading different books and meeting new, exciting, more educated people, I was exposed to a new set of ideas . . . [I was] flying high over [the] heads [of old friends]. . . . I began to silently suffer. As a flying fish, I saw myself, who jumped up in the air but only this time it came down with lungs not gills. Diving in water where it always lived almost killed it, so it jumped up again to get some fresh air. But what is there to do next? It doesn't have wings to fly . . . even if it did, it is a fish not a bird . . . it belongs to the ocean—it can't just fly forever.

But for the best insight into language and language conflict felt *as* language, *in* and *between* languages, we cannot do better than to read the accounts (whether fictionalized or not) of those who combine their experience as bilinguals and as writers. To be sure, these accounts are written by the gifted, published, recognized writers these bilinguals have become; they reflect the sophistication in and about language that the writers' reading and writing and schooling have contributed to. Not to be underestimated, though, is the tremendous advantage that being bilingual has been for these writers. What we will see manifested in their work, researchers have found in studying bilingual children. In their sensitivity to the sound of a language they may not yet understand, such children learn earlier than monolingual children that word sounds can be separate from meaning. Without ever having heard the terminology, they develop an early awareness of the arbitrary nature of linguistic signs; they show a greater ability to reflect on language, as well as greater verbal originality. They have what W. E. Lambert calls "a comparative three-dimensional insight into language, a type of stereolinguistic optic on communication that monolinguals rarely experience."[14] Thus we will find that the source of their most frustrating difficulties can also be the wellspring of their linguistic creativity. Eva Hoffman explicitly relates the "fractures" and "fissures" between her languages to building blocks (*Lost,* 273). As we read these writers, we are grateful for their keen insights into the nature and psychology of language, but surely more important to them must be what these insights did for them as they wrote. We sense in these books that whatever demons the authors had to wrestle with, their victory was in coming to terms in some way with their own between-ness—their interlanguages, their interculture, their "interselves"—and in having made something out of that struggle. If we can even partially trust their memories of past feeling, past intuition about language, past play with words and sounds that heralds the incipient writers in them all, we can begin to enter the bilingual world, to "see it feelingly."

Eva Hoffman titled her memoir *Lost in Translation: A Life in a New Language,* and we notice immediately the absence of a referent telling us what has been "lost in translation"—that familiar term of frustration at the loss of nuance or beauty or rhythm or exactitude when we translate from one language to another. We are left to imagine as referents not only the countless words and phrases that are lost in translation, but a young immigrant who feels *herself* lost—lost in the translation of herself. We imagine both the losses such translation involves—what Hoffman has lost—and translation as a threatening sort of space *in* which she has gotten lost. But just as an Ewa feels lost—in translation, in language—so will an Eva be found there, to use a spatial image, or find her (new) self in the *process* of translation. The subtitle provokes further questions: "A" life presumes that this life is not the only life Hoffman could have been living—an issue, as we have seen, that she discusses with herself: Who would she have been, what would she have looked like, what would she be doing, had she never left Cracow?

14. Lambert quoted in Elizabeth Klosty Beaujour, "Bilingualism," 37. Additional advantages of bilingual children are: greater sensitivity to semantic relationships between words and higher metalinguistic ability; superior ability at detecting syntactic ambiguity; and, more generally, advantages in creative thinking and analogical reasoning. They have also been found to have greater cognitive flexibility, a heightened sense of the relativity of things, more critical approaches to life, and greater tolerance for ambiguity (ibid.; Josiane F. Hamers, "Cognitive and Language Development of Bilingual Children," 55–59; Grosjean, *Life with Two Languages,* 222, 273). See Lvovich on how learning foreign languages and cultures helped her to be more self-reflective and analytical, and "stimulated cognitive, mental, and intellectual growth" (*Multilingual Self,* 27).

Teasing us still more is the concept of a life *in* a language and what that choice of preposition tells us about Hoffman's philosophy of language and her experience with languages. To speak of life *with* a language, or *by means of* it, is to keep language more distant, more separate from the self, than a life *in* it. Obviously, Hoffman is not speaking of anything as superficial as the usefulness of language. To her, language is not simply a tool one needs in order to communicate or to get on in a new life (Gardner and Lambert's instrumental learning); rather, it contains that life, possibly even molds it, a concept not felt by Hoffman alone. In his autobiography *Hunger of Memory,* Richard Rodriguez, too, uses the metaphor of containment: he remembers the painful contrast between his parents' hard-sounding, hesitant English and their soft-sounding, soothing, easeful Spanish, and how he felt "embraced by the sounds of their words" in Spanish, a sound that seemed to say, "You belong with us. In the family." The safe "inside" is a Spanish enclosure; out there, harsh and alien, is the world of English, with its high-pitched, nasal sounds, its "birdlike . . . chirping chatter."[15] Similarly, the newly arrived Hoffman listens to American native speakers and "can't imagine wanting to talk their harsh-sounding language" (*Lost,* 105).

But Hoffman's identification with language goes deeper than needing to feel herself within it: she also needs to feel her language within her, "penetrated to those layers of [her] psyche from which a private conversation could proceed." Once her Polish begins to atrophy, she loses the "interior language" so necessary to half-conscious, spontaneous, flowing nighttime reverie; without an inner language, even the images are blurred. So too is everything and everyone she sees when she cannot process it through language: "What has happened to me in this new world? I don't know. I don't see what I've seen, don't comprehend what's in front of me. *I'm not filled with language anymore,* and I have only a memory of fullness to anguish me with the knowledge that, in this dark and empty state, *I don't really exist*" (*Lost,* 107–8; emphases mine). In such reciprocal inhabiting of language and self we see how inextricably language and identity are intertwined; existence itself seems to depend on language, a vivid illustration of "language ego."[16] If language is not just our medium of communication

15. Richard Rodriguez, *Hunger of Memory: The Education of Richard Rodriguez,* 14–17 (hereinafter cited in the text as *Memory*); Richard Rodriguez, "Aria: A Memoir of a Bilingual Childhood," 518.

16. According to Hoffman, the relationship between language and identity is the whole point of her book; she considers her story to be an example of this issue (lecture presented at Case Western Reserve University, March 16, 1992).

but is also the medium or environment in which we exist ("living in language"), and if, at the same time, we require it within us, there is no way, no place, for us to escape our connection with language, our dependence on it for our sense of who we are—our sense *that* we are. Hoffman's descriptions of herself as empty, hollow, and immersed in an alien medium evoke for me an image of directionless floating, and helps me to understand what she means when she says she "fell out of the net of meaning into the weightlessness of chaos" (*Lost,* 151). Weight, existence, and compatibility can come only if she allows herself to let in this new medium, this English, and let it in deeper than surface learning of vocabulary and syntax; she must be sufficiently permeable during the interlanguage stage if she is to achieve an English "existence."[17]

It was so much easier when English was just sounds. Trained as a musician, she hears in each language "its own distinctive music, and even if one doesn't know its separate components, one can pretty quickly recognize the propriety of the patterns in which the components are put together, their harmonies and discords" (*Lost,* 123). Thus, a performance of the Old Vic in Vancouver rivets her with its majestic speech, its sureness of tone, even though she hardly understands the words; likewise, she is adept at hearing in the tones of speakers their degree of ease or dis-ease. She remains a "skilled diagnostician of voices, and of their neuroses" (*Lost,* 220), hearing not what people say but how they sound, with an ear fine-tuned, presumably, during the years she had spent not fully inside the language, not yet distracted by the meanings of the utterances she was hearing.[18] Once more, Rodriguez proves helpful in illuminating what those fluent in a language seldom experience: the separation of language sounds from their meanings. Freed from meaning, Rodriguez "escaped the prosaic world" in the Latin mass, "great envelopes of sound . . . [that] encouraged private reflection." By contrast, the words of the English mass "enforce attention" (*Memory,* 98–99, 101). Once he had the confidence to speak out

17. I cannot help thinking of the Ugly Duckling syndrome: the child not yet reborn into the new life and language, floating in the amniotic fluid of another species. I realize that to carry this metaphor further would be to recognize that weight and permeability can lead to drowning, a death of the old self—a risk, to be sure, but one that leads to rebirth, an image invoked both by Hoffman and by Mary Antin in *The Promised Land.*

18. In one case, sound, and its association with idiom, may have contributed to Hoffman's fear of what awaited her in Canada. Canada, Hoffman had heard, was a "cultural desert"—who would want to go to a desert? "[T]o me," she writes, "the word 'Canada' has ominous echoes of the 'Sahara'" (*Lost,* 88, 4). As sound only, Ca-na-da and Sa-ha-ra are actually quite similar in their assonance and rhythm—provided one doesn't know where the stresses fall.

loud in English, once conversations became "content-full" and quickened, he concentrated on what people were saying; "sound and word were thus tightly wedded" (*Memory*, 22). Content does enforce attention; when we attend to the *what* of an utterance, we often miss the *how* and the *why*— the phrasing, the undertones and overtones, the rests and pauses. The need to make meaning when many content-pieces are missing forces us back to the music of what we hear, the harmonies and cacophonies, the flows and jolts. To a Hoffman or a Rodriguez, not understanding may have been frustrating, but it was the best sort of training in where meanings often lie, in pragmatics and subtleties.[19]

For Hoffman, the learning stage has its rigors (practicing sounds like "th" or "cat," which refuse to come out sounding American) and its pleasures—for example, the pleasure of possession and accumulation, picking up new words from school exercises, conversations, and library books (*Lost*, 122). She has "strange allergies" to some turns of phrase; to others, she takes "an equally irrational liking, for their sound, or just because I'm pleased to have deduced their meaning" (*Lost*, 106). Even after she has mastered the language (earning her Ph.D. in English literature at Harvard), she is "obsessed with words. I gather them, put them away like a squirrel saving nuts for the winter, swallow them and hunger for more. *If I take in enough, then maybe I can incorporate the language, make it part of my psyche and my body*" (*Lost*, 216; emphasis mine). In these two sentences we see the difference between words as things, possessions, even treasures—outside her body and her psyche—and words as being, as connection to feelings, or people, or experience.

It is this function of language to connect, to be meaningful, not just content-full, that presents the greatest difficulty for Hoffman and that seems to me to precipitate her identity crisis—the crisis of her identity in language. When new words are no longer sounds or games or well-learned lessons but ways of perceiving, conveying, shaping experience, and when they fail in this function, remaining empty of experience or feeling—even when Hoffman *knows* what they mean, knows what they refer to or correspond to in Polish—then language becomes no more than a set of arbitrary signs, signifiers with no felt connection to signifieds:

19. Actually, Hoffman's training in hearing tone as truer than content began in Poland, when she "heard" her teachers' "truths" in tones that contradicted her book lessons: her teachers read of Polish heroes in tones different from those they used in reading from the prescribed Communist texts (*Lost*, 27). In this case she did understand the language, but was disposed to distrust it, dismissing the words to get to the truth in the tones—good practice, as it turned out (*Lost*, 61–62, 65).

> The words I learn now don't stand for things in the same unques-
> tioned way they did in my native tongue. "River" in Polish was a vital
> sound, energized with the essence of riverhood, of my rivers, of my
> being immersed in rivers. "River" in English is cold—a word without
> an aura. It has no accumulated associations for me, and it does not
> give off the radiating haze of connotation. It does not evoke.
>
> The process, alas, works in reverse as well. When I see a river
> now it is not shaped, assimilated by the word that accommodates it
> to the psyche—a word that makes a body of water a river rather than
> an uncontained element. The river before me remains a thing, ab-
> solutely other, absolutely unbending to the grasp of my mind. (*Lost,*
> 106)

For Hoffman, this view of the river, with the realization that experience
has been severed from language, signified from signifier, is the "primal experience," as powerful for her as the Himalayas or confrontation with
death can be for others. It is the kernel, the Jamesian "germ," of her book.[20]
She has arrived at the knowledge that "words are just themselves." For her,
"this radical disjoining between word and thing is a desiccating alchemy,
draining the world not only of significance but of its colors, striations, nuances—its very existence. It is the loss of living connection." If, as she
says, "we want to be at home in our tongue," then to feel unconnected to
the language we are using is to feel homeless, adrift (*Lost,* 107, 124). And
to arrive "home," as she does at the end of her book, is to arrive by means
of language—the English language. She has to experience American rivers
and forge new connections between words and their American connota-
tions—words, as Bakhtin insists, in their social contexts, their heteroglossic
variety.[21] She has to undergo, and not just learn, translations; she must
understand words—and use them—in ways that bear the weight and variety of their cultural and social baggage.

How, for example, are we to understand this oft-quoted passage?

---

20. Hoffman, lecture.

21. Bakhtin writes: "The word, directed toward its object, enters a dialogically agi-
tated and tension-filled environment of alien words, value judgments, and accents,
weaves in and out of complex interrelationships, merges with some, recoils from others, intersects with yet a third group: and all this may crucially shape discourse. . . . The
living utterance, having taken its meaning and shape at a particular historical moment
in a socially specific environment, cannot fail to brush up against thousands of living
dialogic threads, woven by socio-ideological consciousness around the given object of
an utterance; it cannot fail to become an active participant in social dialogue" (Mikhail
Bakhtin, *The Dialogic Imagination: Four Essays,* 276).

Should you marry him? the question comes in English.
Yes.
Should you marry him? the question echoes in Polish.
No.
But I love him; I'm in love with him.
Really? Really? Do you love him as you understand love? As you loved Marek?
Forget Marek. He is another person.

The Polish voice, though, continues to insist on the more totally enveloping, more "romantic" love. Similarly, the Polish voice favors passion over reason as Hoffman debates with herself over her career choices:

> Should you become a pianist? the question comes in English.
> No, you mustn't. You can't.
> Should you become a pianist? the question echoes in Polish.
> Yes, you must. At all costs.
> The costs will be too high.
> The costs don't matter. Music is what you're meant to do. (*Lost*, 199–200)

Like the Japanese war brides in Ervin-Tripp's study, Hoffman gives different answers in different languages, and once again we wonder whether she is two different people in her two languages, if her two languages have created identities so separate that they result in diametrically opposed decisions; or whether, rather, there are words in these dialogues that carry different emotional freight, labels and categories perceived and valued differently, in each culture and hence in each language. In the latter case, Hoffman's bilingualism forces her to hear the words untranslated so that she can choose the meaning that comes closest to her deepest feelings and needs. In addition, she must consider which decision will best fit the life she is leading here and now—in American society as well as in its language. Words like *love* and *costs,* as well as the issue of obligations as opposed to living her life, have different meanings in the two cultures, are ordered according to different priorities, hold different risks and valuations. On the question of career choice, Hoffman decides to listen to her English voice, the voice that values her love of literature and writing, that knows better what her prospects are in each field in America. But on the subject of love and marriage, the Polish voice wins out, though she has told it to "Shuddup." Here her Polish experiences and memories connected with Marek keep her from compromising her former definitions of words like *love, marry, romantic, warmth*.

Perhaps Hoffman sees such words as taken more lightly in America than in Poland. In high school, she requires explanations of *cute* and what constitutes *cuteness* (which is very different from the criteria she is used to) and what it means when a boy is said to be "giving a line" to a girl. In this, her guide is Penny—her friend, by American standards:

> We like each other quite well, though I'm not sure that what is between us is "friendship"—a word which in Polish has connotations of strong loyalty and attachment bordering on love.[22] At first I try to preserve the distinction between "friends" and "acquaintances" scrupulously, because it feels like a small lie to say "friend" when you don't really mean it, but after a while I give it up. "Friend," in English, is such a good-natured easygoing sort of term, covering all kinds of territory, and "acquaintance" is something an uptight, snobbish kind of person might say. My parents, however, never divest themselves of the habit, and with an admirable resistance to linguistic looseness, continue to call most people they know "my acquaintance"—or, as they put it, "mine acquaintance." (*Lost,* 148)

We can assume that Hoffman would not have committed the sociolinguistic gaffe of using *tu* inappropriately, as did Grosjean's English-French bilingual when introduced to her host's *amie*. In both examples, culture and language seem impossible to separate, and "translation" impossible in terms of word equivalences alone. As Hoffman remarks when she compares the farewell messages of her Polish friends to those in her American autograph book, "I've indeed come to another country" (*Lost,* 78).

In this new country, however, she is not content to be a passive learner of new definitions: she challenges American definitions and tries to get her classmates to see the limitations of those definitions, to foster an attitude of relativity that they have never had to assume. Asked by her teacher to describe life under communism, she attempts to counter the class's vision of

22. Compare the definition of another Eastern European, Elie Wiesel: "More than a father, more than a brother: a travelling companion, with him, you can conquer the impossible, even if you must lose it later. . . . It is to a friend you communicate the awakening of desire, the birth of a vision or terror, . . . or of finding that order and justice are no more. . . . Someone who for the first time makes you aware of your loneliness and his, and helps you to escape so that you in turn can help him. Thanks to him you can hold your tongue without shame and talk freely without risk" (*The Gates of the Forest,* 26–27).

darkness, of Poles under the yoke of oppression, with a view of everyday normalcy: "Really there is life there, water, colors, even happiness. Yes, even happiness. People live their lives." She argues against the notion that in Poland people are not free: "More so than here, maybe. Politics is one thing, but what good is freedom if you behave like a conformist, if you don't laugh or cry when you want to?" Her question is greeted with stares of incomprehension (*Lost*, 131–32). What, then, does *freedom* mean? And how does culture—in this case the culture of adolescence in the conformist fifties and sixties—affect our definitions? This is just the beginning of Hoffman's quarrel with her classmates. College is the scene of deeper, more passionate exchanges on terms such as *relevance, dependence,* and *independence:* "There's no common word for 'self-sufficiency' in Polish, and it sounds to me like a comfortless condition, a harsh and artificial ideal" (*Lost,* 176). Is she arguing about culture, politics, or language, or are these terms inseparable? Her interlocutor, a Lutheran girl from Cleveland, "poses problems of translation. She—and many others around me—would be as unlikely in Poland as gryphons or unicorns. In her particular mingling of ideas and sensibility, of emotion and self-presentation, she is a distinctively American personality. Is she as smart as Basia? As spunky? As attractive? But the terms don't travel across continents" (*Lost,* 175).

Hoffman has the same problem translating culture-bound language back into Polish, both to her old friends in Cracow and to her Polish émigré friends. They cannot, for example, understand what she means when she speaks of Americans suffering as a result of an identity crisis. She tries to explain, only to conclude that she might as well be speaking Chinese: "'Identity,' for my Polish friends, is not a category of daily thought, not an entity etched in their minds in high relief." While her American friends are constantly watching and analyzing the fluctuating states of their identities, her Polish friends are more likely to analyze what they have experienced; for them, "an identity, or a character, is something one simply has" (*Lost,* 263). They have just as much trouble understanding why Americans are so obsessed with their mothers: "Things sometimes get uncomfortable in a small kitchen, and the mother and daughter, or son, quarrel. But basically, the mother is as familiar as the slippers with which she shuffles around the apartment, and getting along with her is not a matter for lengthy discussion." One senses the impatience of her Polish friends with such unnecessary fuss: "A mother, for heaven's sake, is a mother" (*Lost,* 265–66).

And so Hoffman, the bicultural bilingual, becomes the (usually) unsuccessful translator—unsuccessful only because in these examples it is to monolinguals that she tries to translate. She understands the multiple meanings—and their untranslatability—precisely because she is no longer monolingual or monocultural:

> Because I have learned the relativity of cultural meanings on my skin, I can never take any one set of meanings as final. I doubt that I'll ever become an ideologue of any stripe; I doubt that I'll become an avid acolyte of any school of thought. I know that I've been written in a variety of languages; I know to what extent I am a script. In my public, group life I'll probably always find myself in the chinks between cultures and subcultures, between the scenarios of political beliefs and aesthetic credos. It's not the worst place to live; it gives you an Archimedean leverage from which to see the world. (*Lost,* 275)[23]

What Hoffman sees as an advantage, Maxine Hong Kingston finds painful. She too occupies a place that allows a Janus view of looking at each culture; a "stereolinguistic optic on communication," in Lambert's words; an "awareness that there is another place—another point at the base of the triangle, which renders this place relative, which locates me within that relativity itself" (*Lost,* 170). But when Kingston turns her attention to Chinese sounds and imagines how native Americans hear them, she finds the familiar words unpleasant, even ugly: "You can see the disgust on American faces. . . . It isn't just the loudness. It is the way Chinese sounds, chingchong ugly, to American ears, not beautiful like Japanese sayonara words with the consonants and vowels as regular as Italian. We make guttural peasant noise and have Ton Duc Thang names you can't remember. And the Chinese can't hear Americans at all" (*Warrior,* 171–72). (So deaf are the Chinese, in fact, to English that when Maxine and her siblings speak English at the dinner table, they are not stopped, even though Chinese custom forbids talking while eating [*Warrior,* 123]. Her parents, it is obvious, are not bilingual and have not acquired her stereolinguistic ears.)

Kingston's eyes are also trained to detect difference—for example, between Chinese and American ideals of femininity:

> Walking erect (knees straight, toes pointed forward, not pigeon-toed, which is Chinese-feminine) and speaking in an inaudible voice, I have

23. Similarly, Vladimir Nabokov wrote of his bilingual, bicultural experience that he was less inclined to rely on rigid and unvarying processing strategies, had a heightened sense of the relativity of things, and had a greater tolerance for ambiguity (quoted in Beaujour, "Bilingualism," 37).

tried to turn myself American-feminine. . . . I had no idea, though, how to make attraction selective, how to control its direction and magnitude. If I made myself American-pretty so that the five or six Chinese boys in the class fell in love with me, everyone else—the Caucasian, Negro, and Japanese boys—would too. (*Warrior,* 11–12)

Hoffman's view of herself—and her definition of *pretty*—undergo a change when she becomes aware of the way the more assimilated Polish ladies see her, seeming to find her "deficient in some quite fundamental respects":

> Since in Poland I was considered a pretty young girl, this requires a basic revision of my self-image. But there's no doubt about it; after the passage across the Atlantic, I've emerged as less attractive, less graceful, less desirable. In fact, I can see that I'm a somewhat pitiful specimen—pale, with thick eyebrows, and without any bounce in my hair, dressed in clothes that have nothing to do with the current fashion. (*Lost,* 109)

Thus begins the labor undertaken by her mentors—plucking her eyebrows, putting her hair in curlers, outfitting her with a crinoline—to transform her into "a princess."

Not long before this, she had judged a girl in the Montreal bus station to be vulgar, in her high heels and lipstick, and the girls in school looked sharp and aggressive with their bright lipstick, their hair stuck up "like witches' fury, and their skirts . . . held up and out by stiff, wiry crinolines" (*Lost,* 99, 105). Now, awkward in her own high heels, crinolines, and lipstick, she feels her body stiff and sulky "inside its elaborate packaging" (*Lost,* 110). The combination of conformity and discomfort with it allows her to see the well-dressed, stylish women of the era looking "a bit as though they have had the services of a taxidermist: meticulously made up, sheathed in stiff dresses and totally matching accessories, smiling carefully" (*Lost,* 140). A combination of awe and strangeness turns her view of a house in Vancouver into a semiotics of suburbia—its trim, open front lawns and symmetrical geraniums signifying subordination to orderliness; its picture windows, low-ceilinged wide spaces, and pastel interiors signifying "open sincerity" rather than privacy or interiority: "there's no mystery, nothing to hide." She senses a lack of imagination along with an aspiration to good taste, with the unintended effect that the house seems thin and unsubstantial—put up today, perhaps to be dismantled tomorrow (*Lost,* 101–2).

Always "at an oblique angle to the proceedings" (*Lost,* 129), Hoffman is the most astute observer, the best ethnographer, that I have ever read on the teenage socializing of that time. The rituals of dating she observes are so rule-bound, so highly standardized, that she is convinced that dating cannot really be much fun (*Lost,* 149). Then there are the elephant jokes, games of spin the bottle, and noisy trips to the drive-in to eat sloppy hamburgers and greasy french fries in the car, all of which she has to pretend to enjoy, when she really wants to tell the other kids how boring she thinks they are (*Lost,* 117–18, 133).

In those cars and at those parties, she feels most deeply what is still missing in her knowledge of English: the extralinguistic, subtle, cultural aspects of language; its levels of heteroglossia; the flavor of its humor that takes years of acculturation to master—in short, communicative competence. She writes of her "titter that comes a telling second too late," the humiliation of failing to amuse, the giving in, finally, to false giggling at jokes she doesn't find funny (*Lost,* 117–18). Years later, admired for her literary criticism and her astute readings of John Donne, she would still not understand *New Yorker* cartoons (*Lost,* 181, 119).

"I am here now," she finally says at the close of the book, a statement of arrival that climaxes and sums up every issue she has been writing about. Unlike Mary Antin, who speaks of herself as suddenly reborn in America, Hoffman "arrives" only after a long and difficult psychic and linguistic journey. Being "here" had to follow becoming "I"; her arrival finally dependent on her becoming comfortable with the intermingling and crossbreeding of her languages and of the language selves that combined to form this "I": "Polish is no longer the one, true language against which others live their secondary life. Polish insights cannot be regained in their purity; there's something I know in English too." She recognizes that the intermingling of languages, of places and cultures, of childhood and adulthood, have made her (and, in fact, all of us) "the sum of my languages—the language of my family and childhood, and education and friendship, and love, and the larger, changing world—though perhaps I tend to be more aware than most of the fractures between them, and of the building blocks" (*Lost,* 273).[24] We realize that much of that education, friendship, and love has taken place in the medium (in both meanings) of English, and that to understand and to be understood required constant translation—of words, of cultural meanings, of herself. When Hoffman speaks of

24. We might apply Bakhtin here as well: "The ideological becoming of a human being . . . is the process of selectively assimilating the words of others" (*Dialogic Imagination,* 341).

having become more "English," as her mother put it, she refers not to language but to her "self-control." Her English self has been influenced by life in America, an individualistic society in which it is important to appear strong (*Lost,* 270). She writes that English is the language in which she became an adult (*Lost,* 272). We may ask once again to what extent these characteristics, this American culture, this stage of maturation, is encased in language. It is telling that Hoffman's mother refers to her change in terms of language, not geography or sociology.

If translation is "where" she was lost, translation is where she will be found; she must find herself by means of translation. If translation is a process of navigating between languages, of learning to live "in" a new language, it is by means of language that she will do so. She speaks of her therapy as "partly translation therapy, the talking cure a second language cure." As she retells her story from the beginning in one language, she seems to be reconciling the voices within her, "translating backward," as she puts it (*Lost,* 271–72).[25] In the process, however, she is not only reconciling Polish and English, but also past and present. She translates her Polish childhood memories into English for her therapist, and in so doing, sees and articulates the past, not only the evolving present, in her new language. She translates her early Polish self into a version that is not simply the adult's view of the child she was, but the English version of that child, her uprooting, and her ongoing translation. And she does so using the first person, the "I" that is so difficult for her to use in writing a journal.

That high-school diary presented a problem, first in language choice: Polish is too much a language of the past, and English, the language of the present, is still too removed from her emotions. (We have seen this paralleled in the difficulty she had in finding a nighttime subverbal language for her fantasies when English did not yet flow, a metaphor I also heard from a ten-year-old bilingual: "Hebrew is like a river—it just flows, but English is more like a fountain—it comes up sometimes.")[26] In addition, Hoffman finds herself unable to use "I" when writing in English—the English-written self is not yet really "I" (*Lost,* 120–21). (Even as an adult, she is filled with the voices of others—they "invade me, as if I were a silent ventriloquist. They ricochet within me, carrying on conversations, lending me their modulations, intonations, rhythms. I don't yet possess them; they possess me" [*Lost,* 220]). At the same time, though, this distanced "I"—

25. Grosjean writes that it is often easier to speak of taboo subjects, or to use taboo words, in the second language. He uses the term *liberating* (*Life with Two Languages,* 276–77). This phenomenon will be discussed in more detail in Chapter 4.

26. Avigail Stein, interview by author, Israel, July 1997.

doubly distanced, as she points out, by language and the act of writing—allows her a more objective view of herself; it allows her more abstract, more rational and objective "English self" to translate her transitional self and help her invent the new self she needs here (*Lost,* 121). (Her discovery, of course, is not new to theorists of autobiography. In Chapter 7 I will go into greater detail on the role of self-writing in "translation," reconciliation, and [re]construction.)

Hoffman's book stands as testimony that she did indeed overcome her inability to use "I," that she can unite past and present not only in her therapy sessions, but also in writing. "I am here now," she writes, and I would suggest that the way she relates *now* and *I* have helped to bring her *here,* capitalizing as she does on structural and grammatical features inherent in language. I refer primarily to the relationship between time and tense, to the inevitable tyranny of time, not only in life, but also in narrative, and to a writer's attempt to exert some control of both by means of language.

Undoubtedly a very sensitive, bright child, Hoffman sensed early on that we want desperately to control time—to hold it, stop it—and that we cannot do so. She recalls walking home from school, traversing the sidewalk cracks and observing the play of sunlight and shadows, when "suddenly, time pierces me with its sadness. This moment will not last. With every step I take, a sliver of time vanishes. Soon, I'll be home, and then this, this nowness will be the past. I think, and time seems to escape behind me, like an invisible current being sucked into an invisible vortex. How can this be, that this fullness, this me on the street, this moment which is perfectly abundant, will be gone?" This intimation of mortality, the recognition that there will not be an infinite number of moments, propel her thinking forward to the future, or rather to a past in the future: "Remember this, I command myself, as if that way I could make some of it stay. When you're grown up you'll remember this. And you'll remember how you told yourself to remember" (*Lost,* 16–17).

In another moment, on another sunny day, she seems momentarily to succeed, not by means of language but of an object in nature:

> I pick up a reddish brown chestnut, and suddenly, through its warm skin, I feel the beat as if of a heart. But the beat is also in everything around me, and everything pulsates and shimmers as if it were coursing with the blood of life. Stooping under the tree, I'm holding life in my hand, and I am in the center of a harmonious, vibrating transparency. For the moment I know everything there is to know. I have stumbled into the very center of plenitude, and I hold myself still with

fulfillment, before the knowledge of my knowledge escapes me. (*Lost*, 41–42)

In both of these moments—the sad one and the full one—there is an acute awareness that this moment will not last. And there is an attempt to hold it—in the hand in the form of a chestnut, or in memory.

Like other children, especially incipient writers, Hoffman plays with language, and she tries to create her own (it has rules and must resemble real Polish, not brute noise): "Bramaramaszerymery, rotumotu, pulimuli." In her nonsense syllables she wants to tell a story. What relates this play to the other two incidents is that she is not only trying out language-making, but also attempting to encompass and contain, to find the story, the word that "says the whole world at once," not content with *a* telling of *a* story. "I want to tell A Story, Every Story, everything at once, not anything in particular that might be said through words I know, and I try to roll all sounds into one, to accumulate more and more syllables as if they might make a Mobius strip of language in which everything, everything is contained" (*Lost*, 11). But of course there is no such word, stories are essentially linear, and time passes.

What struck me as I read this was that Hoffman's narrative of her past, parts of which must surely have been told to her therapist in the past tense, is written almost entirely in the present tense, as if everything that happened in the past is with her as she writes. This means, of course, that the places she has been, the country where she lived, are present as she writes in her American room. Also immediate, by means of present-tense narration, is the process she has undergone: her uprooting, her learning of American language and customs, her quarrels with roommates at college, her love affairs, her trip to Poland, her conversations with her parents and with the New York intellectual set—all part of the process of arriving at the here and now, of becoming the "I" who announces her arrival and who, at last, feels blessed by the return of a "sense of the future." As if responding to her childhood concern for moments in store, she says that "a succession of tomorrows begins to exfoliate like a faith." The present moment once again becomes "a fulcrum on which I can stand more lightly, balanced between the past and the future, balanced in time" (*Lost*, 279–80).

In using the present tense, Hoffman manages to bring her past and her present, her voices and selves, together: the woman writing this memoir in English is still, somewhere, in some way, the young Polish girl who had those feelings and experiences long ago. Poland, while no longer the center of her universe, still exists in a very real and important way for the writer living in, and adjusted to, America. This book is the chestnut, capturing what has gone past, and what is moving inexorably forward, in a present that may only exist between covers, but that nevertheless seems to bind and contain. Time is irreversible, but narration and memory have freedom to move back and forth, and to contain. It seems significant that much of the narration is in the simple present (that is, "we sit"), not the present continuous ("we are sitting"). The simple present is used mainly to express generalities or states of being, a historical or eternal present—the way things *are*.

This could be the language of stasis. Paul Coates, for example, writes of the different modes of narration in *Bleak House:* "Narrative cast in the present tense disintegrates, each action standing on its own in a punctual moment, rather than forming part of a train of events. . . . The absence of the preterite indicates Dickens's inability to put behind him what he sees. . . . Only Esther, to whom is granted the use of the preterite, is seen to go anywhere."[27] At an early point in her narrative, Hoffman, too, fears the stasis of the present:

> I can't afford to look back, and I can't figure out how to look forward. In both directions, I may see a Medusa, and I already feel the danger of being turned into stone. Betwixt and between, I am stuck and time is stuck within me. Time used to open out, serene, shimmering with promise. If I wanted to hold a moment still, it was because I wanted to expand it, to get its fill. Now time has no dimension, no extension backward or forward. I arrest the past, and I hold myself stiffly against the future; I want to stop the flow. As a punishment, I exist in the stasis of a perpetual present, that other side of "living in the present," which is not eternity but a prison. I can't throw a bridge between the present and the past, and therefore I can't make time move. (*Lost*, 116–17)

Her text, though, is dynamic and alive; her use of the present *is* full, and it allows her to extend backward and forward, allows her, in fact, a fluidity of movement in time that sequential past-tense narration would inhibit. Speaking of her difficulty in writing this book, in even deciding that she should write it, she said that her hitting on the present tense was a breakthrough that liberated her. She did not want to write that first this, and then that, happened; rather, she wanted to focus on themes, to break up narrative time, since the past is vivid to her, still very present.[28] It is this quality

27. Coates, *The Double and the Other,* 25.
28. Hoffman, lecture.

that comes through in her writing, the importance of this writing act that she gives too little weight to in the book itself, but that we feel as we read, and that she has acknowledged in speaking about it after the fact.

What we see here is the difference between experiencing an emotional bind and telling about it. We are privy to the thoughts of one who feels caught in a present reality which informs her that she cannot go back either in time or place to where she would rather be. This seems to induce a kind of paralysis in which she cannot see a way out, and therefore cannot see ahead to a future. Hoffman's present narration, on the other hand, is a present that contains all that went before, as well as the seeds of a future. No more than Dickens can she really put her past behind her. Her personal victory lies in her ability to reconcile past and present, to admit her past into her present; her artistic triumph is to have made the past so present and at the same time so vivid. Her art, like Frost's definition of a poem, is "a momentary stay against confusion."[29] Implied in this definition is the work's capacity to sustain and support. The verb *stay* means to arrest, to stop its object; as an intransitive verb, it also means to hold on, to remain or come to rest, to endure. The work of art can contain and endure in a way that life cannot; it can make the timebound timeless. The control an artist exerts over her medium and her text may also be a way of attempting control over what remains inchoate or unruly in her life. Perhaps it can create only an illusion of structure and wholeness, but, in Hoffman's case, we may suspect its making was healing and unifying.

29. Robert Frost, "The Figure a Poem Makes," 777.

4

The Bilingual Text

How Language Signifies

We have been discussing language as a medium, in the sense of an environment surrounding us, enclosing us, or operating within us, the elemental home of our deepest thoughts and feelings; but also as a mode, a channel of communication, a way of making clear what we mean. We have also seen how complex translation from one such medium to another can be. We are accustomed to thinking of the words and phrases of a language as signifiers for all those objects, feelings, and ideas we try so hard to represent—the signifieds. In the context of bi- or multilingualism, though, a particular language itself can become a signifier of issues beyond language: loyalty, prestige, self-esteem, history, culture, identification with a group. In this sense, the way one uses language, one's very choice of language, signifies, is significant. Language, then, becomes not channel but symbol,[1] its referent open, pointing beyond itself to complex and various possibilities, and involving far more than one individual's comfort or discomfort in using it, more than one speaker's identity. It signifies for others in that speaker's world; it signifies for the reader.

In the texts we are discussing, though, language is not simply the medium a writer uses to convey character, situation, idea, and feeling, but also an object in its own right. Bakhtin tells us that language in the novel not only represents, but also serves as the object of representation, is itself represented.[2] This is not always obvious in everything we read. It takes a particular consciousness to view a medium as object, the medium instead of

1. See Winifred Nowottny on symbolism as the missing *y* when metaphor is thought of as *x* expressing *y* (*The Language Poets Use*, 175).
2. Bakhtin, *Dialogic Imagination*, 49, 336.

the message. In texts where bilingualism is a focus, however, where different languages or interlanguages are heard or discussed or at issue, we do indeed see language as represented object even as it also represents and signifies. This can be the case where interlanguage, or the introduction of words or sentences from another language, calls attention to the speaker's foreignness or bilingualism (in discourse, a phenomenon known as code switching). But it is also the case when language is the topic under discussion, as in the following examples.

Because it provides such a clear example of language as a major object of focus and contention, and because that very clarity might illuminate texts where language issues are less overt, I begin by quoting from O. E. Rölvaag's *Peder Victorious*. The conflict between Peder Holm and his mother over his catechism lessons forces the question of what Norwegian and English signify to each of them:

> "Why can't I learn my lessons in English?" . . .
> "You wouldn't put me to shame like that, would you, Permand . . . The idea of a Norwegian boy wanting to talk to God in a language his own mother can't understand."
> . . . Peder came out unto the evening boiling with anger. Now Mother saw no further than her nose—as usual. *He* . . . a Norwegian boy . . . huh!
> Beret . . . listened intently to the minister's remarks. . . . she wanted to get up and protest—Permand was not going to read the Word of God to her in English![3]

Beret Holm does not go quite so far as to claim that God speaks only Norwegian, nor that Norwegian was the original language of the Bible. But in her theology, to change languages is a sin; to have "had so little regard for their language" is surely a part of the reason the ten tribes were lost and never heard from since. And, unexpressed but certainly implied, it is a sin against the Ten Commandments to have so little honor for one's mother as to prefer a language she cannot understand.[4]

Conversely, to speak anything but English (or to eat Chinese food) would show the greatest disrespect to Edna, Kai's Irish stepmother in Gus Lee's *China Boy:* "We are to speak only English henceforth. . . . Absolutely *no* Chinese, in any form. The removal of this *foreign* food will help, since

---

3. O. E. Rölvaag, *Peder Victorious: A Tale of the Pioneers Twenty Years Later,* 204–5. This attitude is similar to that of Reb Pankower in *Call It Sleep,* who doesn't want his students to "talk goyish," meaning English (228).

4. Rölvaag, *Peder Victorious,* 206, 31.

I understand that *no proper words exist to describe it*. Kai, that means no singing songs in Chinese. Jane, that means that you will say nothing behind my back that I cannot understand" (final emphasis mine).[5] Not articulated but obvious throughout is what Chinese symbolizes to Edna—inferiority of language, food, and culture.

The notion that one language is superior to another, that one confers prestige while another signals a lower class, adds yet another complication to the issue of what language choice can signify. Richard Rodriguez's "language divide" from his parents is complex because his parents are not only complicit in his learning English, but also complicit in his valuing it as superior to Spanish; in this way, unwittingly, they contribute to his gradual distancing from them. He writes eloquently about some of the same language issues as Eva Hoffman does, but the contrast between them is an important one. To Rodriguez, the troubling issue is not so much language *as* home (as in Hoffman) as language *in* the home—the language that he associates with his mother and father. Hoffman feels "lost in translation," needs to find herself in her new language, to reconnect objects and experience with words; Rodriguez feels the separation to be between himself and his family. For neither of them does language as an external acquisition, as a learning game, present any problem. Rodriguez, like Hoffman, is sensitive to the sound and arbitrariness of language, and we see the enjoyment he and his family take in language play:

> Excited, we joined our voices in a celebration of sounds. . . . At dinner we invented new words. (Ours sounded Spanish, but made sense only to us.) We pieced together new words by taking, say, an English verb and giving it Spanish endings. . . . Tongues explored the edges of words, especially the fat vowels. And we happily sounded that military drum roll, the twirling roar of the Spanish *r*. Family language . . . voices singing and sighing, rising . . . surging. (*Memory,* 18)[6]

5. Gus Lee, *China Boy: A Novel,* 77.
6. It seems that in their language play the family is pidginizing. As H. Douglas Brown explains it, pidgin is a "mixed language or jargon usually arising out of two languages coming into contact. . . . The vocabulary of at least two languages is incorporated into the pidgin, and simplified grammatical forms are used." Brown goes on to explain that interlanguage can reproduce in an individual, in a shorter time, the same sort of mixing and reducing (*Principles of Language Learning and Teaching,* 191–92). Grosjean calls pidgin a new language that arises from a simplified version of the second language. When it develops lexically and grammatically into a language that is passed on to children as a mother tongue, it becomes a creole (*Life with Two Languages,* 41).

When, urged to do so by the nuns, Rodriguez's parents speak to the children in English, "exotic polysyllables would bloom in the midst of their sentences" (*Memory*, 14). English becomes a family game in which they are all foreign together, creating a family interlanguage: "Laughing, we would try to define words we could not pronounce. We played with strange English sounds, often over-anglicizing our pronunciations. And we filled the smiling gaps of our sentences with familiar Spanish sounds" (*Memory*, 21).[7]

But with the children's improved English, the sounds of the family dinner table change: "as we children learned more and more English, we shared fewer and fewer words with our parents. . . . Dinners would be noisy with the clinking of knives and forks against dishes" (*Memory*, 23). The distance begins when his parents speak seriously to him in "broken—suddenly heartbreaking—English. . . . Those *gringo* sounds they uttered startled me. Pushed me away" (*Memory*, 21). Rachel, the young bilingual I quoted in the previous chapter, spoke of the anger and frustration she experienced "deep inside" when her parents, in an attempt to improve her Hebrew, decided to speak Hebrew in the house. She answered them in Hebrew despite her anger, but after a few sentences the conversation would switch back to English. When her Hebrew-speaking friends came to dinner, it felt "strange" to her to hear her parents speaking Hebrew to them. Lydia, the Ukrainian American university student, reported a similar sensation when her mother spoke English to her piano pupils; it sounded "unnatural," she said. She was bothered when her mother called her "Lydia" in front of them instead of "Lida," her Ukrainian name.[8]

In the case of Rodriguez, the English world exerted its pull at the same time his parents' speaking English lessened the bonds and the security he associated with "inside"—the security of Spanish/mother/father. Thus, his turn to English was a turn away from home. This is a conflict we do not feel in Hoffman. Her distancing herself from her parents seems much less connected with language, and much more with the process of growing up in the sixties a generation removed from her parents, in the interlanguage and interculture that is adolescence. This is another example of the way "immigrant" issues reflect more universal ones, but, because they are

7. On the subject of "trying on" new languages, Schumann makes a delightful analogy between dressing up and trying to speak a new language: children love to do both, but adults—with language as with clothes—fear being thought wrong or inappropriate ("Social and Psychological Factors," 166).

8. Rachel Stein, interview; Kosc, interview.

much more acute, more obvious, to the immigrant, they do so with a magnifying mirror.[9] Hoffman's next "immigration" will be to "college country,"
a move she shares with every other freshman. But even while she is still a
high-school girl at home, she comes under the influence of mentors other
than her parents. They are affluent while her parents are struggling; this
and their influence on her (she begins to shave under her arms and to
wear a brassiere earlier than her mother might have had her do it) give her
some pangs of guilt. But they are also Jewish and also Polish immigrants,
and hence less "other."

Students question why Rodriguez felt he had to abandon Spanish; they
see the contrast between his attitude toward Spanish and Hoffman's toward Polish, and much prefer Hoffman. As I see it, the contrast provides a
valuable example of the way language, economic situation, and cultural
difference may or may not intersect with issues of class. The betrayal by
language that Rodriguez felt, which can be traced to his need to choose
between Spanish and English rather than to feel enriched by his bilinguality, may have its roots in issues of class, and in the way that bilinguality—
Spanish/Mexican working-class bilinguality—was perceived by those in
his white, middle-class school. It may have everything to do with his parents' attitude toward themselves and their language, their issues of self-
esteem, and their valuation or devaluation of their originating culture.
Chinese parents, on the other hand, do not seem to feel apologetic about
their culture, their traditions, or their language, whatever those American
"ghosts" (as Kingston calls them) may think to the contrary. Thus we see
that being "of color" is not necessarily a determining factor in linguistic or
cultural self-esteem. As I observed in Chapter 1, these are too often con-
flated, treated as inseparable. Hoffman's family was struggling financially
in Canada and her father had to take a laborer's job in a lumber mill; however, this was not a cause for shame but for concern and possibly hurt
pride for her father. She did not feel it as a *class* issue: in Poland, her family and those they looked up to lived in quarters shabbier and more
cramped than their home in Vancouver. But in those homes there was classical music—lessons and recitals—and much book talk. Hoffman's love of

9. In her Cleveland lecture, Hoffman noted the same thing: her readers, men as well
as women, have told her they have had feelings similar to those she wrote about; her
answer is that in immigrants they take a more acute form. Perhaps her nonimmigrant
readers feel this connection because of her focus on what she called the internal vicis-
situdes rather than external ones; this focus was an important motivating force in her
decision to write a memoir, as previous immigrant stories had focused on external, not
internal, conflicts (Hoffman, lecture).

books—in any language—did not separate her from her family. To her, Polish and English, Cracow and Vancouver, did not represent lower-higher, worse-better dichotomies. She did not ask "How good am I?" but "Who am I?"—in the English language, in this country.

Another voice relevant to this discussion is that of Gloria Anzaldua. In *Borderlands/La Frontera* she also relates language to identity: "Ethnic identity is twin skin to linguistic identity—I am my language." So far, her point of view is similar to Hoffman's. She goes on, though, to address issues which seem not to be Hoffman's at all: "Until I can take pride in my language, I cannot take pride in myself. . . . I will no longer be made to feel ashamed of existing." This recalls Alexander Z. Guiora's qualification regarding the ease with which a child's ego can adapt to a new language: "as long as there are not undue sociocultural factors such as . . . a damaging attitude toward a language or language group."[10]

The differences between Hoffman and both Anzaldua and Rodriguez can be explained by the findings of researchers in bilingualism that attitudes of the majority culture toward both the native language of the bilingual and bilingualism itself are important factors in the self-esteem of the bilingual, and hence to his or her learning and psychological well-being. Where both languages are valued at home and at school, where the class and prestige associated with those languages are relatively equal, there are not usually signs of personality disturbance or alienation, especially if the parents are also bilingual. In these cases, one does not find children who are ashamed of their parents' accents, or who do not invite school friends home, or (as in one example) who cross the street when walking with their friends in order to avoid meeting their parents. The terms *additive* and *subtractive* are useful here. Because many immigrants perceive the majority language to be the gateway to success and the home language to be used only with family and friends, learning a second language can result in a subtractive "submersion" rather than an additive "immersion" form of bilingualism. The native language (and its cultural and familial associations) becomes submerged, subtracted—an illuminating finding which helps explain Rodriguez as not so unusual after all. Where the second-language learner is a member of a dominant group, or where the two languages share equal prestige and opportunity, the learning is additive, enhancing, valued as an addition to one's linguistic, cultural, and

10. Gloria Anzaldua, *Borderlands/La Frontera: The New Mestiza*, 59; Guiora quoted in Brown, *Principles of Language Learning and Teaching*, 50.

intellectual repertoire.[11] To enjoy such addition implies that one can have a life "in" more than one language. Seen this way, to have a life in only one language (using *in* as Hoffman uses it) is to enclose it in a limited way; conversely, to have more than one language is to break out of mono-lingual boundaries, to live in more than one medium, more than one "life," and to have the freedom to move back and forth. But this freedom de-pends on the security of having both "passports" in order, so that one need not feel like an alien or refugee, leaving one's home in fear of never being allowed to return. Only then can one comfortably make those forays and border crossings, and thus enlarge—"add" to—one's life and possibilities.

In the above examples, languages seem to signify inferiority or superi-ority. Needless to say, there is nothing inherently "superior" about any lan-guage; the issue is how the speaker perceives her language, or how she perceives the way others perceive it—the value she and her surrounding society place on the culture and linguistic artifacts the language contains. Rodriguez associates English, rather than Spanish, with superiority, power, and prestige, whereas we never get this feeling from Lorca or García Márquez. David Schearl, the hero of Henry Roth's *Call It Sleep,* lives in the Jewish section of New York's Lower East Side and never feels self-conscious about speaking Yiddish among Jews.[12] But his later incarnation, Ira Stigman—the hero of Roth's four-novel sequence *Mercy of a Rude Stream*—is different. Ira, a first-generation American, brings home his suave, sophisticated college friend, Larry—also Jewish, but third-generation and assimilated:

> Mom, attuned to sorrow as she was, . . . stroked his arm. "*Mein orrim kindt.* Sit down. Sit down, pleese. . . . So is it *shoyn millt alle fon* us, vee *menshen.* You should excuse me mine English. . . . *Alles* mus' go

---

11. Grosjean, *Life with Two Languages,* 200–202, 163. Analogous, and often related to these attitudes toward languages, is the tendency to greater or lesser trust in and suc-cess in the schools. See Xin Liu Gale, *Teachers, Discourses, and Authority in the Postmodern Classroom,* on different minorities and their success in school. Gale con-tends that "involuntary" groups tend to perform less successfully in school because of their status as outsiders (105). I would make a distinction between being made to feel inferior and being kept as "outsiders." These often go together, but not always, as I hope will be made obvious in chap. 6. See Merrill Swain, "Home-school Language Switching," 243.

12. Contrast this with his trying to pass himself off as the son of a Hungarian janitor when he is accosted by anti-Semitic children: "Yer a Jew, aintchiz?" "No, I ain' . . . I'm a Hungarian." "Talk Hungarian." "Sure like dis. Abashishishabababyo tomama wawa. Like dot" (*Sleep,* 250).

sleep, *mein kindt, tsi* rich, *tsi* poor." [My poor child. . . . So is it now with all of us . . . we human beings . . . all must go to sleep, my child, whether rich or poor.]

. . . "Talk English, Mom," Ira rebuked . . .

"I don't mind your mother speaking Yiddish," Larry assured Ira earnestly. "You seem to think I do. I really don't. I can't tell you why."

"It's atavistic," Ira quipped uneasily.

"No, there's something warm about it. Honestly. Please don't stop her. Don't be embarrassed, Ira. Some of it I think I understand. Your mother is very eloquent, do you know? She's really comforting. I mean it."[13]

For Larry, Yiddish is sufficiently "other" that he finds it attractive rather than embarrassing. It doesn't mark him. Confident in his urbane American-ness, he can feel generous toward Yiddish, which signifies very different things for him than it does for Ira: he associates it with the abstract history of his people and with Ira's mother, whom he likes, whose warmth touches him and helps him in his grieving over his mother's death. It is not part of his own past, and neither is the poverty, struggle, discrimination, and violence that Ira has experienced.

Bilingualism and language choice can be highly charged symbols of conflicting ideologies. The student Lydia related Ukrainian American language practices to political and class issues: the Ukrainian generals, intelligentsia, and upper classes had fought to preserve Ukraine against Russia, whereas the lower classes were willing to join with Russia, and these loyalties and ideologies, she told me, are reflected in immigrants' adherence or nonadherence to Ukrainian in the United States. (Lydia said she avoided speaking Ukrainian in public during the trial of John Demjanjuk, the Cleveland autoworker who was accused of crimes committed as a guard in a Nazi prison camp.)[14]

In her essay "From Silence to Words," Min-zhan Lu writes of growing up in revolutionary China. As the Chinese that was valued in school became a working-class language from which she was excluded—because she was "cultured," as her parents put it, or bourgeois, in the terminology of the school—and as the metaphors of poetic Chinese became the simplified

---

13. Henry Roth, *From Bondage*, vol. 3 of *Mercy of a Rude Stream*, 8–9. There is much more Yiddish in this book than in *Call It Sleep*, but at the same time there is less assumption that the reader knows Yiddish, for Roth appended a glossary of Yiddish words and idioms.

14. Kosc, interview.

and formulaic symbols and slogans of the revolution, it fell to English to "build her resistance to the 'communist poisoning.' "[15] Through English, the family language and the language of Dickens, Hawthorne, Brontë, and Austen, whose books were valued for their internal conflicts and complexities, her parents tried to keep alive their values. Through these Great Books, they wanted their daughter to learn to read and write in the ways they had come to appreciate. At first it seemed simple to keep each language in its place, to use each in its respective milieu, as triggered by their respective associations, expectations, and requirements. But such compartmentalizing between home and school became increasingly difficult to keep "pure." Lu felt she was losing the spontaneity with which she had learned to use both languages; language had become a tool she was no longer active in fashioning, but used passively—a tool that others created for her, to use their way, in order to survive. Her moving, wonderfully analytical essay shows us once again that languages, even when one tries to maintain spaces or boundaries between them, are difficult to separate from one another, from their contexts, from the powerful familial, social, cultural, and, in this case, political associations in which they are embedded, and which they express.[16]

In these examples of what language can signify, its potential symbolism within a text and to its readers, we have, for the most part, been discussing passages that focus on language, and that include dialogue on the subject, but (with the exception of Roth) the language in which these bilingual signifiers are expressed does not call attention to itself *as* language. They do not signify in a bilingual manner. Whatever their speakers or authors may say *about* bilingualism, they are not, themselves, represented bilingually, that is, we do not "hear" the words, or voices, or interferences, from another language, as we do in the following examples:

1. "Let me see book. . . . This American rules. . . . Every time people come out from foreign country, must know rules. You not know, judge say, Too bad, go back. . . . They not telling you why so you can use their way go forward. . . . But they knowing all the time." (*Joy*, 94)

2. "Shakspere is saying what fulls man is and I am feeling just the same way when I am thinking about mine job a cotter in Dress Faktory. . . . For why should we slafing in dark place by laktric

---

15. Min-zhan Lu, "From Silence to Words: Writing as Struggle," 441.
16. Grosjean points out that, unlike bilinguals who can keep two languages safely separate, biculturals cannot manage such complete separation (*Life with Two Languages*, 157–60).

lights and all kinds hot . . . for Boss who is fat and driving in fency automobil? I ask!" (*The Education of H*Y*M*A*N K*A*P*L*A*N,* 13)[17]

3. "A psyche-atricks will only make you *hulihudu,* make you see *heimongmong.*" (*Joy,* 188)

4. "No sanctity anywhere, no faith. It's kosher, she said. Ruchel, his daughter, his thorn. It tastes just as good. In food there should be some trust, he had answered. . . . what enters the mouth, there you must betray no trust. If you're selling 'treifes' say it's 'treife' and men will hold you a man." (*Sleep,* 375)

5. "How many? I god more den you. Shebchol haleylos onu ochlim—. I had a mockee on mine head too. Wuz you unner de awningh? Us all wuz. In de rain."
   "And tell this people, this fallen people—"
   "Yea, and I'll kickyuh innee ass! Odds! Halaylaw hazeh kulo mazo—" (*Sleep,* 229)

In these examples we experience a form of circularity: the foreignness that calls attention to itself by means of language—the language of the text—also calls attention to the foreignness of the speakers through their ways of using language. As with onomatopoeia, the distance between language as signifier and signified is almost erased. To put it another way, such dialogue creates its own closed circle; if we are able to enter it, we share that enclosure and the immediacy experienced with such a text. If the "foreignness" is one in which we already feel at home, or at least recognize a familiar friend or guest, reading of this sort can be an inviting insider experience. We are then already in that circle, and can either feel comfortably at home, or vaguely uncomfortable because we have been trying to leave home, or keep "home" as a private citadel against outsiders, especially outsiders who do not wish the foreigner well. Or we can feel shut out of it, or put off by what is foreign, either *because* it is foreign or simply because it is difficult to understand.[18]

17. Leo Rosten [Leonard Q. Ross, pseud.], *The Education of H*Y*M*A*N K*A*P*L*A*N* (hereinafter cited in the text as *Kaplan*).
18. The concept of "insiders" and "outsiders" in language is brilliantly reversed by Jonathan Safran Foer. In his novel *Everything Is Illuminated,* the insider (a Ukrainian) tries to impress the visiting outsider (an American Jew) with his "premium" English: idiom too literally translated, an elevated dictionaryese. To cull only a few examples: "a petrol store that we passed . . . the night yore. We arrested in front of the petrol machine"; "They are very proximal. Maybe thirty kilometers distant"; "I rotated back around" (108, 109, 117). I found myself imagining what words the Ukrainian had looked up in a thesaurus in order to find "better" ones.

On the other hand, texts are invitations: readers are invited to enter, and if we make whatever effort is required, we are amply rewarded—with a good read, new "friends," a new cultural experience. Once again, though, this raises the question of attitude—are we, as outsiders, gawking, ridiculing, or joining in friendship and, where appropriate, sympathy? In what ways are the authors of these texts creating these attitudes? To what extent is the reader, and to what extent is the writer, a determinant of the nature of this intercultural relationship? In some cases the answers are obvious; in most, they are much debated, determined to a great extent by the attitudes, background, sensitivities, sense of humor, and experiences of individual readers.[19] As Lawrence E. Mintz writes of ethnic humor, much depends on "who says what to whom under what contextual circumstances. The same joke, image, or caricature can have hostile intent and aggressive function, it can enhance group moral[e], it can be an aesthetic comedy-creating exercise, or it can be employed ironically as a sign of friendship and acceptance."[20] In narratives, language is inextricable from the characters and narrators who use it—we as readers engage with them as they speak. To the extent that we read with our ears as well as our eyes, their "foreign" sounds are what we hear and associate with them.

If we examine the examples 1–5 more closely, we will see that they do not all call upon the same linguistic phenomena, nor do they present the same difficulties: In the first two, there are no foreign words—everything is "English," but in its slightly mangled form it is difficult to understand (interlanguage). In examples 3 and 4, foreign words are inserted into the English text (code switching). The last example illustrates both techniques, with whole sentences inserted that will be understood only by those who have participated in the Passover celebration.

Code switching—whether inserting single words, phrases, or sentences into another language, or switching languages in mid-discourse—is a common phenomenon among bilinguals. A bilingual will use the language appropriate to the person or group he or she is speaking with; children seem

19. For an excellent discussion of the ways that the language of *Call It Sleep* sometimes assumes an English-speaking "outsider" reader and sometimes a polyglot reader, and the ways one must read through the English to recover the Yiddish, see Werner Sollors, " 'A world somewhere, somewhere else': Language, Nostalgic Mournfulness, and Immigrant Family Romance in *Call It Sleep*," 133–37. See also Hana Wirth-Nesher, "Between Mother Tongue and Native Language: Multilingualism in Henry Roth's *Call It Sleep*."

20. Lawrence E. Mintz, "Humor and Ethnic Stereotypes in Vaudeville and Burlesque," 26.

automatically to switch languages depending on the interlocutor. What is more interesting is code switching among bilinguals. When one is not as fluent in the second language as in the first, it is natural to insert a word one has at the ready for a word one does not know, or is groping for. But there are other factors that come into play, such as context or topic; a person who has learned chemistry in a second language will more easily use it to speak of chemistry. Other motives for code switching might be excluding a nonmember of the native language group, to emphasize a point, or to show authority. (This can work the other way, according to Rachel: where English is the prestige language, inserting it into another language can have "snob" value.)[21]

More relevant to literary practice is the role of code switching in situations involving emotions; for example, where one is establishing greater intimacy, one may revert to the native language. According to François G. Grosjean, it is not unusual to hear a bilingual revert to the native language when comforting a child. The student Rafael, on the other hand, who came to the United States at age thirteen, found it easier to speak of personal issues such as love in English because his understanding of them was on a level far above what it was at thirteen. This stands in contrast to examples of using the native language for more emotionally charged situations. Grosjean tells of Spanish-English bilinguals who insert more Spanish words into conversations with their English-speaking friends as they become more intimate with them; they desire, as intimacy increases, to speak Spanish.[22]

Other reasons for code switching include the desire to convey anger or stress, or to establish group solidarity. Rachel provided me with a dramatic example of this as it was expressed in her language choice: Even though she was equally fluent in Hebrew and English (she immigrated to Israel at age nine and was fourteen when I interviewed her), she found it more natural to write in English in her personal journal. She had begun the journal in the United States, and it was an outlet for her anxiety about the move to Israel and her homesickness and frustration during the first years of her life there. Even after adjusting to life and language in Israel, she continued to keep the journal in English. This changed on the day of the terrorist attack on the Dizengoff Cafe in Tel Aviv. As she analyzes it, she was so angry—angry as an Israeli—that she wanted to write her feelings in

---

21. Grosjean, *Life with Two Languages,* 52–53; Rachel Stein, interview.
22. Grosjean, *Life with Two Languages,* 202; Rafael Brown, interview.

Hebrew. Contributing to the naturalness of Hebrew for that subject was the fact that the news broadcasts and public discussions of the event were all in Hebrew. But most interesting is the fact that since then she has more often written her journal in Hebrew.[23]

Another phenomenon I have observed, though, is that there is a way in which the second language, just *because* it is less intimate, can be liberating. What is difficult to talk about, or what is problematical because of its association with home and family, becomes easier to discuss in the less natural, more distant, nonnative language. Psychotherapists have found that patients often find it easier to speak of "taboo" subjects—or to use taboo words—in a second language, and this makes absolute sense. The new language may provide the distance necessary for people to see an old situation in a new way; it is also not exactly their own skin they are exposing.[24] This may have been one of the factors in Hoffman's finding English the best language for her therapy. I have noticed this phenomenon with students as well: the second language uses different words from the ones that were taught as taboo, and seems to provide a liberating distance for the person who was taught by his or her parents not to speak that way, or of such things. In *Call It Sleep,* when Genya Schearl confesses to her sister about a love affair, she speaks in Polish so that her son, David, will not understand. But I would imagine that confessing to an affair with a non-Jewish boy is easier for her to do in Polish than in Yiddish, which is not only her mother tongue, and therefore closest to her, but also so Jewish (*Sleep,* 166, 192, 195–99).

Both writing in a nonnative language and code switching in the text can work in some of these same ways for authors. And these choices can help authors establish some of these same relationships with their readers: authority, when using a word foreign to an English speaker; intimacy, when the reader does understand it; or challenge to the reader: how hard are you willing to work to understand, and thus to be included? (Anzaldua's *Borderlands/La Frontera* is a perfect example of the attitude that we must be willing to read in the author's language.) In real-life conversations, some of these switches are deliberate, some automatic or unconscious, especially in children. But in literary texts, they are surely conscious and deliberate, and therefore we should understand how they function in the text—a question related in some way, I suspect, to why they are there.

Foreign words might appear in a text because there is no one-word

---

23. Rachel Stein, interview.
24. Uba, *Asian Americans,* 241; Grosjean, *Life with Two Languages,* 276.

English equivalent. Some words may be untranslatable because they refer to an aspect of one culture which has no equivalent in another. In example 4 above, *kosher* and *treife* refer to Jewish laws concerning permissible and impermissible food. *Kosher* has no equivalent in the majority American culture; it is closer to the Arabic Muslim *halal*. But it has by now entered English among those who have been exposed to Jewish people, texts, or kosher style corned beef. It has acquired a generalized meaning in the majority culture that no longer applies just to food—a business deal can be referred to as "kosher" (honest, legal, on the up-and-up) or "not kosher." Outside Jewish circles, though, one doesn't usually hear the word *treife,* which means nonkosher, impermissible food. (Notice that Roth puts *treife,* but not *kosher,* in quotation marks.) There are ways of using foreign words (sometimes translated for us, sometimes placed in explanatory contexts, sometimes left to us to either look them up or miss something) that convey other, more subtle messages. In some cases, an author might really be saying, as Faulkner's Quentin Compson does of the South to Shreve, his Canadian roommate in *Absalom, Absalom:* "You can't understand it. You would have to be born there." But, like Shreve, we can make the effort anyway.

One message may be that we must be wary of translation—we cannot trust it completely, we cannot perform it adequately, we cannot understand perfectly without intimate knowledge of the language and the culture it is bound up with. I suspect that a term such as "life's importance" is an example of such imperfect translation—imperfect because the English cannot convey either its exact meaning in Chinese nor its significance in Chinese culture. In Amy Tan's *Joy Luck Club,* Suyuan Woo gives her daughter June a jade pendant, saying it represents her "life's importance." It is an important moment because the mother is trying to convey her love, her appreciation of the fine character of her daughter, at a time when June feels inadequate and considers herself to have failed to live up to her mother's high expectations. But June, who does not speak Chinese fluently, doesn't quite understand the term (*Joy,* 197–98, 208). Another such example, in *Call It Sleep,* is when Albert Schearl refers to his son, David, as "the prayer." Considering the context—he is criticizing his wife for being too soft with their son—it seems to be meant in sneering derision of Genya's having made of David a sacred object. Nor is this inappropriate, and it does have this effect. But when one realizes what Albert is actually translating, an important cultural and religious dimension becomes manifest. One of the great values of having a son, in Jewish tradition, is that parents will leave behind someone to recite kaddish, the prayer for the dead, in their memory. It is the son's obligation to recite kaddish daily for a full year after the death of a parent, as well as on every anniversary of the death. A Yiddish speaker may refer, with pride and affection, to his son as his *kaddishl*—his immortality, his memorializer. To know this is to see the juxtaposition of that affection with Albert's derision, which adds to the cruelty and the irony of the term as he uses it. We have seen that even where a word has an "easy" one-to-one translation—for example, *friend* in Hoffman's book—the ways in which it is understood can be so vastly different that it would take many more words to convey exactly what is meant, so that there can be no misunderstanding. The Polish word may, paradoxically, have been more apt, because at least then we would realize that we were not understanding Hoffman's meaning, not really able to translate it.

Tesknota is a word Hoffman uses many times and in a variety of contexts to express a range of emotions for which there is no single equivalent English word: "I am suffering my first, severe attack of nostalgia, or *tesknota*—a word that adds to nostalgia the tonalities of sadness and longing. It is a feeling whose shades and degrees I'm destined to know intimately, but at this hovering moment, it comes upon me like a visitation from a whole new geography of emotions, an annunciation of how much an absence can hurt" (*Lost*, 4). We understand immediately that this word conveys more pain than *nostalgia* ever does; we begin to understand its untranslatability. In the past, in Poland, Hoffman says, she was mistakenly given Boccaccio to read, long before she knew enough to understand its "sauciness" and its temptresses, its "casual couplings [that] set my blood afire; it is a kind of *tesknota*, I suppose, though of a different kind" (*Lost*, 28)—adding an erotic, visceral aspect to this word of loss, nostalgia, and longing.[25] The reader comes to understand its shades and degrees; I find that in class discussions, everyone simply and naturally uses it—untranslated. We not only learn the meaning of a rich Polish word, we also learn that there are words not easily translated, which require many words, several contexts, to be understood—that English (like any other language) cannot say it all.

In example 3 above, the narrator Rose quotes her mother, An-mei Hsu, on the subject of Rose's unhappy marriage and impending divorce—*huli-*

---

25. Milan Kundera, discussing the Greek etymology of *nostalgia*, concludes that the word implies "suffering caused by an unappeased yearning to return." Seemingly close is the Czech word *styska*, used in an expression of love, yearning, pain in absence ("The Great Return," 96).

hudu and *heimongmong* obviously have something to do with her emotional state—and goes on to say:

> Back home, I thought about what she said. And it was true. Lately I had been feeling *hulihudu*. And everything around me seemed to be *heimongmong*. These were words I had never thought about in English terms. I suppose the closest in meaning would be "confused" and "dark fog." But really, the words mean more than that. Maybe they can't be easily translated because they refer to a sensation only Chinese people have, as if you were falling headfirst through Old Mr. Chou's door [the door to sleep and dreams], then trying to find your way back. But you're so scared you can't open your eyes . . . (*Joy,* 188)

After several examples of Rose's unhappiness and her determination not to be further deceived and manipulated by her husband, Ted, we understand what she means when she says: "I saw what I wanted: his eyes, confused, then scared. He was *hulihudu*. The power of my words was that strong" (*Joy,* 196). We know that Rose no longer confines to Chinese experience what she can express only in Chinese. Earlier in her life, when her little brother drowns and she accompanies her mother to the shore to find him, both she and her mother revert to the Chinese language in their state of extreme emotion. Rose repeatedly uses the word *nengkan,* relating it to "fate" and "faith" (they sound the same in her mother's pronunciation)—faith in the self to achieve one's will, a futile attempt in this case, which represents a victory of fate over faith (*Joy,* 121, 124, 126, 130).

In Tan's *The Kitchen God's Wife,* there is a whole chapter dealing with (and titled) *taonan.* Winnie is telling her daughter about Nanking near the beginning of World War II:

> "Hurry. We are soon *taonan*." I added the word *taonan* to make my sister-in-law hurry . . . because that was a word that made everyone jump. This word *taonan*? Oh, there is no American word that I can think of that means the same thing. But, in Chinese, we have lots of different words to describe all kinds of troubles. No, "refugee" is not the meaning, not exactly. Refugee is what you are after you have been *taonan* and are still alive. And if you are still alive, you would never want to talk about what made you *taonan*. . . . It means terrible danger is coming, not just to you but to many people, so everyone is watching out only for himself. It is a fear that chases you, a sickness . . . so your only thoughts are "Escape! Escape!"

From the way Winnie uses *taonan,* we understand that she is describing a very dangerous situation or the state of mind induced by the threat of danger. Grammatically, the word seems to be an adjective, or possibly what we might express adjectivally in a past participle to describe such a state. But there are other possibilities. "We are soon *taonan*": is this something that will be done to us (verb)? Is it something we will be (noun)? If it refers to the "danger," it is a noun. If it refers to the danger's coming, it is a verb. A later sentence—"The money is for *taonan*"—in its English structure uses the word as the object of a preposition, therefore as a noun.[26] We see, then, that in using this Chinese word, Winnie has at her disposal a range not only of definitions but also of syntactical possibilities, hence greater elasticity in what that word, and the situation, means. Chinese is heavily context-dependent, in contrast to English, which is relatively context-free. The above example shows that this is true not only for the meaning of words, but also for their grammatical categories. One Chinese grammar says of the functions of words: "No rules are given for their use, and their proper usage can only be acquired by close attention to the manner in which the Chinese use them."[27] As readers, we are thus expected, as Winnie's daughter is, to give that "close attention" to the way Winnie uses the word, to its range of meaning. We realize that we have to "get it" in Chinese, to appreciate the ways Winnie tries to make it clear to an English speaker, and that there is no simple way to understand it. Even when the chapter ends, we cannot clearly define or categorize the word; we are left only with a complex of feelings, the rush and panic of possible actions— but that is enough, and possibly richer for what it leaves us to fill in.

When words convey cultural values or practices, they are even more resistant to translation, even more dependent on the willingness of the reader or listener to understand, to enter, the culture. Rafael spoke of words that carry tremendous cultural loads, especially of respect. He gave *gaba* in his dialect as an example: it refers to doing wrong to another, and opens upon a range of meaning regarding the way to treat others, with the added implication that the way you treat others will come back to you. *Ga gaba ga* is understood as a sort of threat: "You'll get it—when you are a father!" In *The Joy Luck Club,* we feel *shou* as another such word because it requires a story to make us understand it: An-mei is narrating the painful story of the way her mother's family cast her mother out; she says her

---

26. Amy Tan, *The Kitchen God's Wife,* 207, 209.
27. Chinese grammar quoted in Michael Palij and Doris Aaronson, "The Role of Language Background in Cognitive Processing," 79–81. See this article for more detailed examples.

grandmother told her that her mother had no *shou,* "no respect for ancestors or family." But the word comes at us full force when An-mei narrates
the story of her grandmother's death: how her mother "cut a piece of meat
from her [own] arm . . . took her flesh and put it in the soup. She cooked
magic in the ancient tradition to try to cure her mother this one last time. . . .
This is how a daughter honors her mother. It is *shou* so deep it is in your
bones" (*Joy,* 44, 48).

Part of the poignancy of this story is that there is no evidence of An-
mei's telling it to her own daughter.[28] Only the reader is privy to her memory. Perhaps she is like the woman who came to America with a very
special bird—one that had been a duck and, stretching its neck in hopes
of becoming a goose, had exceeded even its own high ambition and become a swan "too beautiful to eat." The woman wanted to make her
daughter a gift of the bird, "a creature that became more than what was
hoped for," to tell her daughter that what looked like a worthless swan
feather "'comes from afar and carries with it all my good intentions.' And
[the woman] waited, year after year, for the day she could tell her daughter this in perfect American English" (*Joy,* 17). Neither the woman nor An-
mei will ever be able to speak "perfect American English," but what their
stories bring from afar might be better told to a daughter in a voice that
carries echoes from afar. That they are told to us, the readers, in perfect
American English is evidence that they remain unvoiced, for when Tan
quotes these women's conversations with their daughters, we "hear" not
perfect American English, but their Chinese American interlanguage.

To notice the difference between the mothers' interior monologues—
not only perfect, but often poetic—and their quoted English dialogues is
to realize how little of what they are, or what they would want to say, it is
possible for them to convey in English. Just as pidginizing "reduces" language, so must they feel "reduced" in English. Tan writes in her essay
"Mother Tongue" of the way her mother (who reads *Forbes* with ease) is
reduced by others, treated with less respect, her needs given less attention,
when she speaks in her own "broken" English compared with the way she

28. Patricia P. Chu sees Tan as reinventing the immigrant romance as a mother-
daughter romance. She discusses the relationship between what she calls the "mother-
daughter romance" and "the utopian myth of the immigrant's Americanization that
underlies it. [It] typically emphasizes the power of the immigrant's agency and the ultimate attainability of the American dream. . . . Built directly on this foundation is the
mother-daughter narrative, which affirms the desire of each generation for the respect
and understanding of the other, and the importance of maternal legacies of wisdom
and character transmitted from mother to daughter" (*Assimilating Asians: Gendered
Strategies of Authorship in Asian America,* 23, 143).

is treated when her daughter speaks for her in "American" English. Quite rightly, Tan is bothered by the term *broken English*—"as if it were damaged and needed to be fixed, as if it lacked a certain wholeness and soundness"—but she admits to not being able to find a better term, referring at one point to her mother's triumphing over her broker "in her impeccable broken English."[29]

In her books, Tan gives voice to mothers in their idiosyncratic interlanguages, which are mostly English but flavored with Chinese ways of structuring sentences; it is language more enriched and individualized than broken (see example 1 above). She has these mothers speak in what she calls, in her essay, her mother tongue—the English she has always spoken with her mother, so natural to her that even her husband doesn't notice any switch in her English when she says, "Not waste money this way." It is her expressed intention to write using all the Englishes she grew up with (which would be the Englishes of the mothers' quoted words), including what she imagines to be her mother's "translation of her Chinese if she could speak in perfect English, her internal language . . . the essence, but neither an English or a Chinese structure" (which would be the "perfect" passages of internal monologue or unheard narration). We realize that we need both to "get" these characters.[30]

In *The Joy Luck Club,* we hear these Englishes in the daughters' narratives, mainly when the mothers are imparting their wisdom (often unappreciated by their daughters), driving home an admonition or a reproval, or, more rarely, offering words of praise or comfort. These pronouncements are the most memorable ones, the voices the daughters still hear, for better or for worse, as they really sounded. For the reader, they authenticate a fictional voice, giving those black marks on the page life and intonation—and dignity. As a case in point, when Waverly expresses her embarrassment at her mother's proudly pointing out her chess-champion daughter whenever they go shopping, we feel a hurt dignity in her mother's response: "Embarrass you be my daughter?" A quarrel ensues and Waverly

---

29. Amy Tan, "Mother Tongue," 179–80.
30. Ibid., 182. This is not the case in Kingston's *Woman Warrior,* in which we seem meant to assume that Brave Orchid is speaking Chinese. Language and individual voices seem more important to Tan; story, and the interweaving of voices and stories, to Kingston. I suspect that Kingston doesn't want the often unbroken flow of shared narrative, of fact and fantasy blending into one another, to compete with the distraction of language difference. An excellent and well-known analysis of the various ways in which foreign languages are represented in fiction is Meir Sternberg's "Polylingualism as Reality and Translation as Mimesis." See also Wirth-Nesher, "Between Mother Tongue and Native Language."

runs away, returning late for dinner: "Standing there waiting for my punishment, I heard my mother speak in a dry voice. 'We not concerning this
girl. This girl not have concerning for us'" (*Joy*, 99, 100). We may notice
that the mother's use of "concerning" violates not only the rules of auxil-
iary choice and verb forms, but also ignores grammatical categories, as we
have seen Winnie do in *The Kitchen God's Wife*.[31] We could smile at the
awkwardness of the English, instinctively correct its grammar, but we
don't. We are too moved by the pain and dignity of the mother's words,
moved all the more because this dignity is expressed in formal language
not often heard at the kitchen table, but which is being used to impress
upon the child the seriousness of the occasion, the superiority of the
speaking mother to the disobedient, silent child. The pathos lies in the
speaker's attempt at an elevated style she is not capable of handling cor-
rectly. In this discrepancy between position and language capability, we
are reminded of her foreignness, her Chineseness, that she is a Chinese
mother with Chinese expectations of a daughter's respect and behavior.
(We have heard about the meaning of *shou*.) This, and the silent treatment
Waverly gets—hardly a silence of passivity—renders this scene with its "errors" in English more powerful than any "correct" transcription of it could
be.[32] This incident is the beginning of Waverly's loss of her "magical"
power in chess.

In these examples idiosyncratic interlanguage, error and all, does more
than place characters culturally and position us—inside or outside—as
readers. In individualizing these languages, in retaining something of their
foreignness, the author forces us to remember, and above all to hear and
feel, the difficulties and frustrations of being foreign—a situation in which
language, after all, plays a major role. Thus these languages serve to reify
and individualize character and situation for the reader. This is consistent
with our finding in the previous chapter that identity and language are inextricably bound. We are thus given the illusion of authenticity when we
"hear" these characters speak, and the "realities" expressed in language
unfamiliar to us help to create voices we hear during and even after our
reading. If, as Robert Frost said, "the ear is the only true writer and the only
true reader," then these memorable voices—"heard" as we read, invested as
they are with both individual personality and a more generic foreignness—

31. This serves as another example of Palij and Aaronson's analysis of differences
between Chinese and English.
32. See King-Kok Cheung, *Articulate Silences: Hisaye Yamamoto, Maxine Hong Kingston, Joy Kogawa,* on ways silence in Asian American texts can be "articulate," "rhetori-
cal," or "provocative"—"the very antithesis of passivity" (20).

represent as well the author's success in bringing the reader into her bilingual world. Frost was expounding on the importance of capturing speech tones ("sentence sounds") in poetry: "Words exist in the mouth and not in books."[33] The authors who succeed in capturing these voices have lived with these languages and interlanguages "in the mouth" and in the ear—their own being is inextricably bound up with them. This, to me, is a prerequisite for making *us* hear them so clearly.

While we are made to hear the voices that render character and situation more real in a writer such as Tan, we are virtually buttonholed by Anzia Yezierska, who doesn't just speak—she shouts. Often it is "we" in the role of "you Americans" that she is appealing to, accosting, at times almost begging to open our gates of opportunity. Her voice *must* be heard in its "foreignness." Character after character in her fiction (much of it highly autobiographical) is passionate about her ambitions but frustrated by her limitations in English. Vivian Gornick calls this voice Anzierska's "'I want to make from myself a person' voice, the one that made the page jump with violent life." Katherine Stubbs writes of critics who found Anzierska's use of ethnic stereotypes deeply disturbing and considered her use of incorrect immigrant English to be unflattering parody. I agree that her stereotypes are disturbing, making use of "pernicious cliches," especially of Russian Jews, but also of Anglo-Saxons.[34] But with regard to language, whether parodic or not in intention, Anzierska captures voices—anguished, lonely, combative, or filled with urgency and longing—that ring out with the passionate desire to be fully American, in an English structured according to Yiddish syntax and peppered with literally translated Yiddish idiom. Offered the opportunity to learn a trade, to work with her hands, Shenah Pessah, the heroine of *Hungry Hearts,* cries out, "With the hands the best? It's all the same what I do with the hands. Think you not maybe now, I could begin already something with the head? Yes?" After her first visit to the library she "bubble[s]": "Like for a holiday it feels itself in me. . . . Now see I America for the first time!"[35]

Refusing the security offered by a man who loves her, Shenah Pessah explains (partly in well-formed English): "You can't make for me a person. It's not only that I got to go up higher, but I got to push myself up by

33. Robert Frost, *Selected Letters of Robert Frost,* 112, 108.

34. Vivian Gornick, introduction to *How I Found America: Collected Stories of Anzia Yezierska,* ix; Katherine Stubbs, introduction to *Arrogant Beggar,* by Anzia Yezierska, xix.

35. Anzia Yezierska, *Hungry Hearts,* 14 (hereinafter cited in the text as *Hearts;* page numbers refer to the collection *How I Found America,* which includes the full text of *Hungry Hearts.*

myself. . . . I feel the emptiness of words—but I got to get it out . . . there is a something—a hope—a help out—it lifts me on top of my hungry body— the hunger to make from myself a person that can't be crushed by nothing nor nobody—the life higher!" (*Hearts,* 28–29).

Clearly, we are not meant to find these outbursts funny; whatever our positive or negative feelings about this Yiddish-flavored voice, we are not encouraged to laugh at it, to see it as a sort of vaudeville. But what about Leo Rosten's immigrant, Hyman Kaplan, a portion of whose English composition we sampled above as example 2? Do we laugh at his spelling, snicker at his grammar and pronunciation, as do his fellow night-school students when he reads it aloud? Even if we do smile a bit, we are moved more than amused by the difficulties of his labor, both as a "cotter" in a dress factory and as an English student, and moved as well by the inequities of his lot. We are surely meant to laugh, though, at Kaplan's irrepressible zeal to speak English, and at his zany logic. It is difficult to decide whether his teacher, the patient Mr. Parkhill, has failed or succeeded in his lesson on adjectives and their forms:

> "*Bad*—worse. What is the word you use when you mean 'most bad'?"
> "Aha!" cried Mr. Kaplan suddenly. When Mr. Kaplan cried "Aha!" it signified that a great light had fallen on him. "I know! De exect void! So easy! *Ach!* I should know dat ven I vas wridink! *Bad*—*voice*—"
> "Yes, Mr. Kaplan!" Mr. Parkhill was definitely excited.
> "Rotten!" (*Kaplan,* 18)

We laugh, but not at a cardboard stereotype meant to confirm our prejudices against dumb immigrants. Surely mixed with our laughter, as must be mixed with Mr. Parkhill's constant frustration, is affection for this personality—his enthusiasm, his misplaced self-satisfaction. We cannot separate this from the voice, the way it sounds—accent, error, and all.[36]

In another lesson, we hear and feel Kaplan's love of his wife and of nature, as, during "Rasitation and spitch—sp*eee*ch" time, he tells about his week in the "contry": "De sky! De son! De stoss! De clods. De frash air in de longs. All—all is pot fromm Netcher! . . . Ladies an' gantlman, have you

---

36. Mintz describes the ethnic humor of the variety theater, whose core was the construction of caricatures based on both stereotypes and linguistic humor ("Humor and Ethnic Stereotypes," 20–21). I hope it is clear from my examples from Tan, Rosten, and Yezierska that these authors, while exploiting linguistic play and even humor at the expense of their speakers, do not portray—or descend to—stereotypes. Much greater emphasis is on language and immigrant adjustment.

one an' all, or even saparate, falt *in de soul* de trees, de boids, de gress, de bloomers—all de scinnery?" Suddenly our poet is interrupted by embarrassed titters at his malapropism—the word *bloomers,* or underpants, mistakenly used to mean "flowers." We laugh and wince at the same time, I believe; we share his embarrassment and frustration at the interruption of his rhapsody.

> "Hau Kay! . . . So podden me an' denk you! Is de void batter 'flower.' So I love to smallink de flowers . . . I love to breedink de frash air. Mostly I love to hear de boids sinking."
> "You *must* watch your k's and g's," said Mr. Parkhill earnestly. "'Singing,' not 'sin*k*ing.'"
> . . . "An' ven de boids is singing, den is Netcher commink ot in all kinds gorgeous."
> Mr. Parkhill looked at the floor; there was no point in being picayune. (*Kaplan,* 23)

To Mr. Parkhill's credit is his realization that Kaplan's error has a certain logic—he is making a noun out of the verb *bloom,* and in his native language, *blumen* is the word for "flowers."[37]

Similarly, Amy Tan plays on the humor-cum-logic in her characters' occasional malapropisms, or rather, inaccurately used idioms. "Eat, drink, and be married," is not without its logic—to the speaker's way of thinking, being married *is* the way to happiness. The term "college drop-off" makes sense, and changes the mental picture we have of quitting school (*Joy,* 37). In *The Hundred Secret Senses,* Kwan, the Chinese-born half-sister of American-born Olivia, shows us such error and seeming stupidity in reverse. Olivia's friends call Kwan a "retard," and Kwan asks her sister (whom she calls "Libby-ah"): "What this word 'lee-tahd'?" The word reminds Kwan of the time, in China, that she thought the same of her beloved Miss Banner, an Englishwoman:

> "She didn't understand anything. . . . Libby-ah, did you know I taught Miss Banner to talk?" . . . It's true, though. I was her teacher. When I met her, her speech was like a baby's! Sometimes I laughed, I couldn't help it. . . . One day Miss Banner touched her palm on the front of her body and asked me how to say this in Chinese. After I told her, she said to me in Chinese . . . "I wish to know many words for talking

---

37. Leo Rosten was a Jewish Mr. Parkhill, teaching night-school classes in English while he was a graduate student. See Benjamin Harshav's article "The Semiotics of Yiddish Communication" on the role of questions and logic in Yiddish.

about my breasts!" And only then did I realize she wanted to talk about the feelings in her heart. The next day I took her wandering around the city. We saw people arguing. Anger, I said. . . . We saw a thief with his head locked in a wooden yoke. Shame, I said.[38]

In the reference to her as a "retard" and her asking the meaning of "lee-tahd," we "hear" one of many examples of how Kwan sounds to her sister; the rest is narration to herself of her memory, rendered in, or translated into, "perfect American English" for the reader. We are thus reminded once again, as we were in *The Joy Luck Club*, how much of a person—personality, depth, intelligence—is lost in the poverty of an as yet unfamiliar language.

Such a discrepancy is nowhere more sharply and variously drawn than in *Call It Sleep*, a tour de force of language and languages that draws on all we have been discussing: code switching, interlanguage, narrative as opposed to speaking voices, "broken" contrasted with perfectly rendered or translated language. In addition, we are made to feel the psychological impact on David of the different languages in his life: Yiddish, English (in all its varieties), Hebrew, Polish, various street dialects. As readers, we must feel and analyze for ourselves how these languages signify, because we are given the narration from the point of view of a child (six years old at the beginning of the novel), and a troubled and confused one at that. Unlike *Lost in Translation*, in which the narrator is a sophisticated adult who analyzes her being in language and her conflicts in languages, *Call It Sleep* requires us to understand the confusion and conflict that the protagonist himself does not understand in his lonely ignorance, his naïveté, and his terror.[39] Looking for answers, he attempts to express, despite the verbal and conceptual limitations of his age, what is inexpressible for even the most poetic of us. He clutches at symbols, and his symbol-making and hunger for interpretation require us to meet him halfway, to play that serious listening and reading game we enjoy so much.

There are many ways this huge, complex novel can be (and has been)

38. Amy Tan, *The Hundred Secret Senses*, 45, 48.

39. Since my emphasis in this chapter is on language(s), I do not attempt an analysis of narration. For such analysis, I recommend Naomi Sokoloff's *Imagining the Child in Modern Jewish Fiction*, which employs terminology such as "free indirect discourse" and "focalizer" and alludes to the studies of Dorrit Cohn, Gerard Genette, and Brian McHale. See also Naomi Diamant's "Linguistic Universes in Henry Roth's *Call It Sleep*," which combines discussion of narrative and language. Walter Allen calls the book "the most powerful evocation of the terrors of childhood ever written" (afterword to *Call It Sleep*, 444).

seen: as an example of the immigrant novel; as a realistic portrayal of New York's Lower East Side street life near the turn of the century—its poverty, ethnic turfs, and battlegrounds; and as the painful playing out of one family's oedipal drama, whose cast includes a brooding, violent father, a loving, vulnerable mother, and an extremely sensitive son who needs protection from both his father and the streets. In its modes of narration, its interiority, its play with language, its mythic overtones, and its epiphanies, the book shows an obvious debt to Joyce.[40] In its attempt to "shore up the fragments"—which include fragments of speech, the sundry voices of an urban landscape—we hear as well echoes of T. S. Eliot; the land of this book in some ways resembles a "waste land," yet in others teems with life and promise.

But nothing in the book looms larger than language, as we are made to hear it in its multitude of tones and accents and tongues, as its mysteries and complexities illuminate, connect, baffle, distort, empower, or render helpless. I would go so far as to say that no book has done more with languages and language. While this subject deserves a book-length study in its own right, I will necessarily limit myself to examples relevant to this discussion, examples of those "foreign" voices we hear in all their particularity and variety.

Call It Sleep has been called "the noisiest novel ever written,"[41] a description justified by the multiplicity of voices, often loud ones, in multiple languages that clamor for our attention as they invade the mind and sensibility of David Schearl along with "the elements of the ever-present din—the far voices, the near, the bells of a junk wagon, the sing-song cry of the I-Cash-clothes-man, . . . the sloshing jangle of the keys on the huge ring on the back of the tinker" (*Sleep,* 174). The contrast between the noisy street and the quiet of the apartment when only David and his mother are home parallels the contrast between the smooth and lyrical language of their conversation and the harsh "brokenness" of the language of the street, which makes us realize that those mother-son conversations—so poetic, so correct—must be in Yiddish.

> In the street David spoke English.
> "Kentcha see? Id's coz id's a machine. . . . It wakes op mine fodder
> in the mawning."

40. See Brian McHale, "Henry Roth in Nighttown, or, Containing *Ulysses*."
41. Allen, afterword, 445. In her Bakhtinian analysis of child narration, Sokoloff shows how "modern Jewish literature is especially equipped as a laboratory of the dialogic imagination" (*Imagining the Child,* 36). I would add that one cannot find a better-fitted lab than this book.

"It wakes op mine fodder too."

"It tells yuh w'en yuh sh'd eat an' w'en yuh have tuh go tuh sleep. . . . but I tooked it off."

. . . . "I godduh waid hea till duh wissle blows. . . . By de fectory. . . . Cuz dey blow on twelve a'clock an' dey blow on five a'clock. Den I c'n go op." (*Sleep*, 21–22)

Contrast Genya's attempt to explain death:

"They are cold; they are still. They shut their eyes in sleep eternal years" . . .

"Mama, what are eternal years?" . . .

Reaching toward the sugar bowl she lifted out the tongs, carefully pinched a cube of sugar . . .

"This is how wide my brain can stretch . . . You see? No wider. Would you ask me to pick up a frozen sea with these narrow things? Not even the ice-man could do it . . . The sea to this—" (*Sleep*, 69)

Even where interlanguage and code switching do not obtrude themselves into conversations, we, through David's ears and mind, are constantly being reminded to pay attention to language—if not its defects, then its possibilities: its rhythms, semantics, puns, its sound as music.[42] As we have observed not only in the theoretical literature, but also in the narrations of Rodriguez and Hoffman, the bilingual speaker and writer usually has a greater sensitivity than the monolingual to language *as* language, as pure sound, and a greater awareness of the way words sometimes do and sometimes do not represent what we are trying to say. When it isn't frustrating for David, it's a game. He may represent the incipient writer, playing with language, testing it, sensitive to nuances of sound and rhythm.

He greets the telegraph poles as he passes them, racing them as he goes farther and farther from his own familiar block: "Next one. . . . Race him! . . . Hello Mr. High Wood. . . . Good-bye, Mr. High Wood. I can go faster. . . . Hello, Second Mr. High Wood. . . . Good-bye Second Mr. High Wood . . . Can beat you" (*Sleep*, 93). As he imagines himself back home, his wishful thinking takes on the rhythm of his gait: "Borscht . . . Strawberries. . . . Radishes . . . Bananas . . . Borscht, strawberries, radishes, bananas. Borscht, strawberries, apples and strudel. . . . Like it, like it, like it. I—like—it. I like cake but I don't like herring. I like cake, but I don't like what? I like cake,

42. Sollors goes into some detail on Aunt Bertha's puns, the double entendres available to those readers who understand the Yiddish word that sounds so much like the English one ("'A world somewhere,'" 131–32).

but I don't like, like, like, herring. I don't don't—How far was it still? . . . Luter liked herring, don't like Luter. Luter liked herring, don't like Luter (*Sleep*, 95–96; the ellipsis marks after "strudel" are mine, but all others are in the text, where they serve to retard the language, presumably to keep it in line with David's movement).

Even mechanical sounds are "translated" into their likenesses and into alphabetic syllables:

> Uh chug chug, ug chug
> —Cucka cucka . . . Is a chicken . . .
> Ug chug ug ch ch ch—Tew weet!
> —No . . . can't be . . .
> Ug chug, ug chug, ug—TEW WEET!

This is a passing tugboat; its sound, as well as the blinding sunlight on the water, contribute to David's hypnotic, dreamlike state, which comes close to landing him in the water before the whistle wakes him (*Sleep*, 248).

So conscious is David of language and the sounds of different languages that he even ruminates over the bird sounds he hears: "A parrot and a canary. Awk! awk! the first cried. Eee—tee—tee—tweet! the other. . . . He wondered if they understood each other. Maybe it was like Yiddish and English, or Yiddish and Polish, the way his mother and his aunt sometimes spoke. Secrets" (*Sleep*, 174).

The lure of those secrets in their impenetrable, mysterious language is expressed in metaphors of romantic exploration and desertion: "meaning scaled the horizon to another idiom, leaving David stranded on a sounding but empty shore. Words here and there, phrases shimmering like distant sails tantalized him, but never drew near. . . . It seemed to him that his mind would fly apart if he brought no order into this confusion" (*Sleep*, 197). David's growing confusion regarding his own identity and his growing distrust of his only protector, his mother, amid hints of her youthful love affair, is expressed by his confusion in language, having caught between Yiddish and Polish only enough of the conversation between his mother and his aunt to whet his curiosity more, to make "not knowing almost unbearable." He understands "goy," "letters," and "handsome," but what is an "organist"? How can he know what happened if words and predicates are missing? Obsessed, he comes like an archaeologist to language: "But though he pried here, there, everywhere among the gutturals and surds striving with all his power to split the stubborn scales of speech, he could not. The mind could get no purchase" (*Sleep*, 195–96). And so he has to invest the blanks with meaning the best he can, make history out of shards. Out of those snatches, his own frantic needs, and his fertile imagination, he creates a false story of his identity that has disastrous, almost fatal, consequences before its lies bring out the truths that just may have the power to heal.

Unfamiliar words can be hollow playthings or mysterious spaces that must be filled when curiosity, fear, or spiritual hunger create a need for meaning. The "empty" Hebrew words remain only playthings for the boys in David's *cheder* (Hebrew school). They can suggest toilet jokes and sexual puns, letting in small talk and street talk along with the rote chanting. It is when the Hebrew sounds become invested with meaning, as when the rabbi translates the poetic and prophetic words of Isaiah, that the *cheder* books begin to be connected in David's mind with spiritual significance, and to answer a need. He sees that a burning coal—with which the angels touched the lips of Isaiah, not to burn, but to purify—can be redemptive, despite his association of coal with the frightening cellar, with dirt and rats, and with his disgust at his playmate's sister, Annie, "playing dirty" with him in the family's clothes closet. "Angel-coal," he reasons, must be another sort altogether—how to find *God's* cellar? With this new dimension to *cheder,* David strains to hear and understand, and the other boys' reciting and clowning become voices in opposition both to the rabbi's lesson and to the questioning, questing, confused reverie in David's mind. His thoughts, the voices of the boys and the rabbi, and the powerful text of Isaiah's answering the call to prophecy combine to become a discordant, cacophonous chorus, a veritable Babel of voices, languages, and personalities.

Example 5 above is taken from this *cheder* scene, which (like chapter 21 of the section called "The Rail") is a remarkable attempt to do the impossible: to defy the linearality of narrative, the space and time that writer and reader must traverse in sequential order. Roth comes about as far as one can in suggesting simultaneity within the constraints of a linear medium, but ultimately the effectiveness of the scene depends on us as readers: we must visualize—"auralize," actually—as we read. We must imagine that what goes across and down the page is actually simultaneous; that were we there, we would hear not single notes in succession, but a succession of chords, discordant and noisy: the layering recitation of "Chad Gadya" ("One Kid") and the Four Questions, both from the Passover seder service; street talk; the rabbi's disciplinary curses and injunctions to the inattentive students in a mixture of Yiddish and Yinglish; his quiet teaching of Isaiah to the older boy preparing for his bar mitzvah ceremony (the poetic King James English here is surely meant to be understood as a rendering of the rabbi's Yiddish). All of this further stimulates David's active mind; his more than four questions leap between the literal and the metaphysical, soar now to spiritual heights, now involuntarily to dirty words: "Some place Isaiah saw Him, just like that. I bet! He was sitting on a chair. So he's got chairs, so he can sit. Gee! Sit Shit! Sh! Please God, I didn't mean it! Please God, somebody else said it! Please—" (*Sleep*, 230). But after all, didn't the Book say that Isaiah's mouth was unclean? ("Behold my lips are unclean and I live in a land unclean"). And all this against the background of the other voices in the room:

> Why wasn't it clean anyway? He didn't wash it, I bet. So that . . .
> "A lighten', yuh dope. A blitz! Kentcha tuck Englitch? Ha! Ha! Sheor yerokos halaylo hazeh—Dat's two on dot! I wuz shootin chalk wid it. . . . Somm bean shooduh! My fodder'll give your fodder soch a kick—"
> . . . . "And the whole land waste and empty."
> "T'ree is a lie, mine fodder says. Yea? Matbilim afilu pa'am echos halaylo hazeh— Always wear yuh hat when a lighten' gives—"
> —He said dirty words, I bet Shit, pee, ... Stop! . . . It's a sin again! . . . But your mouth don't get dirty. I don't feel no dirt. (He rolled his tongue about) Maybe inside. Way, way in where you can't taste it. What did Isaiah say that made his mouth dirty? Real dirty, so he'd know it was? Maybe—
> "Shebchol haleylos onu ochlim—. De rain wedded my cockamamy! Ow! Leggo! Yuh can't cover books wit' newspaper. My teacher don't let." (*Sleep*, 230–31)[43]

Still, in all this confused chorus, as in all that has gone before (with the exception of the Prologue), there is one unity: David's mind. He remains the focalizer; every voice is in his hearing, entering his consciousness, or giving his consciousness words, sounds, feelings, ideas, to play with or to hide from.

This changes toward the end of the book, where guilt pressures David into lies. His guilt (ironically like his mother's) stems from his attraction to

---

43. The Hebrew phrases are from the Four Questions, asked by the youngest child at the Passover seder. They begin, "Why is this night different from all other nights?" and go on to ask about specific Passover practices, such as the eating of matzo and bitter herbs. The rest of the seder is meant to answer these questions. It is clear the boys have no comprehension of the meaning of these phrases; they are quoted with no regard for their grammatical or logical context. Notice the way Roth clues us into the narrative conventions he adopts: quotation marks give us dialogue as it is heard, and dashes mark David's interior monologue.

a "goy": Leo, the fearless Polish boy who is blessed with freedom and courage. How fortunate Leo is to have no father, and a mother who works all day and leaves him to his own devices; how enviable his courage, which comes, he claims, from a scapular that protects him even when he jumps dangerously off the pier into the river. Jews have no access to such blessings, of course, but for a chance at David's girl cousins, Leo offers him a rosary for protection from harm. This is a temptation David cannot resist, but his unbearable guilt once he has brought Leo to his cousin in her cellar, and his fear at being found out, cause David to "lose himself" in more ways than one.

He runs to the *cheder*, to "lose himself among the rest," "glad to be among them! To forget!" (*Sleep,* 358, 360). He behaves and performs uncharacteristically, answering the rabbi's queries by bursting into tears and babbling a tale fabricated from the snatches of his mother's secrets and, more powerfully, from his need to deny "motherfatherself," to create a new identity, a different David, one with a goy/organist father and who has not done the terrible thing that is consuming him with guilt. Separating himself from the Davy whose mind and guilt and fear and conflict he has been saddled with, he is suddenly free—free to use dirty words with no guilt or apology, to urinate in the street: "I'm sommbody else. I'm somebody else—*else*—ELSE! Dot's who I am. Hoo! Hoo! Johnny Cake" (*Sleep,* 371). But the moment does not last. Tired, he goes toward home. The face he sees in the shopwindows is his, and as we have seen, he takes comfort in the spots between windows where he does not see his reflection: "In between if I stopped, where? Ain't nobody. No place. Stand here then. BE nobody. Always. Nobody'd see. Nobody'd know. . . . carry a looking glass. . . . Be nobody and she comes down. Take it! Take looking glass out, Look! Mama! Mama! Here I am! Mama I was hiding! Here I am! But if Papa came. Zip, take away! Ain't! Ain't no place! Ow! Crazy!" (*Sleep,* 379).

Once he has become a David he cannot bear to be, once his lies and subsequent events move out of his control, so does the narration. We are moved outside David's mind and are now privy to the thoughts of the rabbi, a quarrel between Aunt Bertha and her husband, a conversation between David's parents and the rabbi, that take place, as nothing since the Prologue has, with David absent from the scene. As David's lies spin out of control, what has been warring within him also explodes, along with everyone's secrets, as if all that turbulent fragmentation, those conflicting voices and half-understood tales, have to get out, have to explode, before anything can possibly come together. Once he is out on the street, out of reach of the violence in his apartment, we are told: "He dared to breathe.

. . . For a moment, the wild threshing of voices, bodies, the screams, the fury in the pent and shrunken kitchen split their bands in the brain, flew out to the darkened east" (*Sleep,* 403). We remember that the disconnected words and hints of powerful secrets have threatened the stability of David's mind, which might "fly apart if he brought no order into this confusion" (*Sleep,* 197), an order that only knowledge and control of language can impose.

Mind, identity, a David who is and is not David, narration, language—all of these are unraveling, dangerously fragmenting in the life and family and neighborhood of David Schearl. But in the final chapters of the book they are all brought together, intertwining even as they are disconnecting, working centrifugally and centripetally toward climax and conclusion. As the novel progresses toward the apocalyptic rail scene, all narrative coherence is lost among voices coming from everywhere within seeing and hearing distance of the trolley track where David will create an explosion, nearly electrocuting himself in the process. As David moves toward the tracks with his metal milk ladle, challenging himself to create light, we are given snatches of conversations from all over the area whose languages, dialects, and topics of conversation reflect the speakers: a nightwatchman, Jewish card players, MacIntyre the motorman, an Armenian pushcart vendor, the men in Callahan's saloon and the prostitutes at his family entrance, Salvation Army singers, a Jewish peddler, British sailors on their boat, a communist "preacher." Their voices alternate with one another in a dizzying sequence whose method once again seems a bold attempt to defy the linearality of both time and space in narration.[44]

When David finally succeeds in inserting the ladle into the middle rail of the tracks to create a blinding explosion, all talk from all quarters turns into cries centering on the flash—all movement is toward it. David's monologue is silenced until an unidentified man, using a broom thrown to him by a watchman, pushes him off the track, and another man begins the artificial respiration that a policeman continues. As they labor to restore his breath, David's impressionistic, jumbled inner "narration" resumes—the lyrical, frenzied recapitulation of words and images that he, and we, have been experiencing throughout the book. No longer controlled by sequence, structure, or attempt at logic and understanding, but lyrical, impressionistic, and evocative, it pulls together all the elements in the book. Paradoxically, this most fragmented of narrations resolves in the greatest

---

44. To reinforce this attempt, Roth breaks up David's "narrative" midsentence, even midword: "—*He stole up to the dipper warily* / *On tip—* / 'Shet up, down 'ere, yuh bull-faced harps . . .' [almost half a page follows] / *toe, warily, glancing over his* / *shoulders, on tip-toe, over serried* / *cobbles, cautious—*"

unifications of the book—in David himself, in his family, in the neighbor-hood cacophany of tongues and peoples:

> "Holy Mother O' God! Look! Will yiz!"
> "There's a guy layin' there! Burrhnin'!"
> "Do sompt'n! Meester! Meester!"
> "Oy! Oy vai! Oy vai! Oy vai!"
> "Bambino! Madre mia!"
> "Helftz! Helftz! Helftz Yeedin! Rotivit!"
> "Back up youz! Back up! Didja hea' me, Moses? Back up! Beat it!
> Gwan!"
> "Foist aid yuh gets 'em hea. Like drownin' see?"
> Khir-r-r-r-f S-s-s-s-
> "He's meckin' him t' breed!"
> "Mimi! He's awright! He's awright!"
> "Yeh?"
> "No kiddin'! No kiddin'!"
> "Yeh!"
> "Yuh!"
> "Oi Gott sei dank!" (culled from *Sleep,* 420–31)

Out of this fragmentation of voices, types, religions, languages, normally hostile ethnic groups, classes, and occupations, David unwittingly creates the final unity, drawn as they all are toward the terrific explosion, by their unified/unifying desire to rescue the electrocuted child.[45] Suddenly, they are all gathered at the same spot; their various languages clearly under-stood by them all—they must help save this child.

Back home, in the quiet of his bed, he cannot answer his mother's question:

> "What made you do it?"
> "I don't—I don't know," he answered. And the answer was true. He couldn't tell now why he had gone, except that something had forced him, something that was clear then and inevitable, but that every pass-ing minute made more inarticulate. "I don't know, mama." (*Sleep,* 437)

---

45. Bruce Robbins offers an explanation for this fragmentation in his discussion of David's stream of consciousness when he cannot turn on the tap: "The world seems to break up into private fragments only because children—and immigrants, for the son's helplessness stands for that of the entire family—cannot control its public forces" (Robbins quoted in Karen R. Lawrence, "Roth's *Call It Sleep:* Modernism on the Lower East Side," 116). This observation could certainly be extended to the rail scene—and to the world of the whole book.

His nonanswer raises two questions: why did he do it, and why is it now so unclear? When we consider the momentary unity of the mutually hostile groups in the neighborhood, the talk switching from sexual vulgarity to how to save David, the prayers in Italian, English, and Yiddish all in harmony, we could conclude that David's body has been sacrificed for community; in all their different languages the neighbors manage to communicate and to understand one another. His family, too, calms into harmony and resolution; indeed, he enters a chastened and quiet home—his father contrite, offering to get the medicine and acknowledging David for the first time as his son. The Christological images are there in enough abundance to support the many readings of David as a Christ figure[46]— even relating the slaughtered goat of "Chad Gadya" to the image of the lamb. But as he approaches the rail, it is not with intent to sacrifice himself—no *agnus dei*, this, *qui tollis peccata mundi*. Nor, despite his desire to "not be" when his father is around, is this an act of deliberate self-destruction. On the contrary, what he is seeking is power, his source— though he doesn't understand it himself, electrical power. The dark window of his apartment has "double-dared" him (*Sleep*, 409)—it will not. turn reassuringly light, and so *he* must create light. Rather than a conscious desire to sacrifice himself, this is the courage and desire to take charge (an unintended pun that is grotesquely apt).

He has sought God before, "seen" Him (it?) when Pedey and his pals tricked him into inserting a sheet-zinc sword into the tracks, telling him he'd see magic: "all de movies in de woil! . . . an' all de angels." What he saw then was "Power! Like a paw ripping through all the stable fibres of the earth, power, gigantic, fetterless, thudded into day" (*Sleep*, 252–53; these words are repeated almost verbatim in the rail scene, p. 419). He therefore already knew how to rouse power from the tracks. But this time he went further than seeking God; he was playing God. Let there be light, his act says, as he accepts the "dare" to create it.

The question of what happened to him as a result is perhaps related to the observation that he seems to have succeeded in unhinging himself from the David he couldn't bear. In his "electric" vision, fragments of mirror reappear:

> *(As if on hinges, blank, enormous*
> *mirrors arose, swung slowly upward*

---

46. See, for example, Hana Wirth-Nesher, introduction to *New Essays on* Call It Sleep, 9; Wirth-Nesher, "Between Mother Tongue and Native Language," 306–7; Bonnie Lyons, *Henry Roth: The Man and His Work*, 53; McHale, "Henry Roth in Nighttown," 85–86.

face to face. Within the facing
glass, vast panels deployed, lifted a
steady wink of opaque pages until
an endless corridor dwindled into
night.)

. . . .

David wept, approached the glass,
peered in. Not himself was there,
not even in the last and least of
the infinite mirrors . . .) (Sleep, 427)

In these mirrors David sees "reflections" of the *cheder* wall; images associated with his father, his father's voice, and his mother's explanation of
death; and finally an ember swimming in light. But in this context it is
enough to notice that he doesn't see himself in any of them. In this
"death," who or what has been born, or reborn? (The inserting of the ladle
and the creation of light makes obvious use of the language of sexual
union and birth.)

The first mirror image in the passage above suggests one answer: the
writer. Instead of the image of his reflected face, David sees "opaque pages."

When David tries to give up his identity, his narrative voice (or the
voice that narrates through his consciousness), other voices take over and
exclude him, and it is as though he has sacrificed not his body, but his
voice, to the community. But his "electricified" inner poetic discourse
leaves almost no image, no major incident, out. The "dream" from which
he wakes, with almost no memory of it, contains every memory, transmuted into poetry. He has had a veritable "shock treatment" and thus
emerges more calm, but without full memory—partially dissociated from
who he has been and what has happened. But though he awakes into a
self that may feel divided from its past, it is not divided within itself.
Perhaps what awakes (as I suggested in the case of Maxine's long illness
in *The Woman Warrior*) is the poet, the artist who will create such a
stream of discourse, such a book, as we have been reading. From the broken shards of mirror, the fractured English, and fragments of languages
and voices, a surer voice arises, able to control and unify and capture
them artistically as one cannot do in life—to create a unified work of art
whose subject is fractured languages and identities and communities.

This is what the artist usurps of God—the power to create. The human
creates in imitation of God the creator—man was created, we remember,
in His image.

Mario Materassi relates that Roth wrote to him in a letter "that he found a connection between the change in the point of view at the end of the novel and his creative paralysis. He changed the point of view, he explained, 'as a transition to the choral part; and probably, in retrospect, subjectively I might add, an indication that the form of the novel was being broken, along with the creative psyche of the novelist.'" This is a fascinating look at the author's view of himself and of his famous forty-year writer's block following the completion of this novel. What I have seen as loss of control on David's part, controlled so carefully by the author, what I have seen as a "birth" into creativity and poetry, Roth saw as related to his subsequent paralysis.[47] Perhaps, having created those final chapters, he realized that he could go no further than he already had. It is tempting to extend this relation of the last scenes to what gets silenced: David is silenced in creating the "shock," but if, as some have said, David is the youth who grows up to write this book, that silence gives rise to a new and powerful voice—Henry Roth's voice. But then Roth becomes silenced in creating David—a literal "death" of the author, or at least a long sleep.

That brings us to those enigmatic words, "call it sleep." We must ask, of course, what "it" refers to, as well as why we are to call it "sleep"—if we are to *call* it sleep, it must in actuality be something else, something perhaps that we, or David, or Roth, or the narrator, simply have no other way of expressing. His mother asks David if he is sleepy, and he answers Yes:

> He might as well call it sleep. It was only toward sleep that every wink of the eyelids could strike a spark into the cloudy tinder of the dark, kindle out of shadowy corners of the bedroom such myriad and such vivid jets of images—of the glint on tilted beards, of the uneven shine of roller skates, of the dry light on grey stone stoops . . . that ears had power to cull again and reassemble the shrill cry, the hoarse voice, the scream of fear. . . . It was only toward sleep one knew himself still lying on the cobbles, felt the cobbles under him . . . the perpetual blur of shod and running feet, the broken shoes, new shoes, stubby, pointed, caked, and polished . . . and feel them all and feel, not pain, not terror, but strangest triumph, strangest acquiescence. (*Sleep,* 441)

47. Mario Materassi, "Shifting Urbanscape: Roth's 'Private' New York," 59. Sam Girgus sees David as awakening into a new American consciousness, working through "Christian light" to emerge with a new Jewish identity—one that will "participate in the recreation of American culture and life through the renewal of language" (*The New Covenant: Jewish Writers and the American Idea,* 96, 105). Wirth-Nesher sees the scene as a birth "into the world of English literacy and culture" ("Between Mother Tongue and Native Language," 309). Closer to my reading is Naomi Diamont's, who sees the scene as a "*rite de passage* into [David's] nature as a poet" ("Linguistic Universes in Henry Roth's *Call it Sleep,*" 354–55).

Genya's question causes David to wrestle with the term *sleep:* He is able to confirm "sleepy," an adjective of generalized feeling, in a way he cannot confirm a noun, which requires naming, identifying more concretely this unnameable state. "Toward" sleep, like sleep*y,* is about as definite as he can get.[48] What he says happens only *toward* sleep happens in a state of mind—perhaps a subverbal state resembling his not-quite-conscious state during his electrocution—wherein logic, reason, and inhibitions are re-laxed, where shutting his eyes strikes sparks of imaginative fire—images recalled with more vividness than they were first noticed. Eyes, ears, touch, all senses operate in a heightened, "charged" state, and memory is transformed. After all the wished-for separation from the self, it is only in this state that "one knew himself" as he had been while lying on the tracks, knew, from the memory of his ground view, the great variety of people crowding around him as he had not "known" it while it was happening. Perhaps "it" is this state of creative mind, this loosening of the hold of re-ality and daylight, that allows creativity its flow, feeling stripped of pain and terror, and "triumph." Triumph can be seen in David's feeling of tri-umph over his father or in his maturing into sympathy with his father, but also, perhaps more important, in the triumph of being able to remember and imagine in this heightened way.

And "acquiescence"? To what? To the reality that life will never be per-fect, to what can only ever be partial triumph, temporary freedom from pain and terror, certainly. In the context of creativity, I would suggest that David is also acquiescing to that state of suspended wakefulness, surren-dering to "it." But even as he finds himself immersed in the creative possi-bilities of language, as Naomi Sokoloff points out, he recognizes its limitations.[49] "Might as well" is a term of acquiescence. When one cannot put an exact label on a feeling, on a hazy sensibility, one "might as well call it" something easy and within reach—like "sleep" or "dream." When one has split the world into fragments of vision and language and then tied them into a magnificent whole whose process cannot be adequately named, when one has taken language as far as one can and cannot trust it further, perhaps the rest is (as in Roth's case for a long, long time) silence. But the text does not allow silence; witness all that has already been writ-ten about it, and all, I am confident, that is yet to be written. Now it is we, the readers, who are stimulated by the book's fragmentation to put the

48. I am grateful to Sondra Baras for pointing out the sleepy/sleep discrepancy.
49. Sokoloff, *Imagining the Child,* 89. Lawrence speaks of the "provisional quality of this final naming ('call it sleep') [as] extend[ing] to the act of narrative closure" ("Roth's *Call It Sleep,*" 122).

pieces together, stimulated by its power to keep talking about it, to "call" and name "it."

Many of us have called the result a "masterpiece," but David has no name by which to call this vision or process. He recognizes that there is no word for it, but there are words, voices, and images by means of which he can attempt to name it. He has, after all, been playing with words in different languages, turning them over in his mouth and in his mind throughout the novel as he tries to piece together the visual and visceral and aural fragments of his experience into coherent sentences and narrations. He does succeed in creating a narrative, albeit a fictional one; yet his fiction forces the facts out of hiding. David's fabrication, which includes his fabricated identity, is the catalyst of truth and recognition not only of his parents' pasts but of his own identity—the verification that he is indeed his father's son. The voices and names we hear are put together in such a way that we are made to share David's experience. In a reading experience we live through—in Keats's words, "burn through"[50]—we share a verbally created inner and outer universe. For both writer and reader, such an experience, not the exact words, is "it."

Which brings us back to what and how language signifies. We have seen how the choice of a language can signify. We have also seen language as signi*fied*, the ways in which language and languages are represented, and to what possible purposes, with what possible motives. But at this juncture we can see that no language can be exact—not in how its sounds are represented by the words on the page, nor in what those words signify to their listeners or their readers. Not in a reference for "it." David's "it" reminds us that at some level both language as represented and language as representing are irrelevant; the only thing that really matters is the way both are attempted and understood. We "might as well" content ourselves with hearing and understanding the voice that the words create. More directly than clearly heard or understood words, it communicates both David's state of mind and his promise as an artist in creating a concrete and eloquent articulation of the inarticulate.[51] Out of words: experience, tone. Out of languages: language. Out of voices: voice. Out of fragmentation: unity, but a unity that radiates outward to still further pos-

---

50. In using this term I am indebted to Louise M. Rosenblatt, who invokes Keats's "On Sitting Down to Read *King Lear* Once Again" to define her term *aesthetic reading* (*The Reader, the Text, the Poem: The Transactional Theory of the Literary Work*, 26–27).

51. Robert Frost would have called this "the sound of sense." One of his analogies for this phenomenon is hearing voices through a closed door, when we cannot make out the words but "get" more meaning from inflections and tones (*Selected Letters,* 80).

sibilities. The resolution for David within the narrative is tenuous, but for this work it is perfect: the novel, which powerfully interrogates language, closes on the impossibility of closure and definiteness, of exactness of meaning, of a neat equivalence between David's experience of power and our perception of it, of finding the word that can express that experience in English or Yiddish or any other language. In this, the work parallels reality and represents it—whether a social and cultural world or an individual's psyche—as always in process, un-unified, unstable, always negotiating its fragmented identities and uncertain futures, always in danger of being misunderstood. One senses that David, drifting off, contenting himself for the moment with "might as well" and an unspecified "it," will never really rest from mounting his "raid on the inarticulate," trying out words to create and understand his world. Like the physical world, this verbal world also entangles us within its dynamics and its processes. Roth constantly challenges us to translate, and while for us, as for him, "there is only the trying,"[52] this is the way we effect the book's ultimate unification—that between writer and reader.

52. T. S. Eliot, "Four Quartets: East Coker," lines 179, 189.

5

Heaping Bowls and Narrative Hungers

Around the Family Table

Call It Sleep is permeated with references to Passover preparation and liturgy, but, curiously, we are never "present" at that most celebrated, best-known aspect of Passover, the seder. Genya cleans the house for the holiday, ridding it of any trace of the forbidden leavened bread, or *chometz;* David is sent out to perform the ritual burning of the last remaining pieces. In Hebrew school, the children recite "Chad Gadya" and the Four Questions in preparation for their family seders. As noted in the previous chapter, it is during these lessons that David "hears" the call to Isaiah; it is in searching for a place to make his little bonfire of *chometz* that David has his "vision" of light. But there is no seder scene, perhaps because the essence of the seder—the story of Exodus, the children's questioning and singing, the reading of the Haggadah, all traditionally led by the father— seems totally out of reach and out of character for David's father. Such a scene would be inconsistent with the psychological atmosphere of the book.

We can easily imagine Genya preparing the symbolic foods for the seder plate—bitter herbs as a reminder of the bitterness of slavery in Egypt; salt water for the tears shed by the Israelites; *charoset,* the apple-and-nut mixture whose reddish color is reminiscent of the mortar used in building for the Egyptians; a roasted bone as a reminder of the sacrificial paschal lamb. Surely, she would also prepare a festive, traditional meal that would include chicken soup with matzo balls and conclude with fruit compote and sponge cake. On the table would be lit candles on a clean white cloth.

But the seder is not just a meal, or even just a time for family to gather around a table to celebrate a holiday. The meal is only part of the seder; the word literally means "order," and, according to the order of the seder, the meal comes at the midpoint, preceded and followed by the reading (reciting, singing, discussing) of the Haggadah, the text of the seder, whose main purpose is to tell the story of the exodus from Egypt and to praise God for having brought the Jewish people out of slavery and into freedom. The narrative begins only after the youngest child has recited the four questions, which are introduced by the more general question: "Why is this night different from all other nights?" Albert Schearl would most likely have trouble getting through the Haggadah, both because his Hebrew education is minimal and because he would be impatient with the long text. His attitude toward Hebrew education and religious observance is perfunctory. Even more to the point is the emotional environment he creates, compounded by ignorance, that precludes questions in general.

But throughout the book, we see David questioning, not just out of curiosity but out of a hunger for understanding. What is death? What is God? What are "eternal years"? His desire for spiritual knowledge is merely whetted by what he hears of the call to Isaiah. The hunger he would bring to the seder table could not be satisfied by matzo balls and chicken soup. As if anticipating generations of Davids, the Haggadah contains not only the story of the exodus, but also stories of the telling of that story, of ancient rabbis who were so engrossed in their telling, and asking, and interpreting of the biblical texts that their students had to come to remind them that it was time for the morning prayers.[1] And the Haggadah helps parents to be teachers, providing guidance in how to answer the questions of very different sorts of children—the wise son, the wicked one, the simple one, and the one who does not know enough to ask. (Literally, the Hebrew term could also be translated as "who does not know to ask.") The parent assumes that this last child has questions and "answers" them, showing the child that it is all right, even appropriate, to ask.

I have gone into detail about the seder because it combines food, family, and a story that transmits tradition. Questions are asked, debated, and answered—by book and parent—and good food, as well as symbolic food,

---

1. In both the Haggadah and *Call It Sleep,* we can see the way story and questions function in Jewish communication; questions are answered with more questions or with stories. For a more detailed discussion, see my "'God Loves Stories,' Jews Love Questions: I. B. Singer Questions God." Benjamin Harshav writes that Yiddish internalized some essential characteristics of Talmudic dialectical argument; he notes that there are hundreds of question marks in *Call It Sleep* ("Semiotics of Yiddish Communication," 145, 160). In much Jewish literature, to question is the point. Even modern Jewish writers not schooled in Talmud show the influence of its questioning and dialectic, as well as that of midrash, the genre of rabbinic literature consisting of exegesis, sermons, laws, and narratives known as Aggadah (literally, that which is told).

is an integral part of the experience. The seder is designed to satisfy both kinds of hunger, or if not to satisfy the hunger for historical and spiritual knowledge, at least to provide a forum for questioning and debating, for story and interpretation. It validates, in other words, the processes of asking, of telling, and of interrogating what has been told. And it is all repeated annually, so that the songs, the menu, the very dishes and serving pieces that are reserved for Passover become part of the family tradition, and memories of seders long past become an important part of the family legacy. Of course, much of this is true of any family holiday gathering—family stories get repeated, arguments resurface, and foods related to the holiday are placed on special dishes, such as those brought out every Christmas. What is unique to the seder, and different from all other (even Jewish) holidays, is its focus on narrative—a prescribed one, to be sure, but one meant to stimulate discussion. It is a narrative that explicitly connects the participants to the text and to their history: Tell your son that God did this for *him.* Teach him that he must think of the deliverance "as if he himself went out of Egypt," for had God not redeemed your ancestors, you and your children would still be slaves in Egypt. The wicked son is considered wicked because he asks, "What does this service mean to you?" In saying *you* and not *me* or *us,* he separates himself from his history and his people; he asks, Why do I need to know this?

Inescapable in both Chinese and Jewish American literature is this centrality of family and community—its pulls, its claims, and its stories collective and traditional, particular and familial. Whether the protagonist embraces family and tradition or tries to flee them, they are never irrelevant. Food and foodways, so often connected with family stories and gatherings, exert similar holds and incite similar rebellions. It cannot be a coincidence that food so often accompanies story, that hunger is so often a metaphor of the desire for stories about old or new ways of life, that language so often links food and story. James W. Brown writes: "Eating and speaking share the same motivational structure; language is nothing more than the praxis of eating transposed to the semiosis of speaking: both are fundamentally communicative acts by which man appropriates and incorporates the world."[2] While I would quibble with the reductive view of lan-

---

2. James W. Brown, *Fictional Meals and Their Function in the French Novel, 1789–1848,* 13. This passage is quoted in Sau-ling Cynthia Wong, *Reading Asian American Literature,* 18. Joan Chiung-huei Chang quotes the same passage and goes on: "In Chinese American literature, this deed of compensation or replacement of food for speech usually happens on the occasion of story telling" (*Transforming Chinese American Literature: A Study of History, Sexuality, and Ethnicity,* 150).

guage implied by "nothing more," the connection is apt, especially if one extends "communicative acts" to include the desire for communication and the hunger to belong, be it inside a community and its traditions or outside to new ones.

Like the wise son, David, as well as Maxine in *The Woman Warrior*, Jing-mei in *The Joy Luck Club,* and so many others,[3] says, "Tell me!" Tell me when, and what, and why. This urgency for the story, especially on the part of those who are trying to forge an identity between cultures, is at times matched by an urgency to tell. Perhaps this is the reason so many of these narratives focus on the telling itself, on those who tell and those who hear the stories.[4] In an act that is analogous to feeding, the giving is combined with the receiving of something that becomes ingested, incorporated. At times, though, the demand is answered by a refusal to tell, perhaps out of fear that the child/listener will not understand the story's significance or will ridicule it, or out of fear that one is inadequate to the task, or because the story is a secret, like Winnie's first marriage in *The Kitchen God's Wife* or what really happened to the "no name woman" in *The Woman Warrior.* Or perhaps because forging a new identity necessitates silence about the past. An example of this occurs in Lynne Sharon Schwartz's "The Opiate of the People": a father who has worked hard to create himself as an accent-less American and to put his painful European past behind him consistently rebuffs his daughter's question, "What was it like back there?" At other times it is the listener who refuses the story. The telling, requesting, or rejecting of narratives becomes part of the larger narrative's drama, not just its frame.

"God created man because he loves stories," concludes Elie Wiesel in an epigraph based on the Chasidic tale of the rabbi Baal Shem Tov, who interceded to save his people from terrible suffering by going to a certain place in the forest, lighting a fire, and saying a special prayer. His successors were able to perform this miracle even though the "keys," one after the other, were lost. The followers could not find the right place, were not able to light the fire, or did not know the prayer. Then it was the turn of Rabbi Israel of Rizhin, who lamented that he could perform none of the necessary acts: "'All I can do is to tell the story, and this must be sufficient.'

3. For example, Vivi and her children in Tillie Olsen's "Tell Me a Riddle," Lucy in Lynne Sharon Schwartz's "The Opiate of the People," and the narrator/son in Jerome Weidman's "My Father Sits in the Dark" and Gilbert Rogin's "What Happens Next?"

4. Victoria Aarons speaks of "a deeply ingrained history of bearing witness in Jewish culture and letters" to individual and community survival. She also speaks of "the drama . . . in the very act of telling stories . . . that bond communities" (*A Measure of Memory: Storytelling and Identity in American Jewish Fiction,* 4–5).

And it was sufficient."[5] When David asks Genya about death and God and what happens after death, she does not know the words, she has lost the "fire," and can only reply by means of metaphor: she tells him a story—moving, deeply felt, poetic—of her grandmother's death in the season of falling leaves, answering the most profound questions with a story (*Sleep*, 66–68). Is it sufficient? Not really. Her limited education and lack of faith cannot satisfy her curious, troubled, and spiritually hungry son. But pieces of her story keep recurring in David's thoughts; her metaphors of God and eternity inspire his vision of light. The story continues to work on him and he builds on it. The seder, too, tells a story. It also includes a hearty meal, and thus has the potential to feed both body and spirit. It teaches metaphor and symbol, the importance of questions asked and stories transmitted, identity and history.

Let the seder, then, stand for the ways in which food, family, and what Maxine Hong Kingston calls "talk-story" have the potential for strengthening identity and cultural ties.[6] What happens, though, when food alone is offered, or offered as substitute, a symbol emptied of significance? What if the seder becomes a meal without a story? What if so few other stories have been shared that no one wants to hear a "canned" one that only delays the meal?

A student of mine wrote a story that caricatures such a seder:

> Finally, everyone was there. Of course Grandma wasn't ready . . . . My father, grunting obscenities . . . was the first to be seated. The intense rumbling of his stomach, matched with the snide remarks from his mouth, betrayed his attitude. He took his usual place at the foot of the table, a length of five mismatched chairs separating him from my grandfather. . . . The Khaners were next. After carrying through with her threat, Aunt Judy turned off the sports channel and the men had no choice but to migrate from the television toward the food. . . . Brad, nineteen, scanned the table as he chose his seat for anything that he could easily grab and munch on until the meal would begin. Seth laughed at his baby brother's ignorance, "Loser, put the gefilte fish back. You gotta wait until after the wine."

Amid snatches of conversation ranging from recipes and make-up to the stock market, the seder is about to begin:

5. Wiesel, *Gates of the Forest,* epigraph on unnumbered page.
6. Kingston, interview in *Conversations,* ed. Skenazy and Martin, 149.

"Pop, just start on twenty-seven, drink a few, then it's time for the 'festive meal,' " Uncle Denny proclaimed to the table. . . .

"No, we start on page one. We always start on page one. We started on page one before there was a page one." . . .

"Relax, Grandpa. We don't have to start on page one. God's heard it all before, anyway. He knows what we mean."

Several conversations and a business phone call later, Grandpa compromises: "Page four. In English. Shane, you read."[7]

Disconnected from story and from tradition, the seder has become just another meal, and delay is therefore not easily tolerated. It is not simply that food and story have been disconnected, nor even that the story has become meaningless and irrelevant to the gathered family, but that food has become the substitute for story. Food is no longer the accompaniment to or reward for hearing the story, and interest in food has replaced interest in story. The only questions asked at this seder are those related to worldly affairs and gossip, the only answers, wisecracks and "pass the chopped liver." A few trips in and out of the kitchen to fill the platters will easily assuage the hungers at this table.[8]

Not so the narrative hungers of those who ask what a symbol or ritual means, who want to know the stories that inform the culture and the symbol system, who ask where the family came from, what Grandfather did back there, and what it was like for Mother. The latter are questions not so much of ritual as of history and community, and they are surely more urgent for the bicultural person trying to create an identity and find her place in a history that is not the same as that of her classmates or officemates, that is different from that of the (perceived) majority, that is in reality more like a hydra-headed, multiple history. For the bicultural is attempting to navigate between—no, to weave together—the environments and communities of home and what lies outside, and she needs to understand her own background before she can decide how it does and does not "fit" with the larger fabric of America. It is a commonplace that we cannot change our grandparents, but we can ask who and what our grandparents were. This may be a question totally separate from questions of tradition,

7. Betsy Davis, student assignment, Case Western Reserve University, 1999.
8. This sort of seder meal, like countless other ethnic gatherings and loyalties to particular foods, can serve as an example of what Werner Sollors, citing Herbert Gans, refers to as "symbolic ethnicity," wherein "modern ethnic identification works by external symbols rather than by continual activities that make demands upon" their ethnic constituents (Sollors, *Beyond Ethnicity*, 35).

or it may be that our grandparents are invested with tradition, represent it for us, and, at a table very different from the one in my student's story, tell us their own stories as well as the stories—and histories, and beliefs—their grandparents told them.

When Maxine's mother opens the front and back doors and "mumble[s] something," Maxine asks:

> "What do you say when you open the door like that?"
> . . . "Nothing. Nothing," she would answer.
> "Is it spirits, Mother? Do you talk to spirits? Are you asking them in or out?"
> "It's nothing," she said. She never explained anything that was really important. They no longer asked. (*Warrior,* 121)

Consequently, they no longer know well enough how to behave like proper Chinese children.

In some texts, where stories or traditions are missing, the frustrated protagonists fill the void by creating their own: The protagonist of Cynthia Ozick's novel *The Puttermesser Papers* has a conversation with her great-uncle Zindel, who, "it seemed," is teaching her Hebrew, telling her about his father's Sabbath table, giving her advice about meeting a husband in Israel. Suddenly a metanarrator interrupts:

> Stop. Stop, stop! Puttermesser's biographer, stop! Disengage, please. Though it is true that biographies are invented, not recorded, here you invent too much. A symbol is allowed, but not a whole scene: do not accommodate too obsequiously to Puttermesser's romance. . . . Uncle Zindel lies under the earth of Staten Island. Puttermesser has never had a conversation with him; he died four years before her birth. He is all legend. . . . But Puttermesser must claim an ancestor. She demands connection—surely a Jew must own a past. Poor Puttermesser found herself in the world without a past. Her mother was born into the din of Madison Street and was taken up to the hullabaloo of Harlem at an early age. Her father is nearly a Yankee. . . . Of the world that was, there is only this single grain of memory: that once an old man, Puttermesser's mother's uncle, kept his pants up with a rope belt, was called Zindel, lived without a wife, ate frugally, knew the holy letters, died with thorny English a wilderness between his gums. To him Puttermesser clings. America is blank, and Uncle Zindel is all her ancestry.[9]

9. Cynthia Ozick, *The Puttermesser Papers,* 16–17.

What her mother and father never gave her, perhaps did not have enough of even for themselves, Ruth Puttermesser creates, gathering and combining out of imagination and need the history she hungers for. In this she is like the Kingston of *China Men,* who must work harder and imagine more fully than any recorder or chronicler her father's pre-America past: "I'll tell you what I suppose from your silences and few words, and you can tell me that I'm mistaken. You'll just have to speak up with the real stories if I've got you wrong."[10] Or: "I tell everyone he made a legal trip. . . . But there were fathers who had to hide inside crates to travel to Florida or New Orleans. . . . Yes, he may have helped another father who was inside a box. I think this is the journey you don't tell me: The father's friends nailed him into a crate" (*China Men,* 15, 48–49). "*Demands* connection," "*have to* speak up"—this is the language of necessity, of hunger.

Obviously, hunger that is not physical, that doesn't "demand" food for the stomach, is metaphorical hunger, just as nourishment that provides not calories, but a past or a tradition or a myth—that satisfies what I call *story-hunger*—is a metaphor. And yet so often are literal food and story-food connected that it can be difficult to separate the literal from the metaphorical, especially when they carry messages—sometimes welcome, but often dreaded and avoided. Sau-ling Cynthia Wong writes of the ways "the resources of metaphoric language (traceable eventually to 'human' functions like eating) have afforded [Chinese American writers] a shared means to present complex, ambivalent meanings about the [immigrant family] experience."[11] Chicken soup can call out a much-needed "welcome home" or a stern "where have you been?" Conversely, matzo balls or rice cakes unaccompanied by story can frustrate metaphoric hunger. When they are substitutes for story, they become sterile, mere food for the digestive tract and as easy to eliminate, as easy to make jokes about or disparage: witness all the Jewish-mother jokes about eating and Maxine's angry determination to "live on plastic!" (*Warrior,* 92). Before looking at hunger and nourishment metaphorically, then, it is important to look at some of the communicative uses of literal food and at some of the messages it conveys. We tend to

10. Kingston told an interviewer: ". . . having four or five versions of your immigration—that's not just the way my head works, that's the way narration and memory and stories work in our culture. So, that's a gift given to me by our culture, and not something that I imagined on my own. I invented new literary structures to contain multiversions and to tell the true lives of non-fiction people who are storytellers" (*Conversations,* ed. Skenazy and Martin, 74–75). She also said: "I tell the imaginative lives and dreams and fictions of real people. These are the stories of storytellers" (ibid., 37).
11. Sau-ling Cynthia Wong, *Reading Asian American Literature,* 39.

think of these as messages from parents to children, ways of expressing love or of carrying on tradition.[12] But if there are messages in what Mother serves at a traditional table, so can there be messages in what is sought away from it—the choices one makes in eating "out." In some cases, that other food or table is inviting for the opportunities it affords to enter mainstream culture; it may be attractive just because it's different from home, or it may signal rejection of what the family table offers or represents.

Wong's book *Reading Asian American Literature* is subtitled *From Necessity to Extravagance.* The terms "necessity" and "extravagance" as she applies them to food in Chinese literature convey both pain and embarrassment. Poverty in China necessitated the saving or using of every part of available plants or animals; it ingrained the habit of including whatever was edible into the diet, as well as a horror of waste. Such food habits carry stories of starvation in China (where, throughout its history, hundreds of thousands at a time have literally starved to death). This resulted in insecurity about real or feared poverty in the new country, fears not easily forgotten by those who actually experienced hunger, and so easily ridiculed by their well-fed children. This is an insecurity that Jewish immigrants (as well as others) naturally shared, and those from Eastern Europe shared remembered poverty as well. One major difference, however, is that the laws dictating what is kosher made Jews exclude rather than include in their diet the sort of foods that Kingston and Wong refer to.[13] If starvation forced Jewish parents to eat whatever they could find, they would have done so guiltily, transgressively; they would not have carried the story forward to their tables or to their children. Poverty was common and food scarce in the ghetto and the shtetl, but, except for wartime (the Nazi death camps are another story altogether), it was not starvation, such as the Chinese suffered, but deprivation that Jewish immigrants remembered, that made them frugal. They were more likely to tell of how they had sacrificed their way of life, including religious observance, for mere shelter and sustenance, or of how they scrimped on food all week in order to honor the Sabbath with a decent meal, for which one served the braided challah loaf, made from the more expensive white flour. A haunting photograph in the Jacob A. Riis Collection shows a bearded Jewish man sitting alone at a mi-

12. For an exploration of the relationship between food (and its preparation) and tradition, see Elizabeth Ehrlich's *Miriam's Kitchen: A Memoir,* complete with recipes.

13. In addition, rules governing the slaughter of animals prohibited much of that food: the killing must be as humane and swift as possible, and only a pious man, well informed about the laws of ritual slaughter, may serve as slaughterer.

nuscule table in what looks like a coal cellar, with the Sabbath challah on the table. Hunger, yes; want, yes; but famine is something else.

Whether challah in a cellar, a multicourse holiday feast, or a weekend at Grossinger's (that now-departed epitome of borscht-belt gustatory extravagance), celebratory Jewish eating falls under William Boelhower's description of the "ethnic feast" that serves to affirm and reinforce group identity. Boelhower uses the example of Italian American feasting, which, as Wong points out, serves a very different purpose from that of the Chinese restaurant that purveys the exotic to mainstream America. In Boelhower's description of the Italian feast, the purpose is more intraethnic than interethnic, more to attempt cohesion than to attract, or make oneself attractive to, outsiders. This is not to deny the appeal to others of Italian restaurants, nor the existence of the intragroup feasts of Chinese families (more about this later). But Wong sets up a contrast between these groups and the depictions of food and eating in their literatures. She concedes that Asian American immigrants "do share some similarities with the experiences of European ethnics: dislocation, poverty, prejudice, as well as conflicts between first and second generations." But she goes on to point out that for Europeans "there is enough cultural congruence with the Anglo mainstream, and enough cultural reality in the promised rewards of assimilation to validate the rhetoric of consensual nation building . . ."[14]

The Jewish immigrant is not quite the same as those other Europeans, though, and to see this is once again to put Jews and Chinese face to face—one Other facing another Other—and once more to see their commonalities. For despite their more Caucasian skin and features, the "cultural congruence" of the Jews is neither "enough" to help them merge with the mainstream (whether because of exclusion by the mainstream or because of Jews' own religious restrictions), nor always desirable. "I will . . . talk with you, walk with you, . . . but I will not eat with you [or] drink with you," says Shylock, for to do so would be to transgress the food laws binding upon the Jewish people (and at the same time binding them to one another).

Of course Jews do transgress those laws—very often in Chinese restaurants, as a matter of fact—and herein lies a major difference between the groups Wong describes and that described by, for example, Gaye Tuchman and Harry Gene Levine in "New York Jews and Chinese Food: The

14. Boelhower, *Through a Glass Darkly,* 113; Sau-ling Cynthia Wong, *Reading Asian American Literature,* 70–71, 43.

Social Construction of an Ethnic Pattern." What stands out as different from the mainstream pattern Wong describes are both the transgressive (read: rebellious) nature of the Chinese-restaurant experience for Jews and their need to seek some comfort and commonality in their marginalization. What can be seen as exoticizing in a negative sense had an additional attraction for immigrant Jews in that it indulged their desire to become more cosmopolitan. They wanted to transcend their ghettoization, to prove that they were not provincial "greenhorns," and, without a national home they could identify with, they gravitated toward an image of themselves as cosmopolitan and worldly. Hot dogs at the ballgame signaled "American," which was also desired, to be sure; but the Chinese represented the wider world, one not peopled with Europeans, who were historically threatening and often anti-Semitic, having been taught to regard Jews with suspicion. Indeed, Jews were not treated as unwelcome outsiders in Chinese restaurants, as they might have been in eating places that mainly served as bonding spaces for fellow countrymen (many of whom, unlike the Jews of Eastern Europe, expected to return to their country of origin). Wong writes: "Ingestion is the physical act that mediates between self and not-self, native essence and foreign matter, the inside and the outside."[15] One way to see the attraction of "foreign" food—Chinese food to Jews, hot dogs and hamburgers to both Jewish and Chinese children—is to see eating as a way of navigating between the familiar and the unfamiliar, physical assimilation of the foreign as easier to accomplish, and less threatening to attempt, than social assimilation.

There were other factors that drew New York Jews in large numbers to Chinese restaurants and that, later, drew Chinese restaurants uptown to Jewish neighborhoods:[16] The foods, with their flavors of garlic, onion, celery, sweet and sour sauces, and of course chicken soup, were redolent of home even as they were so pleasingly different. They were affordable to immigrants who liked eating out to socialize but who couldn't afford fancier places. "Eating Chinese" became the Jewish ethnic thing to do of a Sunday evening in New York. Among others who were also looked down upon, Jews felt safe and comfortable; they could push tables together, engage in intense talk, bring the children. They liked to engage in long

15. Gaye Tuchman and Harry Gene Levine, "New York Jews and Chinese Food: The Social Construction of an Ethnic Pattern," 171–72, 167–68; Sau-ling Cynthia Wong, *Reading Asian American Literature,* 26.

16. Tuchman and Levine found that Jews were more likely to go to Chinese restaurants than to those of other non-Jewish ethnic groups, and that beginning as early as the 1890s and becoming "a love affair" in the 1940s, Jews were more likely than other immigrants to go to Chinese restaurants ("New York Jews and Chinese Food," 163–84).

negotiations about what to order in preparation for the communal sharing of a meal. And they could transgress food taboos with greater ease; forbidden food somehow seemed more tolerable when it was chopped up unrecognizably—"safe treyf," Tuchman and Levine call it. Of course these Jews *knew* they were breaking a taboo, but food habits and revulsions can be more deeply ingrained than rules and prohibitions, and if it didn't look like pork or shellfish, it wasn't rejected. Likewise, the prohibition against mixing dairy products with meat, culturally binding long after religious observances were shed by these eaters, never presented a problem in Chinese restaurants, where no dairy products were used. One could have one's rebellion and eat it too where the food *looked* okay and where its ingredients hid behind "exotic" Chinese terms on the menu. Tuchman and Levine quote Raymond Williams's penetrating observation: "[A] culture spawns the terms of its own rejections. Rebels can disavow the strictures of a food-oriented culture by eating forbidden foods. But a food-oriented rebellion cannot be accomplished with just any forbidden substance. It cannot be food that looks so like prohibited fare that it triggers revulsion, nor can it be food that requires some expertise to eat"—lobster, for example.[17]

As both groups became more accepted and more financially stable, their eating establishments became more luxurious, and their feasts and celebrations more elaborate. Neither group can be blamed if in America, in a more comfortable, secure life, the ability to provide food is not only physically, but also emotionally, satisfying. No one can blame them for using food to nurture their pride of accomplishment as well as their children's growth. Food in this case is a symbol of their ability to provide for their families, a symbol that they have made it in America. But extravagance, as epitomized by the Chinese banquet and Jewish wedding, became the embarrassment of the children and the butt of their jokes. Maxine and her brother try to distance themselves as far as possible from the spread of food their mother brings to the airport when they "camp out" for the day to await Moon Orchid. Not only do they distance themselves in space, but also in menu; they leave the spread to "sneak" hamburgers (*Warrior,* 114). Such distancing and embarrassment turned into satire in the hands of the young Philip Roth, whose Jewish characters were very American, affluent, and living in suburbia. In his early novella *Goodbye, Columbus,* Roth satirizes their empty lives, mainly through the observation

17. Ibid., 169–70; Williams quoted, 169. A more recent phenomenon is the kosher Chinese restaurant—no pork or shellfish, of course, and religiously supervised, so that now even observant Jews can taste Chinese food.

of his protagonist, Neil Klugman, who nevertheless is seduced as much by their easy luxury as he is by the beauty of Brenda Patimkin. Indeed, no description of Brenda is as rapturous and sensual as the one of the Patimkins' basement refrigerator: "it was heaped with fruit, shelves swelled with it, every color, every texture, and hidden within, every kind of pit. There were greengage plums, black plums, red plums, apricots, nectarines, peaches, long horns of grapes, black, yellow, red, and cherries, cherries flowing out of boxes and staining everything scarlet. . . . and on the top shelf, half a huge watermelon, a thin sheet of wax paper clinging to its bare red face like a wet lip." To Mr. Patimkin, that refrigerator symbolizes what he has been through and what he has achieved, his pride at having made his family's life easy and luxurious: "A man works hard he's got something. . . . Success don't come easy."[18]

While food as a show of success may be embarrassing for the children of the formerly poor and displaced, food as an expression of love may, in fact, be the heavier burden. Wong speaks of the message of sacrifice that food conveys: sacrifice on the part of the parents to provide, and, inseparable from that "story," the burden this places on the children—of duty, of sacrifice ("one sacrifice calls for another")—to the point where, according to Wong, "[t]he American-born children often have reservations about the parents' food choices (and by implication their life choices); they identify with the creatures slaughtered for food; . . . they frequently feel themselves sacrificed—made into a food source—for the parents." In this case, of course, we are back to food as metaphor—a metaphor of expectation that might take the form of straight A's, or a degree from MIT in engineering, or readiness to take over the family business so that Father may retire. We remember the expectations of Amy Tan's mother—that Amy was to be a physicist and a concert pianist on the side. Jewish boys were to be both doctors and rabbis—and play the violin on the side. Again, Roth turns this to bitter satire in *Portnoy's Complaint,* when the neighbor's son, a fifteen-year-old pianist with "golden hands," a boy who loves his mother like nobody else's boy, hangs himself in the bathroom with a note pinned on his shirt: "Mrs. Blumenthal called. Please bring your mah-jongg rules to the game tonight. Ronald."[19] The story, of course, is told to the accompaniment of Sophie Portnoy's food, her melodramatic exhortations to eat it, and her dramatizations of how she slaved to prepare it. In Roth's vicious caricature of the stereotypical Jewish mother, food is real—it smells delicious; it is

18. Philip Roth, *Goodbye, Columbus,* 30–31, 66.
19. Sau-ling Cynthia Wong, *Reading Asian American Literature,* 33, 37; Philip Roth, *Portnoy's Complaint,* 108, 135.

plentiful and always served up on schedule; but it is also a symbol of controlling love and of Sophie's expectations for her son's future. Without it, how will little Alex be strong enough, healthy enough, to become all she hopes for? Not on the *chazerei* he always wants to eat—junk like American hot dogs and hamburgers.

Even when love does not call for sacrifice, when it nurtures without handing the child a bill, it nevertheless implicitly asks for love in return. It may ask not for A's but for attention or obedience or adherence to tradition, and these can be even more burdensome than striving for good grades. In Ang Lee's film *Eat Drink Man Woman,* for example, a father's elaborate, exacting preparation of a Sunday dinner is followed by scenes depicting his daughters' chafing under the obligation of coming to the dinner, of never missing it; such an elaborate expression of love must be received, it cannot be rejected.[20] In this example, and many others like it, food assumes symbolic dimensions of strings that bind to, instead of binding together; food symbolizes not exodus and freedom, but entrapment and control.

Binding, bonding, bounding—how close in form, how intertwined in meaning, these terms are. Like one's home language, food, along with the places the family gathers, helps to create the familial and community bonds that bind and bound. Of course this is true even of descendants of the *Mayflower* pilgrims. But when those within the home speak, look, and behave differently from those outside, what is inside becomes at once more problematic and yet so much more necessary. The home becomes a refuge from the strangeness outside even as it limits its members, makes them self-conscious, and creates guilt-ridden conflicts that arise from their desire to escape their bonds, to wander beyond the boundaries. Enclosures and boundaries limit, but also protect. (In Robert Frost's famous, enigmatic words, they "wall in" and "wall out.") They constrain, which has its positive as well as negative aspects. To be bounded is to be enclosed, which can mean safety and/or confinement.

Historically, in America, many Chinese immigrants were held on Angel Island or "bonded" by deceptive contractual agreements for their labor. Free as they are today, many Chinese continue to live in "Chinatowns," even

---

20. Sheng-mei Ma quotes Ang Lee's explanation of this meal: "Sometimes the things children need to hear most are the things parents find hardest to say, and vice versa. When that happens, we resort to rituals" (*Immigrant Subjectivities in Asian American and Asian Diaspora Literatures,* 62). Ma goes on to say: "Food as 'a metaphor of love' is poorly produced as the chef can no longer control the right amount of seasoning and is poorly received as the daughters contemplate a move away from the family prison" (ibid., 151).

when they can afford to leave. They choose to be in a safe haven of familiar language, sounds, smells, customs, and like-minded neighbors. Such diaspora communities are a relatively recent phenomenon in a history that goes back thousands of years. Whatever hardships their forebears faced in China, they looked and spoke and dressed like everyone else around them. The long history of Jewish diaspora, dating back to the Roman empire, is one of enforced ghettoization. While the term *ghetto* has become generalized and is used to describe the homogeneous quarters of non-Jewish groups (urban African Americans or Hispanics, for example) and the voluntary gathering of Jews or other "ethnic others" into secluded areas, until recently it referred to urban areas where Jews were compelled to live.[21] Usually such an area was surrounded by walls whose gates were locked at night, and it was a punishable crime for a Jew to be found outside them after dark. It isn't difficult to imagine, where walls were fact, not metaphor, how attractive freedom would have seemed—freedom to leave the ghetto, to wander at will through the city. (This would apply equally to the invisible walls that kept Jews within the "pales"—the areas in rural Eastern Europe where Jews were allowed to live.)

But, as we noted in connection with bilingualism, one wants also the freedom to return, to go in as well as out of those gates at will. To go back in, to return home, whether every evening or after days, months, or years, is to find the place and the people one belongs to, the place where one feels wanted, not rejected. In that place, a shared past and shared tradition permeate the very air we breathe. There we find nourishment, both alimentary and metaphorical—the nourishment of legend and history and family stories associated with remembered smells and tastes, encapsulated in familiar tongues and voices. Home can both arouse and appease our hunger for story. But where such nourishment (of either kind) is seen as a tie that traps and restricts, one may want to go beyond its reach, to eat hamburgers in places where only English is heard. Out there are so many *other* stories—seductive stories of romance and success whose heroes we may long to be. Whether our story-hunger is met with silence—perhaps caused by ignorance, perhaps by unwillingness to remember and to tell— or whether the old stories cannot accommodate those exciting new stories, those new dreams, unsatisfied story-hunger can lead to rejection of the place—the table, the hearth, the community—associated with it.

21. There has been much speculation as to the origin of the term. It most probably originated in sixteenth-century Venice, where the Jewish quarter was located near a foundry (*getto* or *ghetto* in Italian). The institution, however, antedates the term; see "the Jewery" of the vicious tale told by Chaucer's Prioress.

Anzia Yezierska's protagonists, so close in their lives and dreams to herself, are hungry for heroic roles in those "American" stories, and seem at times to be desperately starving; witness the title of one of her short-story collections, *Hungry Hearts*. In the autobiographical essay "Mostly about Myself," she admits: "My one story is hunger."[22] She goes on to speak of "[h]unger driven by loneliness," but the language of hunger and eating, whether used literally to describe food or figuratively to describe other "hungers," is everywhere in her stories. Clearly she has experienced both: "I used to think there was no experience that tears through the bottom of the earth like the hunger for bread. But now I know, more terrible than the hunger for bread is the hunger for people" (*America*, 136). Her narrators speak of "love-hunger" and hunger for education ("I need school more than a starving man needs bread"); she writes of being fed "defeat with the milk of her [mother's] bosom into the blood and bones," and hints at being eat*en*, devoured by "the maw of the [sweat]shop" where her protagonist sits amid "the clatter and the roar, the merciless grind of the pounding machines" (*America*, 119, 137, 114). One of her heroines reads Shelley over lunch at her machine, and in story after story, her protagonist dreams of being loved by an educated, refined, tall, slim Anglo-Saxon (probably modeled upon Yezierska's mentor and partner in romance, John Dewey). In *Salome of the Tenements*, the protagonist hungers for style in fashion, for beauty in all her surroundings. And none of these hungers are easily appeased. About herself, Yezierska wrote: "I used to be more hungry after a meal than before. Years ago, the food I could afford to buy only whetted my appetite for more food. . . . Now I no longer live in a lonely hall-room tenement. I am invited out to teas and dinners. . . . I wonder, is my insatiable hunger for people so great because for so many centuries my race has been isolated in Ghettos, shut out of contact with others?" (*America*, 137).

Only with others, outside, can the hunger be satisfied, only away from home and family—in school, in the arms of a suave "goy," in a spotless apartment—never within the family, never in the tenement. Here we see mediation "between self and not-self, native essence and foreign matter" expressed not in the act of eating foreign food, but, metaphorically, as hunger for what lies "outside"—separate from the familiar. This separation is the natural sequel to Yezierska's story "The Miracle," where everything sacred is sold to purchase the daughter's ticket to America and the hope it

22. Anzia Yezierska, *How I Found America: Collected Stories of Anzia Yezierska*, 136 (hereinafter cited in the text as *America*).

promises. It seems unthinkable that Father can sell his Torah scroll and Mother her silver Sabbath candlesticks, both handed down for generations and symbolizing what is most exalted in their roles and their heritage. We are surely meant to see this sale as a selling *out,* a selling of the characters' souls for, and to, "America."

But not everyone sold out. We can only wonder what Yezierska or her protagonist might have found in a home that valued her nonmaterial dreams, with parents whose yearnings matched her own and who could see in their daughter what they could readily see in a son: an insatiable desire to live a life of the mind, a life whose ultimate achievement would not necessarily be marriage to someone who could put a roof over her head without the help of a hopelessly unavailable dowry. Repeatedly Yezierska's narrators complain: "Does America want only my hands—only the strength of my body—not my heart—not my feelings—my thoughts?" "Us immigrants want to be people—not 'hands'—not slaves of the belly! And it's the chance to think out thoughts that makes people" (*America,* 115, 121). Ironically, in several of her stories, and most pointedly in *Bread Givers,* though the narrator vilifies her scholar-father for not earning money, for lacking "proper" table manners, for trying to restrain her, and for trying to get her married to someone who can help support the family, she and her father are more alike than either of them realize. The father could have shared his scholarship with his daughter had he thought her capable, had he thought a life of the mind suitable for her. But her passion for study, because it lay outside Torah (which was never taught or offered her), could not be valued or supported by one who had no idea of its worth, indeed, who saw it (rightly, in these stories) as alienating his daughter beyond possibility of reunion.[23]

Sadly, the deepest alienation between daughter and parents occurs once food has become plentiful enough to satisfy physical hunger. In the story "The Fat of the Land," Hanneh Breineh feels imprisoned in her silks and furs, in the luxury apartment her children have provided, where she can only relax on the maid's day off. Her successful children provide every physical and material comfort, but will not introduce her to their friends or associates; she cannot participate in their triumphs. Once having had to fight for and carefully dole out every mouthful, now, "deprived of her

23. Yezierska's 1950 autobiography, *Red Ribbon on a White Horse,* draws a much more sympathetic portrait of her father (this will be discussed more fully in Chapter 7). Her own daughter has written of the extent to which Yezierska sacrificed family life on the altar of her writing life and ambition. The price to her was loneliness (Louise Levitas Henriksen, *Anzia Yezierska: A Writer's Life*).

kitchen, [she] felt robbed of the last reason for her existence. Cooking and marketing and puttering busily with pots and pans gave her an excuse for living and struggling and bearing up with her children." In the quarrel that ensues between Hanneh and her daughter, a quarrel of mutual recrimination and ingratitude, her daughter shouts out her memories, cursing and "yelling that we were gluttons"; there are no memories of love (*Hearts*, 91, 93). In the tenement there were evidently no sustaining stories, only want and worry—unsatisfied hunger of every sort.

In the story "Children of Loneliness," Rachel Ravinsky and her parents also have enough food, but Rachel, newly returned home with a teaching degree from Cornell, cannot bear the way her parents eat, nor the mess and dirt of their tenement (they are more characters in Yezierska's gallery of what Katherine Stubbs rightly calls "pernicious cliches"). She refuses the meat and lotkes (potato pancakes) her mother has made in honor of her homecoming, and she moves out. But in her spotless apartment she is besieged by loneliness and guilt, and comes to conceive of herself as one of the "millions of immigrant children, children of loneliness, wandering between worlds that are at once too old and too new to live in" (*America*, 190). In a scene more cruel than sad, Rachel returns to the tenement and watches her parents from the air shaft opposite their kitchen window, alternately feeling revulsion at the mess and guilt over her parents' sadness. When she overhears her father at prayer, "the sobbing strains of the lyric song melted into her veins like a magic sap, making her warm and human again. All her strength seemed to flow out of her in pity for her people. She longed to throw herself on the dirty, ill-smelling tenement steps and weep: 'Nothing is real but love . . . Nothing so false as ambition' " (*America*, 184). But revulsion wins out. She leaves unseen, as if, in similar revulsion and rebellion, she is carrying out Maxine's threat to eat only plastic. It is the familiar food that neither one can abide. In Rachel's case, the food she rejects is that of Eastern Europe; as Yezierska expresses it in "Mostly about Myself," she is at once too full, and yet "starving." Yezierska's hunger is not only for what lies outside her "pale," but for words:

> I feel like a starved man who is so bewildered by the first sight of food that he wants to grab and devour the ice-cream, the roast, and the entree all in one gulp. For ages and ages, my people in Russia had no more voice than the broomstick in the corner. . . . And here, in America, a miracle has happened to them. They can lift up their heads like real people. After centuries of suppression, they are allowed to speak. . . . All the starved, unlived years crowd into my throat and

> choke me . . . and all those dumb generations back of me, are crying
> in every breath of every word that itself is struggling out of me. (*Amer-*
> *ica,* 132)

Once given the right to speak, Yezierska begins by devouring words in-
discriminately, leaving them undigested; her "grabbing greed for words
has choked the life out of them" (*America,* 134). She hates what she writes,
and all that is still bottled up pushes to be expressed.

Maxine also "chokes" on all that she has bottled up, although what she
needs to do is speak out loud, literally to find her voice. She does not yet
realize that she will find her strongest, most powerful "warrior" voice in
writing; first, she must speak out: "Maybe because I was the one with the
tongue cut loose, I had grown a list of over two hundred things that I had
to tell my mother so that she would know the true things about me and to
stop the pain in my throat . . . I felt something alive, tearing at my throat,
bite by bite, from the inside" (*Warrior,* 197, 200). Her list includes confessions and questions, as well as anger and resentment that finds its outlet in
screaming, at a time when the family is eating dinner and conversation is
banned.

The occasion for finally speaking is her (mistaken) fear that her parents
plan to have her marry the "mentally retarded boy" who follows her
around, as if she and "that hulk" are "two of a kind" (194). The message is
her own growing self-esteem:

> My throat hurt constantly, vocal cords taut to snapping. One night
> when the laundry was so busy that the whole family was eating dinner
> there, crowded around the little round table, my throat burst open. I
> stood up, talking and burbling. I looked directly at my mother and fa-
> ther and screamed . . . "There's nothing wrong with my brain. Do you
> know what the Teacher Ghosts say about me? They tell me I'm smart,
> and I can win scholarships. . . . I can do all kinds of things. I know
> how to get A's, and they say I could be a scientist or a mathematician
> if I want." (*Warrior,* 200–201)

Her mother shouts back at her, explaining for the first time that calling
Maxine ugly is "what we're supposed to say. That's what Chinese say. We
like to say the opposite" (*Warrior,* 203). One imagines that this explanation begins a process of going back to other resented words, other misunderstandings that require time and distance to figure out. Maxine the
narrator seems not to realize what Kingston the author surely does: that
there are many ways of telling and knowing and learning "truth."

"You lie with stories. You won't tell me a story and then say, 'This is a true story,' or 'This is just a story.' I can't tell the difference. . . . I can't tell what's real and what you make up." . . . My mother, who is a champion talker, was, of course, shouting at the same time. . . . "you dummy. You're still stupid. You can't listen right. . . . You can't even tell a joke from real life. You're not so smart. Can't even tell real from false." (*Warrior,* 202)

The Maxine who sees the world only logically, who "think[s] that mysteries are for explanation," who "enjoy[s] simplicity," who imagines that "concrete pours out of [her] mouth to cover the forests and freeways and sidewalks," who asks for "plastics, periodical tables, t.v. dinners with vegetables no more complex than peas mixed with diced carrots" and for "floodlights to shine in dark corners: no ghosts"—this is not yet the Maxine who writes this book (*Warrior,* 204). Maxine the author has come to understand her mother's ways of telling and her own hard-won ways of knowing—the place of story in nourishing, in telling, how "by indirections [one finds] directions out."[24] The girl who cannot "see how they kept up a continuous culture for five thousand years" has not yet learned this: "If we had to depend on being told, we'd have no religion, no babies, no menstruation (sex, of course, unspeakable), no death" (*Warrior,* 185). But of course one need not depend on being told directly or logically; perhaps for those five thousand years, in a homogeneous and traditional culture, knowledge and the ways the culture transmitted it were acquired, absorbed, in some other way. Stories were "talked," and mysteries respected. The author of this book has not only learned storytelling from a master storyteller, she has also learned the power of story both to teach and to shape a life. Not in statements or explanations or exhortations do the real life lessons lie, but in stories. Handed-down sayings such as "It is more profitable to raise geese than daughters," epithets such as "ugly" and "bad girl," are goads to respond, to speak out in anger, but they are not lessons to grow on.[25] The saying "A woman without talent is a woman of virtue"

24. This can certainly be related to the role of Aggadah in Jewish teaching; see note 1 above.

25. Amy Ling cites the geese/daughters saying and quotes other traditional Chinese proverbs: "If women are given work that requires contact with the outside, they will sow disorder and confusion throughout the Empire"; "Give a woman an education and all you will get from her is boredom and complaints" (*Between Worlds: Women Writers of Chinese Ancestry,* 1, 3). Ling focuses more than I have done on Kingston's anger (ibid., 24), but I feel that along with resentment there is much admiration for her mother, and ultimate recognition of her as a role model for female strength and for storytelling—qualities Ling concedes (ibid., 128–29).

did not discourage modern women from developing their talent and proving themselves with it. By means of her intelligence and talent, the "useless" girl Maxine comes to feel "worthy": "When I visit the family now, I wrap my American successes around me like a private shawl; I *am* worthy of eating the food" (*Warrior,* 52). That the "shawl" she wraps herself in is private suggests that her successes give her the personal armor and warmth of self-esteem, protecting her from her fears of inadequacy and attack; it is not clear whether the family can see it, or whether those successes assume some other shape for them—their own personal laurels, perhaps. Perhaps the successes are totally invisible to them. Maxine recognizes, however, that they love her "fundamentally," but she needs to go "afar," "out of hating range." She ends this section almost prayerfully: "The swordswoman and I are not so dissimilar. May my people understand the resemblance soon so that I can return to them" (*Warrior,* 53).

Proverbs, statements, morals of the story, exhortations—these ultimately pale in significance and influence beside what Maxine learns by hearing her mother sing of the swordswoman in "The Ballad of Fa Mu Lan," not only because of the content of the words, but also because she hears them from her mother, Brave Orchid, who is quite a swordswoman herself. More important, hearing the chant again as an adult, she remembers: "[A]s a child I followed my mother about the house, the two of us singing about how Fa Mu Lan fought gloriously and returned alive from the war to settle in the village. I had forgotten this chant that was once mine, *given me by my mother,* who may not have known its *power to remind.* She *said* I would grow up a wife and a slave, but she *taught* me the song of the warrior woman, Fa Mu Lan. I would have to grow up a warrior woman" (*Warrior,* 20; emphases mine).

The distinction between "said" and "taught" is crucial. Stephen D. Krashen distinguishes between learning a language and acquiring it, between rule-taught learning and "natural," more subliminal, context-related, indirect, deeper acquiring, and it is in this latter way that Maxine takes in her mother's most meaningful message, given and acquired in song sung together.[26] The storyteller, Walter Benjamin reminds us, passed on experience "from mouth to mouth," and had "an orientation toward practical interests . . . [Thus] every real story contains, openly or covertly, something useful."

---

26. Stephen D. Krashen, *The Input Hypothesis: Issues and Implications,* 1–33. This message is a good example of what Thomas J. Ferraro speaks of as "traces of women's dissent in the interstices of tradition and family history." The daughter's ability to identify the mother's courage and to speak out is what he calls "courageous daughtering" (*Ethnic Passages,* 159).

Benjamin goes on to stress the importance of listeners integrating the stories they hear with their own experience, retaining and retelling them. The art of storytelling

> is lost because there is no more weaving and spinning to go on while they are being listened to. . . . When the rhythm of work has seized [the listener], he listens to the tales in such a way that the gift of retelling them comes to him all by itself. This, then, is the nature of the web in which the gift of storytelling is cradled. This is how today it is becoming unraveled at all its ends after being woven thousands of years ago in the ambience of craftsmanship.[27]

We cannot but assume that when young Maxine follows her mother about the house, they are engaged in some sort of household task—sweeping, washing, or other domestic activities whose rhythms are adapted to the rhythm of the ballad. (Fa Mu Lan was a weaver.) Stories are also told in the family's laundry while sorting and ironing. Brave Orchid as teller, Maxine as listener and reteller, seem perfect examples of the storyteller-artists Benjamin describes, and what Maxine absorbs is an example of the way in which the unforced lessons of stories make the deepest connections with and within the listener.

Besides the Fa Mu Lan ballad Maxine hears many other stories, some overheard as the adults talk, some told to the children at bedtime so that she "couldn't tell where the stories left off and the dreams began" (*Warrior,* 19). Unlike the pat, insulting statements, epithets, and unanswered questions she hears, which cause resentments that tear at her throat and choke her until she screams them out, the songs and stories nourish her, help her to grow into the swordswoman she dreams of becoming, and find their way "out," transmuted into new song that "translate[s] well," that tells a story in her own way. Only when the adult Maxine tells her mother that she also "talks story" does Brave Orchid tell her the story of her grandmother, who valued plays more than things. Despite the danger of bandits, her grandmother left her home unprotected and took her family to the theater; the house was not robbed, thus proving the worth of going to the theater (*Warrior,* 207). Amy Ling sees this final story, begun by mother, ended by daughter, as a metaphor of the resolution of the conflict between Maxine and her mother. The story of Ts'ai Yen, the captive poetess,

27. Walter Benjamin, "The Storyteller," 84, 86, 91, 89. On the several versions of a story Kingston says: "I ask that question: which one is true? But then I also ask: which one of these is most useful?" (interview in *Conversations,* ed. Skenazy and Martin, 41).

symbolizes both their lives, both victims and victors.[28] Ts'ai Yen, as victim, suffered by being forced to live among barbarians just as Brave Orchid suffered in coming to America and in being misunderstood by her children; similarly, Maxine has suffered alienation in American schools. Ts'ai Yen the victor sings in a way that touches her captors and her children, who sing with her, as does Maxine, ultimately, with her mother; and it is Maxine whose retelling of her mother's stories "translated [them] well" (*Warrior,* 129–30).

In contrast to the lack of inspiring stories in Yezierska's home and her hunger for stories in the world outside, the stories Maxine hears at home nourish her, give her "food" for her own growing creativity, her own separate needs as a woman and as an artist, a point that her critics seem to miss. She doesn't just "use" the legends; the stories she heard were her food: they grew with her, in her, feeding her hunger for story, for self-esteem, and ultimately for the raw material of her creating. Even in the style of her telling, Kingston demonstrates the way in which this works. It is impossible to sort out exactly where, in the "White Tigers" chapter, story heard becomes perhaps dream, perhaps wistful fantasy, and ultimately Kingston's superbly crafted narrative. Much of this blurring is accomplished with brilliant manipulation of modals and modes:

> The call *would* come from a bird that flew over our roof. In the brush drawings it looks like the ideograph for "human," two black wings. The bird *would* cross the sun and lift into the mountains (which look like the ideograph "mountain"). . . . I *would be* a little girl of seven the day I followed the bird away into the mountains. The brambles *would* tear off my shoes . . . but I *would* keep climbing. . . . I *would* not know how many hours or days had passed. . . .
>
> The door opened, and an old man and an old woman *came* out carrying bowls of rice and soup and a leafy branch of peaches.
>
> "Have you eaten rice today, little girl?" they greeted me.
>
> "Yes I have," I said out of politeness. "Thank you."
>
> ("No I haven't," I *would have said* in real life, mad at the Chinese for lying so much. "I'm starved. Do you have any cookies? I like chocolate chip cookies.") (*Warrior,* 20–21; emphases mine)

The story begins in the hypothetical mode of the wish, the unreal, the conditional—"if I were that girl" or "if I could be that girl in the future," this is how it would be. But then, with the appearance of the old couple,

---

28. Ling, *Between Worlds,* 129.

the fantastic becomes the "real"—the story as it is, the adventures as they "happened." The only exception is the narrative voice intruding, now in the hypothetical mode, as if what Maxine "would have said" is the fantastic intruding upon the reality of the mythic story. (We may also note that what she asks for is very American—chocolate chip cookies—as is the desire to be frank—"I'm starved." But in fact, for those who understand subtle cultural cues, such honesty is not necessary—the rice will be given.) In this blurring of "real" and "unreal," of wish and fact, of dream and ambition, an inextricable merging is also accomplished of the stories, their source in Brave Orchid's talking story, Maxine's imagination, her present reality, her attention to the written word and ideograph, and her becoming.

As Maxine "feeds" on her mother's stories, so too is her talent and ambition nourished by her mother's medical career. True, Brave Orchid now helps in the laundry and picks tomatoes, and tries to "teach" her daughter the traditional virtues, but then there are those documents in the metal tube—her diploma among them—that she brings out periodically to show her daughter; there are her stories of her schooling, her doctoring, her bravery, that speak louder and more memorably than any rules to the incipient "word warrior." Her stories are family stories, told not around the dinner table, where talking is not allowed, but around the work table, where story and family and responsibility and cooperative work are not kept separate, where the act of storytelling is a valued family activity that can mitigate a harsh reality:

> When the thermometer in our laundry reached one hundred and eleven degrees on summer afternoons, either my mother or my father would say that it was time to tell another ghost story so that we could get some good chills up our backs. My parents, my brothers, sisters, great-uncle, and "Third Aunt," who wasn't really our aunt but a fellow villager, someone else's third aunt, kept the presses crashing and hissing and shouted out the stories. Those were our successful days, when so much laundry came in, my mother did not have to pick tomatoes. For breaks we changed from pressing to sorting.
>
> "One twilight," my mother began, and already the chills traveled my back and crossed my shoulders; the hair rose at the nape and the back of the legs . . . (*Warrior,* 87)

Here too, narrative technique blurs distinctions, but this time more specifically between Brave Orchid as teller of the incident and Maxine as narrator. The story begins with Brave Orchid's "One twilight" and continues for a paragraph that contains some highly poetic description of the river. But then the quotation marks close, and the narrative voice picks up the story: "One twilight, just as my mother stepped on the bridge, two smoky columns spiraled up taller than she" (*Warrior,* 88). The mother's sensations are graphically reported, as are her words to the ghosts. Whose words are whose? Whose story, finally, is it? That very blurring, and the merging it effects, is exactly the point. What Maxine has "ingested" has become hers—her.

But perhaps most important is the fact that what becomes part of Maxine, what is not rejected, choked on, spit out, is a story that empowers her as a woman and as a storyteller. It is also significant that story and its ability to "chill" in a suffocatingly hot room turns what could be a painful memory into one of the most harmonious moments in the book—not a memory of child labor or poverty, but a happy family memory.

Similarly, the family shop on Friday night when Herbert Gold was a young child listening in on the grown-ups, participating in their work as well as their joking and gossiping, provides his protagonist, Herbert, with some of his happiest memories. *Fathers,* once the narrative voice catches up in maturity with its author, is a kind of love song to Herbert's father, Sam Gold. At the same time, we hear quarreling, resentment, anger, hurt, and rebellion. Since the family business is a grocery store, food is ever-present—both as source of income and literal nourishment. So are almost all the other issues discussed in this chapter: stories told or withheld, family, tradition, community, and hunger; these issues are at times presented as positive, at times as negative or lacking. Thus we constantly find either similarities or contrasts to one or another of the texts already discussed. *Fathers* in many ways pulls together their thematic threads, but always with a difference: Jewish religious tradition has long gone out the window, including observance of dietary laws, but the importance of food and family talk at the dinner table remains, as does the stereotypical Jewish mother cooking and serving the food and giving lectures on its importance (non-kosher though it is). As Gold explains in a subsequent novel, *Family,* in the context of family history in Kamenets-Podolsk, Poland: "Much of a child's discipline in virtue, obedience, awe and worship was joined to the duties of food: of cleanliness, of care, of prayer over food. . . . Milk and meat were never eaten at the same meal or with the same utensils; the blessed white bread, queen of the Sabbath, was taken with joy and wine on Fridays at sundown; pork and shellfish were abominations, cursed, forbidden." After the family has come to America, Herbert violently vomits up the breakfast his mother has prepared for him of eggs fried in bacon grease: "You know we don't keep kosher. I was out of chicken fat . . . A little nourishment for you, skin and bones."[29]

Traditions, legends, ancient rites, sacred texts, stories of Passover and the exodus—nothing like these are in evidence, but family stories manage to exert their fascination and make their weight felt. The tradition of what family means, what obligations it carries—that remains. One obligation put upon Herbert is that he shoulder a small share of the effort to provide for the family's needs by helping out in the store. Ironically, as he approaches the age of thirteen, while there is no plan for a bar mitzvah ceremony, he is nevertheless sharply reminded that he is to "be a man" and must give up the childish privileging of "play" and assume some responsibility for his family.[30] His forefathers who were slaves in Egypt have played no great part in Herbert's education, but what it means to be a Jew in Poland—that seems carried in blood and memory. In *Fathers* too, though Herbert's great hunger is for what lies outside (Pattie Donahue and the world she represents—slim fathers with portfolios, who golf and take their kids fishing), there is no fulfillment out there. This next-generation book seems a good example of Irving Howe's analysis (applicable to Chinese American writers as well) of the way "even a lapsed tradition, even portions of a past that have been brushed aside, even cultural associations that float about in the atmosphere, all have a way of infiltrating the work of American Jewish writers. Tradition broken or crippled still displays enormous power over those most ready to shake it off. And tradition seemingly discarded can survive underground."[31] Ultimately, the story of Sam's exodus from Poland (and family and Jewish observance), which carries a message that is the opposite of his daily exhortations (as with the subliminal messages of Brave Orchid's stories), helps to empower Herbert to find his own life and achieve reconciliation with his father, who later says: "Listen, I'm glad you went into your own line. We're not so different. You take your pleasure. Which it is you make it your own way" (*Fathers*, 282).

After all, Sam Gold "had created Friday Night as God had ordained a day of rest and as the florists of America created Mother's Day," and a very different Friday night it is from the one God intended for him (*Fathers*, 101). There is not much Jewish religious tradition in these Friday nights, which are a prelude to the grueling Saturday workday, but feasting there is, and family, though "family" extends to the regulars who work in Sam's

---

29. Herbert Gold, *Family: A Novel in the Form of a Memoir*, 303, 72.
30. Herbert Gold, *Fathers*, 178 (hereinafter cited in the text).
31. Irving Howe, introduction to *Jewish-American Stories*, 13.

store, who "dined richly on foods taken from the store at the verge of spoiling, avocado pears with one bad spot and a hump of succulence, canned strawberries with soiled labels, heaps of tomatoes . . . later came platters of fried liver and onions, the jeweled sauce running." As "a special bonus" there is wine—"cheap, red, sedimented, and strong, made with a loving lack of skill in Uncle Izzy's basement" (*Fathers,* 103). Food and story—stories from the grocery, family stories, food as nourishment, commodity, and sign of love: all these are bedrock to young Herbert, whose greatest enemy is his father's pinochle deck, the cards that steal his father's attention from him even when he is invited to sit near him and watch, even when he accompanies his father to the *shvitz* (Russian steam bath) on Sunday mornings.

Inevitably, though, it is that very store and the weight of family that the adolescent Herbert fights in his battle to grow up in middle-class America. The food that is their stock in trade, that his father relishes and knows intimately, that his mother prepares and enjoins upon him, is more than nourishment, more even than a show of burdensome love: it represents an even more burdensome responsibility that he does his best to shake off, and a hope for the sort of future he has never wanted to share. He wants to read books, he admires men with briefcases; he would never accept the gift of his father's partnership or his grocery business, nor even, later, of his real estate business. He has "smoke in the head," according to his father; he is unambitious, lazy, and unrealistic, reading books in the basement of the store on busy Saturdays when he is needed upstairs to help customers. In his mother's view, he is not as good a boy as his aunts' sons, who always offer to relieve their mothers in their stores, to bring rest to their "waricose weins," and hope to bring their families greater security in their choices of professions or wives.

This autobiographical novel manages to contain both the adolescent's anger and the adult writer's love and admiration for the father he battled for the right to become what he had to become. In the Gold family it is not only the mother who is associated with food, with *ess, ess, mein kinde* (eat, eat, my child), but also the father, a food connoisseur: "He ate with silent respect for food, a great deal, and not out of gluttony but with appreciation for his own labor in it. He knew the cost. In each spoonful of soup carried with music to his mouth I heard the winds whistling through the . . . *knaedloch* trees;[32] I saw the farmers' trucks laden with chopped liver. . . .

---

32. "Knaedloch [matzo-ball] trees" is possibly an ironic and telling allusion to the cottonwood trees of "Don't Fence Me In," a song that seems apt to Herbert as he longs for freedom from his father and the store.

'Eat,' he pronounced at intervals, easing his love for us, 'eat, eat'" (*Fathers*, 155–56). But such love for family, food, and the expertise that goes with it cannot compete with Pattie Donahue and Poe's "Ulalume" for Herbert's heart:

> My father had the gift of listening to the artichokes at the top of a load in such a way—they informed him in a language which only he and the artichokes spoke—that he always knew when their brothers at the bottom were defective, defeated, edged with rust or shriveled from a stingy soil. Silent in their hampers they communicated by the violence of love. . . . They accepted the gift of himself which my father made, their shoots curly for him, their unbaked hearts shy in a bra of ticklish felt. Buy us! Sell us!—they asked for nothing more. Artichokes understood my father, his sympathy for vegetables arose to meet theirs for him. Devotion—he gave this freely. He accepted too, being stuck with thorns.
>
> Unfortunately I, even in those days, was not an artichoke—perhaps not so rewarding, my heart not luscious with a dab of Miracle Whip. (*Fathers*, 179)

Herbert begins to realize that it is for his children that Sam struggles so, that it is for his future, that his father sees "Sam's Fruit and Vegetable in terms of immortality for both of [them]" and that he asks "only a sign of recognition for this gift"; but Herbert "refuse[s] his gift daily" (*Fathers*, 181).

In Gold's narrative, as in Kingston's and Tan's, it is not orthodoxy but obligation that incites rebellion even as it also creates the ties and the guilt; it is family—for better and for worse. Howe writes of the centrality of family in Jewish life:

> An agency of discipline and coherence, the family has given the children of the immigrants enormous emotional resources, but also a mess of psychic troubles. To have grown up in an immigrant Jewish milieu is to be persuaded that the family is an institution unbreakable and inviolable, the one bulwark against the chaos of the world, but also the one barrier to tasting its delights. In American Jewish fiction, the family becomes an overwhelming, indeed, obsessive presence: it is container of narrative, theater of character, agent of significance.[33]

He goes on to ask: "[W]here is the family in Emerson and Thoreau, in Whitman and Melville? Where is it in Hemingway and Fitzgerald? . . . rarely

33. Howe, introduction, 8.

a dominating and enclosing presence." (One would never ask this of Chinese American fiction; what Howe says of family would sound very familiar to Wong and to the writers she discusses.)

Gold's adult narrator recognizes the complexity of the struggle, the hurt that his refusal caused his parents, and the worry about how he would turn out. But at the same time he sympathizes with his young self: "He worked! Mother worked! Like dogs! They were right, but they could not see through to my rightness, forgetting a child's *hunger to belong*" (*Fathers*, 177–78; emphasis mine). Of course this could be any adolescent's struggle to be accepted by peers, any boy's struggle with his hormones as they prod him on toward a Pattie Donahue, so beautifully packaged in angora sweaters. But in this case, as in others we have been discussing, it is everyone's struggle writ large, exaggerated and made more difficult because of differentness, marginality, otherness. How can Herbert explain to his proud, hardworking, self-made father his shame that Pattie and her mother might see him in an apron, behind a counter, while the other guys are out playing ball?

> I could not explain to him the disgrace of working in a store in a neighborhood where boys had important unexplainable things to do . . . while their fathers managed offices . . . or handled law cases for insurance companies downtown. I wanted him to commute instead of work, like the others.
>
> . . . My father's will was already developed, he spoke a language in which existed no vocabulary to explain that among the people with whom he chose to bring me up, it was more important to run end in a pickup touch football game . . . than to fill orders in sour old orange crates on Saturday afternoons. We all paid, in our various ways, a price for those [suburban lawns and] trees. . . . He did not draw the consequences of his ambition for me. If he judged our neighborhood to be better than that of his childhood, then our neighborhood would judge his world. (*Fathers*, 170–71, 177)

Herbert is not imagining things. The day he sneaks out of the store to the class field trip, and ends the afternoon by buying Pattie an ice cream and declaring his feelings for her, "[h]er laughter tinkled in the July calm . . . 'you're just a grocery boy, you. You just grub around a certain store I could name.' " At this moment he realizes that, unlike his father, he has no compensating history—whatever stories he has were only heard, and from an impassable distance: "She put her hand to her mouth and delicately closed it. Tee-hee. She looked at me unblinking. My father, knowing he was a foreigner, could have accepted this in the perspective of history. I had to discover a fact without a past; it leapt out at me like some fierce fish from the glittering shale of Pattie Donahue's economical eyes" (*Fathers*, 195). Nor does he have a compensating kindred community. What makes it even more difficult for Herbert is the fact that except for his family and the grocery store, the very restraints he is trying to throw off, he has nowhere to retreat to, no sense of where he came from that might welcome him back, if only to lick his wounds, no friends and neighbors going through the same thing, for this isn't Jewish New York, nor is it Chinatown to the Chinese—the voluntary "ghettos" that shelter their wounded and preserve community. It is Lakewood, Ohio, a west side suburb of Cleveland, miles away from the east side Jewish neighborhoods of greater Cleveland, almost like another country, and Herbert goes to a school that, in 1938, has an exchange program with students from Germany:

> The murder of Jews had already begun in the great center of civilization across the sea. It was barely noticed. . . . I sat stiffly through assemblies where the returned exchange students delivered reports on their year in the renovated Third Reich. "I didn't see any Jews being beaten. Of course I didn't see any Jews either." (Laughter.) Or solemn, precisely enunciating German children explained to us why the elimination of racial pollution was essential to German survival. (*Fathers*, 64)

One cannot know, of course, what difference it might have made to Herbert's commitment to tradition had he grown up in a Jewish, or simply a more diverse, neighborhood. Certainly he would have felt less alienated. Henry Roth considered his family's move from New York's Jewish Lower East Side a disaster: ". . . as long as I lived on Ninth Street, in the Lower East Side, I thought I was in a kind of ministate of our own. It never occurred to me that the world could be any different. But moving into this Irish-Italian neighborhood . . . was a terrible shock. I came to believe we were all the things the goyim called us."[34] In an essay entitled "No Longer at Home," Roth writes of himself in the third person: "Continuity was destroyed when his family moved from snug, orthodox Ninth Street . . . to rowdy, heterogeneous Harlem; normal continuity was destroyed. The tenets, the ways, the faith were discarded too rapidly. . . . That which

---

34. Henry Roth, *Shifting Landscape*, 66.

informed him, connective tissue of his people, inculcated by *heder,* coun-
tenanced by the street, sanctioned by God, all that dissolved when his parents moved . . . No longer at home."[35]

One cannot know, either, whether the alienation that these writers felt
contributed to their writing, or whether they, like other writers discussed
in this study, needed to create wholeness and "home" through their writing, and so make their homes on the page, *because* of their feelings of
fragmentation and dislocation. (How much more terrible was Roth's writer's
block in that case, since it would have kept him from "home" as well as
from his vocation.) Howe writes: "Tradition as discontinuity—this is the
central fact in the cultural experience of American Jewish writers." We
might say that discontinuity from tradition and location has created a tradition *of* discontinuity, and with it, a literature of discontinuity and its consequences—one of which is that literature itself. Childhood alienation as
practice for the alienation writers come to feel as artists, the distance they
need from what they are observing, and their outsider status—this is not
unique to bicultural writers, but it has certainly enhanced the keenness
and multiplicity of their vision. Kingston claims: "Exclusion plays right into
the hands of the American writer. There have been amazing coincidences
of exclusion, so that I have become a person who is able to look at everything from an interesting perspective. The alienated, individualistic writer
or hero or heroine is a tradition in American literature. I take that stance
very easily."[36] Fragmentation, alienation, distance, rootlessness, dissocia-
tion—these sensations are certainly not unique to the bicultural writer, but
as we have seen, they are highly prevalent, even typical, in their texts.

The sociologist Marcus Lee Hansen noted the phenomenon of third-
generation Americans adopting the traditions of their grandparents: "What
the son wishes to forget, the grandson wishes to remember." Recently,
there seems to be a sort of literary Hansen's Law operating, whereby the
children of the rebellious children of immigrants are saying, Why have you
robbed us of our stories? Or, Why couldn't you have made our stories

35. Ibid., 168, 170. In his fiction, Roth writes of this discontinuity: "The child expected that those things implanted into his psyche would flourish as he developed: the
landscape, the field or farm or village or barrio, would also comprise his larger world
as he grew up. And the language: how important a factor that was. Yiddish in his case.
He witnessed its drying up, his mother tongue shriveling in a single lifetime." He goes
on to say that the same could be said of Rudolfo Anaya, Pietro DiDonato, and the
Southern Black, and laments the disappearance of the parochial world in (or its dis-
placement by) the cosmopolitan world (*From Bondage,* 28).
36. Howe, introduction, 13; Kingston, interview in *Conversations,* ed. Skenazy and
Martin, 50.

more interesting, our traditions more adaptable to life in America? These
are the children (or grandchildren) who sign up for courses and majors in
the Yiddish or Chinese that their parents rejected, as does Callie in Gish
Jen's *Mona in the Promised Land*.[37] Or they are the grown children of immigrants, realizing that what they have rejected has value, and seeking it
academically, impersonally, in a "neutral" environment where the only
strings are doing their homework. In Kingston's interviews, we hear a more
mature, more appreciative, version of the younger self she created in her
autobiographical narrative:

> [My parents] have a life-force that is so passionate and dramatic and
> strong. They can do drama before your very eyes, and I don't see peo-
> ple like that all the time . . . they truly love literature. All my life they
> sang Li Po and Tu Fu, and I didn't know that. . . . So I was raised on all
> this classical Chinese poetry, plus the chants, like the chant of Fa Mu
> Lan, and I grew up with those rhythms. . . . As a writer, these were
> priceless gifts that they just strew in their path and I was just in the
> way, picking it up.

> I want to credit my ancestors for *The Woman Warrior* and *China Men*
> . . . it's not as if I made up these forms. It's because I am open to hear-
> ing talk-story. It's part of my culture. This is what my family does.[38]

In *From Bondage*, Henry Roth, referring not only to his own situation
(or Ira's, rather), but also to the larger "ethnic" one, writes of the mind
newly aware of the cosmopolitan world, chafing rebelliously against
"prohibitions that only yesterday were *nurturing traditions,* but now
newly perceived as constraints. . . . Thus, when the revolt . . . succeeded
. . . *he simultaneously abandoned his richest, most plangent creative
source: his folk, their folkways . . . the very elements of his formation*" (emphases in original).[39]

Some more recent Jewish American writers, like Allegra Goodman and
Cynthia Ozick, grew up knowledgeable and comfortable enough to make
Jewishness central to their writing. Ted Solotaroff distinguishes between a

37. Amy Ling writes: "[A] minority individual's sense of alienation results not only
from rejection by the dominant culture but also rejection of parental strictures. Minority
parents' own fear of losing their cultural heritage is intensified by the fear of losing
their children to the 'foreign' culture, and therefore they insist with greater vehemence
on their children's acceptance of family traditions and Old World ties" (*Between
Worlds*, 123).

38. Interviews in *Conversations,* ed. Skenazy and Martin, 41–42, 149.

39. Henry Roth, *From Bondage,* 29.

"post-immigrant culture," whose goal was acculturation, and a post-acculturated one coming into being in "our increasingly pluralistic society." He is referring to Jews, but he could just as well be talking of the Chinese.[40] Once more, Gish Jen's light touch and good humor come to mind: the Chinese Mona becoming Jewish in "Scarshill"; her parents still very much Chinese, but open to new ideas; her Chinese loyalties coming to the fore when a drunken white guest at a neighbor's party makes racist remarks and when the country club cannot find space to include her family as members. In the evolution of a single writer, we might consider Kingston's narrative "Maxine" voice to be post-immigrant and her voice in her interviews (even in *Tripmaster Monkey*) to be post-acculturated. In neither cultural group can we mistake where these writers are coming from; they know who and what they are, and they write out of that knowledge. Nessa Rapoport speaks of "a Jewishly educated and culturally confident community of writers"; Kingston speaks of having claimed America in her writing. Writers more secure in their place in America, more elastic and creative in their approach to tradition, can write not *out of* hunger for the world *outside,* but *about* the hunger created by the *absence* of stories and tradition.[41] In two examples, such absence is dramatized in the context of hunger.

Lan Samantha Chang writes of "unforgetting" in a story of that name she collected in a book titled *Hunger,* wherein each immigrant story chronicles some form of hunger or loss. Different from merely remembering, unforgetting is the unraveling of the deliberate effort of forgetting. When Ming Hwang drives his wife, Sansan, through the hills and fields of Iowa toward their new home, he feels "overwhelmed. . . . Surely no Chinese man had ever laid eyes on this place before. . . . He wanted to say 'This place has nothing to do with us.' " Instead, he points out their destination, Mercy

---

40. Ted Solotaroff, "The Open Community," xv. See Thane Rosenbaum et al., "The Jewish Literary Revival," a symposium that includes many voices and gives the lie to Howe's 1977 prediction that American Jewish writing had already begun its demise (Howe, introduction, 16). Gerald Shapiro's recent collection *American Jewish Fiction: A Century of Stories* likewise "answers" Howe. See also Sara Horowitz, "Portnoy's Sister—Who's Complaining? Contemporary Jewish-American Women's Writing on Judaism," and Furman, "Immigrant Dreams and Civic Promises," which discusses how Jewish and Chinese American authors have recently portrayed a zeitgeist very different from that of earlier immigrant writers, a new cultural confidence, and a desire to distance themselves from the "toothless" mainstream rather than to assimilate (212, 214–15).

41. Nessa Rapoport, "Summoned to the Feast," xxix; Kingston, interviews in *Conversations,* ed. Skenazy and Martin, 71–72, 144. Both Kingston and Ozick address these issues eloquently, but are louder and clearer on the need to value tradition in genres outside their fiction: Kingston in her interviews and Ozick in her essays.

Lake. "'We're getting old,' she said. 'How will we make the space in our minds for everything we'll need to learn here?' Without a pause, he answered her, 'We will forget.' . . . And so the Hwangs forgot what they no longer needed."[42] They put into the basement their precious rice bowls (once used in the emperor's household), along with Ming's old chemistry textbook (a way to forget his dreams and hopes in order to make room for concentrating on his job selling copy machines). Sansan "forgets" her Chinese classics, which also find their way to a shelf in the basement, and learns how to cook American food from a Betty Crocker cookbook; she buys a Jell-O mold and bright-colored plastic dishes, which she and Ming learn to eat from with a knife and fork. Ming forgets the taste of yellow watermelon, his grandfather's hopes that he will return to help rebuild China, and his own hopes for a Ph.D. to help humanity. Even though they are now speaking English to their son, Charles (as his teachers have suggested), they cannot forget their own language: "'So much is missing,' [Sansan] told Ming. Her English world was limited to the clipped and casual rhythm of daily plans. 'Put on your tie.' 'Did you turn on the rice?'" (*Hunger,* 146).

Meanwhile, Charles is excelling in school, especially in the humanities. He has less and less to say to his parents, and applies to distant colleges. He is interested in history, and asks his father about Chinese history, but Ming is unable to remember the history he learned in China. "How could he explain to his son that the past was his enemy?" (*Hunger,* 142). But there are things he and Sansan cannot forget: the colors of the Beijing sky, Uncle Lu's scrolls, the meal they shared the night of a flood.

> Their memories seeped under the doors and sifted through the keyhole. They had taken root in the earth itself, as tough and stubborn as the weeds in the garden. It seemed to Ming that after seven years in Mercy Lake, the world of his past had grown larger and more vivid until it pressed against his mind, beautiful and shining. And he wondered if perhaps this world had pushed his own son out of the house—if they had lost their son because of their stubborn inability to forget. (*Hunger,* 148)

Perhaps Ming and Sansan's futile effort to forget could have been turned to unapologetic remembering and a sharing of their memories with their son—not to keep out Iowa, but to incorporate their Chinese past into their

---

42. Lan Samantha Chang, *Hunger: A Novella and Stories,* 134–35 (hereinafter cited in the text as *Hunger*).

American present and speak to Charles in a language they would all understand, so that history and classics, and not just "put on the rice," can be part of the conversation. Charles doesn't socialize at school, so all three—each alone—are locked into an Iowa isolation, the parents with their stubborn memories and stories, Charles with none. About China, he has been told nothing. "Did they realize [he asks them] how little he knew about the world? He needed to know what the world was like outside of their house, outside of Iowa, so that for the rest of his life he would not remain entirely lost" (*Hunger*, 149). When he announces his intention to go to Harvard, all the thoughts Ming and Sansan have pent up come out; they shout at each other and plastic plates fly and shatter, until Charles comes downstairs and whispers: "I wish you would be happy for me." His look of sorrow, Ming realizes, is like his own—Charles is indeed his son.

"I want to go back," Sansan says for the first time. "Why did you have to bring me here?" The question brings them full circle to Ming's silent observation their first night in Iowa: "This place has nothing to do with us." The thought and the question constitute a dialogue Ming and Sansan never had, but should have. What they came to was not just America, not some diverse urban center, but Mercy Lake, Iowa, where "surely no Chinese man" could have been before, where there is no one with whom to share memory, language, culture, or homesickness—no community. "What would happen? He had no one to ask—no friends, no parents—no one who could have understood the language of his thoughts" (*Hunger*, 151). Unspoken but implicit is the question we have all at one time or another asked ourselves in a strange place: "What am I doing here?" If we are not eventually able to answer this question, we can either move to a place where an answer becomes apparent or remain isolated and unhappy. What we gain from a move to Iowa or anywhere else had better be worth what we have lost or given up; at least the gains, the goals, and the terms of the bargain should be clear. Sansan drives off, alone, but "she had nowhere else to go. Nothing remained of the stories and meals and people they'd known, nothing but what they remembered. Their world lived in them, and they would be the end of it." They have only each other. The next morning, her car is back home, grains of yellow Iowa wheat embedded in the tires (*Hunger*, 153).

That question "What are we (or you) doing here?" in tension with a hunger to belong echoes throughout Philip Roth's *American Pastoral*. Feeding that hunger may exact a price no one can anticipate, since one cannot know when alleviating a hunger in one quarter might cause starvation in another.

Merry (Meredith) Levov, the greatly loved, privileged daughter of seemingly perfect, all-American Seymour Levov (aka "the Swede") and his Irish Catholic wife, Dawn, a former Miss New Jersey, is quite literally starving herself, living in filth and poverty in the worst slum of burned-out Newark, New Jersey. She has become a Jain (a religion she discovered and studied in the public library), living for spiritual perfection, so reverent of all life that she wears a veil over her mouth and goes unwashed for fear of disturbing the smallest microorganism; her goal is one day to do without even disturbing vegetables for her food.[43] Just as incomprehensible as all this is to the father who wants to rescue her and care for her is the fact that in her anti-Vietnam-war zeal she has blown up the town's tiny postal station, killing the town doctor in the process; thereafter, seemingly without remorse, she has gone on to kill three other people in her crusade against "America."

A model family living in a historic house in the quiet town of Old Rimrock, Morris County, New Jersey: "What is wrong with their life? What on earth is less reprehensible than the life of the Levovs?" These questions (unanswered) are the final words of *American Pastoral*. Failing to establish any causal link between the terrible deed and the seemingly sane and stable life, Seymour "had learned the worst lesson that life can teach—that it makes no sense."[44] This is the narrative voice of Nathan Zuckerman, who, through information from Seymour's brother Jerry but mainly through his own imaginative (re)construction, tells the story and tries to understand it but ends up with only those final questions. Were Jerry asking them, his tone might very well be sarcastic; Seymour's would be genuine bewilderment. Indeed, how could the Levovs' life be reprehensible when so much love and attention have been lavished on Merry, the apple of her father's eye? Jerry tells Zuckerman, "My brother was the best you're going to get in this country by a longshot," adding, "that bomb detonated" the lives of Merry's parents, causing unending misery and grief; it sent her mother into psychiatric wards and broke her father's heart (*Pastoral*, 66, 69).

The name Levov combines two Hebrew words: *lev*, or heart, and *av*, or father; together they mean "the heart of a father"—a major theme of the book. In a dialogue between the brothers, an anguished Seymour cries: "If

43. Jainism is a religion of India whose ideal is to realize the highest perfection of the nature of man, who in his original purity was free of pain and the bondage of life and death. A cardinal principle is the nonhurting (*ahisma*) of living things of both higher and lower forms, but there is no tradition of veiling or suicidal starvation. In fact, some Jainists are wealthy.

44. Philip Roth, *American Pastoral*, 81 (hereinafter cited in the text as *Pastoral*).

what you are telling me is what I was . . . wasn't, wasn't enough, then . . . I'm telling *you*—I'm telling you that what *anybody* is *is not enough*." "You got it! Exactly! We are *not* enough. We are *none* of us enough! Including even the man who does everything right!" Jerry goes on, taking up another theme: "Out there playing at being Wasps, a little Mick girl from the Elizabeth docks and a Jewboy from Weequahic High. The cows. Cow society. Colonial old America. And you thought all that façade was going to come without cost. Genteel and innocent. *But that costs, too, Seymour. I* would have thrown a bomb. *I* would become a Jain and live in Newark. That Wasp bullshit! I didn't know just how entirely muffled you were internally. But this is how muffled you are" (*Pastoral*, 280). Jerry is by no means an innocent. He has been married four times, each time to a nurse from his medical practice. Nor is he the voice of idealizing sacrifice: he makes a million dollars a year. A cardiac surgeon, he cuts at hearts, but to mend them; he constructs bypasses and helps people with heart failure to get on with their lives. He may cut with his words, but one never has to dig for their meaning; he tells it as he sees it. He hides nothing, nor does he hide behind anything, and he practically accuses his brother of having lived behind a mask—as a good man, to be sure, doing what is right, living according to well-defined codes. But his *being*—what is that? And how can one ever penetrate such "opacity," a life so carefully constructed and protected (*Pastoral*, 77)?

On one hand, we have the agony of unanswerable questions, insane, irrational behavior inexplicable by any logic or causal analysis; on the other, judgmental analyses such as Jerry's, attempts to reason and find cause. What saves the book from being a parable, a morality tale, is that these pronouncements come from a brother who ought not to throw stones, whose rancor can be attributed at least in part to jealousy of his favored demigod of a brother and whose view of their father, Lou Levov (so different from Seymour's and even Zuckerman's view of a reasonable, lovable, loving man, tough though he was), is that he was "one impossible bastard" (*Pastoral*, 66). As usual, Roth has it all ways—and no one way. His narrator, Zuckerman, makes no secret of his boyhood adulation of the Swede, which he has still not quite outgrown, nor of his admiration for the daring, outspoken, brilliant Jerry, nor of his own vocation of making stories, as he makes up what he envisions as Seymour's story. As for all that Jerry and Lou say, we are free to take it or leave it, to see possible cause or "no sense." Roth, again as usual, undermines his narrative with unreliable narrative voices. (Even when he uses his "own voice" in *The Facts: A*

Novelist's Autobiography, he appends a lengthy letter from his longtime narrator, Zuckerman, urging him not to publish the book!)

But whatever our view of narrative unreliability, of towns such as Old Rimrock, of the Vietnam war, or of Jerry's accusations, we, like some juries, have already heard what may be inadmissible as evidence; we cannot unhear the language of façade, of self-delusion, of denial, of "mistaken" identity—and of hunger in the midst of God's plenty.

Seymour's hunger is the hunger to belong, but to his credit, he has never denied his Jewishness; he never changed his name (it was his school coach who dubbed him the Swede), and it was not his fault that he looked like a Viking and became the town hero in three sports and a war. The fact that he is Jewish *and* all that is no small part of his standing with the Jewish community of Newark—he is their golden boy, their hope in America. However, he hungers not simply to belong to the America that he and his family inhabit, but also to belong to an American past they simply have not shared, to claim roots deep in the soil of his property, when in fact he has only just recently set himself down upon it. His American dream takes the form of the Old Rimrock stone house that, as a high-school boy, he had seen from the bus on the way to a game. Built just after the Revolution out of stones collected from the fireplaces of the Revolutionary army's campsites (Washington had wintered in nearby Morristown), the house is to make Seymour temporally as well as spatially a part of America.

Lou Levov can't understand why Seymour would prefer this "decrepit mausoleum" to a luxurious modern house in suburban South Orange, where Merry would have some Jewish friends. What he is really asking is: What are you *doing* here? (a question so similar to Ming's "This place has nothing to do with us"):

> "Heat this place, cost you a fortune, and you'll still freeze to death. . . . What are you going to do with all this ground . . . feed the starving Armenians? You know what? You're dreaming. I wonder if you even know where this is. Let's be candid with each other about this—this is a narrow, bigoted area. The Klan thrived out here in the twenties. . . . This is rock-ribbed Republican New Jersey. . . . Why did they hate Roosevelt out here, Seymour? . . . because they didn't like the Jews and the Italians and the Irish—that's why they moved out here to begin with. They didn't like Roosevelt because he accommodated himself to these new Americans. . . . But not these bastards. They wouldn't give a Jew the time of day . . . this is where the haters live, out here." (*Pastoral,* 309)

Seymour is told that before the war, swastikas were painted on a nearby Jewish resort. Dawn seems to understand her new neighbors better than Seymour does. When Bill Orcutt offers the Levovs a tour of the neighborhood, Dawn decides to stay home: "Something in Orcutt's proprietary manner had irritated her . . . something she found gratingly egotistical in his expansive courtesy, causing her to believe that to this young country squire with the charming manners she was nothing but laughable lace-curtain Irish . . . ludicrously barging into his privileged backyard. . . . 'I know it's just my Irish resentment, but I don't like being looked down on'" (*Pastoral,* 301). The tour turns out to be a name-dropping history lesson, a "cemetery tour" of Orcutts dating back to the Revolution (ironically, they originally came from Ireland), with Orcutts as supporters and even classmates of Jefferson, Jackson, and Adams. The history lesson bores Seymour, but the fact that his neighbor is a walking history book, a living part of American history, seduces him:

> His family couldn't compete with Orcutt's when it came to ancestors—they would have run out of ancestors in about two minutes. As soon as you got back earlier than Newark, back to the old country, no one knew anything. . . . But Orcutt could spin out ancestors forever. Every rung into America for the Levovs there was another rung to attain; this guy was *there.* Is that why Orcutt had laid it on a little thick? Was it to make clear what Dawn accused him of making clear simply by the way he smiled at you—just who he was and just who you weren't? (*Pastoral,* 306)

The irony, of course, is that while Seymour is seduced by Orcutt's history, hungry for history, he is totally unaware of *his*/story—his own people's history, which (like Ming's) stretches back thousands of years into antiquity. Here's Jerry on religion in the Levov household: "She's post-Catholic, he's post-Jewish, together they're going out there to raise little post-toasties" (*Pastoral,* 73). When Bucky Robinson, a Jew Seymour has met in touch football matches, invites the Levovs to join his temple—more for social than for religious reasons—Dawn thinks it would be a good idea but Seymour refuses and proceeds to avoid Bucky and touch football: "With Robinson . . . he felt like Orcutt" (*Pastoral,* 315). But, as Lou Levov tells Orcutt years later in another context: "You don't have to revere your family . . . you don't have to revere where you live, but you have to know you *have* them, you have to know that you are a *part* of them. Because if you don't, you are just out there on your own and I feel for you" (*Pastoral,* 365).

Lakewood, Ohio; Harlem, New York; Mercy Lake, Iowa—they all force the question: "What am I doing here?" To ask oneself this question implies an emphasis on that "I," raising the questions of who and what I am and what I am not. Unbeknownst to anyone, Seymour identifies with Johnny Appleseed. In his springtime exuberance, walking home with his Sunday *Times* from the general store (which his daughter later blows up), he even waves his arms in great arcs, as if spreading around all those apple seeds, helping to create a bountiful America. Seymour, in his own view, has indeed created a self that "belongs." But his brother sees no "self" at all, and assumes that to be a major part of Merry's problem: "You're the one who does everything right . . . that's what your daughter has been blasting away at all her life. You don't reveal yourself to people, Seymour. You keep yourself a secret. Nobody knows what you are. You certainly never let *her* know who you are. That's what she's been blasting away at—that façade" (*Pastoral,* 275). Zuckerman asks: "[W]hat did [Seymour] do for subjectivity? . . . There had to be a substratum, but its composition was unimaginable" (*Pastoral,* 20).

Indeed there is a substratum, but we are led to believe that before the bomb it lay untouched and unexamined. Like that other dreamer of the American dream, Jay Gatsby, who also ended up starring in his own American nightmare, Seymour Levov creates the Seymour of his dreams, one that his physical attributes and prowess allow him to create. Nick Carraway says of Gatsby, "There was something gorgeous about him," and that adjective is applied to the Swede as well (*Pastoral,* 79). Good son though Seymour is, following his father into the family business, retaining his name and his family loyalties, nevertheless he, like Gatsby, creates and guards an idealized (American) self.[45] But to be self-conceived is to deny history, to deny family in some fundamental way. It is worse than rejection in that one sees nothing to reject: there is no need to refuse a family and its stories, for they seem to bear no vital connection to what one is, what one has constructed out of other materials, other stories—romantic dreams and wishes, heroic roles. Self-conception is concerned with external beauty and prowess, all that magnificent appearance and seamless decorum that others see and admire so intensely.

45. Idealization is, of course, typical of pastoral, and is usually ironic: its view of a green place and golden age shows up the tarnished present and corrupt society the writer inhabits. Old Rimrock as green place in contemporary America can only be a *seeming* ideal. Roth is probably also playing on the "past" in "pastoral," the American past out of which Seymour tries to fashion himself anew—another false ideal, Gatsby-style.

The self-abnegation of Seymour's Jain daughter is, in some grotesque, parodic way, an extension of her father's self-denial and self-creation. Merry has sought objects to worship all her life: her father, the Virgin Mary (under the influence of her Irish grandmother), Audrey Hepburn, and then the communist party, along with the Viet Cong and the antiwar movement, as love and worship turn to hatred (of Lyndon Johnson) and destruction (of the government's post office). Ultimately, though, she seeks purification through self-denial and worship of all life, ironically willing to sacrifice her own. If Jerry is right—that all her life she has been trying to "blast" her way in to penetrate what her father really is (that explosive imagery is also carried out in her incurable stuttering, which becomes angry sputtering against the war, the government, her parents, their capitalist way of life, and finally, the violent outburst of her bomb), if a search for truth and identity is at the core of the family's destruction—then Seymour's self-denying self-creation and Merry's increasing self*less*ness are of a piece.

To the questions Who am I? What am I doing here? Where do I belong? must be added: Where does my (not Orcutt's or Johnny Appleseed's) story fit into the larger story I want to become a part of? I cannot think of a better answer than Maxine Hong Kingston's, as she asserts her "claim to America":

> Actually, I think that my books are much more American than they are Chinese. I felt that I was building, creating, myself and these people as American people, to make everyone realize that these are American people. Even though they have strange Chinese memories, they are American people. Also, I am creating part of American literature . . .

> Chinese culture is part of American culture. I mean, all those transcendentalists at the beginning of American writing. . . . It's always been part of America.

> No, we are not outsiders, we belong here, this is our country, this is our history, and we are part of America. We are part of American history. If it weren't for us, America would be a different place.[46]

Evidently, though, this has not always been acknowledged in American history courses. The twelve-year-old eponymous hero of Frank Chin's *Donald Duk* is horrified when he discovers that the Chinese part of American history is missing from his textbooks; the names of the Chinese who arrived first at Promontory Point, Utah, when the transcontinental railroad

46. Interviews in *Conversations,* ed. Skenazy and Martin, 71, 39, 25.

was completed are not in the library books either (though there are eight Irish names). There are Chinese in the pictures snapped there on May 8, 1869, but no Chinese faces are to be seen in the pictures taken on May 10, the historic day the tracks were joined with a golden spike. Donald's discovery is no news to his father, King Duk: "Fair? What's fair? History is war, not sport! . . . You gotta keep the history yourself or lose it forever, boy. That's the mandate of heaven."[47] But Donald will do more than keep it himself: he teaches it, as Chin does in this book (and as Kingston insists on doing—aesthetics be damned—in the "Laws" chapter of *China Men*).

King Duk is one of the best restaurateurs in San Francisco's Chinatown, an artist in the kitchen. On the occasion of the Chinese New Year, he works his singing woks like an orchestra conductor and flies between them like a dancer, explaining his intention: "[L]ike Confucius himself, I will restore ways that have become abandoned and recover knowledge that has been lost" (*Duk*, 63–64). Food (plentiful as well as meaningful), history, culture, story, ritual, family, and the friends that become "family" for the occasion all come together, as they do in the Passover seder. The occasions are different, as are the historical, religious, and culinary particulars, but in spirit, it is as if, through the Duk household, Chin is creating a sort of "Chinese seder"—a meaningful, prescribed order of celebration that, in this book at least, focuses as much on legends and history as it does on holiday festivities.

But the main focus is Donald's progression from angry, resentful, rebellious, embarrassed Chinese boy in a white preppy school to proud, vocal "teacher" of his history teacher, the condescending, ill-informed (though probably well-meaning) Mr. Meanwright. Donald never attends his already paid-up Chinese school, and "doesn't like speaking . . . Chinese. He doesn't have to—this is America" (*Duk*, 3). According to his father:

> "Donald Duk may be the very last American-born Chinese-American boy to believe you have to give up being Chinese to be an American. . . . These new immigrants prove that. . . . They learned French. Now they're learning English. They still speak their Cantonese, their Chinese, their Viet or Lao or Cambodian, and French. Instead of giving anything up, they add on. They're including America in everything else they know. And that makes them stronger than any of the American-born, like me, who had folks who worked hard to know absolutely nothing about China, who believed that if all they knew was

47. Frank Chin, *Donald Duk*, 123 (hereinafter cited in the text as *Duk*).

100 percent American-made in the USA Yankee know howdy doodle
dandy, people would not mistake them for Chinese." (*Duk*, 42)

(This would have been the perfect answer to Ming and Sansan as they
began their hard work of forgetting.) Donald is not the only Chinese in the
school, but none of them have a name like his, and he and the others
avoid one another: "This school is a place where the Chinese are comfortable hating Chinese." He hates his name—he does not live in Disneyland,
and he is not a duck. "Looking Chinese is driving him crazy!" So is the big
deal all his teachers make of Chinese New Year. But the lesson Mr. Meanwright reads the class (out of *his* teacher's book) on the Chinese, their
Confucian nonassertiveness in the face of competition, their passivity,
makes him want to "barf pink and green stuff all over the teacher's
teacher's book." What the teacher is saying, Donald whispers to his (non-
Chinese) friend, Arnold, is the "same thing as everybody—Chinese are
artsy, cutesy and chickendick" (*Duk*, 1–3).

What Donald seems desperately to need are Chinese heroes, legendary
or historical, role models other than his father, whose name is as silly as
his. His romantic hero is Fred Astaire, and though he cannot look like him,
Donald aspires to dance like him, taking lessons from "the Chinese Fred
Astaire" (he refuses to participate in the traditional lion dance, though).
Fred Astaire invades his dreams and accompanies him on his walks; he admires Donald, encourages him, and even glorifies him, but of course he
isn't Chinese. At this stage, Donald needs "white" approval, and Fred certainly gives it, but Fred is pure fantasy—Donald's own personal dream.
Arnold cannot possibly compete with this dancer, actor, and purveyor of
grace and romance.

Chinese art forms and legends enter into Donald's life with the arrival of
the opera master he was named for—Uncle Donald. Not only is Uncle
Donald revered by all the "opera people," but as the opera mentor of
Donald's father, he tells Donald what a great actor King has been. King has
played—and will again play—the great and powerful Kwan Kung, god of
war and literature, a role so demanding that he was required to seclude
himself for three days with no meat or sex and concentrate on *becoming*
Kwan, dangerous to anyone whose eyes he looked into. Woven through
this story, by means of the legendary double role of Kwan, is the relationship of art to power. In Donald's railroad dreams, Kwan becomes the foreman who humbles the railroad executive Charles Crocker, whose white
trousers and white horse become splashed with mud, into an apology (*Duk*,

76–77) and inspires his workers to break the tracklaying record.[48] In this way art, imagination, power, and history begin to take shape in Donald's dreams, which come to be shared by his white friend, Arnold. Genuine interest is surely what separates Arnold from the gawking Chinatown tourists. Arnold stays with the Duks throughout the fifteen days of the New Year, and we suspect that his interest in every aspect of the celebration, and King's patient explanations, have a lot to do with Donald's growing willingness to listen and to participate. Arnold and Donald go together to tai chi and learn how to become part of the great dragon in the parade. Kwan, lion dancing, the music of gongs, drums, and sizzling woks, exploding firecrackers—all these enter into Donald's dreams of the railroad and his part in it (or the part of that ancestor who wasn't much older than he and who bore the same name).

He dreams truth, he dreams history, he dreams the world record for laying the most tracks in a ten-hour day is won by the Chinese in a furious competition against the Irish. His dreams make a lie of the stereotype of the weak, passive, noncompetitive Chinese; they create the final spike that wasn't driven—the one with ten thousand Chinese names carved into it. Donald's and Arnold's dreams lead them to the public library, where they discover the truth of what they dreamt.[49] They recognize the 108 Outlaws of the Water Margin and the Monkey in Chinatown comic books. But Donald also dreams himself an important role—dancing (in the lion) at the head of the railroad workers. In his dreams, driving labor, the push to set the record and beat the Irish, turns into celebration with food, music, and dance. Chin creates a triumph of onomatopoeic detail:

> Kwan lights the fuse, the rocket goes off leaving a trail of sparks and explodes. Work starts. The crossties thump off the wagons and stomp into the roadbed. The tampers tamp, the rails clang, the tongs clink and ting and the rail sings as steel tools set and gauge. Then the hammers hammer, the pike bites home and the rail sings fishplates and

48. There is an irony in Chin's "use" of Chinese legendary figures after vociferously criticizing Kingston for tampering with received myths ("Come All Ye Asian American Writers of the Real and the Fake," 3). True, Chin does not change stories or conflate heroes, but all the same, he allows Donald to use heroes as he needs them in creating a mythology that empowers him, just as Maxine finds power and Kingston finds metaphor in the legendary heroes. Surely Kwan Kung never worked as a railroad foreman.

49. In criticizing the didacticism of *Donald Duk,* Susan B. Richardson points out that Chin has not learned from his own example—that of letting the "learner" or reader discover truths, as King Duk does for Donald ("The Lessons of *Donald Duk,*" 74).

nuts and bolts wrenched tight with tools as long as a man is tall, made
of solid steel that gets hot in the sun, hot with the work and cooled by
the grease and sweat of the handlers. (*Duk,* 111)

This dreamworld is rendered real through its connection to the material
and familiar; food and body imagery give life to the very rails as they expand: "Just sitting alone on the flatcars, the rails sing and ping, stretching
in the sun, warming up, getting hot. . . . snap like knuckles, crackle like
hot oil in the wok. The steel radiates the cold of last night and sounds like
liquid, sounds like bone and chilled muscle" (*Duk,* 98). Donald "wakes to
dream and takes his waking slow," wanting to continue the adventure and
his role in it. "Donald Duk dreams he's sleeping at night and wakes up
dreaming, and wakes up from that dream into another, and wakes up into
the real" (*Duk,* 118). When he tells of his dreams, no one laughs at him,
and King tells him:

> "[Y]ou know the truth. The truth came looking for you in the dreams.
> You go look for truth in the library. You know what is true. You know
> what is true. . . . That makes your life hard, kid. You have the choice.
> If you say Chinese are ching chong, you have to choose to do it and
> lie about what you know is true. And you remember one thing too:
> Soong Gong, the Timely Rain, came to you in your dreams and asked
> you to . . . join his heroes. Boys and girls don't dream like that over
> here. You must be something special. Maybe." (*Duk,* 139)[50]

As if responding to the clear challenge of that "maybe," Donald challenges his teacher in a voice "louder than he expects," a sharp contrast to
his whispers the last time Mr. Meanwright lectured on the Chinese. Mr.
Meanwright's lecture on "sojourners," passivity, and noncompetitiveness is
illustrated with a slide show, and as the class is looking at the photo of the
golden-spike ceremony, Donald bursts out:

> "Yessir, I am offended. . . . You are . . . sir, Mr. Meanwright, not correct
> about us being passive, noncompetitive. We did the blasting through
> Summit Tunnel. We worked through two hard winters in the high
> Sierras. We went on strike for back pay and Chinese foremen for Chi-
> nese gangs, and won. We set the world's record for miles of track laid

50. Compare Kingston's: "I tell the imaginative lives and the dreams and the fictions
of imaginative people. . . . I tell you what their dreams are and what stories they tell"
(interview in *Conversations,* ed. Skenazy and Martin, 37).

in one day. We set our last crosstie at Promontory. And it is badly informed people like you who keep us out of that picture there."

The class follows Donald's gesture toward the screen, where an old, grainy picture is projected: Chinese above the snowline, working with picks and shovels in the Sierra Nevadas. In the center is a smiling boy with Donald's face. "We didn't do all that being passive and non-competitive, sir. . . . April 29, 1869. . . . A Thursday, as I remember . . . Chinese set the record— 1200 of us—and the history books don't have one of our names down [as they do] the eight Irishmen who lifted rail off the flatcars with us"—facts that Arnold brings out the library books to corroborate (*Duk,* 151–52).

Besides Donald's newfound courage, supported by his newfound knowledge, what is striking in his "speeches" is the "we," the "us," and the "I remember." Whether the boy in the photo just looks like Donald, or is his ancestor, or actually *is* Donald—the one who remembers not just what he read in books, but what he *lived* at Promontory in 1869—doesn't matter, for it is "as if he himself went out of Egypt," or, in *this* story, helped his ancestors at Promontory. To continue the analogy with the Passover Haggadah, it is as if Donald begins as the "wicked son" who wants to dissociate himself from his people ("What is all this to me?"), progresses through the questions and curiosity to know, and ends up, like the "wise son," totally involved in his people's history, as if he himself had been there. The New Year celebration marks Donald's journey to freedom, his journey from shame to pride in his heritage.[51] The order (seder) of his progress is constantly punctuated by food, which happens to be the final word of the book: ". . . like everything else, it begins and ends with *Kingdoms rise and fall. Nations come and go,* and food" (*Duk,* 173).

Finally, another vital aspect of the Haggadah is represented in *Donald Duk:* the narrative of narrating—not only the story itself, but the centrality of the act of telling. Once Donald and Arnold have learned the story, they are not content simply with the knowledge. They must tell it, and not just to one another, not just to other Chinese in their class, but also to the whole class and to the teacher, Mr. Meanwright. (*Does* he mean

---

51. This progression signals a maturation as well. Uncle Donald comes to the Duks on this New Year because it is to be the twelfth birthday of his namesake, Donald. As Uncle Donald explains it, twelve is a significant birthday in that it marks the completion of the zodiac cycle, a sort of life cycle, or coming-of-age, event. In this respect it resembles the "becoming a man" theme of the bar mitzvah at a similar age, thirteen, both coinciding with the approximate age for the onset of puberty.

well? construct meanness? require meanness to be set right? As with other stereotypers, we cannot always know which it is.) As teachers of the teacher, they bet they're "the first kids to make Mr. Meanwright read books" (*Duk*, 159). They are classroom heroes, backed up by King's booming entrance as Kwan, inviting one and all to the opera. In "feeding" teacher and class the Chinese stories appropriate to the lesson of the season, they stage a dramatic reversal of the roles of teacher and pupil and of the typical acculturating classroom. They are now the history teachers, but even more important than *what* they tell the class is *that* they tell, and especially that Donald has become a teller of "his" story.

6

"My Pearly Doesn't Get C's"

The Centrality (and Cost) of Education

If called upon to identify the single institution most responsible for helping bicultural young people to fashion an American identity, most of us would name the American public school system. While it has been guilty of discriminating against, even for a while excluding, Asians, while some of its teachers seemed to care more deeply about clean teeth and fingernails than they did about the minds of their charges, while its "Americanizing" goal often rode roughshod over the sensitivities and traditional identities of its students (a sure prescription for conflict between children and parents, or within the children themselves), the school system opened America—its language, its tradition and history, its opportunities—to bicultural students. But such opportunities were not taken without cost—witness Theodore Roosevelt's credo, published in a Board of Education bulletin: "We have room for but one language here, and that is the English language . . . and we have room for but one sole loyalty, and that is loyalty to the American people."[1] In facilitating the transformation of immigrant children into "real Yankees," the schools (and the society they represented) required that they give up the external signs, for example, of being Jewish. Often it was upon entering school that children became aware they were different, and that difference was a hindrance to acceptance by teacher and classmates. It was in school that children learned to feel ashamed of their language, their parents, and their way of life. Even their accents were seen by some

---

1. Sydney Stahl Weinberg, *World of Our Mothers: The Lives of Jewish Immigrant Women,* 112. See Diane Lei Lin Mark and Ginger Chih on the exclusion of Chinese students in the nineteenth century, followed by the establishment of schools for the Chinese (*A Place Called Chinese America,* 92–93).

overly zealous, insensitive teachers as a stubborn refusal to learn English. Where accent and dress became fully Americanized, some young people could "melt" into the American pot; but the Chinese, no matter how well they conformed, could not change their faces, nor could many teenaged white immigrants lose the accents that marked them as indelibly "foreign" as any Asian.[2]

As will be seen in the texts under discussion, becoming American enough to fit in, even to merely survive, in the public school exacted a price. Students were made to feel stupid when they could not understand directions or questions or books; other students ridiculed them, calling them "chink" or "kike" and telling them to go back where they came from. At times the price was paid by both parents and children as conflicts arose over old and new worlds, tradition and modern America; the gap yawned wider and deeper between the languages of parents and children, between the sorts of knowledge parents had and treasured and what their children were learning in school. At the same time, the parents needed what their children were learning in school; at the very least, they needed their English-speaking children to interpret for them at doctors' and government offices and to fill out official forms, which created role reversals that caused discomfort for both parents and children and upset the normal balance of power. Because they were able to get things done, children's status in the family became higher, and some even assumed "head of the family" functions. Sydney Stahl Weinberg writes: "With children often the teachers and parents the learners, no wonder that many immigrants called America a 'godless country. All the wrong side up. The children are fathers to their father. The fathers children to their children.'"[3]

Children also learned about American democracy and its emphasis on the importance of the individual, which conflicted with home cultures that emphasized the greater importance of membership and place within the group, not to mention the respect relationship expected between children and their parents. (This was equally true of traditional Chinese and Jewish homes.) Of course, even in the United States minors don't get to vote, but in many cultures, one never loses "minor" status relative to one's parents or elders. There must have been many conversations that resembled this one from Gish Jen's *Mona in the Promised Land,* modern living notwithstanding:

2. Hana Wirth-Nesher has spoken of Mary Antin's obsession with pronunciation, her frustration that she could not be fully "passed," and her view of her spoken language as "mongrel" ("'Passing' in the Promised Land," paper presented at a conference of the Israel Association of American Studies, Jerusalem and Tel Aviv, May 1999).

3. Weinberg, *World of Our Mothers,* 115.

"Context! Social problem! What kind of talk is that?"

Mona closes up the dishwasher. "It's a free country, I can talk however I want. It's my right."

"Free country! Right! In this house, no such thing!" More social analysis:

"That's exactly the problem! Everywhere else is America, but in this house it's China!"

"That's right! No America here! In this house, children listen to parents!" (*Mona,* 250)

Mona Chang's parents want Harvard and suburbia, and are paying the price of their children's assimilation.[4] Other families made the same choice, and, like the Changs, did not realize the cost until it had already been paid. Others resisted, trying to keep their children separated from the mainstream, and still others, knowing the price, gladly paid it. After all, it was to the schools that parents looked to provide their children a way out of the sweatshop, or the laundry, or the fields. If America was the gold mountain, then school was the castle on the hill. America was the land where there was not only gold in the mountain and on the streets, but golden opportunities that education would make possible, treasures it would unlock, and all of it free. And books! heretofore unavailable, or forbidden—they too were free to use, an important promise in Mary Antin's *The Promised Land:*

> Education was free. That subject my father had written about repeatedly, as comprising his chief hope for his children, the essence of American opportunity, the treasure that no thief could touch, not even misfortune or poverty. It was the one thing that he was able to promise us when he sent for us; surer, safer than bread or shelter. On our second day I was thrilled with the realization of what this freedom of education meant. . . . No application made, no questions asked, no examinations, rulings, exclusions; no machinations, no fees. The doors stood open for every one of us.

> To most people their first day of school is a memorable occasion. In my case the importance of the day was a hundred times magnified, on account of the years I had waited, the road I had come, and the conscious ambitions I entertained. . . . I may have been ever so much an exception . . . none the less were my thoughts and conduct typical of

4. Obviously Andrew Furman's point about parental desire to assimilate (see 25 n. 14 and 154 n. 40) does not hold up when values such as parental authority are challenged; assimilation must not go that far.

the attitude of the intelligent immigrant child toward American institutions. And what the child thinks and feels is a reflection of the hopes, desires, and purposes of the parents who brought them overseas. . . . Your immigrant inspectors will tell you what poverty the foreigner brings in his baggage, what want in his pockets. Let the overgrown boy of twelve, reverently drawing his letters in the baby class, testify to the noble dreams and high ideals that may be hidden beneath the greasy caftan of the immigrant.[5]

Such opportunity, whether actual or mythical (and it most certainly could be either), found fertile soil among Chinese and Jewish children and their families. As we can see in the texts under discussion, these children came out of cultures that placed great value on scholarship and learning. In both cultures, ancient texts were revered, and those who knew them well, who spent their lives acquiring and teaching their wisdom, were held in esteem bordering on reverence. We find no evidence in these texts of disdain for the sedentary occupation of reading, or for soft, rather than callused, hands.[6] That a family could afford to educate its sons, or to keep the hands of at least one son "soft"—to sacrifice the others, perhaps, so that there might be one scholar—is an ideal in the Chinese families of these stories.

Sui Sin Far provides examples of such attitudes in her stories, articles, and interviews. Of a wife whose husband admires a white woman who had been his teacher, she writes: "There is a jealousy of the mind more poignant than any mere animal jealousy." Elsewhere, she notes: "Many of the Chinese laundrymen I know are not laundrymen only, but artists and poets, often the sons of good families. . . . [M]any of the Chinese who come to this country to work as laborers are oftentimes cousins of government students, and, in several cases . . . brothers of students, it being the custom among the Chinese to educate but one boy of a family if domestic economy

5. Mary Antin, *The Promised Land,* 186, 198. Abraham Cahan tells of his willingness as an adult to sit in an elementary-school classroom so that he would be better able to master correct English pronunciation. He reasoned that in night school, exposed almost exclusively to peers whose English was as bad as or worse than his own, he would not do as well (*The Education of Abraham Cahan,* 39–40).

6. Weinberg writes that Italian and Polish immigrants wanted their children to get to work fast to help the family save money for land or a house; education was sometimes viewed with suspicion as a competitor for a child's allegiance. She explains that since Jews were seldom allowed to own land in Europe, property was not seen as security for the future in the way an education or a business would be (*World of Our Mothers,* 6). Gay Talese notes the relative paucity of Italian immigrant literature, citing suspicion of education on the part of the mainly peasant immigrants ("The Italian-American Voice: Where Is It?" 319).

necessitates that course." Interviewing a cook in a hotel kitchen, Far finds that in China he had been a scholar:

> "I thought a scholar in China was not supposed to know anything about work."
>
> "True," answered Wang Liang; "a scholar must be helpless in all ways in spite of his learning. But my mother was ill and needed ginseng and chicken broth, and my father was getting old, and we were poor. . . .
>
> "Then one day I read in my Classics, 'Those who labor support those who govern,' and I reasoned that if those who labored supported those who governed, then the laborer must in no wise be inferior to him that governs. So I decided to work with my hands, and in order *that my parents might not be made to feel ashamed, I came to America.* . . . When I have enough to live on for the rest of my life I will return to China and again *take up my studies and do honor to my parents as a scholar.*" [emphases mine][7]

In the "Father from China" section of Maxine Hong Kingston's *China Men,* a boy is coddled by his mother, kept back from working the fields as his brothers have to do; at his one-month party, he is given the Four Valuable Things—ink, inkslab, paper, and brush:

> "Your little brother is different from any of you. . . . This kind of hand was made for holding pens. This is the boy we'll prepare for the Imperial Examinations." The other boys were built like horses and oxen, made for farmwork.

> Instead of acrobatics and shuttlecock, he liked studying. Ah Po kept her boy close. She sewed little scholar's caps and scholar's gowns. She used the leftover black scraps for knee patches on her other sons' pants. Even before Bibi could talk, she fed and lodged itinerant scholars, who stayed the night or week to read to him. . . . When he was old enough for lessons, his brothers sometimes came inside from their chores to rest on the floor at the tutor's feet. Ah Po did not stop them. . . . Soon the farming brothers' heads nodded. . . . [O]ne by one they withdrew to slop pigs, draw water . . .[8]

In the Jewish community, it was worth a large dowry to a prospective father-in-law to have a learned young man as a son-in-law, for "a boy

---

7. Sui Sin Far, *Mrs. Spring Fragrance and Other Writings,* 51, 232, 237 (hereinafter cited in the text as *Spring*).

8. Maxine Hong Kingston, *China Men,* 16, 23 (hereinafter cited in the text as *Men*).

stuffed with learning is worth more than a girl stuffed with banknotes."[9] Conversely, to match one's son with the daughter of a great scholar was itself a dowry. Scholars were provided with sleeping space in the study house or synagogue and meals at the tables of often poor shtetl dwellers in communities that prided themselves on supporting such a worthy cause.

We find evidence that books and learning were romanticized not only among immigrants, but back in the old-world villages and cities; most romanticized were works of the larger world that threatened fidelity to tradition and traditional texts—tempting, challenging, redolent of forbidden fruit. In Cynthia Ozick's *The Cannibal Galaxy,* the school that represents the culmination of Principal Brill's dream, that of a dual curriculum combining Jewish and secular Western studies, has its beginnings in the yearnings and discoveries that tempt the youthful Brill in Paris. Living in the Marais district, the boy thinks the Rue Vieille du Temple refers to the Temple of biblical Jerusalem rather than to the crusading knights who slaughtered Jews; he rationalizes visits to the statue of Rachel—the legendary actress of the red slippers whose Phèdre was a precursor of Bernhardt's—thinking that she is the matriarch Rachel weeping for her children. (At least she was a Jewish actress, he tells himself when he realizes his mistake.) On his walks home from school—home to his father's fish store, the back room of which doubles as the Hebrew school where he studies with his rabbi—he discovers the Musée Carnavalet. Not a church (that would frighten him too much), but a palatial home, where Madame de Sévigné lived and slept and wrote letters to her daughter, and where hangs a portrait of Madame de Sévigné herself: "[H]is mother had been nearly right [in warning him about images of unclothed women]—she was almost completely nude, down to the very top of her bosom, where the lace frill made a pretty border. Pearls were sewn into the voluptuous sleeves of her gown—ah, these had the shapes of crosses at last." Only years later, as a student at the Sorbonne, does he learn of the greatness of her letters and their influence on French literature. By then Brill is a serious student of literature, that is, until he learns that neither his friends nor the texts he studies can be trusted to be hospitable to Jews. Thus he reaches out to the beyond; "he looked for a place without taint": the stars.[10]

The Nazi roundup of his neighborhood claims his family and his rabbi,

---

9. Antin, *Promised Land,* 32.
10. Cynthia Ozick, *The Cannibal Galaxy,* 10, 16 (hereinafter cited in the text as *Galaxy*).

but miraculously Brill escapes capture and is hidden for a while in a convent-school basement, along with the books of a dead priest. The bishop is a bit embarrassed by the liberal character of the priest's library, and is glad to have them out of his way. While the good sisters keep Brill alive, these books keep him sane in his solitude and further his education as well, especially when he discovers among them, annotated by the priest, the works of Edmond Fleg, a French Jew who wrote of Jesus, Jews, and Palestine.[11] He also reads the sacred text his rabbi had entrusted to his care before he was taken away, reads it juxtaposed with, of all things, Proust's *Sodome et Gomorrhe:* "How different they were! *And neither told a lie.* This was a marvel, that two such separated tonalities, so to speak, could between them describe the true map of life" (*Galaxy,* 28). And thus is born his theory—in truth not very original—and his school.[12] Unfortunately, in middle America his dream of uniting two grand traditions is "beleaguered by middling parents and their middling offspring," and becomes a watering down of each tradition rather than a glorious combination (*Galaxy,* 6). He has long before left behind his studies of astronomy, and the school's motto, *ad astra,* is only that—a motto.

But the vision, the dream, the romance of great books and great minds, the educated one as hero—such goals and attitudes were indeed brought over the ocean in immigrant baggage. In his autobiography, Abraham Cahan takes us back to Vilna, Lithuania, and his discovery of its library:

> "With a feeling of awe I approached the catalogue. . . . I was in the library four or five hours every day. I remember the smell of the books, the stillness of the reading room, the feel of the book bindings. I remember the taste of the brass check which I held in my mouth while reading. In my mind, its cool, metallic taste is especially associated with the taste of Turgenev's lines. . . . My enjoyment was in the beauty of his language and the enrichment of my own that resulted from constant resort to the dictionary. The Vilna Public Library became for me a temple of learning and inspiration."[13]

11. Edmond Fleg (né Flegenheimer, 1874–1963) was a prolific poet, playwright, and essayist. His weakened ties to Judaism were dramatically strengthened as a result of the Dreyfus affair and the Zionist congresses. Some of his most famous works are a verse cycle, *Ecoute Israel,* the "biography" *Jesus, raconté par le Juif Errant,* and the essay *Pourquoi je suis Juif.*

12. In nineteenth-century Europe there were already such schools, and they are numerous now in the United States. Their quality varies, as does the emphasis on Judaic studies relative to secular studies.

13. Abraham Cahan, *The Education of Abraham Cahan,* 95–97 (hereinafter cited in the text as *Education*).

"Awe," "temple"—Cahan is not merely romanticizing scholarship, but elevating books and learning to sanctity. (That the works of secular gentiles such as Turgenev are seen as the new Torah has significance that will be dealt with in greater detail below.) He refers to the Vilna teacher training institute as the "holy of holies" (*Education*, 103).

In Cahan's novel *The Rise of David Levinsky,* the chapter that describes Levinsky's move into manufacturing, and thus away from his goal to enter City University, is named "The Destruction of My Temple."[14] This development is especially cataclysmic when we remember the way Levinsky's impoverished, widowed mother reacted when the villagers advised her to have him learn a trade:

> Sending me to work was out of the question. She was resolved to put me in a Talmudic seminary. . . . Nor was she a rare exception in this respect, for there were hundreds of other poor families in our town who would starve themselves to keep their sons studying the Word of God. Whenever one of the neighbors suggested I be apprenticed to some artisan she would flare up. . . . [P]ointing at some huge volumes of the Talmud, she said: "This is the trade I am going to have you learn, and let our enemies grow green with envy."[15]

Such dreams, however, were not always strong enough to withstand the frustrations of the workplace and the temptations that beckoned one toward easier, faster money. It is obvious that to persist in the intellectual life means to defer financial stability and, in most cases, to give learning priority over wealth. In Levinsky's case, his "temple" begins to crumble over a spilled bottle of milk: When his superior chastises him severely, humiliates him, and charges him damages over the spilled milk, Levinsky begins to think creatively and determinedly about never having to be in such a position again and becoming, instead, a manufacturing boss.

In Jen's *Typical American,* Ralph Chang, Ph.D., finally tenured (not without help from a friend who is chair of his department and always ahead of him in study and publication), has his great epiphany of career dissatisfac-

14. To emphasize the magnitude of the destruction of Levinsky's plans, Cahan evokes events that are central to Judaism and Jewish history: the destruction of Solomon's temple in Jerusalem by the Babylonians in 480 B.C.E. and the destruction of the rebuilt temple by the Romans in 70 C.E. So began the Jewish diaspora and loss of sovereignty. The site of the temple was not to return to Jewish hands until 1967, and is now the site of the Moslem Dome of the Rock. To this day, Jews the world over fast and mourn on Tisha B'Av, the ninth day of the month of Av, anniversary of the date of both destructions (as well as of the expulsion of Jews from Spain in 1492).

15. Cahan, *Rise of David Levinsky,* 23 (hereinafter cited in the text as *Rise*).

tion in a stuffy, cramped classroom. Facing once more a class of bored, vacant-looking faces, he wants to flee, to drive and never stop. And so he finds himself looking up a number, dialing it, and accepting an almost forgotten invitation from a man that everyone but he can see for what he is— a con man with a shady past, a seductively irresponsible and reckless manner, and lots of highly visible luxuries. The result is Chang's leaving his professorship to become the owner of a fried-chicken take-out restaurant. The Chicken Palace becomes the repository of his dreams, that is, until it collapses—literally—when Chang, against advice, builds a second story. It seems his "friend" has unloaded a "palace" built on a covered pit filled with rotting logs. The cracks that begin to form ("a little settling") win the battle against the pints, then buckets, of joint compound Chang valiantly applies, and finally the walls come tumbling down.[16]

Once, Chang was as determined as Levinsky to conquer the Everest of an American education, to bring a Ph.D. home as a trophy to a father who never imagined that his ordinary son, Yifeng, could amount to very much, certainly not to be a source of parental pride. Determination fueled his journey to America, occupying every waking moment of the long Pacific crossing:

> On the way to America, Yifeng studied. He reviewed his math, his physics, his English, struggling for long hours with his broken backed books, and as the boat rocked and pitched he set out two main goals for himself. He was going to be first in his class, and he was not going home until he had his doctorate rolled up to hand his father. He also wrote down a list of subsidiary aims. . . .
>
> He studied in the sun, in the rain, by every shape moon. The ocean sang and spit; it threw itself on the deck. Still he studied. . . . Even when islands began to heave their brown, bristled backs up through the sea (a morning sea so shiny it seemed to have turned into light and light and light), he watched only between pages. For this was what he'd vowed as a corollary of his main aim—to study until he could see the pylons of the Golden Gate Bridge.[17]

Of course it would be naive to ignore the obvious fact that these narratives are written by *writers*—those to whom words and texts are vital, and the means to them (books, teachers, places of learning) to be treasured and cultivated. Irving Howe reminds us that not all immigrant Jewish children

---

16. Gish Jen, *Typical American,* 243–46.
17. Ibid., 6–7.

"burned with zeal to learn"; at the same time, though, he acknowledges the "fierce attention and hopes lavished on those who did comprise that layer of brilliance." Lecturers were in great demand and lecture halls were filled; cafes ("the universities of the ghetto") on the lower east side of New York buzzed with the talk of intellectuals, political reformers, and artists, and were attended by wanna-bes who felt enriched by merely listening to or rubbing shoulders with these great talkers. Many sweatshop workers carried books (often in Yiddish or Russian) to their sewing machines, seeking the "glamour of the spirit" that made their daily drudgery easier to bear. It is impossible to know just how much young men and women were drawn to lectures by pure intellectual curiosity and how much by the need to socialize and seek romance. (Housewives, not yet liberated, seldom had the time or the freedom—or the courage—to spend evenings at lectures or cafes.) Still, Howe speaks of the hunger for knowledge that rose, in a few, to "a fierce and remarkable passion." He quotes one self-educated worker:

> "How can I describe to you, you who live with a mountain of books, the hunger that I and my friends felt? The excitement we shared when we would discuss Dostoevsky? . . . For us it was books and only books. . . . By the time I came to America, I had to pull my nose out of the books to get a job, but . . . I would go home in the evenings and read. . . . I went to night school, and picked up a little English, so I could read the easier books. But it never seemed enough. I was like a hungry man. . . . And I went to lectures."[18]

Cahan writes of tutoring businessmen, peddlers, and manufacturers in their offices (*Education,* 280).

It is likewise difficult to separate the motive of intellectual curiosity from the desire to get ahead, whether to escape poverty or rise above the prejudices of the majority culture. Getting into one of the professions was the main task of children who had the benefit of a school education, an op-

18. Irving Howe, *World of Our Fathers: The Journey of the East European Jews to America and the Life They Made,* 278. Although New York intellectuals such as Howe grew up speaking Yiddish, they never walked the few blocks from Greenwich Village to converse with the Yiddish-speaking intellectuals at the Café Royale on New York's Lower East Side (David Roskies, conversation with author, Tel Aviv University, May 26, 1999). It was as if they had to distance themselves from Yiddish and the "ghetto." For more detail on this issue see "The Restlessness of Learning," chap. 7 in *World of Our Fathers;* Howe relates those in the New York scene to the self-educating workers in England and Europe from the nineteenth century on.

portunity parents made certain to impress upon the children and their teachers. Such ambition became one aspect of the stereotypical Jewish mother, satirized so savagely by Philip Roth but remembered by Pearl Whitman with love and admiration that transcends the embarrassment of the moment:

> The notion that one could argue with [my teacher] was unthinkable. And here was my mother questioning my idol's judgment. It's true that I had come home in tears the day before because of the grade; that it was the first "C" I had ever received. . . . Mama was a fairly tall, dignified woman who spoke English correctly with a slight Yiddish accent and turn-of-phrase. . . . She rarely raised her voice and had the reputation in the family and the neighborhood as a peace-maker. But her soft demeanor belied her determined ways and when it came to her children, no one was permitted to do them wrong. So I should not have been surprised to see her appear. . . . For a moment she spoke with tremulous voice reflecting old-world awe of teaching authority, but quickly her posture straightened. . . . She said simply and clearly, "My Pearly doesn't get C's."[19]

Myla Goldberg's recent novel *Bee Season,* whose nine-year-old Jewish female protagonist, Eliza, and her father are obsessed with winning the national spelling bee, serves as a reminder that academic aspiration and competitive spirit did not die with the immigrant generation. True, mysticism plays a part in Eliza's winning, but the vehicle to success is still words and letters.[20]

Not surprisingly, most parents were ready to make untold sacrifices for education. Said one Chinese father to his son: "I've worked my finger to the bones for you to get an education. If you cannot be better than they are, try to be their equal anyway, because that way, one of these days, you can be up there too." It is obviously not just economic gain this father is talking about, but also the prejudice he knows his son will encounter. While Jews encountered the same problem, and therefore had a similar need to demonstrate superior knowledge and skills in order to compete for university places and jobs, Asians were at a far greater disadvantage, as racial exclusion laws made painfully obvious. No subtlety there, no quiet

19. Pearl Whitman, "My Pearly Doesn't Get C's," 8.
20. For the story of how the daughter of a Jewish family of championship spellers lost in the nationals to a child of Indian immigrants, see Bruce Grierson, "Spellbound," *New York Times Magazine,* September 1, 2002, p. 56.

"gentleman's agreement," but openly expressed and legislated exclusion.[21] To some it was surely a disincentive to strive for education when employers were color-conscious and Ph.D.s became grocers.[22] But to others, education was a hedge against prejudice and a way of maintaining personal and cultural self-esteem. To this end, Chinese traditional culture was invoked as a source of pride: "Be proud that you're Chinese," parents told their American-born children. "Yes, legally you are Americans, but you will not be accepted. Look at your face—it is Chinese. But don't worry. Just show them how smart you are because you have a superior heritage. . . . Don't pay attention to the names they call you. They're just barbarians! Just be as nice to them as possible, because you have a superior culture." Gerald Haslam writes that "the knowledge that their ancestors had created a great and complex civilization when the inhabitants of the British Isles still painted their fannies blue" enabled the Chinese to endure rejection without anger or injury. (The same could be said of those Jews who were schooled in their own ancient heritage, history, and tradition.) Thus, doing well and behaving well had a dual function: it enabled young people to break out of menial lives, and it protected their dignity—and, not incidentally, the dignity of their parents. According to Ronald Takaki, Asian parents often vented their own frustrations on their children, counting on them to recover the family's dignity and urging them to get ahead. "Furnish your mind. . . . You don't have to be poor inside, too," says the father in *The Jade Peony*.[23]

21. The Chinese father is quoted in Mark and Chih, *Place Called Chinese America*, 75. For more details on exclusion, see Ronald Takaki, *Strangers from a Different Shore: A History of Asian Americans*, 265–69, and Kingston, the "Laws" chapter in *China Men*, 152–59. Perhaps racial prejudice and the consequent narrowing of opportunity—which led to advice (before the Communist revolution) that students return to China to practice careers—affected the degree to which Chinese parents encouraged their children to become "real Americans." In looking at the literature under discussion, it seems to me that there is less of this push to English-language facility, to being a "Yankee"—less pride in children becoming Americanized.

22. Takaki, *Strangers*, 265–68. It must be noted, however, that differences in socioeconomic class, and in eras, are involved. Comparing Chinese American levels of education with the majority culture, Morrison G. Wong finds that at the lower end of the socioeconomic scale, more whites finish high school and even some college, but at the higher end, more Chinese are likely to have one or more degrees ("Chinese Americans," 80). Pyong Gap Min points to a dramatic increase in Asian American students at prestigious universities (*Asian Americans: Contemporary Issues and Trends*, 49). See Lisa See, *On Gold Mountain: The One-Hundred-Year Odyssey of My Chinese-American Family*, for a family saga involving great wealth in Chinese exports/imports.

23. Several Chinese parents quoted in Takaki, *Strangers*, 255–56; Haslam quoted in Kim, *Asian American Literature*, 69; Takaki, *Strangers*, 256; Choy, *Jade Peony*, 139.

Jen turns such ambitions to humor, though the pressure so many of these young people feel to live up to their parents' expectations, and to make their sacrifices worthwhile, is clearly not funny. The humor (like so much satire) carries an aura of bitterly remembered truth:

> [N]ow Mona's been signed up for the family project too. After all, one generation is supposed to build on the last, ascending and ascending like the steps of a baby bamboo shoot; and how nice for the parents to be able to say, "The girls go to Harvard"! Mona realizes this herself, the misty elegance of the sound—it lingers in the air like something of a perfume spritzer. (*Mona*, 100)

> Mona cannot help but hear what [her mother] would say: *What do you mean, not going to college? You kill your parents, you talk like that....* "[T]hey think that's the exact job of the parents, to make sure the kids go to college.... And the kids' job is to go and not hack off. Our job is to remember how hard our parents worked, and to get all A's to make it up to them." (*Mona*, 258–59)

In case these sentiments are not familiar enough, here's a quotation that will make almost any Jewish reader laugh nervously in recognition:

> Ralph and Helen have something to discuss with [Callie]—namely, the dread subject, Medical School. They discuss this in their various ways. Helen concentrates on filial piety. Here her parents slave all day to pay tuition, think of that.... Also think of how her poor parents have no son to send instead. Ralph goes with a more philosophical, nature-of-the-world approach: *"You got to have a meal ticket.... You got to earn your own money, otherwise your husband treat you like a slave."*

And to Callie's lack of interest in medicine: *"Medicine is very interesting.... Life is about work, and since when is work supposed to be interesting?"* (*Mona*, 233).

Helen Zia writes of the desire of Asian parents for children who, as physicians, will be able to care for them in their old age; Phoebe Eng writes of *expectations* as "a key word in the Asian American coming of age lexicon" and of the role that a child's educational success plays in family honor. Eng theorizes that American and European parents are more likely to credit success to good school training, whereas Chinese parents are more likely to attribute it to good upbringing at home. The corollary to this, of course, is that Chinese families take failure much more personally, and feel dishonored. Success is thus the minimum standard.[24] In addition, and common to many immigrant groups, school success and career choices that lead to financial promise and security become a whole-family concern, one, understandably, that grows out of the insecurity and often real difficulty of being an immigrant.

Even back in the home countries, scholar/sons who had achieved some recognition were able to escape menial labor and poverty. It is crucial to keep in mind that this was true only because in those societies scholarship was valued: that which is considered valuable can serve as currency, whether it be to obtain community support, a wealthy father-in-law, or a position of influence or esteem or greater ease. In pre-1905 China, a high ranking on the Imperial Examination brought one access to the most lucrative bureaucratic offices and immense social prestige. Theoretically, since this access was determined by an examination, the "aristocracy" was determined not by birth or wealth but by mastery of classical texts and commentaries, and facility in verbal expression and calligraphy. In actual practice, of course, reaching those high levels required that one's family could afford not only to release their son from labor, but also to hire tutors who themselves had passed the examination with distinction.[25]

Kingston's family were village people; they were not wealthy, and they did not come from a line of scholars. But BaBa, her "Father from China," was still encouraged to pursue his studies. In *China Men*, BaBa, seeking poetic inspiration from the trees, branches, and flying geese, chooses to walk for two days to the place where the examinations are given. He finds an idyllic scene where scholars converse quietly, help one another study, and tell riddles, talking "about what happened in books as if it were real. They were a different race from the splay-fingered village men, whose most imaginative talk was about the Gold Mountain" (*Men*, 25). How ironic, then, is BaBa's ultimate decision to heed the villagers' talk and go to the Gold Mountain.

He indeed succeeds in escaping the fields, but, as he takes his examination in the final year it is given, he cannot, as many scholars did, try again (and yet again) to reach a higher rank, and he is not able to do better than become a humble village schoolmaster. Had he ranked higher, the

24. Zia, *Asian American Dreams,* 56; Eng, *Warrior Lessons,* 18, 23. Morrison G. Wong criticizes as unwise for the long term the trend of these students considering "risk aversive factors" in choosing their major, favoring those where English presents less of a problem ("Chinese Americans," 81). Amy Tan also discusses this issue in "Mother Tongue," 181.

25. Jonathan Spence, *The Search for Modern China,* 46.

narrator tells us, he would not have had to come to the Gold Mountain; he would never have run a Chinese laundry—and, we assume, he would at least have been able to teach boys different from the sons of the village men. As a teacher he fails dismally to understand his pupils, and his nightmare experience is made especially poignant by the efforts he makes (futile though they are) to bring some beauty into the lives of these children—some poetry, some imagination. He thinks to please and inspire them by making for each boy his own handwriting pattern and using each boy's special words; he explains things in the common language ("students should have marveled that they had a teacher who knew the meanings of the texts and not just the rote"); he tries to point out correspondences of nature and history, but produces either sleepiness or wild behavior (*Men,* 33–34). As the year goes on, we are told, "he used the rest period to read his own books before he forgot how. Someone had to enjoy reading in this school. The students . . . spoiled the songs of the birds. . . . Teaching was destroying his literacy. . . . He shrank the poems to fit the brains of peasant children, who were more bestial than animals; when he used to plow, the water buffalo had let him prop a book between its horns" (*Men,* 39). It is difficult to decide which is the greater contrast: that between BaBa's teaching and his hopes when he pinned his pigtail to a ceiling hook the night before his examinations, the better to stay awake to study, or that between those hopes and his work in the laundry. Privy to his love of reading, his making everything he sees into poetry, we may also find it difficult to separate learning for position from learning for the sheer love of it.

Sara Smolinsky, in Anzia Yezierska's *Bread Givers,* seems to me a pivotal character in this context. One in the gallery of Yezierska's passionate female characters yearning for a better life—cleaner, more refined, more American, but also more educated—Sara's educational odyssey begins with a story in the Sunday paper about a shopgirl who went to night school, then to college, where she "worked and studied, on and on, till she became a teacher in the schools. A school teacher—I! I saw myself sitting at a desk, the children, their eyes on me, watching and waiting for me to call out the different ones to the board, to spell a word, or answer me a question. It was like looking up to the top of the highest skyscraper while down in the gutter." Even at this early stage, her desires are not merely material or social, but connected somehow with her romantic vision of "school" and those who are educated. Later she recalls "the inspiring sight of the *teacherin* . . . how thrilled I felt if I could brush by Teacher's skirt. . . . If I was lucky enough to win a glance or a smile from that superior creature. I had it ingrained in me from my father, this exalted reverence for the teacher." Hunger, dirt, noise, fatigue from working all day in a laundry—these become the demons she must fight with determination to reach her goal. Geometry and tedious definitions of parts of speech are likewise her enemies. It is only after she realizes that the man who is pursuing her has no appreciation for who she is and what she wants that she returns to her books as her best friends: "I looked at the books on my table that had stared at me like enemies a little while before. They were again the life of my life. *Ach!* Nothing was so beautiful as to learn, to know, to master by sheer force of my will even the dread squares and triangles of geometry. I seized my books and hugged them to my breast as though they were living things."[26] She has made the transition, despite the importance of her economic and career goals, to valuing knowledge and study for its own sake. At this point she is like Yezierska herself, who in her autobiography writes of her "capitalist courage" in buying lessons from her janitor's daughter:

> "Say, Minnie! What are you learning?"
> "Synonyms," she grumbled.
> "Synonyms? What's that?"
> "It's words about words . . ."
> "I'm crazy for words!" I bounced into the basement, seized the book from her hand. Words about words weren't just words to me. . . . Synonyms spread before my eyes a feast of language. . . . "Look!" I waved a shining half dollar before her eyes. "All this is yours if you tell me everything you learn in school." And so my education began. Evenings, Sundays, and holidays, I labored over Minnie's schoolbooks. A nickel a lesson, ten lessons for fifty cents bought me the right to read all her books.[27]

The Rise of David Levinsky presents us with two characters hungry for knowledge: the title character and Dora Margolis, the only woman who reciprocates his love. Whereas in some characters it is difficult to find the line dividing material and practical considerations from a passion for learning, Levinsky is a character torn between these two ambitions. To his eternal regret (though regret not strong enough to make him give up his power), he sells out one for the other, rising financially at the expense of his original ambitions and dreams. What makes him sympathetic despite his ideological and moral lapses is that his yearning toward those dreams

26. Anzia Yezierska, *Bread Givers,* 155, 269, 201.
27. Anzia Yezierska, *Red Ribbon on a White Horse,* 76 (hereinafter cited in the text as *Ribbon*).

never really changes; rather, the chasm between what he values and what he has become widens. He begins his story by referring to his metamorphosis as

> nothing short of a miracle: . . . I was born and reared in the lowest depths of poverty and I arrived in America . . . with four cents in my pocket. I am now worth more than two million dollars [in 1917!] and recognized as one of the two or three leading men in the cloak and suit trade in the United States. And yet when I take a look at my inner identity it impresses me as being precisely the same as it was thirty or forty years ago. My present station, power . . . seem to be devoid of significance. (*Rise,* 3)

In the final pages of the novel, he admits his loneliness, saying of immigrants who have distinguished themselves in science, music, or art, "these I envy far more than I do a billionaire" (*Rise,* 529). In his case, it is not education that exacts a cost; it *is* the cost. Financial success and power come at the expense of education; scholarship is bartered for financial success. Levinsky concludes: "I cannot escape from my old self. My past and present do not comport well. David, the poor lad swinging over a Talmud volume . . . seems to have more in common with my inner identity than David Levinsky, the well-known cloak manufacturer" (*Rise,* 530). We must ask, though, how long an "inner" Levinsky can remain so uncontaminated by the outer self who acts—so impermeable, so separate? But the need for that illusion—for that remembered ideal which seems still to hold the promise of some possible future—is genuine, and its impossibility more sad than ironic.

Levinsky remembers the fierce determination of his mother to make a scholar, a fine Jew, of him, and he is haunted by the fears of his rebbe (rabbi) in the Russian town of Antomir when he told him he was going to America: "To America! . . . Lord of the World! But one becomes a Gentile there" (*Rise,* 61). And he remembers his rebbe's expectations: "Be a good Jew and a good man. . . . Do not forget that there is a God in heaven in America as well as here" (*Rise,* 81). But even back in Antomir, his drive to learn had been partly fueled by the desire to be number one, to outstrip others, a competitive spirit his mother also shows ("let our enemies grow green with envy"). The target of his envy is a boy in the yeshiva who is not only rich but has an extraordinary memory. He can recite five hundred leaves of Talmud: "[T]hose 'five hundred leaves' of his gave me no peace. Five hundred! The figure haunted me. Finally I set myself the task of memorizing five hundred leaves" (*Rise,* 45). In America, education (now secular) becomes his goal: he is interested in "business"—peddling—only to live, all the while practicing English and dreaming of furthering his education. His peddler-supplier advises him: "If you want to make a decent living you must put all other thoughts out of your mind and think of nothing but your business" (*Rise,* 105). Yet when he is given a Dickens novel, the first novel he has ever read, he reads it through, struggling with its English, and allows his pushcart business to run itself into the ground.[28]

A friend introduces him to the craft of tailoring, which he regards only as a stepping-stone to a life of the intellect, a way to save money for the university, which he now calls his temple, "the synagogue of my new life" (*Rise,* 169). In the off-season, he studies with a passion. When the businessman he tutors asks him what he intends to do after college, he explains that he wants to become a doctor of philosophy: "I am not going to be a doctor *and* a philosopher, but a doctor *of* philosophy." To which the businessman replies: "I never learned to write, but I have a learned fellow in my office. . . . Yet who is working for whom . . . ?" (*Rise,* 180). (Conversely, Ralph Chang is a Ph.D., but he capitulates to his uneducated friend.) Being bossed becomes so intolerable to Levinsky that he decides to become his own boss. Once he puts his intelligence and drive and energy and time toward that end, his passion for success gains the upper hand over his passion for study. For a while he fools himself—he tells himself he will go to university later—but in retrospect he sees his decision as the tragic destruction of his dream, the betrayal of a sacred mission.

The irony of his decision, and his wealth, is that it was not money or what it could buy that spurred him on. The spirit of competition (not unrelated, of course, to ambition), of challenge, which could have been satisfied in intellectual pursuits, seems a far more potent motivation: "I visioned myself a rich man, of course, but that was merely a detail. What really hypnotized me was the venture of the thing. It was a great, daring game of life" (*Rise,* 189). The impossibility of Levinsky's reconciling his two selves, of ever feeling whole and content, is epitomized by his failure to find the right woman. His only mutual love relationship—with Dora— can never be consummated because she is married and honorable. He has his choice of fine, traditional daughters from prosperous homes, but he is unable to commit himself to them. The women he does admire and yearn

28. Compare Younghill Kang's *East Goes West: The Making of an Oriental Yankee,* in which Kang sees Shakespeare's plays as "a talisman . . . a symbol of the elusive ideal of Western Civilization" (Kim, *Asian American Literature,* 39), but reading Shakespeare loses him jobs, and he becomes too hungry to concentrate on *Hamlet* (Kang, ibid., 30).

for are those who represent intellect, political involvement, or artistic accomplishment, but of course they look down on him. They obviously do not share his view of himself: "I am essentially an intellectual man, I think" (*Rise,* 524).[29]

To Dora, though, he represents not only refinement in contrast with her boorish husband Max, but also learning—Levinsky can read and write English; he has read Dickens and, before coming to America, Tolstoy. On Levinsky's first visit to the Margolis home, Max makes his daughter, Lucy, "test" her mother on spelling for Levinsky's benefit. Both mother and daughter are quick pupils; in fact, a contest has developed between Dora and her "teacher," little Lucy.

> The day when she took Lucy to school—about two years before—was one of the greatest days in Dora's life. She would then watch her learn to associate written signs with spoken words. . . . But that was not all. She became jealous of the child. She herself had never been taught to read even Hebrew or Yiddish, much less a Gentile language, while here, lo and behold! her little girl possessed a Gentile book and was learning to read it. She was getting education, her child, just like the daughter of the landlord of the house in Russia in which Dora had grown up. . . . When the little girl could spell half a dozen English words she hated herself for her inferiority to her. . . . "She'll grow up and be an educated American lady and she'll be ashamed to walk in the street with me." (*Rise,* 242–43)

This is not the same sort of competition that Levinsky had with his yeshiva rival; this is jealousy of one person's literacy on the part of another who desperately wants to be literate. It is also fear on the part of a mother that her daughter, if allowed to outstrip her, will no longer respect her (another example of parental fear in the face of children who, literate in English, assume "adult" roles). And so Lucy has to teach her mother so that Dora will, at the very least, be on her level. Of course, the little teacher is not always

29. Cahan was not Levinsky. His sidelocks were cut long before he came to America, and he had attended a teacher training institute in Vilna (now Vilnius), Lithuania. As editor of the *Jewish Daily Forward,* he became a great influence on Yiddish-speaking immigrants, helping them to become Americans. He deintellectualized the paper so that, with its stories and its Bintel Brief (letters to the editor), it would appeal as well to the poorly educated girls at the sewing machines in New York. In his replies to readers' letters he offered advice on everything from the workplace to a broken heart in a sympathetic but authoritative voice, urging his readers to educate themselves, learn English, become American. He encouraged them to be intellectuals, not just doctors and lawyers (Howe, *World of Our Fathers,* 247).

able to explain things well, and this can lead to disagreeable scenes arising from mutual frustration. Cahan describes, with an almost Dostoevksean intensity, Dora's consuming passion and its effects on her relationship with her daughter:

> Her mother wanted her to go over her last reading-lesson with her, and the child would not do so, pleading a desire to call on Beckie.
> "Stay where you are and open your reader," Dora commanded.
> Lucy obeyed, whimperingly.
> "Read!"
> "I want to go to Beckie."
> "Read, I say." And she slapped her hand.
> . . . "I don't want to! I want to go downstairs," Lucy sobbed defiantly.
> "Read!" And once more she hit her . . .
> Dora did not relent until Lucy yielded sobbingly.
> . . . She beat her quite often, sometimes violently, each scene of this kind being followed by hours of bitter remorse on her part. Her devotion to her children was above that of the average mother. Lucy had been going to school for over two years, yet she missed her . . . as though she were away to another city; and when the little girl came back, Dora's face would brighten, as if a flood of new sunshine had burst into the house. (*Rise, 253*)

What is so moving here is the terrible bind of Dora's ambivalence—the intensity of her love for her daughter, her pride in her accomplishments in school, her hopes for her American future, but at the same time her own desperate need, and her recognition that what is readily available to Lucy will never be possible for her. The never-quite-satisfactory resolution: "She had formed a theory that the child was born to go to school for her mother's sake as well as her own—a little angel sent down from heaven to act as a messenger of light to her" (*Rise, 246*).

So idealized a vision of school could not possibly be sustained in the reality of the classroom, where there were neither cherubs sitting in the rows of little desks nor an angel of mercy at the big desk in front. Certainly there were pupils who were bright and eager to learn and teachers who were selfless, hardworking, and giving, such as Antin's Miss Dillingham and the strict but understanding Miss Doyle in *Jade Peony*. But there were also teachers with little patience, especially for students who looked or talked or thought in ways they had not experienced and were ill prepared to tolerate; in some cases they were simply ill prepared to engage students' interest at the level at which they entered their classrooms. In the literature under discussion, classroom situations are often dramatized—sometimes as comic (Hyman Kaplan's night school, for example), sometimes as touching, and sometimes as painful.

Elaine M. Mar's experience is only one of countless examples of the high emotional costs sustained by immigrant children who must endure that unavoidable period of transition during which they are made to feel stupid by all they do not understand and frustrated by being, in turn, misunderstood. Unfortunately, such difficulties are often compounded by ridicule or rejection they suffer from classmates. Elaine (the American name given to her by her teacher) was tormented on the playground, with children bouncing balls off her and calling her "chink eyes."[30] In one poignant classroom incident, a genuine misunderstanding caused both frustration and ridicule: Elaine was far ahead of the other children in arithmetic, but when the teacher called on her to give the sum of 3 + 4, she was unable to remember the English for "7." Her solution was to write "7" on the blackboard, but when she stood up to do so, the teacher said, "You can't go to the bathroom now," and the class giggled. "I felt trapped inside my body," she writes. "Language seemed a purely physical limitation. Thoughts existed inside my head, but I wasn't able to make them into words" (*Paper,* 66).

There was also an additional burden:

> [I] couldn't explain these difficulties to Mother. Our language didn't leave room for such a conversation: The Chinese don't ask their children, *How was school today?* They say, *What did you learn?* And *Did you understand your lessons?* In Cantonese I could only describe the equations we'd solved that day. I was able to show her my spelling list. And I could honestly say that I *did* understand, on paper at least. It was harder to explain that kids groaned when I was chosen to be "it," that I hated dodgeball, and that I was largely mute. As far as Mother was concerned, the first two complaints were just silly—she didn't send me to school to play with the ghost children. Nor did she view silence as a problem; in our culture, a student *should* be quiet, the better to hear the teacher's wisdom.... Mother created her own homework assignments—shocked that first grade had no homework—to practice calligraphy for hours on end—"First grade, what is this first grade? ... No work at all. You're learning simple addition, how lazy!

30. Elaine M. Mar, *Paper Daughter: A Memoir,* 117 (hereinafter cited in the text as *Paper*).

Why did we come here, to have you learn nothing? . . . in Hong Kong
. . . you'd be learning long division by now, not one plus one. You're
forgetting everything. . . . San doesn't even know multiplication, that's
what America does to children!" (*Paper,* 69–70)

Clearly, Mar's mother was unable, or unwilling, to sympathize with her
daughter's language and social difficulties in school; one reason may have
been her own lack of experience in trying to study and socialize in English, but another reason was surely her very different expectation of
what—and *only* what—school is intended to accomplish. Friends and
games obviously had no place in her "curriculum."

Parental attitudes were different back in the "old country," as Cahan
also shows us in his autobiography. Even a despotic rebbe was respected,
and even a cheder where students were whipped was a "holy place. The
children dare not tell of the punishments and the parents dare not interfere
with the melamed's [teacher's] authority. How can authority be effective
without slaps, pinches, and blows?" (*Education,* 26). The teacher was
revered, and the student's task was to make the most of what the teacher
had to offer. In *Jade Peony,* Wayson Choy writes of Sek-Lung's education
and his family's view of play:

[H]ow foolish to waste away those hours. . . . Though he knew better,
Father saw each of his three sons as Confucian scholars. . . . [I]n Sun
Wu village . . . if a boy was not too poor, after his labours in the family
shop or after his toils on some ancestral field, he looked forward to an
encounter with reading and writing. . . . At least that was what the elders told the Chinatown sons. In old China, no scholarly child actually
played after age six. He put away childish things, found in learning his
recreation and inspiration. "In China," Third Uncle told me, "there was
a poor boy who caught a hundred fireflies and kept them in a jar . . .
so he could have enough light to study at night." I thought it would be
fun to catch the flies, but too much of a strain to read at night.[31]

Teachers can be idealized or demonized, students can be inspired or
disenchanted, and in the books under discussion both sorts of students
and teachers can be found in both the old-world traditional classroom and
the new-world classroom. If the traditional teacher back in the home village has been idealized, as was David Levinsky's beloved Rabbi Sender,
the American scene can represent a fall from grace—replete with the guilt

31. Choy, *Jade Peony,* 186.

of having forgotten or ignored what is sacred and valuable for the "ungodly" pursuits that tempt one here. More often, though, we are given the Hebrew school or the Chinese school as places that students either dread or refuse to take seriously, while the American school is what matters—it is what hurts when the students are embarrassed or unaccepted; it is what seduces when they are welcomed.

Mary Antin's autobiography, *The Promised Land,* provides the most idealized version of this education plot, both with regard to her experiences in the classroom and the lack of conflict in her home. Despite her frustrations with English pronunciation and her stint in the "baby" class, she blossomed in school. Miss Dillingham became her angel and George Washington her new Moses; it was her good fortune that her father's loyalty to the "old" Moses had long been severely compromised. He basked in his daughter's achievements and excused her from earning money so that she could continue her schooling, a decision for which the landlady reproached him bitterly, though the druggist extended him further credit. The goal of the educational system was Americanization, an example of the homogenization, melting-pot metaphor of assimilation, and it found an appreciative pupil in Antin and an appreciative parent in her father.

Pardee Lowe's father, as portrayed in *Father and Glorious Descendant,* was like many immigrant parents: he wanted his son to have an American education whose influence, however, was to halt at the threshold of their home. Just as Father Lowe "was as Chinese in Chinatown as he had been American in East Belleville," Pardee was to behave "Chinese" at home; he was also expected to learn calligraphy and Chinese classics.[32] He began his studies at a "progressive" Chinese school where the ancient classics were ignored in favor of simplified texts and Chinese characters were equated with objects they resembled in nature. After an hour spent on the fundamentals of Chinese language, history, geography, and philosophy, the following two hours, ostensibly devoted to memorizing these lessons, were more often spent "reading Western novels and magazines borrowed from East Belleville's Public Library behind our Chinese textbooks" (*Descendant,* 107–8). How familiar this sounds to those of us who were sent, unwilling, to Hebrew school. Lowe's next school—one that stressed classical education—was run by a teacher who refused to simplify Chinese diction or philosophy: Tutor Chun "prided himself that he had learned it the hard way and . . . it was the only way he would teach it" (*Descendant,* 111). Pardee

32. Pardee Lowe, *Father and Glorious Descendant,* 35 (hereinafter cited in the text as *Descendant*).

spent six years in this school, but again, as with so much after-hours Hebrew education, its students graduated having learned something of ancient texts but unable to speak or write in the language and with little appreciation of its connection to their American selves. Once Pardee began high school, he was faced with the choice to do well in one area or the other, for "students who were outstanding in Chinese classics stood low" in their American classes, and those who excelled in American high school were not the ones who spent their evenings studying Chinese (*Descendant*, 116). America won out.

Like many a cheder rebbe, Tutor Chun was a misfit in this country. Despite the inefficacy of his methods, he "continued blindly to plug us with classical Chinese characters which required a dictionary to decipher. Even when the meaning was clear, it was impossible to bring it down to earth" (*Descendant*, 111–12). We might remember how the oppressive, noisy cheder came to life for Henry Roth's David Schearl when he discovered that a text in Hebrew held *meaning*, when the Hebrew babble became not boring noise, but the call to Isaiah, the prophet's feeling of unworthiness, and his mission. In these examples we can see that, in addition to the pulls exerted by America—with its grade competition, scouting, and athletics—there was that in the traditional school which pushed children away. Some of the teachers should never have been teachers, and even those who had been good teachers in the home country had such lofty standards and so exalted a view of what they had to teach that they were unable to meet their young American charges on common ground. We see this clearly in Reb Pankower's thoughts about David. The pinching, insulting Reb Pankower seems to become a different person when he muses on David's "iron head" and his spiritual potential; once privy to the rebbe's internal monologue, we understand his pain, his fear that his Jewish students will become as nothing in godless America (*Sleep*, 373–76).

Cahan speaks with affection of teachers who did not depend on slaps and blows, in particular, one who taught him Talmud with love and understanding and engaged his mind in ways that trained him well for reasoning in math once he entered the secular world of the Russian gymnasium (*Education*, 72).[33] It is ironic that it was in the secular institutions that lessons were learned by rote and memory, taught by teachers who themselves had learned by the same means; the Talmudic studies that Cahan gave up in favor of the secular had provided much more mental stimulation.

33. For another example of the need for teachers who can meet students intellectually at the level of their questioning, see Antin's *Promised Land;* for a more recent example, see Philip Roth's "The Conversion of the Jews" in *Goodbye, Columbus.*

Once he ceased to be a believer, however, and became acquainted with secular literature, his interest in Hebrew "evaporated" and his Russian studies became all-consuming (*Education,* 78).

The lure of the modern world, whether in Vilna, Paris, or New York, whether focused on material or intellectual wealth, proved irresistible to many and forced radical choices on those who were not prepared for them within their own traditions. Cahan, through Levinsky, expresses the failure of his orthodox faith to "trim its sails" to fit the winds of the modern world. Jews of his "type" and origin had not learned to "bend" so that their faith would not "break." As Levinsky tells it: "The very clothes I wore and the very food I ate had a fatal effect on my religious habits. A whole book could be written on the influence of a starched collar and a necktie on a man who was brought up as I was" (*Rise,* 110). Such a strict dichotomy between the ways of the shtetl and the ways of New York accounts for Levinsky's inability to believe that his fiancée's brother, who looks and acts so modern, so American, can possibly be learning Talmud properly. "That an American school-boy should read Talmud seemed a joke to me." But Levinsky finds that the boy, Rubie, is "reading the text and interpreting it in Yiddish precisely as I should have done. . . . He even gesticulated and swayed . . . as I used to do. To complete the picture, his mother, watching him, beamed as my mother used to. . . . I was deeply affected" (*Rise,* 397–98).

What we would call the middle ground, finding one's place or identity between two worlds, knitting them, weaving them, or falling in confusion between them (one's choice of metaphor can be revealing) is precisely what I am discussing in this book. Rubie is on his way to succeeding, Levinsky is failing, and somewhere between the two poles of total assimilation and total rejection of the new culture we will find almost every bicultural protagonist. Each has somehow to wrestle with this issue anew, find his or her own way of negotiating this betweenness that is always in process, never quite uniform from one context to another. So often, as evidenced in these texts, school—its content, its method, its teachers—is the site of the most powerful contestation. As we have seen, students often have to bear the pain of teachers who do not understand them—their language or their needs—and some who do not care to try.[34] (Immigrant and colonial literatures are rife with stories of children who are slapped for speaking languages other than English.) But it is also evident that rejection

34. The library at Ellis Island has many moving examples of both the pain and the joy of immigrants facing American schools. Some of these interviews are available on tape; some have been transcribed.

from without is not the only problem. Much more difficult to deal with can be the fears that students bring to school, the limitations and differences their "foreignness" creates, and the way those differences between home and school create conflict in the minds and homes of students.

The gaps widened as the level of education increased. As Vivian Gornick tells it in *Fierce Attachments:*

> Benign in intent, only a passport to the promised land, City [College] of course was the real invader. It did more violence to the emotions than . . . Mama . . . could have dreamed possible . . . provoked and nourished an unshared life inside the head that became a piece of treason. I lived among my people, but I was no longer one of them. I think this was true of most of us at City College. . . . [S]ecretly we had begun to live in a world inside our heads where we read talked thought in a way that separated us from our parents. . . .

> [Mama] would shout at me. "What *are* you talking about? Speak English, please! We all understand English in this house." . . . Wasn't she pleased that I could say something she didn't understand? Wasn't that what it was all about?[35]

Even when there is no open conflict, a student whose education is taking her farther and farther away from a common language with her family feels both loss and resentment. Elaine Mar writes of such distancing as she felt it at Harvard: "I called home every Sunday, just to check in. The conversations were always the same, always five minutes long: *'How's the weather? Are you eating enough? What are you eating? Do you understand your lessons?'* I wanted to tell my parents about my revelations, but I didn't have the language for it. How could I describe my essay on Narcissus as metaphor for the artist?" (*Paper,* 273).

Here again we see the conflict of a Chinese daughter to be simply a more heightened, more dramatic, form of what many college students go through when their education, or form of education, or chosen discipline, is not within the experience of their parents. Witness what Peggy Johns, a mainstream American student in my Immigrant Experience class, wrote in response to some of the texts we had read:

> Because I study both theater and English, I spend many hours alone working. In theater the work is done in the preparation, not the performance. English is the same. I sit alone wrestling with a book and

35. Vivan Gornick, *Fierce Attachments,* 105, 108.

finally come to a startling revelation only to write it down, but not discuss it with anyone. Last Christmas I went home wanting to share so
much with my family. How could I expect them to understand a connection that I had made between a character I was playing and a novel
I was reading for a class? But I did expect them to understand, and for
a while I was angry and hurt that they wouldn't or couldn't share my
excitement. How dare my parents see a play that I had worked months
on—spending entire nights unable to sleep because I was obsessed
with a particular moment in the piece—how dare they say afterwards
in the lobby: "How did you memorize all those lines?" I spent a lot of
time feeling guilty because I was angry with them for not understanding.

And yet, her parents had crossed the country to see her performance, and
took great pride in her—more fuel for guilt. After describing a moving dialogue with her mother, Peggy concluded: "I understood for the first time
that I would have to give up a part of myself to continue to learn and
grow. I wanted to hold on to it so badly, but I knew I couldn't. I cried all
the way to Cleveland."[36] No villains here, but education as "immigration"—to the academy, to the arts, to adulthood—a "moving away" from
home that will develop into loving visits back and forth, but only visits,
nevertheless.

Kingston's first classes had no villains either, but her own self-
consciousness silenced her, and she "flunked kindergarten" because she
never opened her mouth. She writes: "My silence was thickest—total—
during the three years that I covered my school paintings with black
paint." Her teachers *were* concerned, and called her parents to school:
"The teachers pointed to the pictures and looked serious, talked seriously,
too, but my parents did not understand English" (*Warrior,* 165). Still, it was
at school that she was praised and made to feel esteemed, not at home,
and because she did not sufficiently understand the "Chinese-ness" of not
praising one's children, she thought it was only at school that she was valued, which, of course, made her resent her parents. The greater resentment was still to come, expressed at a later time but obviously long
accumulated within: "I flunked kindergarten because you couldn't teach
me English, and you gave me a zero IQ.[37] I've brought my IQ up, though.

36. Peggy Johns, untitled essay in *The Immigrant Experience: Voices and Visions,*
ed. Lisa Chiu, Judith Oster, et al., 75–76.
37. Amy Tan writes of the way "home" English can lower SAT verbal scores and of
the way Asian students are thus often steered into math and science, which is what almost happened to her ("Mother Tongue," 181). See also Morrison G. Wong's comment
above in note 24.

. . . And at college I'll have the people I like for friends. . . . I don't care if they were our enemies in China four thousand years ago. . . . I'm going to college. And I'm not going to Chinese school anymore." But no one was trying to stop her. As her mother reminded her: "What makes you think you're the first one to think about college? I was a doctor. I went to medical school" (*Warrior*, 201–2).

This was not always the case. We read of others whose parents—whether because of financial hardship, gender bias, or ideology—fought their "Americanizing" children who wanted to acquire more education. Fathers in Yezierska's narratives fear American education for all three reasons. "Pfui on your education! What's going to be your end? A dried up old maid?" This is the reaction of Reb Smolinsky when Sara turns down an eligible suitor.[38] Yezierska's own father was hurt by her pursuit of what he saw as the wrong education and the wrong goals, and by her having written *Bread Givers,* whose ugly portrait of a father wounded him deeply, as Yezierska recounted in her autobiography:

> "What is it I hear? You wrote a book about me?" His voice and the sorrow in his eyes left me speechless. "How could you write about some one you don't know?"
>
> "I know you," I mumbled.
>
> "Woe to America!" he wailed. "Only in America could it happen— an ignorant thing like you—a writer! What do you know of life? Of history, philosophy? What do you know of the Bible, the foundation of all knowledge? . . . If you only knew how deep is your ignorance. . . . My child!" His eyes sought mine, as if something in me had touched him. "It says in the Torah: He who separates himself from his people buries himself in death." (*Ribbon*, 216–17)

Yezierska's stories are filled with characters who leave the old neighborhood only to feel torn, lonely, and guilty like ungrateful and neglectful children, who cannot be happy anywhere else—much, it seems, like Yezierska herself. In *Hunger of Memory*, Richard Rodriguez writes of the unanticipated costs of education, the price paid by families who feel estranged from their educated children because they no longer have much in common; success even in lower school can cause conflicts when a child's love for school and teacher threatens the harmony and stability of the family. The pain of rejection and the fear of sounding stupid or foreign was for many easier to bear than the conflict engendered by education.

38. Yezierska, *Bread Givers,* 205.

The conflicts in Jade Snow Wong's 1945 autobiography, *Fifth Chinese Daughter,* are mild in comparison to Yezierska's, but they are by no means absent, and they take varied forms. Mr. Wong wanted his daughter to go to school and learn American ways; he was not so afraid of foreign influence that he wanted her to stay away from American schools. Nor did he object in principle to education for a girl; it was only an expensive college education that he was unwilling to provide for her. He could not afford to educate both his son and his daughter, and it seemed more important to spend his money on one, as he put it, who would "perpetuate our ancestral heritage by permanently bearing the Wong family name and transmitting it through their blood line . . . make pilgrimages to ancestral burial grounds and preserve them forever. Our daughters leave home at marriage to give sons to their husbands' families to carry on the heritage for other names." Jade Snow was educated enough to become a stenographer—which was more educated than most Chinese girls of that time—but Older Brother was to be a doctor. At that, Jade Snow for the first time felt bitterness toward her father: "Perhaps I have a right to want more than sons! I am a person, besides being a female!" Determined, she took jobs cleaning houses and began her higher education, even though she had to compromise on a cheaper junior college for the first two years.[39] In the persons of Mr. Wong and his daughter, the motives for education are clearly delineated: it was practicality that finally convinced Mr. Wong to allow Jade Snow to go to college; it would afford her more job opportunities. Jade Snow's priorities were just the reverse: jobs enabled her education. She thirsted for knowledge without regard to its instrumental value. Ironically, her career as a ceramist evolved from her most "liberal," seemingly least practical, college course—Art Studio.

Happily for the family, there was no conflict over the relative importance of Chinese and American educations: from the time Jade Snow was very young, Mr. Wong taught her Chinese history, reading, and writing. She not only went to Chinese school but, unlike Pardee Lowe, also long considered it more important than her American schooling, as she planned to "return" to China (before World War II made that an impossibility). Conflicts

39. Jade Snow Wong, *Fifth Chinese Daughter,* 108–10 (hereinafter cited in the text as *Daughter*). It must be acknowledged how exceptional it was at that time for a Chinese woman to go to college. In 1940, American-born Chinese men had an average of 6.2 years of education compared to 8.3 years for their counterparts in the general population; American-born Chinese women had 8.6 years compared to 8.5 years for their counterparts in the general population (Takaki, *Strangers,* 265, 260), but these figures reflect high-school, not college attendance. Mr. Wong was also not typical: he was a businessman and a Christian.

arose in more subtle ways: it was not *what* Jade Snow was taught in college but *how* she was taught that created distance from her family; she was encouraged to think more independently and to examine assumptions she had always taken for granted. The first such "revolution" in her thinking came when her sociology teacher "shatter[ed] her Wong-constructed conception of the order of things" by stating: "Parents can no longer demand unquestioning obedience from their children. They should do their best to understand. Children also have their rights." All that day, Jade Snow "was busy translating the idea into terms of her own experience. . . . Could it be that Daddy and Mama, although they were living in San Francisco in the year 1938, actually had not left the Chinese world of thirty years ago? . . . Was it possible that Daddy and Mama could be wrong?" (*Daughter,* 125). Predictably, her professor's theory did not sit well with her parents when she tried to act on it:

> "A little learning has gone to your head! How can you permit a foreigner's theory to put aside the practical experience of the Chinese, who for thousands of years have preserved a most superior family pattern? Confucius had already presented an organized philosophy of manners and conduct when foreigners were unappreciatively persecuting Christ. . . . You think you are too good for us because you have a little foreign book knowledge." (*Daughter,* 128–29)

Mills College was to take Jade Snow's habits of mind to a new plane. There she discovered that although she had been exposed to some new ideas, and much knowledge, she had not really been expected to think independently or analytically, or to express her ideas. One of her instructors insisted on a "conversational" method, "to develop your minds, not to give you a set of facts" (*Daughter,* 162). The single essay question on his exam left her floundering amid her memorized dates, names, and places. "In the ensuing hour, her heretofore unshaken faith in the effectiveness of the Chinese study method collapsed entirely." Over the term, she began to learn how to analyze, evaluate, and express what she thought. "Her mind sprang from its tightly bound concern with facts and the Chinese absolute order of things, to concern with the reasons behind the facts, their interpretations and the imminence of continuous change" (*Daughter,* 163).[40]

40. Gish Jen's Mona, raised both Chinese and Catholic, explains what is, to her, an important attraction of Judaism: "I like it that you tell everyone to ask, ask, instead of just obey, obey. I like it that people are supposed to be their own rabbi, and do their business directly with G-d. I like it that they're supposed to take charge of their own religion, and they even get to be general-rabbi-for-a-day when they get bar and bas mitz-

But she also learned to keep home and school in separate compartments of her life. When her professor arranged to bring the class on a field trip to her father's factory, she found herself feeling suddenly estranged, "observing the scene with two pairs of eyes—Fifth Daughter's, and those of a college junior" (*Daughter,* 165).

In reality, such "twoness" had begun long before, when her kind, blond teacher comforted her on the playground by putting her arms around her, something her parents did not do. It was her first lesson, and an uncomfortable one, that American ways were different from Chinese ways and would involve her in a choice. The differences in educational philosophy were also becoming clear, if not analyzed, even when she was learning to draw in elementary school: "Daddy had severely nipped her early efforts to draw pictures instead of square characters. 'You can learn nothing from your own pictures,' he had reprimanded. Now in the low-third grade she was encouraged to draw. She decided that the American school was going to be continuously different in more and more ways from Chinese studies and that there would be little point in wondering why" (*Daughter,* 18).

Wong's conflict between two educational philosophies that are based, as such philosophies always are, on fundamental values in their societies, is not simply typical of the 1930s. We all know the bright freshman who excels in objective test-taking but is frustrated when she is not given a specific question to respond to. (Equally telling is the student in an introduction-to-literature class who suddenly feels liberated when the teacher does not impose a single reading on a poem.) It is when we try to stimulate engagement of both mind and feeling in our less experienced students, and ask that they express the results of such engagement in conversation and essays, that we may encounter the most resistance. William C. Perry, studying ethical and intellectual growth in Harvard students over the four years of their degree programs, developed a scale ranging from dualistic thinking (right/wrong; the Teacher has the Answers) through increased relativism and on to the realization that teachers and students alike are continuously searching for truth, for answers, and that professors invite students into a community of seekers. Not surprisingly, the humanities, especially the study

---

vahed. In the Catholic church, you know, you're always keeping to your place and talking to God through helpers" (*Mona,* 34). Compare Cahan's complaint about his Russian institute's rigid methods of teaching and learning by rote amd memorization with his description of the yeshiva in *The Rise of David Levinsky,* where Talmud studies were not only about, but conducted through, disputation (*Education,* 111–14, 124; *Levinsky,* 27–29). Of course, the disputation stayed within the bounds of the religious life, and it was only open to males. See also my "'God Loves Stories,' Jews Love Questions."

of literature, posed the greatest problem for the "dualists."[41] These students do not represent our highest values in independent thinking, and they tend not to be the ones who have attended America's finest prep schools.

However, I have taught students from other cultures who have had the best schooling that their countries offer; who have mastered a great quantity of material and arrive here far ahead of American students in math, for example; who have an impressive command of English and top scores, yet who are classic examples of Perry's dualists—more rigid in their thinking, even, than those in his study. They are armed with superb memories and a readiness to receive the best possible education they can at the hands of Teachers they would not dream of arguing with. I had the privilege—and challenge—of working with two such students who took courses with me over the years of their undergraduate education, beginning with freshman composition and on through courses in literature. George was an international student from a top school in Hong Kong (which meant that his problems in language were minor); James was an immigrant from Taiwan, who had come to the U.S. at the age of fourteen and succeeded brilliantly in math, but suffered language difficulties for years. They graciously allowed me to interview them and to present the results of our conversations,[42] which are not only relevant to the issues faced by Jade Snow Wong, but are also, once again, a more sharply dramatized, more extreme and obvious example of what we see in so many mainstream students. To hear their voices is to better understand how conflicting and painful the educational process can be even for the brightest bicultural students.

These students (who were eventually to describe the experience of their freshman course as a "breakthrough," as "the first time I really touched American education") both confessed to having thought at first: "This is not a class. I am learning nothing." George, who prided himself on "testing" all his teachers in Hong Kong and who assumed that the purpose of an English class was to produce facts and accuracy, had trouble assessing the class. He hadn't learned many facts in our discussions of literature ("If they are not facts what are they?"). On whether I passed his "test," he said:

41. William C. Perry, *Forms of Intellectual and Ethical Development in the College Years: A Scheme.* Perry outlines ten positions in intellectual and ethical maturity; the major breakthrough (position 5 on the scale, with hardly anyone going beyond 8) occurs when relativism is seen as a way of thinking about problems.

42. The papers presented were "Rigidity→Resistance→Emergence: A Chinese Engineer Becomes a Writer," TESOL (Teachers of English to Speakers of Other Languages) international convention, San Francisco, March 1990, and "What ESL Students Can Teach Us about Perry and Iser," Conference on College Composition and Communication, Boston, March 1991.

"[It] seems the questions I asked you ... I couldn't confirm your answer because the thing you told me doesn't appear in the book. I don't know where you learned those. . . . I usually look for material that are printed in books. What you told me couldn't be proved on paper." He also confessed: "A class like yours make me very uneasy because it requires some thought, requires probably more creativity. We must hook up to the subject the others were discussing. It required more mental activities. The way I thought was different back in Hong Kong—not so much imagination and creativity." George, an electrical engineering major, ended up taking a number of courses in English. He wrote poetry, learned to analyze literature in sophisticated ways, and went on to earn a master's degree in journalism at a top school, after which he became a writer at Bell Labs.

James was able to be more analytical about the problem my course was posing:

> A typical example will be my chem lab. I had lots of conflicts between Western education and Oriental education, and some things [that] really bother me will be exactly similar things. . . . In Taiwan we supposed to listen exactly what instructor say . . . and do exactly whatever we supposed to do. We are not even have to touch the equipment, we are not allowed to. . . . If I do something for myself I probably kick out of the class. . . . Here I have freedom. Of course I have a lot of responsibility. When I step in . . . I keep waiting for instruction. And it took me at least two or three years to recognize this problem. And I started to realize that, *aha*, that's a difference between Oriental and America. [In literature and writing classes there] we just memorize the whole thing . . . all you have to do is memorize exactly, and that's why I kinda mixed up myself. I get lost myself because I try to memorize and then I realize it's impossible to memorize it, and then I say, if I don't memorize it, what shall I do?
>
> The author . . . never say anything about his personal opinion, but he makes the readers to think a lot of things. And that's why I want it, okay? And then the same, you. I realized you try to tell me something . . . but I just can't figure it out, it's so unclear to me . . . the whole method. So brand new. I never had that kind of teaching before.

It was not that I was holding out on James, but rather that I was telling him there was no simple answer to his open-ended questions. I was attempting to draw out student responses to stories that were also "open," that required more from the reader. Notice the analogy James drew between what the texts required of a reader and what the class required of a student, the way the reading experience brought him to a greater under-standing of the learning experience and of the educational philosophy underpinning it. At first he thought he was learning nothing, but, as he put it: "[S]uddenly . . . I started to realize that I know how to think . . . to orga-nize. And that's a learning. That's a different kind of class . . . today you say something here, and tomorrow you come up with something else, and then I try to focus it. . . . And that's why I wanted to know *so badly.* Because once I figure it out, I'm gonna figure out lots of things for my life . . . a general solution that applies to lots of questions." He claimed that everything began to improve—chemistry, social adjustment, even his way of analyzing his family problems: "The way I view things is more clear." It seemed to me that one transferable skill he was talking about was an atti-tude toward problem solving, a strategy of defining problems and seeking solutions. His own metaphor—what he termed a "scientific example"—for this transfer says it best: "[L]ike the atomic bomb—it's very difficult to acti-vate one electron to explode, but once it explodes, it keeps exploding, keeps exploding. All I have to do is get it to explode. That's why I kept thinking."

What these two students dramatized most poignantly, though, was the unease, the pain and struggle, that was the cost of this "brand new," "dif-ferent" educational experience.[43] George said in his freshman year: "If a person thinks frequently, he may sometimes get lost in the thinking pro-cess, and I don't think that would be a good process in his development . . . because there is nothing solid to grasp, which will give him a sense of insecurity. So if I continue to think in that way I might get lost. I think it's essential to stick on something solid—a solid idea." In a similar vein, James spoke of the feeling he had initially had of "floating."

While these students provide the examples, and Perry a schema of stages, Wolfgang Iser, whose works do not deal at all with pedagogy but with theories of reader response, nevertheless gave me the clearest insight into what George and James were going through. In his analyses of the phenomenology and act of reading, he details what must go into the "pro-

---

43. Perry is right when he points out: "The most difficult instructional moment for student and teacher occurs at the transition from the conception of knowledge as a quantitative accretion of discrete rightness to the conception of knowledge as the qual-itative assessment of contextual observations and relationships. In approaching this point of transition the student generally misconstrues what his teacher is doing, and both suffer. It is a crucial moment; and for intelligent action, the teacher requires the clearest understanding of his, and the student's predicament. . . . The good teacher be-comes one who supports in his students a more sustained groping, exploration, and synthesis" (*Forms of Intellectual and Ethical Development,* 210–11).

duction" of a reading when texts are "indeterminate": the reader must "wander" backward to what has been read in order to readjust it in light of the newest information and forward to what is anticipated, which, of course, will require modification in light of what is actually written in the text. In tension with this wandering viewpoint is what Iser terms consistency building, the impulse to synthesize and seek consistency, a vital aspect of the reading process. The security of consistency, though, must be deferred in such texts; readers (and students *are* readers) must be willing to defer resolution, to live a while with ambiguity, and remain flexible as each page requires modification of assumptions previously made. When this process is combined with affect—the reader empathizing or identifying with characters or situations in the text—the urgency to resolve it is intensified, and the reader becomes entangled (Iser's term) in the text, both intellectually and emotionally. Iser speaks of texts "shattering" a reader's frames of reference, of emerging from a reading as if "awakening back into the real world," viewing the text "as a thing freshly understood." When this new understanding forces a reader to question her previously held values, the result can be open rejection of the book, and, I would add, of the teacher, process, or course that has required the reading.[44]

While such experiences can be exhilarating, they can also be threatening, especially when they are unfamiliar. Texts that can have such an effect and require such a process leave what Iser terms gaps that the reader must fill in order to derive or create meaning from them; in entering into these gaps, in attempting to close or fill them, readers thus become producers or performers of the text. As a reader becomes more and more absorbed in what he himself has been made to produce, as he combines what is given with what must be inferred or imagined, he cannot help but be affected by his own production. He has become one with the text, for the time being; the reader, "in constituting the meaning, is also constituted."[45] Or perhaps we should say *re*constituted. Someone like George, who has heretofore believed in the concept of a closed-in, bounded, fixed and determined self, will fear its erosion. When George realized he was "more susceptible to others' ideas," he felt it to be a sign that he was deteriorating, losing self-confidence. Ironically, what many would regard as growth was not yet seen or felt that way by the person whose rigidity was crumbling before a new strength had formed. At that point he could not know that he would be feeling more confident—able to argue with critics, able to read with

44. Iser, *Act of Reading,* 140, 202.
45. Ibid., 140, 150.

greater openness still other texts, even those nonprint, nonliterary texts of
real characters and real situations.

James eventually found his literary and writing experiences to have
been beneficial in the real world:

> Even my own parents, they make mistakes. . . . I realize that I make
> some mistakes. . . . [T]hat story made me realize that there is nothing—
> nothing, I would say not a single thing—[that] is definitely good, or
> definitely bad or definitely right or definitely wrong [the midpoint in
> Perry's scheme—relativism that precedes a concomitant commitment],
> and that's what made me feel more comfortable . . . that's why I love
> the story so much . . . I realize that it's not everything totally wrong, it's
> not everything totally right make me really calm, and I say, well, *try to
> stretch as much as you can* . . . that's why I feel more positive, more
> comfortable. (Emphasis mine)

James spoke of his parents' mistakes and, yes, the conflicts and resentments that he was feeling, but at the same time of his newly developing
ability to distance himself from them even if just momentarily, to see himself and these issues more calmly—how similar this sounds to Maxine's
getting herself "out of hating range" so that she can return home in peace
and calmly communicate her feelings to her mother. What is this distance
she travels that takes her out of hating range? Surely it is not only spatial.
That it is the distance of time, of further maturation as well, seems obvious. But I would suggest still another "distancing" range: her education,
experience with the process I have been discussing, a reading (and analytical) process that enlarged her perspective and that gave her the same
sort of double vision Jade Snow experienced when she accompanied her
classmates to her father's place of business, and that must also have given
her the ability to "read" her family differently and with greater understanding, even as she might still be smarting under hurts that are too close to be
read.

I would go farther and posit that many such acts of reading, many such
constructions of self into text, might have aided that construction and
transmutation of self into text that became her writing. Even George and
James, on their own, began to write about their own experiences, their
family struggles—in George's case, his anger at (and his grief over) his father's death. The decontextualizing and recontextualizing that can be exciting or disturbing ("shattering"), or both, as one constitutes self while
constituting meaning in a reading has the potential as well for constructing
meaning and self in texts yet to be written. The educations that cost so

dearly paid great rewards for the students, not only, as their parents hoped, in career opportunities, but also in new ways of seeing those parents, of seeing their own cultures. Paradoxically, that which had the power to alienate had, in a new way, facilitated a return. That the authors and students we have been "hearing" could "read" their lives, families, and cultures anew and write about them provided not only distance, but structure. To write is to form, even if the form is imposed and even if ragged reality eludes it. I think we can assume that education, whether in classes or libraries, enabled these authors to become creative and productive readers, who, having written themselves into so many texts as readers, also began to write the texts of themselves. Words on paper become in some measure separated from the inner worlds that give rise to them, so that fashioning and constructing selves and lives can give authors greater distance and more perspectives from which they are able to see themselves and their lives newly—more coherently and more peacefully. In the next chapter we will look more closely at these tensions and that process: at the autobiographical act and the texts that emerge from it.

7

Writing the Way Home

For the writer who is forming not only a text but a bicultural identity (especially one who is still asking "Where do I belong?"), the page might very well be the place where she feels most "at home." For me, Sandra Cisneros expresses this connection best: "Only a house quiet as snow, a space for myself to go, clean as paper before the poem." This is Esperanza's wish at the end of *The House on Mango Street;* in connecting house and paper, she implies that her home can be the page. Mango Street—its impermanence, its disappointing inadequacy, its surroundings—cannot "hold [her] with both arms" once she "put[s] it down on paper."[1] We assume she will now be in charge, will make a home for herself regardless of where it happens to be or how much rent she can afford.

The page as home, and the act of writing as a way of finding one's place, has surely helped Eva Hoffman, too, to feel "at home." "I am here now": So Hoffman ends her struggle to find "a life in a new language." "Here" is a garden in Boston, and "now" the time she feels herself finally to have arrived. But "here" is also a location on a page, and not just any page, but the final one in her autobiography. "Now" is also the final moment of her writing (or at least the reader's sense that it is, as well as the reader's final moment sharing Hoffman's experience). Hoffman concludes her book almost with the same sentence that opens Czeslaw Milosz's essay "My Intention." It was from him that she drew the inspiration to use it as her focal point.[2] Her book is a journey—in space, time, and print—to arrive at that point; as opening words, though, "now" must point backward

---

1. Sandra Cisneros, *The House on Mango Street,* 108, 110.
2. Czeslaw Milosz, *To Begin Where I Am: Selected Essays* (New York: Farrar, Straus, and Giroux, 2001), 1; Hoffman, lecture. Milosz's opening sentence is "I am here."

to "then," and "here" to "there." In either case, such declarations are hard-won; such words on a page most likely have been—or will be—earned by all the other pages in the book. And the reader senses that what it took to write that book was no small part of being able to utter a sentence at once so simple and so forceful.

Hoffman's words help me to look backward and forward in this study: back to all the *heres*, *theres*, *nows*, and *thens* through which every protagonist we have discussed has had to navigate in order to move toward "I am"—be it declared, interrogated, or sought. Back to those elements of bicultural identity construction: self-image(s), language(s), traditions and stories old and new, education(s). Back to the rending and mending at work in those pluralities, and the ways in which facing and communicating those tensions have aided, often painfully, in approaching "I am." Forward to focus more pointedly on the act of self-narration, drawing more fully on ways theorists of autobiography view such constructions (identities *and* texts, identity-forming through text-forming) and to examine narratives through those lenses. The motives and acts of self-narration have already been seen as a "doublement" of the "I" in time or imagining, as a reconciling of past with present and of an internally viewed self-image with an external one; let us revisit them in contexts other than self-imaging, taking into consideration factors underlying and inseparable from such reconciliation.

While Cisneros suggests the page as a new home and Hoffman writes of arriving there, other bicultural writers are in some way returning home, coming home at least to visit, or revisiting places and memories in the attempt to do so. The sense of who I am in bicultural narratives is inseparable from where I am, or have been, or want to go. Crossings, journeys back and forth, chasms, bridges—these are the common and almost unavoidable spatial metaphors that enter into the discussion of who I am and where I belong. I would go so far as to say that the need to reconcile or navigate spaces (literal, emotional, cultural) as well as times, the importance of finding or creating one's place(s), is a distinguishing characteristic of these narratives.

Writing one's way home—whether to create a home on the page, to narrate a journey to the new home, or to narrate one's way back home after a necessary "journey" away (physically, culturally, psychically, or through education)—is also to write of the people there. One's being in relation to those people, the importance of one's relations, and whether relationality is important to the narrative and to the protagonist have been seen in gendered terms, but they can just as well be seen in cultural terms. Paul John Eakin, in *How Our Lives Become Stories: Making Selves,* writes extensively about "relational lives." He invokes Nancy Chodorow's and Carol Gilligan's theories, which posit that women tend to think and make decisions based more on relationality and connectedness than do men, who tend to see themselves more individually, competitively, and hierarchically. Elsewhere, Eakin quotes Joy Hooten's finding that autobiography that is "related rather than single and isolate is . . . the most distinctive difference between male and female life writing."[3] This ties in with what feminist life-writing theorists say of conventional autobiography, based on male models, which tends to be linear and focused on the individual and his achievements. But to see relational writing as "female" is to assume as universal the Western (white, Christian, heterosexual) male life narrative, and to assume that gender, and not just as likely culture, is responsible for these tendencies. We will look at male and female narratives in which relation to family plays a crucial role because the writers come from cultures where family and home are crucial.

What Jerome Bruner says of the importance of place in the life narrative—in this case, in the narratives of men and women in a Brooklyn Italian family—has particular relevance here:

> Place is not simply a piece of geography, an established Italian neighborhood in Brooklyn, though it helps to know its "culture" too. [For his subjects] its central axis is "home," which is placed in sharp contrast to what they refer to as "the real world." They were [from] a "close" family. . . . Consider the psychic geography. . . . "[H]ome" is a place that is inside, private, forgiving, intimate, predictably safe. "The real world" is outside, demanding, anonymous, open, unpredictable, and consequently dangerous. But home and real world are also contrastive in another way . . . home is to be "cooped up," restricted by duties and bored; real world is excitement and opportunity.[4]

Bruner, a narrative psychologist, does not confine his studies to ethnic subjects, but in this case conflicts and issues arise that, while certainly not

3. Hooten quoted in Paul John Eakin, *How Our Lives Become Stories: Making Selves,* 48. Chodorow posits that since female identity is formed in a context of ongoing relationship with primary caretaker/mothers, who experience their daughters as more like and continuous with themselves, and since male identity is formed as separate from the mother, male development entails greater individuation. In girls, the basis for empathy and relationship is built into their definition of self, and thus girls are more likely to see themselves "as more continuous with and related to the external object world and as differently oriented to their inner world as well" (*The Reproduction of Mothering,* 167, 169).

4. Jerome Bruner, "Life as Narrative," 25.

exclusive to "others," are nevertheless more prominent and more deeply conflicted because of "home" and "real world" differences. One feels, therefore, an even greater urgency to try to reconcile or at least to articulate these pluralities.

Also often coded "female" is writing that is nonlinear, more experimental, more reflective, more fragmented. But those qualities, too, may come from an experience of dislocation or betweenness (consider Faulkner in the postbellum South, Joyce in self-exile from Ireland, or Proust) and a need to be more reflective about who and what and where one is. Philip Roth experiments daringly in shifting perspectives, narrative voices and doublings, and structure. Frank Chin blends dreams, history, and the movies. In *A Walker in the City,* Alfred Kazin narrates walks that weave past and present, and divides the book according to locales and their associations, their conflicting pulls. Still, Jan Welsh Hokenson—writing of intercultural autobiographers that each is alone in literary history in creating "an amalgam of two cultures," a bridge spanning a particular individual, "a singular self with uniquely intercultural perspectives and experience"—relates "plurality" of perspective and voice to women's experience and, therefore, their mode of writing (referring specifically to *The Joy Luck Club*).[5]

None of this is to deny what theorists of women's self-writing have discovered, but to notice that marginalization or fragmentation of self or text cannot be seen as exclusively "female." Françoise Lionnet, for example, points out that Montaigne and Nietzsche used fragmentary writing to convey dispersion and dissemination of self in language. She speaks of "women writers who seek modes of discourse which reflect by analogy the traditionally stratified nature of their lives as 'heroines' and as women, lovers, daughters, sisters, mothers, writers." I would say, more explicitly, that those males *and* females who navigate between cultures share plurality and stratification with these "heroines," and share also their ability to see their world from a new perspective, for which, according to Lionnet, "exile and marginality are the necessary preconditions." Often one feels that their narratives arise from the necessity of incorporating their "marginal" perspectives with what they are looking at, or moving into. They bridge, they weave. Lionnet's term *métissage* is perfect—and has multiple meanings—in this context: she explains that it derives from the Latin *mixtus,* which means mixed (literally, a cloth made of two different fibers). While her primary purpose for using this term is to neutralize "racial" mixtures, its relation to living at borderlines, to everything that the metaphor of weaving

5. Hokenson, "Intercultural Autobiography," 99, 101.

implies (including the creation of a work of art or function), makes it most useful for this discussion. Not only do different psychic locations require connection but so do past and present if an identity is to be woven into some sort of whole. When Lionnet speaks of confronting limiting images and stereotypes and suggests finding new directions, she resorts once again to the weaving metaphor: new directions are not to be made out of totally new cloth. One must understand that perceptions of self are influenced by the past; in narrating the self (whether to oneself or publicly) one must weave threads of old stories into new images of one's own, weave texts into and out of a métissage of voices and textures. Of such "weaving" Maxine Hong Kingston is once again a perfect example. Fa Mu Lan, her warrior hero, is, after all, a weaver. Besides, Kingston is well aware that "text" derives from *textus,* another weaving metaphor: "One of the things I wish I'd have said about Fa Mu Lan, the Woman Warrior, was that she was a weaver. . . . Also I love it that the word 'texture,' which has to do with weaving, comes from the same root word as 'text'—'text' in writing. So weaving and writing have a connection."[6]

The subtitle of James Olney's book *Memory and Narrative: The Weave of Life Writing* makes obvious his use of the weaving metaphor to link memory, narrative, and text. He discusses weaving as Augustine's metaphor of memory and as similar to the rumination metaphor used by Augustine for thought and memory, and goes on to elaborate the weaving metaphor's connection to his subjects:

> As weaving has little of the rote about it, so also with memory, which is more imaginative in its operation than mechanical, more adaptive than simply or only reactive. The justification for bringing interpretive practice together with the operation of memory and the making of narrative lies in the Latin *contexto,* "to weave together," which permits us to speak of a text of memory and a text of narrative, both woven forms amenable to interpretive unraveling and reraveling in the pursuit of meaning.[7]

Textures and voices, past and present, home and the world out there woven into identity, into narrative text—that connection of self and self-narration is no longer the province only of literary scholars interested in autobiography. We *live* autobiography, perform it in our daily lives, define

---

6. Françoise Lionnet, *Autobiographical Voices: Race, Gender, Self-Portraiture,* 85, 209, 94–95; Kingston interview in *Conversations,* ed. Skenazy and Martin, 131.

7. James Olney, *Memory and Narrative: The Weave of Life Writing,* 20, 65–66, 419.

and constitute ourselves in the act of narrating ourselves, practice autobi-ography in our inner conversations.[8] While a memory of the past may flash unbidden into a present moment, only tenuously connected or per-haps even unconnected to anything we are presently experiencing, recon-structing it into its original context, or finding it relevant to the present, is an autobiographical act.[9] The "self" that we feel to be continuous and rel-evant over time is established in narrative—"a significant resource for cre-ating our internal, private sense of self." Patricia Meyer Spacks puts this another way: "Man's need to understand his life as a story and his need to tell that story suggest that the subjective faith in continuous personal iden-tity depends on the explanations provided by the imaginative process of story-telling as well as the bare recollections of memory." In anyone's life, "logic seldom emerges in immediate experience. Putting a life into words rescues it from confusion, even when the words declare the omnipresence of confusion, since the act of declaring implies dominance."[10] If this is true in the confusion and illogic of anyone's life and memories, how much more true is it for the person who is constantly made aware of the "dou-bleness" of her identity, her need to span or weave together aspects of her identity and her society (or societies).

Putting a life into words, of course, may take the form of interior mono-logue, stories we tell family and friends, letters, journals, autobiography, or fiction. As theorists such as Bruner, Eakin, and Charlotte Linde remind us, our cultures validate different kinds of narrative; we are immersed in an environment of stories and ways of telling them which provide founda-tions for the narratives we fashion out of fragmentary memories and expe-riences. Mary Antin and Eva Hoffman were provided by their cultures with biblical topoi—promised land, exile, paradise—which, as Sau-ling Cynthia Wong points out, were not the topoi or narratives through which Asian im-migrants saw their journeys to America.[11] But Hoffman, though she alludes to the importance of Antin for her, is not able to write in that mode today. For one thing, she and we realize that the glorified myth of America as Promised Land has been tarnished since Antin left Polotsk; in fact, Antin herself, looking back from the vantage point of turning thirty and having written *The Promised Land,* could no longer see it that way either, even in

8. Eakin, *Lives,* 101, 21; Jill Ker Conway, *When Memory Speaks,* 178.

9. Barrett J. Mandel, "Full of Life Now," 51.

10. Linde, *Life Stories,* 101, 99; Patricia Meyer Spacks, *Imagining a Self: Auto-biography and Novel in Eighteenth-Century England,* 18, 21.

11. Jerome Bruner, "The Remembered Self," 46; Eakin, *Lives,* 52; Linde, *Life Stories,* 47; Sau-ling Cynthia Wong, "Immigrant Autobiography: Some Questions of Definition and Approach," 153–54.

1912. Folk stories and fairy tales we have heard, novels we have read, and plays we have seen provide the narrative and dramatic frames through which we can see in retrospect the "turning points" Bruner speaks of: the conflicts, conquests, and defeats that I-as-hero experience become, in retrospect, constructed dramas in even the most factual recollections. Stories change with circumstances, with interlocutors; they may be of the possible selves we wish or fear to be. Our view of an event may be shaped by the way it can be told; Bruner quotes Henry James as saying, "[A]dventures happen to people who know how to tell it that way," presumably to illustrate the difference between an "adventure" and something that just happens. But, as Leigh Gilmore points out, what inspires autobiographies is often other autobiographies, and those are products of their cultures—the American individualist success, the Christian or intimate confession, the tale of communal exploits rather than internal struggle.[12] Recent literature provides other models, however, and Kingston and Amy Tan, for example, are also members of a literary culture, one that includes modernist and postmodernist texts; Hoffman is clearly well schooled in contemporary theories that ground "reality" in language.

Putting such a life narrative *on paper,* however—hoping to get it between the covers of a book—is obviously a far more consciously structuring act than everyone's daily self-narration. We know that even the most factually faithful life narratives employ selection, heightened drama, the imagined thoughts of others—in other words, fictional techniques. Spacks begins the passage quoted above as follows: "To turn lives into words— *whether those words claim to render fiction or fact*—involves some act of the mind that discovers the logic of happenings in memory or imagination . . . " (emphasis mine). I do not mean to imply that there is no difference between an autobiography and a novel, but I submit that there are genres other than conventional autobiography that render what has been real to an author, that organize into narrative form the issues, feelings, and types of experience that she shares with her protagonist, and that may very well be a way for her to "rescue [her life] from confusion." Gilmore prefers the term *autobiographics,* claiming that autobiographical writing can be expressed in a variety of genres. Olney uses the term *periautog-*

12. Bruner, "Remembered Self," 49–51; James quoted, ibid., 48; Leigh Gilmore, *Autobiographics: A Feminist Theory of Women's Self-representation,* 25. Barrett J. Mandel, while he firmly states that autobiography is not fiction, nevertheless warns that "the problem results from leaving out readers, without whom we are left with a false dichotomy: fiction/non-fiction. We find books cut adrift from the very subjectivity that gives them their reality and without which they are left embalmed forever in dry logic and academic rules, neat but unconvincing" ("Full of Life Now," 55).

raphy—"writing about or around the self"—precisely because of "its *inde-finition* and lack of generic rigor, its comfortably loose fit and generous adaptability."[13] Not only do some of the texts under discussion (*The Woman Warrior,* for example, or autobiographical novels such as Gold's *Fathers*) blur genre boundaries, but one suspects that in some cases writing fiction has been a way to avoid using real people and real events while still writing a book that is heavily invested with the author's experience. This seems to apply to Chinese American narratives, where so few are "autobiographies," yet so many share their authors' situations.[14] One can only assume that writing narratives either of one's own life or of protagonists who share one's culture, environment, and conflicts indeed helps to structure confusion; perhaps it gives them another chance in life, influences their present or gives direction to their future.[15] I would not presume that to be the case as I discuss an author any more than I would presume to decide which incident or character is "true" to an author's life. What I will discuss is the texts themselves, and, where appropriate, comparisons between what their authors have called fiction and what they have called autobiography or biography.

I also want to make clear once more that continuity of a protagonist in a text, as well as the evidence of our own "feeling" of "selfhood," validate for me terms such as *self* and *identity,* given that they are always in process—as Eakin notes, "dynamic, changing, and plural."[16] Were there no such continuity, no relation between past and present, between the narrating self and what happens to that person, we could, as Macbeth hoped to do, pluck out a bad memory or guilty deed. But feelings such as love, loss, loyalty, guilt, and responsibility do continue in us over time, whether we accept what they put on us or not, and putting such feelings into perspective, giving them context or justification or meaning, aids writers—or any of us—to come to terms with ourselves and our worlds.

"And now," as Alexander Portnoy's psychiatrist says, "ve may perhaps to begin." And begin—why not?—with Philip Roth and the evidence in his work of "writing in relation," of coming home, as well as of his excruciating self-consciousness about what it is that a writer such as he is doing.

---

13. Gilmore, *Autobiographics,* 14; Olney, *Memory and Narrative,* xv.

14. See the biographical sketches in Wendy Ho, *In Her Mother's House: The Politics of Asian American Mother-Daughter Writing,* 42–46; see also Janet Handler Burstein on a similar phenomenon in the writings of Jewish American daughters in *Writing Mothers, Writing Daughters: Tracing the Maternal in Stories by American Jewish Women,* 13, 17.

15. Bruner, "Life as Narrative," 20, 31.

16. Eakin, *Lives,* x, 98.

One is struck, in reading bicultural narratives, by how often getting back *to* so often goes together with getting back *at*. Maxine has to clear her throat of the two hundred things on her list, an outburst that precedes a quiet conversation in her bedroom with her mother, and presumably has to precede, as well, the writing of *The Woman Warrior*. Anzia Yezierska's strident narrators shout at genteel teachers and editors who would reject or look down on them, at parents who would stand in the way of their desire to escape and assimilate. In Philip Roth's narratives we read more than once of the dreadful wife, the tortured, inescapable marriage.

Roth's Nathan Zuckerman, author of a *Portnoy*-like novel called *Carnovsky,* sends letter after letter to the critic Milton Appel—manic, Percodan-mad, vengeful diatribes. To Zuckerman, Appel is not just Appel, he is also the rabbis who excoriate Zuckerman for making Jews look bad in his writing. And all of them are also his father, fiercely loyal to the Jews, and his forefathers, the dead in the cemetery, who represent what Zuckerman sentimentalizes: the last generation of old-fashioned men who fathered old-fashioned sons.

> Who that follows us will ever understand how midway through the twentieth century, in this huge, lax, disjointed democracy, a father— and not even a father of learning or eminence or demonstrable power— could still assume the stature of a father in a Kafka story? . . . [W]ithout even knowing it, a father could sentence a son to punishment for his crimes, and the love and hatred of authority could be such a tangled, painful mess.[17]

This driving need to get back—back *to* after all the bad-boy getting back *at,* or simply ridiculing mercilessly—is what Zuckerman sees in the manuscript of Roth's *The Facts: A Novelist's Autobiography*. This book begins with a letter from Roth to his character Zuckerman, asking his opinion, and concludes with Zuckerman's long reply. His judgment: the book is sentimental, needy, and a falling off from the wit, comedy, and vitality of Roth's earlier work. You need me! he tells Roth in no uncertain terms, not only to save himself from extinction, but because through Zuckerman, Roth is liberated, set free to be outrageous. The real Philip Roth confronting an aging father and grieving over his dead mother tries too hard to be "good," and good is just not as much fun, nor, Zuckerman comments,

---

17. Philip Roth, *Zuckerman Bound: A Trilogy and Epilogue,* 686 (hereinafter cited in the text as *Bound*). This book comprises *The Ghost Writer, Zuckerman Unbound, The Anatomy Lesson,* and *The Prague Orgy.*

as honest. There follows some of the best discussion I have ever read on the differences between self-writing in one's "own" voice and fiction. Fiction, Zuckerman claims, has more of the author's real life in it than Roth will ever admit, more conflict, rebellion, and guilt than Roth in his own voice allows his readers to see. Don't publish this, Zuckerman advises. It's inferior to everything else you've done.[18] Roth has asked Zuckerman's opinion, but he doesn't answer him; he just publishes the book anyway, winning the argument over publication, but not necessarily on literary judgment—there, Zuckerman is much more perceptive.

Of course, "Zuckerman" is a fiction Roth has created, setting in motion a mind game he plays with the reader as to who Portnoy/Carnovsky/Zuckerman/Roth really is, ridiculing readers silly enough to ask that question even as he keeps setting us up for it (and he will go on to pit Roth against Roth in *Operation Shylock*). In *Deception,* the character "Philip" complains: "I write fiction and I'm told it's autobiography, I write autobiography and I'm told it's fiction, so since I'm so dim and they're so smart let *them* decide what it is or isn't." In *The Facts,* though, Roth presents a self-critical dialogue: the artist who agrees with Zuckerman in conflict with the son who needs to get his version of himself down—and out.[19] As in his other dialogues of difference—between brothers, between Philip Roths, between fathers and sons—both voices are simply left there, unreconciled, very possibly because they remain so for the writer, whose inner divisions and concerns with large philosophical and political debates must out. The tension between what his characters and his narrative voices represent creates tension as well between text and readers, especially Jewish readers, who bring their own family backgrounds, expectations, embarrassments, fears, and sense of humor (often guiltily indulged) to the text. What Roth does seem to have resolved is that Jewishness—secular, American, forties and fifties Newark, holocaust-affected Jewishness—is central to his being and to his art; he may, nevertheless, like Zuckerman, remain locked in the paradox of being a "Jew set free even from Jews—yet only by steadily

18. Philip Roth, *The Facts: A Novelist's Autobiography,* 161–65, 173, 191, 194 (hereinafter cited in the text as *Facts*).

19. Philip Roth, *Deception,* 190. Roth speaks of "how somebody, in this case me, becomes a writer," and then another voice "comes along that questions . . . the ability of the writer to be revealing in this form." It's the muse saying, "You can't do this, you're better at the other thing." Roth cautions against taking Zuckerman at face value—he has a vested interest, and "makes a good case as to why he's a better vehicle. The autobiography consists in part in the clash of those points of view, of being torn between the facts and the fiction, of being torn between the autobiographical impulse . . . and the fictionalizing impulse to understand something" (interview in *Conversations with Philip Roth,* ed. George J. Searles, 227).

maintaining self-consciousness as a Jew" (*Bound*, 209). In *The Facts* Philip the son recognizes that, more than he ever admitted to himself in his youth, he is the heir of his parents; he has internalized and made art from what they stood for—limited, unsophisticated, and annoying though it might have been, battling it though he does. He recalls a drive that occasioned his father's memories of family struggles, dissension, tragedies, disappointments: "It wasn't exactly the first time I was hearing these stories. Narrative is the form that his knowledge takes, and his repertoire has never been large: family, family, family, Newark, Newark, Newark, Jew, Jew, Jew. Somewhat like mine" (*Facts*, 16).

In his letter to Zuckerman, Roth wonders if "a breakdown-induced eruption of parental longing in a fifty-five-year-old man isn't, in fact, the Rosetta stone to this manuscript" (*Facts*, 9)—a desire to "come home" if ever there was one. For the writer, the path must consist of page after page, filled with words.

But Zuckerman remains skeptical about Roth's idyllic childhood, the paradise of his Weequahic neighborhood, and the flawless, nurturing parents. He senses a huge gap, too much missing: how did that secure boy end up in such a disastrous marriage? What brought him to a psychoanalyst—and what did they actually talk about? How did such a good boy come to write *Portnoy's Complaint*? He finds Roth in his own voice too inhibited. Roth is as aware as any theorist that "the facts are never just coming at you but are incorporated by an imagination that is formed by your previous experience. . . . It isn't that you subordinate your ideas to the force of the facts in autobiography but that you construct a sequence of stories to bind up the facts with a persuasive *hypothesis* that unravels your history's meaning" (*Facts*, 8). In *The Counterlife*, Nathan refers to "that ever-enlarging storage plant for my narrative factory, where there is no clear demarcation dividing actual happenings eventually consigned to the imagination from imaginings that are treated as having actually occurred—memory as entwined with fantasy as it is in the brain."[20] But in *The Facts*, Roth seems to want to set some records straight, to record in his own voice his youth, his hurts, and his loyalties. He also seems to need, in his own voice rather than Zuckerman's, to pay some debts, vent his anger.

So what, then, is Zuckerman? Sander L. Gilman points out: "Zuckerman is not Roth or even a Roth surrogate; he is what his readers expect the author of *Portnoy's Complaint* to be." Alan Cooper calls Zuckerman Roth's alter ego, but goes on to make very clear distinctions between Roth and

---

20. Philip Roth, *The Counterlife*, 264 (hereinafter cited in the text).

his creation.[21] True, they share backgrounds, schools, and incidents; they have written similar books that have provoked similar outcries; they even have some similar brushes with death, marriage, breakdown, and psychiatry. But unlike the Zuckerman of *Zuckerman Unbound,* Roth's mother was not threatened and his father had not died, and his parents expressed only pride in him and defended him and his books loyally. Roth's brother, far from calling him a bastard for portraying their parents as he did, designed the jacket for his first book; he was an artist, not a dentist. As Zuckerman explains: "People don't turn themselves over to writers as full-blown literary characters. . . . Most people (beginning with the novelist—himself, his family, just about everyone he knows) are absolutely unoriginal, and his job is to make them appear otherwise" (*Counterlife,* 156). Gilman posits that "Roth's strategy was the ironic mode: to accept the myth, confess to the charges. Instead of protesting that he was not Jew-hating, family-abusing, and misogynistic, he would let Zuckerman seem to be all those things and induce readers to experience [*Zuckerman Unbound*] as if they were getting the goods on Roth." Zuckerman becomes "unbound" from all his roots—family, neighborhood, Jewish community, in a way that Roth never feels himself to be.[22] (Zuckerman does, though, become bound once again in *The Counterlife,* once he has experienced British anti-Semitism.)

Through Zuckerman, Roth is able to render as exaggerated or comic or absurd the hurts he seems still to be feeling—at his first wife, at Irving Howe for an essay that criticized him, at the rabbis and hostile audience he faced at Yeshiva University. But it is Zuckerman who vents his rage so obsessively, and whose pain, in *The Anatomy Lesson,* becomes so all-absorbing as to turn into a metaphor of entrapment, the crippling entrapment of unrelieved self-absorption that is the pain's inevitable consequence. Or has the pain been its cause? Well-meaning comforters suggest to this Job that his suffering has been brought upon him by the sins he committed in

21. Gilman, *Jewish Self-Hatred,* 355; Cooper, *Roth and the Jews,* 179. Roth himself has said: "Nathan Zuckerman is an act. . . . Making fake biography, false history, concocting a half-imaginary existence out of the actual drama of my life *is* my life" (interview in *Conversations,* ed. Searles, 166–67).

22. Gilman, *Jewish Self-Hatred,* 186–87. One need only read Roth in his own voice to see how connected he is to his Jewish roots and community, how serious, at bottom, is his comedy. He has written: "I have always been far more pleased by my good fortune in being born a Jew than my critics may begin to imagine" (*Reading Myself and Others,* 20). When he taught an English course on guilt and persecution, he emphasized the comedy in Kafka's "morbid preoccupation with punishment and guilt" (ibid., 21–22). More recent has been his mission to publish the works of Eastern European writers and his friendship with and interviews of writers like Aharon Appelfeld (collected in *Shop Talk: A Writer and His Colleagues and Their Work*).

treating his parents so shamefully. His father has died with a word on his lips that *may* have been "bastard," a possible accusation that leads Zuckerman's brother, Henry, to call him a murderer. Later, when his mother dies, Henry uses the opportunity to eulogize her for over an hour, presumably to assure readers so naive and ignorant as to confuse fiction with real life that she was in no way like Carnovsky's mother (*Bound,* 450).

The parents Roth describes in *The Facts,* though, bask in their son's glory, enjoying their celebrity status in Florida among fellow Jews from New York and New Jersey. And yet couldn't there have been those who wondered how much like Sophie Portnoy Mrs. Roth really may have been? How different *were* they from the parents who sent Alex to Dr. Spielvogel? How similar were their chauvinism, their pride, and their ghetto fears? We may ask to what extent Zuckerman liberated Roth by absorbing so much of the guilt for any embarrassment he may have caused his parents, not to mention the pain they must have suffered at his choice of a wife—not only a *shiksa* but a pathological lower-class parasite who, it didn't take a mother's instinct to see, would ruin their son's life.

Even Appel/Howe seems to be an internalized voice of Zuckerman/ Roth.[23] "Je m'appelle Appel," Zuckerman says (*Bound,* 579)—echoing Flaubert's statement "Emma Bovary, c'est moi," which could be Roth's realization as well regarding the voices he sets in counterpoint. Appel and all the Jewish dead have their hold on Zuckerman. Zuckerman gets his jaw broken at a cemetery as he crazily attacks yet another old Jewish father. His mouth—that trouble-making mouth—is wired up so that he cannot speak, and he is forced to do what he thought he had foresworn—write. It is Zuckerman, not Roth, that this has happened to, but what these voices and actions represent are surely Roth's demons and inspirations. It is Roth who has written of them; it is Roth who wrote Zuckerman's criticism of his failure to include enough explanation, enough of what lay inside, in a book he called *The Facts.* Perhaps, as with many another novelist, and as Zuckerman points out, more of that is in the fiction, *un*factual though it may be. We have no reason to doubt Roth's word that Alex Portnoy's feelings of restriction and suffocation were inspired by the writings of Roth's Jewish students in a writers' workshop,[24] but we may also suspect that something in Roth caused him to respond to them as he did, to incorporate those feelings in his creation of Portnoy.

And so the need to "come home," to write his way home, as Roth does

---

23. Cooper, *Roth and the Jews,* 195.
24. Roth, *Reading Myself,* 39, 142–43.

not only in *The Facts,* but more movingly, more "relationally," in *Patri-mony: A True Story.* In reading *Patrimony* we can really believe, finally, that Zuckerman is not Roth. Here is a son whose grief and agony over his father's brain tumor can make us weep, who seems to have reversed roles with his once powerful father (a familiar reversal), to have gone from young son to an almost parental nurturer of an increasingly frail parent, but who still cannot erase the power of his father's hold on him, nor his need for his father's love and approval. His frequent trips to visit his ailing dad bring not a forgetting of past struggles and hurts, but acceptance and reconciliation. And recognition—of the fact that "the huge job he did all his life, that that whole generation of Jews did, was making themselves American"; of how much Roth the writer owes him: "*He's* the bard of New-ark. That really rich Newark stuff isn't my story—it's his." And: "[H]e taught me the vernacular. He *was* the vernacular, unpoetic and expressive and pointblank, with all the vernacular's glaring limitations and all its durable force."[25] Driving with his son through "poor old Newark" to the hospital for a consultation, Herman Roth relates stories and people with every spot and building they pass: his school and his favorite teacher, the places where friends and relatives had their shops. "You mustn't forget any-thing—that's the inscription on his coat of arms. To be alive, to him, is to be made of memory—to him if a man's not made of memory, he's made of nothing" (*Patrimony,* 124).

How, then, to memorialize not only the father and *his* memories, but also the newfound—or, rather, recovered—closeness to the father? To ren-der and make public also can be to betray—this is the writer's dilemma, the subject of conversations "real" and imagined in *The Counterlife* and *Deception,* books Roth was writing and completing during his father's ill-ness. Six weeks after Herman Roth's death, his son had a dream in which Herman, buried in the shroud mandated by Jewish tradition, reproached him: "'I should have been dressed in a suit. You did the wrong thing.' I awakened screaming. All that peered out from the shroud was the dis-pleasure in his dead face. And his only words were a rebuke: I had dressed him for eternity in the wrong clothes." Roth concludes that his fa-ther was alluding to "this book, which, in keeping with the unseemliness of my profession, I had been writing all the while he was ill and dying. . . . [I]n my dreams I would live perennially as his little son . . . just as he would remain alive there not only as my father but as *the* father, sitting in

25. Philip Roth, *Patrimony: A True Story,* 125, 181 (hereinafter cited in the text as *Patrimony*).

judgment on whatever I do" (*Patrimony,* 237–38). The "unseemliness" Roth alludes to includes, I would imagine, both the subjects he has written about and the very act of writing. Roth is certainly not the only one who describes experiencing a grief and at the same time thinking of how it will be used, being both a mourner and a reporter at a loved one's funeral, distancing himself from grief by the very act of putting it into words as it is being experienced. (In *The Counterlife* and *Deception,* the writer/protagonists' lovers complain of the appropriation and distortion of their conversations and confidences.)

One wonders how Herman Roth would have felt if he had read two scenes at once so private and so central: those of his incontinence and subsequent bath.[26] At this point in the book, recovering from a biopsy and a bout of constipation, Herman excuses himself from lunch to go to the bathroom; not quite making it all the way to the toilet, he suffers what might be termed an explosion, which he then attempts to clean up, only making matters worse—excrement is spattered and smeared everywhere, including the walls and toothbrushes. Lovingly, Philip washes him, puts him to bed, cleans the mess, gathers the clothes, scrubs the walls. Approaching the task, he thinks: "It's like writing a book . . . I have no idea where to begin."[27] He promises not to tell the family about the incident: "I won't tell anyone" (*Patrimony,* 173). And he doesn't. But here it is in the book. Rightly or wrongly, the incident is absolutely crucial to the author and his book:

> I thought I couldn't have asked anything more for myself before he died—this, too, was right and as it should be. You clean up your father's shit because it has to be cleaned up, but in the aftermath of cleaning it up, everything that there is to feel is felt as it never was before. . . . [O]nce you sidestep disgust and ignore nausea and plunge past those phobias that are fortified like taboos, there's an awful lot of life to cherish. . . . And *why* this was right and as it should be couldn't have been plainer to me. Now that the job was done. So *that* was the patrimony. And not because the cleaning it up was symbolic of something else but because it wasn't, because it was nothing less or more than the lived reality that it was. There was my patrimony: not the money, not the tefillin, not the shaving mug, but the shit. (*Patrimony,* 175–76)

26. See Eakin, *Lives,* 182–86.
27. Roth has referred to his experimenting with writing as "playing (in the mud)" (*Reading Myself,* 36).

Roth, whose "dirty books" were so staunchly defended by his father, seems to be coming full circle. This patrimony symbolizes nothing but its own reality; nevertheless, that very reality, in all its stink, in the opportunity it gives the son to play parent, creates a bond "to cherish." If writing autobiography is a sort of salvation or second chance,[28] then this "lived reality" is an important trial in the process.

The satisfaction Roth gets from bathing his father can be related to the intimacy of the parent-child relationship and its reversal here. In another full circle, the author of Portnoy's penis obsession and of Zuckerman's impotence expresses his pleasure at seeing his father's still young-looking organ. "'I must remember accurately,' I told myself, 'remember everything accurately so that when he is gone I can recreate the father who created me.' *You must not forget anything*" (*Patrimony*, 177). As I see it, these two scenes bear a highly complex relation not only to one another, but also to the image Roth later creates as he describes lying in bed recuperating from quintuple-bypass surgery at the same time his father is dying—that of giving birth. He feels himself reborn, envisioning his "heart as a tiny infant suckling itself on this blood coursing unobstructed now through newly attached arteries borrowed from my leg." Imagining himself as a nursing mother, he has never been happier. These reveries bring him close to "being the double of my own nurturing mother. . . . I had come to feel myself *transposed,* interchangeable with—even a sacrificial proxy for—my failing father. . . . I was never a heart patient alone in that bed: I was a family of four" (*Patrimony*, 225–26). Earlier in the book, we hear Herman telling a friend that Philip is being a wonderful mother to him. Cooper takes this as a sign that Herman, while acknowledging the parental role his son is now playing, will not give up his own role as *the father*. Perhaps so, but the maternal aspect, the nurturing and giving birth, the "reality" of that most primal bond, is also being recognized, as is the indissoluble familial bond that in the birth image transcends and blends all roles.[29] Roth expresses a oneness with his father in still another context: At Bucknell, he feels that he is also getting an education for his father, who had no such

28. Alfred Kazin writes: "For the nonfiction writer, as I can testify, personal history is directly an effort to find salvation, to make one's own experience come out right" and "[T]o write is to live it again, and in this personal myth and resurrection of our experience, to give honor to our lives" ("The Self as History: Reflections on Autobiography," 78, 89).

29. Cooper, *Roth and the Jews,* 249. In *The Counterlife,* Zuckerman asks: "Why do I so passionately want to become a father? Is it entirely unlikely that from the latent paterfamilias coming to the fore, it's the feminized part of me, exacerbated by the impotence, that's produced this belated yearning for a baby of my own?" (203).

opportunity, as if his father is a homunculus he carries within him to school; ironically, with every class and every book he experiences, the gulf between them widens (*Patrimony,* 160). (How sharp the contrast between this maternal/paternal/filial Roth and the ailing Zuckerman of *The Anatomy Lesson* on his playmat being distracted and coddled by the sexual partner/mothers who come to attend and amuse and feed him.)

More vital than nurture, though, is creation. Roth wants to re-create the father who created him, and he has this thought at the moment he muses on his father's organ of procreation, of generation, which "generated" him. He does not comment on the fact that his father's penis, like his own, has been circumcised; in *The Counterlife,* however, circumcision is crucial (Zuckerman's denial to an Israeli journalist of the importance of his circumcision to his "I" notwithstanding). In that book, Zuckerman informs his Christian wife, Maria, that he insists on it for their "son" to be. The final two pages of the book—Nathan's "posthumous letter" to his Maria, in which he affirms the comfort of returning to his own people—focus almost entirely on circumcision: "Circumcision makes it clear as can be that you are here and not there, that you are out and not in—also you're mine and not theirs. There is no way around it: you enter history through my history and me. . . . Circumcision confirms that there is an us, and an us that isn't solely him and me" (*Counterlife,* 323–24). The mark of the biblical covenant is not simply indelible and ineradicable: it is placed on the organ of generation, to be a sign and connection to all future generations. Despite Zuckerman's disclaimer of his fidelity to the biblical connection, his circumcision and his insistence on his son's circumcision binds him to past and future generations. Roth, musing on his father's organ of generation and his own determination to "re-create" his father in *Patrimony,* is looking at one who, like himself and Zuckerman, is circumcised, and thereby covenanted not only to *his* father, but to his people, to his ancestors all the way back to Abraham.[30]

---

30. In discussing Chinese-language stories that deal with Jewish Americans, Xiaohuang Yin cites "Circumcision" by Zhang Xiguo, wherein the Chinese protagonist, Song, a former student immigrant now an assimilated department chair, has been invited to a *bris* (circumcision ceremony). Xiguo grasps so well the generative/generational aspect of Jewish circumcision: Song "cannot calm down tonight. What he saw this afternoon has greatly stirred him—the baby's tender and red penis appeared again and again in his sight. The baby's penis looks weak and tiny with the skin at the tip peeled off . . . but Song is aware of the potential strength of the small penis, and he can picture its magnificent shape years later: growing from a defenseless bloody flesh sprout to a giant and powerful root of life." He begins, as a result, to ponder his attitude toward his own tradition. Yin comments: "The circumcision has provided a powerful awakening for Song's long-repressed ethnic consciousness" (*Chinese American Literature,* 193).

Roth *in* the book wants to re-create the father who created him; the *writing* Roth is of course also creating the writer who wants to re-create the father, while at the same time forming the writer's possibly inchoate feelings into articulated intention that becomes (and facilitates) both this book and an ever-closer relationship with the father. Roth does not ruminate much on these distinctions in *Patrimony;* he leaves that to the reader, especially the reader who has read *The Counterlife,* where a writer's self-consciousness about what it means to write a self and to use friends and family in fiction is most out in the open. *The Counterlife* constantly circles around these questions and others: how to differentiate fact from fiction, memory from imagination; how to invest oneself in fiction, and still separate the self from the fictions it spins. And is there even such a thing as an "I"? The writer writing, trying out different fictional and not-so-fictional versions of himself, his family, his values, now projecting and displacing, now revealing—this is the issue Roth dramatizes in *The Counterlife*. In this book a more thoughtful Zuckerman seems to be the reliably reporting and confessing protagonist, but before long we realize that Zuckerman is experimenting with different versions of a book, with different versions of characters who are called Nathan, Henry, and Maria. In effect, Roth is not just splitting himself, doubling aspects of himself in Zuckerman, but creating a writer, Zuckerman, who is doing the same thing within *The Counterlife,* and, further, within the book that Zuckerman-in–*The Counterlife* is trying to write. In addition, the characters are also readers reacting to what they are reading.

The book is in five parts: "Basel," "Judea," "Aloft," "Gloucestershire," and "Christendom." The first part has Nathan trying to write a eulogy for his brother Henry's funeral, but what results instead is material for his book about Henry, totally unusable as a eulogy. It tells of Henry's heart condition and death: the beta blockers Henry was taking rendered him impotent, which created a problem for him with his mistress. As a result, Henry risked coronary surgery and died. Nathan also remembers Henry's agonized confidences about the love of his life, Maria from Basel, for whom he did not leave his wife and move to Switzerland, as well as his feelings of suffocation in his marriage. When Nathan declines to give the eulogy, Henry's unsuspecting wife does the job, speaking of her late husband's heroism in undergoing the surgery so that he could be a full husband to her.

In "Judea," Henry (now going by his Hebrew name, Hannoch) is alive and living in Israel, where he is either making his escape in a more acceptable way or sincerely finding himself among his people, having landed in a settlement of extreme nationalists. Nathan now assumes the role of good brother, trying to rescue Henry from himself and bring him home to his family. In the process, Nathan—and the reader—are presented with highly charged, highly articulate lectures, both from the far left and the far right of Israeli politics. As is typical of Roth, these viewpoints are left unreconciled. A large issue here is where "home" is, where one can have "a life free of Jewish cringing, deference, diplomacy, apprehension, alienation, self-pity, self-satire, self-mistrust, . . . hypercriticalness, hypertouchiness, social anxiety, social assimilation" (*Counterlife*, 120). To Nathan, "home" is the Weequahic section of Newark, the New Jersey of his childhood; to Henry, it is Israel: "There's a world outside the Oedipal swamp," he tells Nathan of the settlers, "something more to go on than their hilarious inner landscape! Here they have an *outer* landscape, a nation, a world!" (*Counterlife*, 140).

"Aloft" takes place on a plane: Nathan is writing a long letter to Henry about his telephone conversation with Henry's wife the night before, reading a letter from a left-wing Israeli friend, and sitting next to a crazy fan of his, who is about to attempt a hijacking with a hand grenade. What follows is a madcap scene in which security plainclothesmen grab the grenade, the fan, and Nathan.

The real surprises begin in section four, "Gloucestershire," in which we learn that *Nathan* is the one with the heart condition that renders him impotent, and that, inspired by an affair with an Englishwoman (another Maria) in the apartment above his, it is *he* who is to undergo fatal surgery to restore his potency. We leave Nathan facing his surgery and continue on to Henry, alive and well and never having been in Israel, trying and failing to compose a eulogy for Nathan's funeral. Since his accusation that Nathan killed their father with *Carnovsky*, the brothers have not been speaking. After the funeral (where the eulogy is delivered by Nathan's editor—a eulogy that sounds like an exonerating book review, written in advance by Nathan), Henry sneaks into Nathan's apartment and reads his notes and the draft of a novel containing all the Henry stories we have read up until this point. Henry steals and destroys the incriminating sections. Next, Maria comes downstairs to mourn Zuckerman. There ensues a dialogue—mainly short questions followed by Maria's long answers—which could be between Maria and Nathan's visiting ghost or Maria's internal dialogue. She is drawn to the section of Nathan's manuscript entitled "Christendom," which takes place in Gloucestershire and London and projects a marriage with Maria and life in England, where for the first time Nathan feels rejected as a Jew: he experiences two viciously anti-Semitic outbursts, and at other times encounters strong though politely veiled anti-Semitism. What is more alienating, though, is the way Maria and others simply cannot understand what all the fuss is about; they make remarks of the "you Jews are too sensitive" variety. The book ends with Nathan and Maria's separation (with hope for reunion) and an exchange of letters that might be posthumous or written into the novel by the still-living Nathan, the last of which contains the affirmation of circumcision quoted above and discusses the importance of "the Jewish question" to Nathan and his relationship with Maria.

Attending a London Christmas service with Maria and her family, Nathan realizes: "I am never more of a Jew than I am in church . . . I have the emotions of a spy in the adversary's camp and feel I'm overseeing the very rites that embody the ideology that's been responsible for the persecution and mistreatment of Jews" (*Counterlife,* 256). In *Deception,* "Philip," newly returned from England, realizes there is something he was longing for—Jews, but not the kind he saw in England; rather, "Jews with force . . . with appetite. Complaining Jews that get under your skin. . . . New York's the real obstreperous Zion." To which his lover replies: "So you've returned to the bosom of the tribe . . . The one who has gone home," alluding to the *Odyssey*.[31] But the road "home" is rocky, and the travelers are torn between directions. So is the reader. Rather than attempting to shore up the fragments as we have seen other bicultural authors do, Roth deliberately splits identities. He not only splits his own conflicts into characters who express opposing viewpoints, different ways of being a good boy and a good son and a good Jew—creating a Nathan and a Henry, with Nathan acting out the worst of Roth—but also gives us Henry, the good boy, acting out rebellion in his love affairs. But wait a minute—is Henry alive or dead? Is this Nathan's story, Nathan's Maria—and is *he* alive or dead? Within the narrative, has any of this actually happened, or is this a book about Nathan trying to write a book in which nothing he recounts has actually taken place?

What emerges as Roth's principal subjects are the importance of narrative construction, how the autobiographical and the fictional are related, and what identity—individual, familial, or "tribal"—really is. To quote what Roth has written, and put into his characters' mouths:

> *You are your brother!* (*Counterlife,* 304)

> The treacherous imagination is everybody's maker—we are all the invention of each other, everybody a conjuration conjuring up everyone else. We are all each other's authors. (*Counterlife,* 145)

---

31. Roth, *Deception,* 204–5.

How [brothers] know each other . . . is as a kind of deformation of themselves. (*Counterlife,* 80)

Being Zuckerman is one long performance and the very opposite of what is thought of *being oneself.* In fact, those who most seem to be themselves appear to me people impersonating what they think they might like to be, believe they ought to be,[32] or wish to be taken to be by whoever is setting the standards. . . . I realize that what I am describing, people divided in themselves, is said to characterize mental illness and is the absolute opposite of integration. . . . But there are those whose sanity flows from the conscious *separation* of those two things. . . . [T]he natural being may be an innate capacity to impersonate. . . . There's no you, Maria, any more than there's a me. There is only this way we have established . . . of performing together. . . . It's *all* impersonation—in the absence of a self, one impersonates selves, and after a while impersonates best the self that best gets one through. . . . I, for one, have no self. . . . What I have instead is a variety of impersonations I can do, and not only of myself—a troupe of players that I have internalized . . . I am a theater. (*Counterlife,* 319–21)

If the issue is the relationship between fact and fiction, between the possibility and impossibility of an irreducible identity, given that identity may be composed of learned and created roles, does that give us greater license to speculate about the relationship between Roths and Zuckermans even as we are generalizing and theorizing truth-to-life and character? If we all play roles and create our own ongoing, past, and future narratives, can we not assume kernels of truth in Roth's fiction, which may be as true as—possibly truer than—the facts he gives us straight? Cooper writes: "Zuckerman stands for the view that no man can tell the truth about himself because his fiction-making capacity is always at work"—a conclusion not so different from that of theorists of autobiography and memory. He goes on to say: "Roth's subject matter, whatever else it may also have been, had been fiction—the fiction we are asked to live, the fiction we create to survive, the fiction we oppose to the fictions imposed, the writing or rewriting of ourselves."[33] This means that readers are presented with an unsettling oeuvre, for even if we understand that fact and fiction cannot be neatly set apart from one another, that our suspension of belief and disbelief are being deactivated and reactivated by a cunning author, we have

32. For very similar theories, see Daniel Albright, "Literary and Psychological Models of the Self," 33, and Kenneth J. Gergen, "Mind, Text, Society: Self-Memory in Social Context," 97.

33. Cooper, *Roth and the Jews,* 53, 62.

still to reckon with the implication of such narrative instability for our own life stories.

Consider where Roth has taken us: In *Patrimony* we have met the real Philip, the good son who frequently flies home to see Dad, even from across the globe. This is the Philip who has created Nathan Zuckerman, the kind of man readers imagine as the author of a book like *Portnoy* or *Carnovsky*, and put him out there, or over his own face like a carnival mask, to do and say all that one would imagine such an author to do and say, while keeping the "real" Philip safe behind closed doors in his loving, attentive, real-son life. In *The Counterlife*, he has created for Nathan a brother, Henry, whose perfection as a son and stability as a respectable suburban Jewish dentist is first undermined by his adulterous flings and then by what Nathan sees as another escape scheme: transforming himself into a Zionist extremist, returning to Judea, substituting a Jewish/national-istic/biblical "we" for the egoistic, goy-pleasing "I." But Henry's fatal sur-gery turns out really to have been Nathan's, whose death (*whose* death?) becomes part of a narrative being written—a fiction perhaps? A fiction within a fiction whose subject may not be Zuckermans or Roths or Jews, but fiction itself? Is this only a game played with readers, a sort of hide and seek, or Where's Waldo (all over the place, if you are thorough and precise and minute in your seeking)? Or is it all a serious unmasking of masking? Is Nathan just a figment of some Red King's dream? Are we all?

The dream of Herman Roth arising to complain that he was buried in the wrong clothes, and Roth's interpretation of "clothes" as narrative—as his book, the wrong memorial, the wrong presentation of his father—invites us to speculate, like Roth, on the many ways we have of distorting others, seeing or presenting them in one way rather than in so many other ways that would be just as "true." This is not to mention Roth's guilty admission that everything he and his father were going through together was simul-taneously being turned into narrative by a son who was at one and the same time cleaning up the shit and standing apart from the mess and the love and the nurturing, observing it and himself and turning the whole drama into words on a page that made him the good son and hero of the bathroom, guardian of the secret that would soon be public. And all of this took place, Roth tells us, as he was breathing life into those interchangeable Zuckerman brothers—role-exchanging, even life-and-death-exchanging, to the point where life becomes a manuscript that outlives the grave.

Bury him naked, that's what Roth really wanted to do with his father— no decision about orthodox shroud or assimilated business suit. Naked, real, unadorned Dad, unadorned truth in the telling of him. But of course there must be some covering, some presentation, selection, decision, in any "dressing" or narrative, in any characterization, factual or imagined. And any one of them overlays, clothes, adorns, and possibly masks. Zuckerman may be what readers imagine the writer of a book such as *Portnoy* or *Carnovsky* to be, and not the real author, but the real Roth did write *Portnoy,* and then proceeded, eighteen years later, to deconstruct the fictional, flak-taking Nathan of *Zuckerman Bound,* turning him first into Henry and then into manuscript. Along the way, he put Nathan in dialogue not only with a Henry who acts the good-boy part, but also with a Henry in a yarmulke who repudiates his former self to return to Zion, his newfound home, coming home not to Jewish Weequahic, which is no more, but to biblical Israel, choosing its most extreme incarnation. It is in this role that he argues with Nathan and puts into question everything that both their lives had stood for.

Where is the naked father? The author? The fictional creation? When fiction itself becomes so elevated, so invested with questions and identities, so absorbing and at the same time so stripped and unmasked, is it even possible to extricate the "real" from the masked? Zuckerman says: "I can only exhibit myself in disguise. All my audacity derives from masks" (*Counterlife,* 275). I suspect this is Roth's real subject. The wrong suit, the right suit, the impossibility of suitlessness—are we returned to Eli and the greenie? "You are us, we are you," Tzuref reiterated in that story. Is Nathan/ Henry/the posthumous manuscript saying the same thing? Is this what it means to write one's way home—putting masks in endless confrontation, creating dialogues that cannot resolve into a single truth any more than any one outfit can wholly express or represent the complicated, often conflicted, person who puts it on and who can just as easily take it off, have it cleaned, or replace it with one that is more in fashion? Even nakedness— were it possible to parade around in public that way—can never reveal all that goes on under the skin. And so, what we have in *Patrimony* and *The Counterlife* is unabashedly relational—the autobiograph*ical* that is not just autobiography, but also fiction and literary theory and history, and that is asking not only Who am I? and Where do I belong? but also What is my relationship to my family, to my people, and to my history? Nathan and Henry act as doubles not just of one another, but also of the protagonist of *The Facts* and *Patrimony.* It is not a simple one-to-one correspondence, to be sure, but a fundamental relationship with a larger "us" in all its varied suits and hats.

We cannot possibly know to what extent Roth's growing oeuvre and its composition affected his "coming home" and to what extent it merely reflected it. To ask this question is to ask yet again how art influences life, how telling and writing a self influence self-perception and direction, influence not only one's view of the past, but also of the future; it is to ask whether art can make things happen. We must chalk up to eerie coincidence that Roth underwent a quintuple-bypass operation *after* he wrote of Nathan/Henry's cardiac surgery. In addition, he suffered a Halcion-induced, suicidal, psychotic episode following knee surgery that rendered him even more helpless and mentally unbalanced than was Zuckerman in *The Anatomy Lesson,* and that too was after he had written about the experience. Of course, we are left with only irresolvable conjecture on the parallels between life and art.

Bruner's theory that ways of telling become recipes for structuring not only past but future experience, for directing a life narrative into the future, and his statement that "we *become* the autobiographical narratives by which we 'tell about' our lives" is more easily traced in the writing of Anzia Yezierska, admittedly not the complex, sophisticated writer that Roth is—not even in his league—but perhaps because of her "simplicity" much more transparent. She also illustrates aptly Daniel Albright's discussion of the subject as object: an "I" may write about a "me," but the relationship between the spectator/writer who does the remembering and the actor, remembered and constructed out of an aggregate of "me"s, does not go in only one direction. We can easily assume with Albright that the "I" always leaks into the object, but more telling for this discussion is his claim that the subject cannot be confined to the nominative realm. The remembered "me" has projected a self into the future. The remembered self is also nominative—in the subject position—in that it intended the present self, an imperfectly realized object. Bruner says: "Experience has altered the rememberer as well as the remembered self."[34]

In her highly autobiographical stories, Yezierska's heroines reiterate their battle cry and hers: "I want to make from myself a person!" And so she does. The "I" writing anticipates *and* forms the "I" who becomes what she has written—a writer, and a success. Writing her determination before anyone ever reads it, then publishing it to catapult her to fame, she *is* that same poor, uneducated immigrant, and even once she becomes more educated and famous, she continues to write her hungers and ambitions. She becomes the "sweatshop Cinderella" she had dreamed and written of being, celebrated and thrown into Hollywood luxury, into more luxury

---

34. Bruner, "Life as Narrative," 31, 15; Albright, "Models of the Self," 35, 37. See also Olney on memory as both recollective and anticipatory (*Memory and Narrative,* 343).

than any she fabricated in her hungering narratives. Once there, she sometimes put her fictional self and her lived self in reciprocal relation, capitalizing on her Cinderella rise to exaggerate her story in interviews, and
leaving out important stages (such as her degree from Columbia Teachers
College). "Spinning . . . fairy tales about herself was one of the pleasures of
authorship Anzia was just beginning to appreciate," her daughter wrote.
"Affected by the force of her own creation, she often could not remember
what was real and what was invented in . . . her . . . stories and books."[35]
She was not above incorporating the "real" into her fiction—for example,
by lifting sentences from John Dewey's poems and letters to her.

But most important is the way that Yezierska, in the guise of fiction,
writes a self, as Albright theorizes, wrapped in dignity and erotic power, a
self she craves to be.[36] In some stories, there is only the craving; in others,
an illusory fulfillment; in still others, fulfillment in romance, wealth, power,
or all three (as in *Salome of the Tenements*), but in almost all of the stories,
the end is disappointment or disillusion. In some (and most prominently
in her autobiography, written much later), dislocation is the sad ending:
the protagonist cannot find her place in the new environment, nor can she
any longer return to where she came from. Yezierska wrote for herself a
person, but not a home. Sadly and ironically, in the comfort of Hollywood
or uptown Manhattan, away from want and hunger, filth and poverty, she
realized where her sources lay, that the noise and squalor of Hester Street
was her well of inspiration. She published six books between 1920 and
1932 (the last, *All I Could Never Be,* was poorly received), and was then
virtually silent until her "fictional autobiography," *Red Ribbon on a White
Horse,* appeared in 1950, when she was about seventy. There she writes:
"I had lost the human ties and emotions that sustained others. Without a
country, without a people, I could live only in a world I had created out of
my brain. I could not live unless I wrote. And I could not write any more.
I had gone too far away from life, and I did not know how to get back"
(*Ribbon,* 127). Her "rag and bone shop" was not only of the heart, but of

35. Henriksen, *Anzia Yezierska,* 143, 217. It is telling that even though Yezierska's
daughter, Louise, wanted to correct what she saw as the tendency of a new generation
of scholars to take her mother's fictional characterizations of herself as literal truth (see
Alice Kessler-Harris, foreword to *Bread Givers,* vii), much of the evidence she brings to
bear on her mother in her biography relies on quotations from her mother's books.
One wonders whether this is because there is much truth in the fiction or because
there was not much else available in the way of evidence. (Henriksen does acknowledge the help of Dewey scholar Jo Ann Boydston.)

36. Albright, "Models of the Self," 33.

her "junk-shop brain . . . a sort of Hester Street junk shop, where a million different things—rich uptown silks and velvets and the cheapest kind of rags—were thrown around in bunches" (*America*, 155).

She had had to leave home to write and become a person, but in so doing, she was not only making her new home on the page, she was also finding it to be the only real home she had. Homelessness, lostness, and rootlessness became her subject and then her "cage," as she suggests in her late story "The Open Cage." To discuss Yezierska in a chapter titled "Writing the Way Home" is to see the emphasis, on one hand, on writing, and on the other hand, on the way home.

She writes a self and she writes a writing self, writes about her hunger to write and her frustrations with language and with cold-blooded Anglo-Saxon editors and teachers who do not understand that what and how she writes is *real* and must get out—out of her, and out to Americans who need to get her message.

> [A]ll those dumb generations back of me are crying in every breath of every word that itself is struggling out of me. . . . Writing to me is a confession—not a profession . . . I can never touch the surfaces of things. I can only write from the depths. . . . I am so in love with the changing lights and shades of words that I almost hate their power over me . . . (*America*, 132–34)

> I am thinking . . . of Victor Hugo and his immortal book. . . . It's great literature, but it isn't the dirt and the blood of the poor that I saw and that forced me to write. (*America*, 139)

> Why is it that only the thoughts of educated people are written up? . . . We who are forced to do the drudgery of the world, and who are considered ignorant because we have no time for school, could say a lot of new and different things, if only we had a chance to get a hearing. . . . With me my thoughts were not up in my head. They were in my hands and my feet, in the thinnest nerves of my hair, in the flesh and blood of my whole body. (*America*, 154–55)

She writes of how important to the writer is a connection to the smells and sounds around her. In "My Own People," Sophie keeps trying to get rid of her talkative landlady so that she can write the dry exercises she has set herself, but finally she really listens to her and to "the whole range of human emotions, from bitterest agony to dancing joy" that is in her conversation: "'Ach, if I could only write like Hanneh Breineh talks!' thought

Sophie. 'Her words dance with a thousand colors. Like a rainbow it flows from her lips.' Sentences from her own essays marched before her, stiff and wooden" (*Hearts,* 104).

This, of course, is the lesson Yezierska learned: once educated, she returned to Yiddish ghetto idiom to capture "their cries—my own people . . . 'Ach! At last it writes itself in me!' " (*Hearts,* 107). As she recalled, "Here was life, right here on my own block. . . . In all of them I saw a part of myself. . . . In the intoxication of this sudden recognition, all my hunger and longing for love turned to ambition. I saw a place for myself"—a writer's place, her "home" as she was to create it on the pages she would write (*Ribbon,* 119).

It is ironic and almost prophetic the way her prize-winning story, "The Fat of the Land," anticipated Yezierska's own future. In her youth she struggled to escape a family and a mother so like Hanneh Breineh in her story, only to become herself like Hanneh Breineh, the now-rich lady who cannot adjust to East Side doormen, who misses her old ghetto but can no longer endure its discomfort and its smells, who cannot hope for sympathy from those who still live in poverty and envy her wealth.

It is in the much later *Red Ribbon on a White Horse,* however, that Yezierska's desire to come home and reconcile herself with her family and her people is given clearest articulation. So are her guilt and regret and attempts to justify her neglect of her parents. The poignant scene in which she attempts to explain herself to her father, to share her wealth with him, only makes her realize that he will never accept or understand her. At the same time, by the time she wrote this book, she realized how much she was her father's daughter—how she, like him, sacrificed her family for her ideals, for being what she felt she had to be, just as she sacrificed her parents' acceptance when she moved out to become independent and educated. In this book, as Alice Kessler-Harris points out, the father is no longer portrayed as tyrannical, but as traditional.[37] Even *Bread Givers,* though, dramatizes the desire for reconciliation: the happy ending has Sara marrying a Jewish version of the refined, educated male of her romantic plots, and the newlyweds inviting her father to live with them in a home that they will make kosher for his sake.

Nostalgia is evident even in the narrative structure of *Red Ribbon,* for throughout her stories of New York and Hollywood she is carried back from present scenes to a past redolent with happy memories. On the Hollywood set for *Hungry Hearts,* she escapes the smell of paint by thinking

---

37. Kessler-Harris, foreword, x.

back to the remembered smells of fresh-baked halleh and gefüllte fish in Plinsk. "I closed my eyes and could almost see Mother spreading the red-checked Sabbath tablecloth . . . Mother blessing the lighted candles, ushering in the Sabbath" (*Ribbon*, 49). The father that Sara Smolinsky of *Bread Givers* seemed to hate so, for placing his studies of sacred writ above providing for his family, is in his remembered person now idealized for those very qualities:

> This ancient past that I had despised and rejected with the ruthlessness of youth now had me by the throat. I had never really broken away. I had only denied what was in my blood and bones. . . . I remembered waking up before dawn in our straw-thatched hut in Poland and seeing Father at his table of sacred books. His black skullcap setting off his white face . . . We had been hungry, in rags, but the poverty we suffered had been because Father chose to have his portion in the next world. In the depths of our want was glory—pride in Father because he was not like other fathers. He had worked for God. (*Ribbon*, 92–93)[38]

In the face of such conflicted memories and frustrated desire for reconciliation, writing autobiographically not only gave Yezierska's life a seeming coherence, but also a way "to explain her experiences to herself," as her daughter put it. Kenneth J. Gergen writes of the way memories of the self are constructed (as well as recited) in a social context, whether in their telling, as in stories told to children, or in the way they sustain one's identity within relationships, establishing oneself as a particular kind of person with particular privileges and duties. It is not difficult to imagine that Yezierska's memories with regard to duty may have been difficult to entertain, that she needed also to claim the privilege of the artist who must have freedom even if it means sacrificing others and their needs. Gergen goes on to relate autobiographical writing to challenge: telling the self, with its personal remembering, can be felt as a necessary response to the questioning of one's authenticity. In Yezierska's case, establishing her authenticity as an artist and her continuing relationship to those she left behind *through* her writing, as a voice crying out on their behalf, surely helped her as she constructed an Anzia—both alone and in relation—in her own mind. Yet another example of Gergen's view of self-memory and telling as socially stimulated and constructed is the role of audience *within* Yezierska's

---

38. The scholarly father is also idealized in *All I Could Never Be*, which was written as early as 1932.

narratives. Her first published story, "The Free Vacation House," was almost a collaboration with her sister Annie, who provided not only some of
the experience, but also a listening, participating audience for Anzia as she
told stories, putting her drama lessons into practice as she and her sister
assumed the various voices.[39] She wrote of reading her stories to Zalmon
the fish peddler and Hayim Shmerel the plumber, asking them as well as
the other girls in the shop for better words, more authentic language
(*Ribbon,* 77).

A similar collaboration is implied in the dedication to *China Boy: A
Novel,* where Gus Lee writes: "The book began as a summer's tale to our
seven-and-five-year-old children, and resulted in our collaborative work. It
is a moral lesson for myself—*a father's reminder of the purpose of life, the
need for both parents' love,* and the everpresent opportunity for redemp-
tion" (emphasis mine). If Lee's book is about anything, it is about the
search for missing parents, the way fathers or father substitutes are needed
to guide a boy to manhood. The search for a father in the face of an absent, inadequate, or failed father is not new, nor is it particular to cross-
cultural narratives, but where identity has already been fractured, where
dislocation in place, culture, and language have rendered the outside
world threatening in its very difference and incomprehensibility, such absence is doubly threatening.

When relation—home and family, father, mother—assume great importance in a culture and its texts, it should not be surprising to encounter
narratives where loss of a family member, far from being simply an important and traumatic incident, actually drives the narrative. In *China Boy,* for
example, and in Fae Myenne Ng's *Bone,* one is struck by the almost physical presence of absence. "Mother's presence was palpable," says Kai of
his dead mother in *China Boy;*[40] in *Bone,* the suicide of Ona works both
centripetally and centrifugally, at once tearing the family apart and cement-
ing its bonds. (Lost siblings—and even more, the silence and secrecy that
their stories are buried beneath—also weigh heavily on Kingston's Maxine,
on Tan's June, and on Kim Chernin's protagonists.) *China Boy*'s Kai begins
his life enveloped in love. This changes dramatically with the death of his
mother and the remarriage of his father: his life undergoes not only the
pain of loss, but also physical and psychological brutality, rendering him
ripe for seeking and accepting a series of parent substitutes, an ongoing
odyssey that results in fortunate rescue operations and thrilling triumph.

39. Louise Levitas Henriksen quoted in Kessler-Harris, foreword, ix; Gergen, "Mind,
Text, Society," 89–90, 88, 97, 98; Henriksen, *Anzia Yezierska,* 22.
40. Lee, *China Boy,* 83 (hereinafter cited in the text as *Boy*).

The jacket photo of a smiling, cheerful-looking Gus Lee is the antithesis of the pain between the covers of the book, but then so is the narrator's humor in recounting it. While the book is labeled a novel, Lee and Kai seem to have more in common than languages and family origin in Shanghai. For example, Lee went, as Kai does, to West Point (the setting of his sequel, *Honor and Duty*). Kai's father was a fellow officer and World War II buddy of a Maj. Gen. H. Norman Schwarzhedd; in his acknowledgments, Lee thanks his teachers, among them H. Norman Schwarzkopf (*kopf* is German for "head"). "Toos," Kai's first friend and protector, is also thanked by name in Lee's acknowledgments. But what struck me with the greatest force was Lee's acknowledgment to his family: "To Mah-mee, for love; to Father, for guidance; to my stepmother, for English; to my sisters, for caring." If Kai ends up writing splendid novels in English, he can indeed thank his Irish stepmother for teaching him the language, but at what cost did he learn? As discussed in Chapter 4, Edna's method is to perform a sort of linguistic/culinary "ethnic cleansing" that not only robs Kai of his language and culture, but also of all tangible reminders of his mother. Edna burns the crate containing his mother's favorite belongings, the "crate that had been hauled across the world . . . a treasure trove of books, photos, clothing [including her wedding gown, saved for her daughters], and memorabilia" (*Boy*, 8). "English only" is enforced with beatings and destruction of precious toys; brussels sprouts, liver, cabbage, and other British delicacies suddenly and completely replace the food Kai is accustomed to. In addition, the previously coddled five-year-old Kai is put out onto the street to play until suppertime, in a black San Francisco neighborhood where one has to be tough and know how to fight bullies and avoid racial beatings. No amount of terrified banging on his door, not even blood and bruises, can induce Kai's stepmother to open the door to him before supper is ready. Such treatment usually takes place in his father's absence (which is most of the time); even when home, his father seems to have totally capitulated to his blond beauty of a trophy wife. (Lee does not leave it to our imagination to relate this scenario to the story of Hansel and Gretel; he has Kai do so explicitly. In fact, Edna throws that storybook out and punishes Kai and his sister for retrieving and reading it.)

Clearly, Kai has to find ways to survive, literally. Toos tells him, "You'se *gotta* be a streetfighta," and "don't havta *win*, jes *fight*" (*Boy*, 2, 106). As Kai puts it:

> Fighting was a metaphor. My struggle on the street was really an effort
> to fix identity, to survive as a member of a group. . . . The jam was that

> I felt hurting people damaged my *yuing chi,* my balanced karma. . . .
> "Kai Ting," my Uncle Shim said to me, "you have excellent *yuing chi,*
> karma. You are the only living son in your father's line. This is very
> special, very grand!" I *was* special. I was trying to become an accepted
> black male youth in the 1950's—a competitive, dangerous, and harshly
> won objective. This was all the more difficult because I was Chinese. I
> was ignorant of the culture, clumsy in the language, and blessed with
> a body that made Tinker Bell look ruthless. . . . I enjoyed Chinese cal-
> ligraphy . . . and hated . . . my own spilled blood. (*Boy,* 3–4)

If, as Kai says, "[f]ighting was a measure of citizenship" (*Boy,* 98), he is
forced to choose a "country" and, accordingly, the mentors to guide him in
its ways. Although conflicted between the realities of the street and the
idealistic, scholarly, aristocratic values of Uncle Shim (his mother's best
friend and philosophy sparring partner as well as Kai's teacher in calligraphy and classics), Kai is not left with much choice. His father tells him:

> "You must decide. . . . Be American. Or Chinese. And never change
> your mind. . . . Na-men Schwarz'd taught me that. It is what West Point
> had taught him. When you have to make a decision, *make it!* . . . then
> . . . don't look back. . . . It took courage to come to America. Courage
> to stay here, when I could have joined the American Army as inter-
> preter . . . for Korean War! Ayy! Even courage to have a mixed mar-
> riage!" I nodded my head. I understood. "I pick Y.M.C.A.," I said to
> myself. (*Boy,* 212–13)

The Y enters Kai's life after he is brought home by a neighbor in so bloody
and wounded a state that his father can no longer remain blind to what is
happening; as a result, Kai begins to train in what is to be haven and
"home" for years to come. The Y (also acknowledged by Lee) is Kai's
place of nurture in both senses of the word, for motherly Angela begins to
feed him without charge at the cafeteria once his boxing teachers tell her
he needs to put more calories into his skinny body. The boxers teach their
young charges moves, rules, and discipline with love and concern. "Each
of the three men who were about to become my putative godfathers was
a former pugilist. . . . They grew up in the Depression, when the certainty
of a meal was a question mark. They were the equivalents of my father, . . .
who saw an entire society, hewn from hard soil and violent history for
thousands of years, crumble to dust in the space it takes to say good-bye"
(*Boy,* 147). One of them, Mr. Barraza, gives Kai "gold"—time, the wealth of
his experience, and much patience, "hinting that I was worthy of effort. . . .

I was beginning to be embarrassed with my riches in human contact"
(*Boy,* 177).

At the same time, however, he misses Uncle Shim, who has been made
to feel that his presence and all it represents is most unwelcome in the
new household. True to his sense of honor, he refuses to meet Kai at the
Y until he has his father's permission. Of course, the Y and all it teaches is
anathema to Uncle Shim, and it takes crude, tough Barraza to make him
see that the effort Kai is putting into body-learning, as opposed to the
mind-learning valued by Uncle Shim, is necessary: "See the marks on the
boy's face? See 'em Mr. Shim? 'At don't happen here. . . . If he don't work
his body, what he learns in his brain from school ain't gonna amounta spit.
Mr. Shim, this boy, he lives in a hell's kitchen. . . . Now you, and me, we
don't wanna see this here boy dead. And it don't get no more simple 'n
that" (*Boy,* 235). Away from his father's house, Kai never really has to
choose or look back. The teachers at the Y show him how to stay alive
and to win respect out on the street. Uncle Shim's calligraphy lessons and
Chinese training give him a view "back"—and forward. His uncle takes Kai
to his chess club, where the old, family-less men treat him like a long-lost
prince of the realm. In the sequel, *Honor and Duty,* Uncle Shim continues
to be the voice of both those values, as Kai wrestles with ethical dilemmas
at West Point, where he is also guided by Maj. H. Norman Schwarzhedd,
son of the major general, who has heard of their fathers' friendship. His
own father does, of course, take pride in him and advise him, but these
other "fathers" (son-seeking men themselves) are indispensable to his
coming to manhood.

In *Bone* too, as important as blood ties are, blood is not the only tie to
family. Leila, the narrator, has a different father than her sisters: their
mother's first husband, who went to Australia and never came back. Lei
says of her stepfather, Leon, though: "He's the one who's been there for me.
Like he always told me, 'It's time that makes a family, not just blood.' "[41]
Friends of the family realize this too, telling Lei, "He loves you like a father, that's all I know" (*Bone,* 115). This works both ways. It is Lei, the
only daughter still at home after her sister Ona's suicidal jump from a roof,
who takes responsibility for Leon as well as for her mother. She and her
boyfriend, Mason (son-like even before he and Lei are married), are "there
for" Mah, her mother, and Leon as well, spending much time and energy
looking for Leon as he wanders from home to town square to restaurant.

Blood is not relevant even to Leon's own identity, for he was a paper

41. Fae Myenne Ng, *Bone,* 3 (hereinafter cited in the text).

son, "buying the name Leong . . . like a black-market passport." When Lei needs to find proof of his age, some paper that will do for a birth certificate so that Leon can collect social security, she goes through the suitcase he arrived with from Angel Island. The suitcase, whose contents are listed over three pages, becomes an important symbol and an example of the way relevant details in just the right combination can work to delineate an identity—in this case, not only for the benefit of the reader, but also for Lei, as she sorts through papers she has never seen before. Included in the list are: letters of rejection from the army, job interviewers, and landlords of "unavailable" apartments; letters rubber-banded into decades; newspaper photos of Lei's sister Nina graduating from kindergarten and of Lei herself; aerograms from China; maps; foreign money; menus from steamship lines where Leon worked as a cook; photos of Hitler and Churchill out of *Life* magazine; a certificate of Mah's first marriage, and one of her marriage to Leon; and finally a photograph of a young Leon—his affidavit of identification.[42] All in a suitcase from which "the past came up: a moldy, water-damaged paper smell and a parchment texture" (*Bone*, 57). Lei continues: "I packed everything—letters, official documents, pictures, and old newspaper clippings—back into the suitcase and slammed the old thing shut. I thought, Leon was right to save everything. For a paper son, paper is blood. . . . I'm the stepdaughter of a paper son and I've inherited this whole suitcase full of lies. All of it is mine. All I have is those memories, and I want to remember them all" (*Bone*, 61). As Lei searches for her stepfather around Chinatown, the contrast between Leon, who is being looked for by a daughter, and the other old men with no families is painfully evident, but so is the occasional similarity, which is why Lei cannot bear to see Leon hanging around the square with those old "fleabags." Leon *has* a family, and a home to return to from his wanderings. He has children who love him and a wife who makes celebratory meals when he returns from sea despite their often bitter quarrels. The other men, by contrast, look "like scraps of dark remnant fabric . . . tattered collars, missing buttons,

---

42. This list illustrates perfectly Patricia Hampl's valuing of detail: "The beauty of memory rests in its talent for rendering detail, for paying homage to the senses, its capacity to love the particles of life, the richness and idiosyncrasy of our existence." Accuracy matters less than potential symbolism; Hampl shows how her own inaccurate memory nevertheless "*becomes* the palpable evidence of . . . longing. In other words, it becomes symbol" (*I Could Tell You Stories: Sojourns in the Land of Memory*, 33, 31). Thomas W. Kim discusses the suitcase full of documents in terms of "the literal construction of an identity" which "reveals the conflicts inherent in subjectivation" ("'For a paper son, paper is blood': Subjectivation and Authenticity in Fae Myenne Ng's *Bone*," 43). And this is not to mention that as a paper son Leon's identity is not even authentic.

safety-pinned seams, patch pockets full of fists"—stark reminders, once more, of the importance of family, dramatized in detail by its absence (*Bone*, 8).

If it's time that makes a family, then when time breaks down, so might the family. When Ona dies, "Like that, we all just snapped apart. For me, it was as if time broke down: Before and After Ona jumped" (*Bone,* 15). The fracturing dislocation of time is reflected in the narrative structure of the book, as it jumps backward and forward to events taking place at many different times. Each vignette or incident is told clearly, the way it happened, but the sequential relation of these short narratives to one another is not clear—one must go back through the book and reorder them if one wants to create a chronology. What is always there, referred to in almost every segment, is Ona's suicide and the effect it has had on each member of the family and on their relations with one another.

Out and back, that's the rhythm of *Bone.* The black hole of Ona's suicide explodes the family outward; Mah and Leon's bitterness is shouted out, their words hitting each other and Lei in sorrow and blame, exacerbating the outward-moving pattern already in effect—Leon moving out to old San Fran, Nina flying out as a flight attendant and moving three thousand miles away—but also magnetically drawing the characters back in: Lei moves back from Mason's to be with Mah and spends her weekends going back and forth; Leon ships out but always returns with money and gifts; Nina visits home and journeys to Hong Kong with Mah, quitting her job as flight attendant to guide tours to China, "the map of China in her head." Back and forth; away, but then "backdaire" always.

Mason, the grandson of Louie the herbalist, is clearly one of them, but he lives in the Mission District, constantly driving back and forth. Despite where he lives, he navigates Chinatown emotions, bonds, and mores as only a native of the place can. He understands Mah and Leon and has infinite patience with their needs and demands. He wants only that Lei join him "outdaire": away, but close enough to be, as Mason is, always and totally available—to circle Chinatown in search of Leon, to run interference between Leon and Mah, to help Mason locate his family's bones. He is "at home" in Chinatown; as Leon has told Lei, "the heart never travels" (*Bone,* 193). It is when Lei finally realizes this that she can drive away from Salmon Alley, from the sign that says #2-4-6 UPDAIRE. The sign reminds her "to look back, to remember." Knowing that she always will look back, come back, she is finally able to turn the corner and leave "Mah and Leon—everything—backdaire" (*Bone,* 194).

While looking back and staying close makes leaving possible for Lei, leaving and putting distance between herself and home makes returning possible for Kingston's Maxine. And yet these movements are not really the reverse of one another, for the rhythm of out and back characterizes all the journeys "home" discussed in this chapter and, I would venture to say, all stories of painful maturation (especially when exacerbated by cultural as well as generational gaps), where separation from home and parents results eventually in some sort of adult reconciliation. Maxine has to get "out of hating range," has to keep herself where she won't always get sick the way she does at home. Perhaps she also has to separate her writing of stories from her mother's storytelling before she can weave them together into her "memoir," but woven together they certainly are, even as she recreates them and makes them a vital part of her own story. In Chapter 5, I expressed this fusion (at times *con*fusion) between mothers' and daughters' narratives in terms of ingestion; Maxine has been nourished by her mother's talk-stories of female folk heroism as well as of her own personal bravery in the face of child loss, newfound independence, unusual ambition, and ghost battles.

These "tellings" must now be seen in the context of relational autobiography, where writing the way home is consciously or unconsciously collaborative—what I will term a relational construction of both women's lives. It is no news that *The Woman Warrior* has attracted the attention of scholars who represent a variety of disciplines and theoretical interests, scholars who do not ordinarily study Asian American literature, or any "ethnic" literature at all. Autobiography theorists explore Kingston's blurring of genres, her use of the term *memoir,* and the ways she pushes the limits of any distinctions we might make between autobiography and fiction, verifiable experience and imagination, "what happened" and fantasy. Feminists are especially concerned with silencing and voice, representation and importance of the body, empowerment, agency, and (as discussed above) what "female" autobiography does with and against conventional "male" modes of self-writing. Even ethnographer Michael Fischer finds Kingston important to his field.[43] Of course, scholars of Asian American literature have written on Kingston incisively, at times to answer her critics

43. Fischer, "Ethnicity and the Post-modern Arts of Memory," 208–11. Sidonie Smith devotes a chapter to *The Woman Warrior* in *A Poetics of Women's Autobiography: Marginality and the Fictions of Self-representation,* and Nancy Walker discusses Kingston in her essay "No Laughing Matter." See also Gilmore, *Autobiographics;* Celeste Schenck, "All of a Piece"; and Shirley Nelson Garner's "Breaking Silence: *The Woman Warrior."* Paul John Eakin discusses *The Woman Warrior* in both *Fictions in Autobiography: Studies in the Art of Self-invention* and *How Our Lives Become Stories,* as does G. Thomas Couser in *Altered Egos: Authority in American Autobiography.*

(such as Frank Chin), but mostly to illuminate her work, the warring and merging of her Chinese and American influences, from the point of view of Chinese tradition. They address issues such as silence, autobiographical writing, gender, myths, and mothers from an "insider" perspective.

For example, Shirley Geok-lin Lim expands on Maxine's identification with the outlaw knot-maker to show how the art of knot-making is connected not only with storytelling, but also with Maxine's mother and their shared stories. Kingston originally makes the connection—knots and stories—when she compares her brother's bare-bones account of Moon Orchid's confronting her husband in Los Angeles (heard secondhand) with her own detailed, dramatic narrative: "His version of the story may be better than mine because of its bareness, not twisted into designs. . . . Long ago in China, knot-makers tied string into buttons and frogs, and rope into bell pulls. There was one knot so complicated that it blinded the knot-maker. Finally an emperor outlawed this cruel knot. . . . If I had lived in China, I would have been an outlaw knot-maker" (*Warrior,* 163). Lim writes:

> The narrator's self-consciousness about her writing (storytelling) is a consistent thread . . . she picks up in various metaphors. One figure is that of the forbidden stitch. . . . The knot is what the narrator makes, . . . the metaphor of the knot covers the making of the mother/daughter relationship in the text, a figure so tightly and complexly tied that the greatest skill will be needed to unknot it. . . . In China the knots were made into buttons, frogs (fasteners), and bellpulls, figures of joining, tying, connection, and sound.

Lim goes on to suggest that the daughter identifies with the knot-maker figure in her desire for both art and affiliation. Bellpulls were works of art, but they also caused people to come in response to the sound of the bell. The stories Maxine grows on and incorporates are *heard.* As Lim points out, Maxine will reinscribe maternal talk-stories, oral stories, into written speech, a transcription that can be related to the mother-daughter collaboration in the final pages, where Kingston writes: "The beginning is hers, the ending mine" (*Warrior,* 206).[44]

The knot is indeed a perfect figure, tying together, as it does in its making, all these potential references. The bringing together continues in its

44. Shirley Geok-lin Lim, "The Tradition of Chinese American Women's Life Stories: Thematics of Race and Gender in Jade Snow Wong's *Fifth Chinese Daughter* and Maxine Hong Kingston's *Woman Warrior,*" 262–63.

subsequent functions, all of which enable connection; but the uses to which knots are put—fastening, sounding a call—are all just as easily capable of enabling *dis*connection, *un*fastening, dismissing, or exiting. But this particular knot, the knot that blinds, is the one that Lim says requires "the greatest skill" to unknot. To me, though (admittedly unfamiliar with knots), such unknotting seems impossible, especially if one has been "blinded," unable to see clearly and logically, as we often are in our closest relationships. The knotting will either hold or require cutting to unravel, and I submit that what Lim finds to be "so tightly and complexly tied," in this case, ultimately holds. To relate the figure once more to threads of stories as well as to the mother-daughter relationship, the interweaving of their stories is similarly difficult to unknot. The critic, then, must be the one with "the greatest skill" to separate the threads and follow them to their source, or, conversely, to admit the impossibility of the task. To me, that very un-knotability, the construction "so tightly and complexly" knotted as to make its unraveling impossible, is what is so admirable in the "weaving"—the knot's strength is one of the book's greatest strengths.

In this connection we can analyze the places where we ask whose story this is, who is doing the telling, and whether a story was even told to the narrator. Let us revisit, in this context, those places where teller, listener, and reteller become blurred, for there we find the closest collaboration between mother and daughter. Whose is the poetry describing the river under the bridge where Brave Orchid encounters a ghost? "[T]he river . . . looked like a bright scratch at the bottom of the canyon, as if the Queen of Heaven had swept her great silver hairpin across the earth as well as the sky" (*Warrior*, 87–88). This part of the story is in quotation marks, attributed to Brave Orchid, but then the text continues with a narration in the third person of what happened on the bridge one twilight—the mother's story, told in detail by Maxine. When Brave Orchid tells the story of the ghost at the medical college, the narrator speaks of "my mother" and repeats her quoted dialogue, including this telling of the telling: "'Whup. Whup.' My mother told the sound of new fire so that I remember it. 'Whup. Whup'" (*Warrior*, 74). "So that I remember it"—the sound as Brave Orchid reproduces it becomes, then, a shared aural memory. "I think my mother said" is another way of reminding readers that it is Maxine telling her mother's story, trying to reconstruct it as it seemed to her to have happened, trying to make it come out sounding like an eyewitness account (*Warrior*, 75). At other times she tells her mother's story, including thoughts and quoted speech, with no narrator intervention. When she uses a hypothetical mode regarding what her mother would and would not do (whether one reads "would" to mean that this was her mother's habit or only a possibility), we cannot be sure if she is relying on her mother's account or hypothesizing based on her day-to-day experience with her mother (*Warrior,* 79).

"The beginning is hers, the ending mine," Maxine writes in her introduction to her final chapter, "A Song for a Barbarian Reed Pipe" (*Warrior,* 206).[45] Perhaps because Maxine's story will end in "translation," in yet another transformation of a Chinese poem for Maxine's purposes, and will finally unite Chinese and barbarians through the medium of art, she requires, or is at least inspired by, her mother's tacit permission to value art above all else. This is still another lesson to be drawn from the mother's "beginning" story, that of her grandmother's taking the family to the theater despite the threat of bandit raids. As we have seen, the bandits did come, but raided the theater, not the house. Even though they took one of the aunts, the fact that they let her go and the family all returned safe was "proof to my grandmother that our family was immune to harm as long as they went to plays. They went to many plays after that" (*Warrior,* 207). We remember that Brave Orchid tells stories to warn or to grow on, and this may very well be one of those. For the first time in the book Brave Orchid seems to be recognizing what Maxine is doing, and showing in her subtle, storytelling manner that it has value to her too. Maxine says: "Here is a story my mother told me, not when I was young, but recently, *when I told her I also talk story*" (*Warrior,* 206, emphasis mine). It is as though Brave Orchid is giving Maxine a gift: she has long since given her the gift of storytelling, and now she adds to it the gift of her acknowledgment that they share this treasure. Implied in the telling and in the story itself is Brave Orchid's valuing the gift, and valuing the fact that they share it. Brave Orchid, we have been told much earlier, is a "champion talker." Her talking story, like the swordswoman movies, makes Maxine feel that she "ha[s] been in the presence of great power" (*Warrior,* 19–20). Perhaps the shawl of success Brave Orchid has wrapped about her, success in story, has given Maxine great power as well, a power her mother now seems willing to acknowledge and share with her. Power through words and her family's recognition of her word power will be essential to any

45. Celeste Schenck writes of this chapter that it "is in the fullest sense a collaboration between mother and daughter, a parable in itself of female artistry and achievement that begins and ends in productive, neither annihilating nor symbiotic continuity with the maternal rhythm. . . . [T]he duet performed by mother and daughter . . . retains all the tension implicit in their differences and all the daughter's ambivalence . . ." ("All of a Piece," 301).

sort of homecoming. She has made this clear back in the "White Tigers" chapter, where she concluded her woman warrior story: "The swords-woman and I are not so dissimilar. May my people understand the resem-blance soon so that I can return to them" (*Warrior,* 53).

It is an acknowledgment of Maxine's having that power that seems im-plicit in her mother's story of Grandmother and the theater and inspires Maxine's version of Ts'ai Yen's story, allowing her to render it in a "trans-lation" that travels well. According to Maxine's story, it is only when the captive poetess hears the barbarian's music—the cut reeds that she had as-sociated only with weapons having now become flutes—that she rises to approach them. Here too art and weapon are one, just as Guan Gung is at once god of literature and war. At this point the narration becomes poetic: "She heard music tremble and rise like desert wind. . . . [The barbarians] reached again and again for a high note, yearning toward a high note, which they found at last and held—an icicle in the desert" (*Warrior,* 208). Their music disturbs her, until she joins it; she begins to sing a high, clear song that matches their flutes. Although she sings of China in a language the barbarians cannot understand, they are able to understand the sadness and anger in her songs, just as she is able to understand the yearning of their flutes. Her barbarian children, who laugh at her when she tries to speak to them in Chinese, sing along with her when she sings; the songs she has brought back to China from the savage lands "translated well." Brave Orchid tells the beginning, Maxine tells the end, and together, it seems, they too are uniting in song, in story; through art, they are able to combine what is Chinese with what is "barbarian" as they never really have been able to do in any other way. "You lie with stories," Maxine had shouted. But, as King-Kok Cheung points out: "Though the influence is not openly acknowledged, the consistently inconsistent mother nurtures the narrator's ability to entertain contradictions . . . to see truth as multidimen-sional, and to escape from the scientific authority that sets empirical truth and the voice of reason above the promptings of the imagination." In this story Maxine acknowledges collaboration. And this story, like the song, translates well—from Ts'ai Yen to Maxine, from Brave Orchid's oral stories to Maxine's written text, from lived pain to art. It translates barbarian and Chinese words and ways to one another in and through the medium of art.[46] Brave Orchid begins a story that shows she understands the resem-blance, and so Maxine can come home—she has written the way home.

---

46. Cheung, *Articulate Silences,* 99. Cheung points out the connection between *translate* and *traduce* (to betray or speak falsely) (ibid., 96). The well-known accusa-tion *"traduttore traditore"* refers to the violation of a text when it is translated—what

In My Mother's House: A Daughter's Story dramatizes collaboration overtly: Kim Chernin is not just writing the way home *to* her mother, but also *with* her. The reader is allowed into the process and the dynamics of that collaboration. Eakin's observation that collaborative auto/biography usually includes the story of the telling of the story is certainly true of this book, but much more is at stake, and accomplished, in the process of this particular telling, listening, and writing.[47] As the story of the mother, Rose Chernin, comes to include the stories of *her* mother, Sarah, and also Kim, the story of the telling takes on a much larger role than that of a frame in which a teller reveals her life to her listening daughter; it is more than just another example of the way narrating one's life clarifies and reifies experience for the teller, organizes it, and reveals new truths and perceptions to her. In this story of telling, the listener becomes the indispensable other half of— no, participant in—the telling. The telling/listening that the work entails over a seven-year period provides the occasion as well as the necessity finally to articulate pain that has never been spoken (the loss of a sister/ daughter plays a major, though repressed, role), to put pieces of their lives together, and in so doing to unearth, articulate, correct, and thereby lay to rest misunderstandings that have been long buried but still lie close enough to the surface to make this project fraught with risk and tension. Still, in answering the (until now) unasked questions, in responding to the look, touch, memory of the listener—be that mother or daughter—lives become stories, and stories re-bond the most fundamental, most unshakable relationships in this book: mother and daughter, past and present.[48]

The book is set into motion by an urgent request Chernin's mother makes of her: to write her story. Rose Chernin has been an active and fiery voice for "the people" and their plight, from evictions to deportations, an active and vocal member of the Communist party. To this cause she has dedicated her life and her family's, with the result that she was jailed during the McCarthy era and threatened with deportation. Her fight for herself and others whose citizenship was threatened by the Smith Act went all the

---

gets lost, reduced, or distorted by even a well-meaning translator. It is a warning meant to privilege the original language. But in this case, we are told the songs "translated well." We may ask: In whose opinion—the translator's? And would the original author agree? There lies the ambiguity. I don't take "translation" in this context to be, necessarily, a betrayal.

47. Eakin, *Lives,* 59.

48. In Chernin's later book *In My Father's Garden: A Daughter's Search for a Spiritual Life,* she voices resentment over her mother's quashing any desire for spiritual expression; thus the book is not only a tribute to her father, but also an indication that resentments toward her mother are not over and done with.

way to the Supreme Court, where the act was declared unconstitutional and Rose finally free of the threats of prison and deportation. Rose's story also includes her life in the shtetl under the czar, as well as her mother's life with an abusive husband in an America she could never adjust to. It includes the story of Sarah's attempted suicides, her commitment to a state mental institution, and her continuing paranoia even after Rose brings her home to live with her. It must also include Rose's guilt over having left her mother in her father's hands so that she could continue her education, determined *never* to allow herself to be like her mother. Mother guilt, daughter guilt—not only Rose's, but Kim's, who has not seen her mother for years. Rose's anguished question "Was I not also a daughter?" lays the ground for reconciliation if anything does, for as the stories are told a pattern emerges of "this tragedy of woman, always needing to sacrifice someone else in order to go after her own life." This is from a discussion of Yezierska, and Rose realizes that it "is easier when you hear it about someone else's life. It seems . . . even, forgivable."[49] The implication is that the listener from the next generation, Kim's daughter, Larissa, will have it easier.

Rose's story ranges from shtetl to America and back to a euphoric time in Russia, where her engineer husband works on the Moscow subway and she translates for party publications; it is an era of communal joy and cooperation, singing and dancing—who could have believed it? The people got rid of the czar and were building an ideal world. Then back again to America, where Rose feels she cannot sail away from the plight of her imprisoned friends and comrades. She is an organizer, and she is needed to organize, to speak out, to rescue, to act. Her story darkens with the death of her beloved elder daughter, Nina, from Hodgkin's disease. Nina was not only a daughter, but also a support, almost more a mother to little Kim than Rose, taking over much of her care so that Rose could continue her active party roles. But her death was never spoken of, and Kim, who shared Nina's bed, was never made to understand it, never relieved of her childish burden of guilt and fear that somehow she was responsible, never allowed to articulate her grief at the loss of this beloved sister/mother, as well as the loss, for a while, of her own mother, whose grief plunged her into a depression that rendered her, too, unavailable to her adoring five-year-old daughter. Now, finally, Nina's death is being told—by both of them. Now, at last, tears too long unshed are liberated and flow freely.

Conflicts between Rose and Kim begin, not surprisingly, during Kim's adolescence, but the usual conflicts are exacerbated by Rose's imprison-

49. Kim Chernin, *In My Mother's House: A Daughter's Story,* 108–9 (hereinafter cited in the text as *House*).

ment (read: abandonment and then return to glory and center stage) and, later, by Kim's disillusion with communism. Kim too experiences an intensely emotional, euphoric "return" to Mother Russia as part of an international communist youth gathering. But gradually the singing and dancing, the romances and friendships, become more and more tarnished by hints of repression, fear, and anti-Semitism. "Go back to America," all Kim's new Russian friends tell her. This experience, combined with her reading of the Khrushchev report on Stalin and his purges, causes what, to Rose, can only be considered apostasy and betrayal. Kim leaves the party, disillusioned, while her mother continues to cling to the ideals that have driven her since her own adolescence.

What Kim tries to impress upon her mother is that she too is breaking ground, albeit on issues that Rose cannot quite understand. She says she too is breaking taboos (*House*, 6).[50] The disappointment that Rose feels in this daughter—who once wanted most of all to be like her mother—is that of the activist, doing and accomplishing, looking with disdain upon the self-enclosed, "passive" life of the poet. The task that Rose lays on her daughter, a task that at first she seems to see as mainly stenographic—"to take down the story of my life"—becomes, between them, a "bearing of the flame." It is collaborative in the way one story calls out another, or a memory surfaces in response to a question, evoking any of a variety of responses on the part of the listener. And it raises the esteem of The Writer in Rose's eyes. But to take on this story, to be the author of this project, of her mother's life and, in the process, her own, Kim must once again be willing to surrender to her mother, to risk being swallowed by this powerful woman.[51] "I must keep [the flame] alive, I must manage not to be consumed

50. While Chernin does not mention her lesbian relationships in this book, it seems possible that this could be what she is referring to, and that it could have been a bone of contention in addition to her change in politics and move toward spiritual enlightenment. By the time *In My Mother's House* was published in 1983, she had undergone her second divorce and was living with a woman (Jerilyn Fisher, "Kim Chernin," 56). In 1996's *In My Father's Garden*, she refers openly to her relationship with Renate Stendhal, and her 1986 novel *The Flame Bearers*, dedicated to Stendhal, could very well be the project she says she interrupted in order to work with her mother.

51. Compare Doris Kearns (now Doris Kearns Goodwin) on writing a biography of Lyndon Johnson: "[D]espite the pull of fascination, there was always a counterbalancing need to get away, to leave, not to be owned" ("Angles of Vision," 92). Eakin discusses the shift in power relations that occurs in the course of this collaboration, and quotes Chernin on the way she had to create a voice that sounded like her mother on the page: Rose "had taken over, *or been taken over by*, the voice I had created for her" (*Lives*, 179–80). Marianne Hirsch writes of a similar power shift: "To speak for the mother, as many daughters in this [Hirsch's] book do, is at once to give voice to her discourse *and* to silence and marginalize her" (*The Mother/Daughter Plot: Narrative, Psychoanalysis, Feminism*, 16).

by it," she writes (*House,* 16), as she begins to assume power over the narrative, making from her mother's stories this book she will author and subtitle *A Daughter's Story.* Which daughter? Whose story? For is Kim not also a daughter, just as her mother has said of herself? Kim will take on this task and accomplish the mission, but first she must surrender, not only to her mother's power but also to her own memories, her own role as the child saying, "Mama, tell me a story."

This typical child's request is reduced to "tell me," repeated as a refrain throughout the book, a reduction that is in reality an expansion of "story." "Tell me" asks to share a life, experiences important and trivial, the day's events; it demands information and explanations. No longer a childish request for a well-worn formulaic tale with a happy ending, it implies: tell me the danger, tell me what's wrong with Nina, why she's dying (yes, I do know she's dying); tell me when you'll return to me from your grief, and what the Smith Act is doing to you and us. And now, tell me your story so that I can tell you mine.[52] Tell me my grandmother's story so I'll understand yours. "Take down my story" elicits "Tell me, Mama." Once Rose has told her stories, she says that now Kim must tell, that the rest of the story, covering much of the same time period, must be hers, and of course, hers is quite different from her mother's. Kim suffered, Kim too was required to sacrifice, and wasn't Rose also a mother? And did she not, as a mother, also require sacrifices that were sometimes given and sometimes refused?

This reciprocal telling and the weaving into their narratives of the stories of grandmother and aunts, many of them told as well to Kim's daughter Larissa, who has questions and comments of her own, is indeed an important story in its own right, and, as is already evident, as vital stimulus for eliciting memory and telling. Chernin is masterful in structuring the book to reflect this interweaving and to give prominence to the story of the story as well. Introducing and separating the stories (eight stories "my mother tells," three stories "I tell") are narratives during the "present" of the narrating mother and daughter, stories of the telling and listening, the asking and the reflecting—on tales, on one another, and on themselves as reflected in each other's eyes. Kim observes: "A fine point of light opens into her eyes. And now she stares at me as if she could find the truth of her own life in my face" (*House,* 148).

As Rose revisits her mother's sad life, she begins to realize, in light of

---

52. Burstein writes of the way the mother's story "can open up to embrace her listener. . . . When Kim is enabled by entering her mother's story to see from within the places where it touches and diverges from her own, she is changed" (*Writing Mothers, Writing Daughters,* 169).

her own active life, her daughter's poetic life, and her granddaughter's seemingly limitless future, that her mother's tragedy, perhaps her insanity, was
rooted in the way "she was miscast in life":

> She hated housework, she hated the routine. She wanted only to make
> delicacies, to bake, to embroider, to write letters.... You could see
> she was contented with life. But of course, she looked around, she
> compared herself to those women who were outstanding homemak-
> ers. Their ability was always very highly prized.... Compared to these
> other women who hung out their clothes on Monday and ironed them
> on Tuesday, she seemed to herself an inferior human being. She hated
> the things she thought she should be able to do. And who valued the
> things she loved? ... Who cared then if a mother would write a beauti-
> ful letter? ... Her letters were all she managed to find for herself.
> Whenever she could take the time, always you would see her, sitting at
> the table, writing. That is how you should think of your grandmother.
> This is how I want to give her for you to remember. (*House,* 173–74)

"To give her"—this picture of Sarah is a gift Rose gives to Kim (much like
the gift Brave Orchid gives Maxine). Her grandmother, a writer. Other references have been made to Sarah's literacy—exceptional for a woman of
her place and time—the letters she wrote to America from the shtetl, from
America to the shtetl, for her friends who were illiterate. Her letters were
tales, more fabrication than truth, cloaking truth on behalf of those who
wanted her to do so, and in the process embellishing, imagining, embroi-
dering. Rose laments the loss of her mother's letters; they would have
been a chronicle of a woman's immigrant life in America. Rose (much like
Kingston) realizes that her mother was a storyteller, not only in what she
told, but also in the tales' artistic quality. "What is in the background . . .
this matters also to the story," she quotes her mother as saying. Sarah talks
of "liv[ing] a story" (*House,* 54–55). As Alice Walker goes "in search of our
mothers' gardens," so too Rose and Kim search Sarah's life; her creativity
unappreciated, her talent now flowers in a granddaughter who becomes
her heir. The realization of what Grandmother Sarah could have been adds
to Rose's appreciation of what Kim has become, and where it may have
originated. Walker realizes that the talent rising up in her generation had to
come from somewhere and, stunted in earlier generations, often found its
outlet in madness or what was thought to be madness.[53] Where Rose sees
only madness in Sarah's inability to understand that the czar was dead and

---

53. Alice Walker, *In Search of Our Mothers' Gardens: Womanist Prose.*

that the time and place of the shtetl were long gone, Kim sees this "mad-ness" as treasure: "Just think of it, Mama. That old woman, living here in Los Angeles . . . for her the shtetl still existed. She believed her father was alive there, that Jews could still not live in Moscow, that the czar had not been deposed. That old woman, I tell you, carried a world around in her, still living, the rest of us have lost." What Kim looks back on with nostal-gia is, to Rose, a bitter life gladly left behind, but the potential quarrel does not, this time, materialize. They are seeing with different eyes: "This is a different shtetl than the one I knew. Or maybe . . . maybe I have forgot-ten," is Rose's response (*House,* 105–6).

Might this view of Grandmother Sarah dredge up "forgotten" pieces of shtetl life for Rose? Might her daughter's way of seeing put even those memories that are available in a new light? We are not told, but what is clear is how essential the role of listener has been throughout the book. In *The Woman Who Gave Birth to Her Mother,* Chernin articulates this explic-itly: "A good listener is the first requirement for a good story, the ideal fellow-traveler, the companion sitting across from one, stranger or inti-mate, as the storytelling train starts up out of the station. . . . Stories need listeners who can be there, virtually a part of the story itself as it unravels."[54] Mother and daughter work together to reconstruct, in fact to re-see, their lives and the intricate networks connecting them to one another and to other family members dead and alive, and this process and its role in re-constructing the mother-daughter relationship is the story of *In My Mother's House.* Not as clear to me is why, when it is Kim's turn to "tell," she launches her story with her closest friends as the audience. The occasion is fraught with tension and possibility: Rose comments that it is the first time Kim has introduced her to her friends; she assumes that Kim is ashamed of her, when the truth is that Kim fears her mother will look down on her friends. This preamble to the stories about to be told prepares Kim and Rose—and us—for other realizations and confessions occasioned by the presence of others, listeners who have never been a party to the events in their narratives or to their lifetime of interaction. Perhaps the necessity to contextualize, explain, provide some history and background, brings out explanations they had never before made to one another, even in the long process of collaborating on Rose's story. The agenda for the evening is Kim's reading; she will read the manuscript of her first story to her friends, and also to her mother. But Rose feels she must speak first, introduce her

54. Kim Chernin, *The Woman Who Gave Birth to Her Mother: Seven Stages of Change in Women's Lives,* 40–41.

daughter's story with some background on the life she caused Kim to lead, along with her own realization of Kim's pain, acknowledged for the first time—an acknowledgment born of the necessity to provide the "history" so fundamental to what Kim's friends are about to hear. But this is the result of having an audience outside the family.[55] Did Kim realize as she was planning the occasion that this would happen? Did she somehow feel that to tell a crucial story she had to have listeners who were not in any way a part of the story except as listeners, realizing the importance of listeners to tellers? It is also possible that she realized, and feared, the power of such a storytelling moment: "The storyteller needs to risk an engagement with recollection, a slippery, uncertain text. The storyteller should be wrestling with memory, with its power to call up,"[56] and such risk, such wrestling, such confrontation through her narrative with her mother, who has not yet read or heard it, may have required her to want the presence of "seconds" in this wrestling match, a community partaking of an intimate communion with the hosts of the occasion, witnessing and sanctifying their testimonies. She may have needed to couch the painful and familial in the social, proudly introducing her mother to her friends; may have needed, in so risky a situation, to have friends there to "call her back" from her memories and her narrative, much as Brave Orchid needed the assurance that her schoolmates would tweak her ears and call her back from the realm of ghosts by using her closely guarded private name.

To write one's life requires great self-assurance, or confidence in the importance of one's story, or great motivation—the urgency to tell, the urgency to be heard, or both. Amy Ling writes that Chinese society, for example, would have viewed a woman who writes (not to mention one who writes in another language) as lacking in respectability:

> Modesty and reticence were the ideals established for women; writing was extreme egotism, even self-exposure. Therefore . . . she must be something of a rebel. . . . Also she has to possess two basic character traits: an indomitable will and an unshakable self-confidence. She must also be propelled by the undeniable drive to communicate with the readers and speakers of the dominant language of the society into which she has been transplanted either because of the rightness of her cause or because of the force of her need to express herself.[57]

55. For a discussion of the power of public storytelling to bring out what has been hidden and to "give birth to a new relationship," see Chernin's *Woman Who Gave Birth to Her Mother,* 208–9.

56. Ibid., 43.

57. Ling, *Between Worlds,* 14.

One way of interpreting what Gergen calls the challenge to tell one's life is as the challenge of reaching an audience for whom the writer has an important message. To be a spokesperson, a comfort, an inspiration to others who will benefit, or to give voice to what the "voiceless" need said for them—these too are socially stimulated motives to tell one's story. In this case the audience one is writing *to* may also be the group one is speaking *for,* a justification for telling and especially for asserting the "I" that a less self-assured writer might need. Eva Hoffman speaks of such a motive: expressing the difficulties of "life in a new language" and, more generally, of "translation" of the self, not only for herself but also for the benefit of those who are going through the same difficulties, gave her the incentive and the much-needed license to write about herself and her family. Feeling that she had such a mission relieved her of inhibiting guilt and of feeling that it was presumptuous to write "I" as if she should matter to readers. Joan Chiung-huei Chang finds a similar license in Chinese American autobiographies whose meaning "has moved from the presentation of one's personal experiences and sentiments to that of personal experiences and sentiments among many persons within the private and isolated community of Chinese Americans. . . . [A]utobiography has transformed from the writing of *self* into the writing of *selves*." Patricia P. Chu locates the difficulty in the tension between "the Asian sense of the self as rooted in family and community and the American sense of self as an autonomous being." Similarly, Hana Wirth-Nesher writes of Jewish autobiography: "Given the emphasis on community in Jewish culture, where the act of confession is necessarily a public and communal ritual, a genre that valorizes the individual would not find fertile soil for its sustenance. Celebrating the uniqueness of the individual and attaining freedom from a community has been antithetical to Jewish identity. Thus, the power of community acts as a constraint in Jewish-American self-portraits."[58]

While one hardly imagines Yezierska allowing such considerations to silence her, we have seen in her writing an urgency to speak on behalf of others who suffered as she did—poor, inarticulate by mainstream standards, powerless and unheeded. That she was writing not only herself but also her fellow immigrants and sweatshop workers gave her a self-justifying agenda in the face of another sort of challenge: appealing to "Anglo-Saxon" Americans to accept and appreciate and help those poor and foreign in their

---

58. Chang, *Transforming Chinese American Literature,* 89; Chu, *Assimilating Asians,* 18; Hana Wirth-Nesher, introduction to special issue on Jewish American autobiography, *Prooftexts* 18 (1998): 114.

midst. In this, she, like Jade Snow Wong, for example, wrote to speak in the name of a community or group, what John Beverly refers to as *testimonio,* a function he goes so far as to relate to the symbolic function of the epic.[59]

Phoebe Eng, on the other hand, in *Warrior Lessons: An Asian American Woman's Journey into Power,* tells her story mainly to inspire other Asian woman to journey, as she has done, to whatever power they yearn for. In writing of her own conflicts and struggles, she shows that she understands full well what they are up against, that she encountered the same obstacles, but as she faced and surmounted them, so might they. To telling and listening she adds another important dimension: Asian American women sharing stories in order to connect with one another—a network she worked hard to establish. She writes of the decision she had to make in order to accomplish her mission: "*Warrior Lessons* is also about my own growing process. . . . Some of the personal stories I share will leave me exposed and vulnerable. . . . I had to bring my own voice and my own experience to the table in as truthful and intimate way as I could. . . . [The book] includes stories that I was reluctant to tell." But she realizes that only by such opening of herself can she expect others to do the same with her; only by sharing stories will connection occur. It is not surprising that her warrior lessons—learned as well as offered—were in no small measure inspired by that powerful word warrior Maxine Hong Kingston, which is an important reminder of the influence of reading, of the shift in roles from reader to writer, and of the strength and direction that *writing* can provide. Eng admits that writing her book was a journey and an education for herself as well, and that the stories she has heard helped her "to piece together the road map" she had sought for so long.[60]

Eng details the battles that she and her fellow Asian American women have had to fight on their journeys to power, their "adversaries" often their own feelings of guilt, or fear of disappointing their parents, or just plain fear of "dar[ing] to disturb the[ir] universe." But as so many readers of *any* of these books can attest, one need not be either Chinese or Jewish or female to see oneself reflected somewhere in their pages. So often quoted from *The Woman Warrior,* and relevant here as well, are the questions: "Chinese Americans, when you try to understand what things in you are Chinese, how do you separate what is peculiar to childhood, to poverty, insanities, one family, your mother who marked your growing with stories,

59. John Beverly, "The Margin at the Center: On *Testimonio,*" 95.
60. Eng, *Warrior Lessons,* 6, 7, 11.

from what is Chinese? What is Chinese tradition and what is the movies?" (*Warrior,* 5–6). Absent is any scene or context of a speaker addressing an audience; therefore this passage is made to sound like a direct address to the reader—specifically, a Chinese American reader. What, then, does that make the rest of us? Eavesdroppers? Guests invited and then excluded? Perhaps we are merely observers; perhaps we are being ignored; but if the shoe fits, we are free to wear it. If we do, though, what we are really doing is translating "Chinese American" into our own "language" and identity. And we are reminded of Kingston's own voice, in an interview, acknowledging with great satisfaction the letters she receives from so many *non*-Chinese readers who feel that her words speak to and for them as well.[61]

So, are we invited in after all—as witnesses, as parties to some ongoing conversation? Has opening such a book and wanting to keep reading been our entrée, not only into the book but also into the conversation, and possibly even a world? Yezierska writes of addressing an audience of college sorority girls who wanted to write. Her emotions, as she looked at their "hungry" eyes, switched from terror to envy to hate, until she realized that what she saw in their eyes was the need to question rather than to hear a speech, the need to hear the truth. She tore up her speech and answered their questions with stories of her own experiences. "I had erected a wall of self-defense around me and shot arrows of envy at them. Immune to envy . . . they swept across the hall and conquered me. All at once I loved them" (*Ribbon,* 134). The audience had been there from the beginning, but communication began only when she looked into their eyes and understood what they, privileged and enviable though they were, hungered for: something valuable that she had the power to give them. Audiences within a story can have the effect of making the reader, too, feel included as part of that group, as a listener inside and not just a reader outside the text. Perhaps Chernin, in creating her storytelling scene, with its group of intimate and reacting listeners, was also inviting her readers into this group to hear her story and her mother's introduction, even to notice her friends wiping the tears from their eyes.

Cisneros's "house quiet as snow . . . clean as paper before the poem" becomes the paper written upon when a writer is writing the way home, whether that home on paper is a new and private place or the parental home revisited. It is these pieces of paper, bound and put in front of us, that are extended to us as readers. From various motives and carrying highly individual, infinitely varied baggage we arrive, and we enter.

61. Kingston, interview in *Conversations,* ed. Skenazy and Martin, 178.

8

The Reader in the Mirror

To enter a text—what does that mean? What are we expecting, and what is being expected of us? What does an author risk in inviting us, and what does a reader risk in accepting the invitation? What sort of transaction have we entered into when we open and stay with a book, and how much does it matter whether the milieu into which we are plunged is familiar or strange? The previous chapter has included stories of writing, but what about stories of reading? Here (albeit written by "all-American" Eudora Welty) is one of my favorites:

> You could take out two books at a time and two only. . . . So two by two, I read library books as fast as I could go, rushing them home in the basket of my bicycle. From the minute I reached our house, I started to read. Every book I seized on . . . stood for the devouring wish to be read being instantly granted. I knew this was bliss; knew it at the time. . . . I wanted to read *immediately*. The only fear was that of books coming to an end.[1]

I read this memory, and suddenly I am eight, or ten. I can't wait to get home to open—which book first? To that remembered child on her bicycle, I breathe: "Eudora, c'est moi!" for once again I am in my room with only a few pages left of *Heidi,* and I don't want to leave Grandfather's cottage in the Alps. It's no use telling me there's a sequel. It won't do. The Alpine world I've been wandering in has become for a time my world, Grandfather my kindly tutor, and my own room (surely much more comfortable than Heidi's) so ordinary, so everyday, so lonely. What a jolt to be

---

1. Eudora Welty, *One Writer's Beginnings,* 33.

back there so suddenly, with just the turn of a page and closing of the cover. For a while, though, Heidi still lingers as my companion, or is it I who am Heidi and Grandfather my companion? My room and the Alps merge into an out-of-focus double exposure, hazy until my mother calls me to dinner or a chore.

We learn early on that a book is an invitation, and to read it is to accept. We enter to share in another life, another world. So many of us who wanted books to go on and on, who found compensation in knowing that there were countless others, the next book and the next, have grown up (and into careers) wanting to share that feeling and those countless worlds with others. Long before we were theorists or critical readers, long before we understood "distance" from texts, or that texts and characters are nothing more than verbal constructions, we experienced closeness to those real-seeming constructs—we loved them or hated them, we feared for them and hoped for them; for the reading duration we *were* them, playing the roles the author wrote for us, identifying with them.

But of course the capacity for affective (and affected) response, for identification, never goes completely away. As Inge Crosman Wimmers writes: "What we know in theory to be an illusion is quite another thing while we are immersed in the experience of reading." The knowledge that when we open a novel we enter a fictional world "does not protect us from falling prey to the illusion that fictional entities exist or seem real." Jerome Bruner calls literary texts "magnets for empathy" and cites Wolfgang Iser, who also discusses the ways in which we become "entangled" in a text, and the ways texts have the power, for better or for worse, to change us—the ways in which, as we are constructing a reading, we are also reconstructing ourselves. Wimmers goes even further in privileging empathy, and cites others who also view identification as crucial to interpreting a text, and the understanding of a text as a way of understanding the self. For example, she quotes Paul Ricoeur: "[T]he interpretation of a text is completed in the *self-interpretation* of a subject who henceforth understands himself better, who understands himself differently, or who even begins to understand himself" (emphasis mine). Wimmer concludes: "By opening the interpretive space between reader and text to include both text interpretation and self-interpretation, the frames of reference that come into play are multiplied."[2]

2. Wimmers, *Poetics of Reading*, 19, 4, 154; Jerome Bruner, *Actual Minds, Possible Worlds*, 21; Paul Ricoeur, "Qu'est-ce qu'un texte?" quoted in Wimmers, *Poetics of Reading*, 8. Wimmers also draws on Volker Roloff's studies of role playing in reading fiction, as well as Anselm Haverkamp and Iser.

Autobiography theorists make similar points about the reading of auto-biography. For example, Leigh Gilmore writes that by identifying with an autobiography, the reader constructs an "imaginary relation" to the "situation the text depicts." Barrett J. Mandel writes: "The autobiographer springs open a door and gives me a glance into his or her deepest reality, at the same time casting my mind into a state of reverie or speculation. The being of the author is felt to merge with my own. For a moment I plummet deep into my own veiled assumptions, feelings, and self-meaning."[3]

What these and other reader-response theorists have in common is their emphasis on the importance of the reader's active participation in creating the meaning of a text. Iser considers literary texts as "initiat[ing] performances of meaning, rather than actually formulating meaning themselves." Citing Anselm Haverkamp, Wimmers explains that empathy sets up participatory reading; as the reader perceives analogies between his own disposition and the roles inscribed in the text, he becomes an active participant "in setting in motion analogies between aesthetic experience and his own life. Reading . . . becomes an occasion for further self-awareness." Which seems to be another way of saying that a text can reflect its reader (art holding the mirror up to nature), but actually is saying more: that a text can make us aware of what we may not otherwise have seen in ourselves ("*further* self-awareness"). Wimmers quotes Proust: "In reality every reader is, while he is reading, the reader of his own self. The writer's work is merely a kind of optical instrument which he offers to the reader to enable him to discern what, without this book, he would perhaps never have perceived in himself."[4]

To read oneself in a book suggests looking in a mirror; but if we see more than we are accustomed to seeing, it must be a special kind of mirror, one that penetrates surfaces—perhaps a kind of X ray, showing our bones through a fluoroscope. "Seeing," relative to this study, though, might also relate to another sort of "optical instrument": a lens to bring closer or clarify a subject, or even a simple transparent glass, for the texts under discussion also serve as windows through which we are able to see something of the cultures of others, bring them closer, clarify our view of them, and at times color them. Yet, as we come closer, as we perceive analogies and similarities and therefore identify with more distant or more proximate others, what we are doing, in effect, is turning that window into a mirror,

3. Gilmore, *Autobiographics,* 23; Mandel, "Full of Life Now," 69.
4. Iser, *Act of Reading,* 27; Wimmers, *Poetics of Reading,* 129; Proust, *The Guermantes Way,* trans. C. K. Scott Moncrieff et al., quoted in Wimmers, *Poetics of Reading,* 10–11.

or into an "optical instrument" that allows us to see what is not visible to the naked eye or obvious at a quick glance. Through such a process, and in such mirrors, we may come to see some reflection of our "own" selves.

But first the distance between reader and book must be closed, and to better understand *that* process, it would be helpful to return to Iser and discuss his theories of reading in a bit more detail. It is the openness of a text[5]—the variety of its possibilities, and its very difficulties—that attracts, he tells us. We become entangled in it because of its indeterminacy, the gaps it presents to the reader between what is given and what must be inferred, between what is given on page 1 and what we must remake of those givens by the time we get to page 50 or 300. Our viewpoints must "wander"; we must be willing always to modify what we made of pages past as well as our predictions for pages ahead, to construct and reconstruct. But at the same time we are always seeking consistency, whether in constructing wholeness of the text or reconciling it with our worldview and our experience; we need to make meaning where we do not readily find it, and we become engaged in the making more than in the ready-made. Thus we become entangled as we construct the text. And thus we construct ourselves into it as we read.[6]

While Iser addresses himself mainly to the difficulties of reading modernist novels and to the requirements of constructing meaning in formal, structural terms, we can apply his theory to issues of cultural knowledge as well: when we enter a world that is unfamiliar, we notice what we don't know, what we need to know, and what we must fill in either with the help of our imaginations, our analogous experience, or information outside the text. (In texts such as *Call It Sleep, The Woman Warrior, The Joy Luck Club,* and *The Counterlife,* we must enter into both kinds of gaps.) Of course if a potential reader looks into a book as if through a window, decides that what he sees is too unfamiliar, and lacks the requisite curiosity or motivation to work a bit harder at understanding, or, in Iser's terms, to wander and build and "fill in" the gaps, the relationship ends right there. But the reader who does commit to engagement, through constant oscillation between observing and being involved in a text, will experience the text as a living event. As he becomes more and more absorbed in what he himself has been made to produce, as he combines what is shown and known with what is not shown, but imaged, imagined, he cannot help but be affected by his own production. He has become one with it, for the

5. I use the term *openness* as Umberto Eco does in *The Role of the Reader: Explorations in the Semiotics of Texts.*

6. Iser, *Act of Reading.*

time being: "the meaning of the literary text . . . does not exist independently of him; just as important, though, is that the reader himself, in constituting the meaning, is also constituted."[7]

Such an experience can be exhilarating or threatening, or both, especially if the reader is being (re)constituted to re-view his own environment.
A work of literature helps this to happen because it "takes its selected objects out of their pragmatic context and so shatters their original frame of
reference; the result is to reveal aspects (e.g., social norms) which had remained hidden as long as the frame of reference remained intact." The
reader is thus placed in a position from which he can take a fresh look at
"social forces and norms he may have accepted unquestioned and unexamined." In the context of cross-cultural literature, the reader who shares
the culture in the book and the one who is seeing it in contrast to her own
will have strikingly different "norms" to reexamine, but the potential disturbance can be very similar. So might the "awakening" Iser discusses:
once absorbed in a book, in producing its meaning, and hence "temporarily
isolated from the real world," the reader, on "returning" to her real world,
can suddenly, if momentarily, view it "as a thing freshly understood"—
again, an enlarging but also (as discussed in Chapter 6) a potentially threatening experience.[8]

When Iser speaks of "social norms," he seems to presume norms shared
by text and reader, the familiar becoming not confirmation but the basis
for forming something new, the old given a new significance, new life.
Umberto Eco assumes a model reader in the mind of the writer "that enables the author to set up a culturally based system of reference in the
text," which, in turn, enables the reader "to deal interpretively with the
cultural codes inscribed in the work."[9] In cross-cultural reading, we can
make no such assumptions. The reading audience is aligned along a con-
tinuum from intimacy with the culture of the author to total unfamiliarity.
We have seen non-English words, idioms, and structures written into
English-language texts that may or may not be translated, and we must assume that both language and cultural codes are read very differently by
those who share them and those who do not. Who, then, is Kingston's

---

7. Ibid., 128, 140, 150. Wimmers too uses the term *event:* "Novels . . . are not simply
verbal constructs whose illusion building we can rationally dismiss; they are experienced as events while they engage us in a particular process of world building, feeling,
and thinking" (*Poetics of Reading,* 21). Louise M. Rosenblatt, a reader-response theorist
positing a "transactional" theory of response to "aesthetically" read texts, describes "the
poem" as "an event in time" (*The Reader, the Text, the Poem,* 12–21).

8. Iser, *Act of Reading,* 109, 74, 140.

9. Ibid., 132; Eco quoted in Wimmers, *Poetics of Reading,* xvi.

"model reader"? Yezierska's? Henry Roth's? Tan's, or Chin's? Surely authors like these are aware that their "in-group" audiences will react in very different ways from their "majority" readers; that what is inside knowledge and connection to one reader will be an exotic experience or, at least, new information to another.[10] Jade Snow Wong clearly wanted to teach non-Chinese readers, show them how "civilized" the Chinese really are. Her ambassadorial agenda seems quite clear, and innocuous; yet an Asian American student of mine found *Fifth Chinese Daughter* to be extremely unsettling because aspects of it cut too close to home. Frank Chin, on the other hand, sees Wong as pandering to the worst white stereotypes of Chinese, especially those of white men.[11]

Being inside or outside a culture, then, is not the only basis for difference in response, for within any cultural group there is not only a broad spectrum of familiarity or nonfamiliarity with that culture, but also different degrees of loyalty, different personal memories of relations with the "majority" culture, and certainly different experiences with literary conventions and ways that texts are read by one's peers. Witness the ire that Philip Roth has raised among Jews who feel he gives ammunition to anti-Semites, not to mention their feeling that their own mothers have been besmirched by his portrayal of "the Jewish mother." And witness his hurt responses to them, as well as his derisive remarks about readers who take a novel to be sociologically reliable or autobiographical, who take straight what is meant to be a satirical critique of hypocrisy. Recall the Chinese American student in my class who was angry with *The Woman Warrior* until he was allowed to air his feelings, to discuss them in the context not only of his legitimate sensitivity but also of narrative conventions and of Kingston's agendas. Still, his fears of the "wrong impressions" created by the book never went completely away, and I'm sure he could have gone on and on in dialogue with Kingston's books and interviews. Most conflicted was the young Chinese American woman who was an English major (and a creative writer as well), and who responded in two radically different ways:

10. Wendy Ho, while acknowledging that Kingston, Tan, and Ng could be narrowly and reductively classified as sentimental or as "women's" writers and thus trivialized, and while likewise acknowledging their books' potential as exotic "chic," writes of the ways these writers contributed not only to the reading pleasure of Asian American women, but also to their lives. She describes the outpouring of stories and tears by the Asian American female actors at the casting of the movie of *The Joy Luck Club,* and quotes from letters all three authors have received from readers acknowledging their strong identification with their books (*In Her Mother's House,* 49–55).

11. Chin, "Come All Ye Asian American Writers," 25–26, 29.

as a disturbed Chinese daughter and as an appreciative literature and writing student.

In all of these responses, identification plays a part, and the experience can be enlightening, disturbing, empowering, threatening, healing, or all of the above. The student who found *Fifth Chinese Daughter* upsetting was one of the quietest students in my very talkative Asian American literature class. In my office she confessed to her discomfort with the course: "I may not be ready yet," was how she put it. Jade Snow Wong was "too close." To her own surprise, tears welled up and began to get away from her, and then we—mainly I—talked (she preferred neither to talk nor to end our conversation). I told her about other students like her, and about the value they found in taking the option to write one of their papers in an autobiographical mode. End of conversation; but her next paper was a beautiful narrative about herself, her "identity" conflicts and her father, recently deceased. After I returned her A paper, she came to my office to tell me, "That was a hard essay to write," but would I be willing to read a longer version some time (what a question!)—there was so much more she wanted to include. This time, she walked out smiling.

In Chapter 2 we observed how protagonists in texts confront mirrors; as readers, it is we who confront the mirror: not the mirror *in* the text, but the text as mirror. And what is it we see? On one level, we may see aspects of our selves or our situations "mirrored" in the book. If we share the culture of the protagonist, we may feel better understood, or, as we have seen, more angry, more protective, more hostile to what may be a negative portrayal. And yet whatever truth or distortion there may be in the (re)presentation, it is close to us and personally affecting. But when we are not in the same minority culture, or even more removed—not in any minority culture at all—the identification triggers an altogether different kind of recognition: surprise that there can be any identification with this book at all. This other kind of person is not one I could ever have imagined as "I"; this life seems to have so little in common with mine, and yet there *is* something of me here. This "other" and I are not as "other" as I had thought. Such recognition is of an altogether different order. It is the recognition of similarity in difference that we have seen throughout this book.

But on another level, the text mirrors us as *readers*. Not just in the act of identifying, but also in reaction to a text, a reader may, in Proust's words, "discern what, without this book, he would perhaps never have perceived in himself." What a reading experience suddenly forces us to confront may be our own ignorance—of other cultures, of our own—or perhaps our un-acknowledged need for likeness and community. It may be our parochial-ism, or unconscious prejudices about others; it may be remembrance of hurts long ago thoughtlessly inflicted—on "others," or on our own. It may be embarrassment and self-hatred we have never before acknowledged, or a new appreciation of our own traditions. At best, such jolts of percep-tion do not simply "shatter" previous "frames of reference," but also en-large, modify, and reconstruct them to include the new self-knowledge, the new "relationships" we have formed, with and through texts.

We speak of entering a text, constructing it, seeing ourselves reflected. What a mixture of metaphors! To reconcile them I visualize a scene that I wish I could capture in oils, but can only attempt to paint in words: I see a figure—me—standing at a doorway. The upper half of the door is made of glass, through which I see a roomful of people—men and women, boys and girls, of all types and shades. One wall is darkened floor to ceiling by shelves crammed with books. Before the door is opened to let me in, be-fore I step over the threshold, I look closely through the glass, and in it I see not only those people on the other side, but, as if superimposed, a faint reflection of myself. No impressionist painting this, no abstraction or blurred edges: each face retains its individual features; every outfit, every expression, is clear. At the same time, so is mine. The door has remained a door and the glass has remained transparent, even as it has also become mirrorlike. And I realize this phenomenon is possible not only because I am willing to come close to the threshold, but also because of that wall—that wall of books.

Bibliography

Aarons, Victoria. *A Measure of Memory: Storytelling and Identity in American Jewish Fiction*. Athens: University of Georgia Press, 1996.

Abrams, M. H. *The Mirror and the Lamp: Romantic Theory and the Critical Tradition*. London: Oxford University Press, 1953.

Albright, Daniel. "Literary and Psychological Models of the Self." In *The Remembering Self: Construction and Accuracy in the Self-Narrative*, ed. Ulric Neisser and Robyn Fivush. Cambridge: Cambridge University Press, 1994.

Allen, Walter. Afterword to *Call It Sleep*, by Henry Roth. New York: Avon Books, 1962.

Alter, Robert. *After the Tradition: Essays on Modern Jewish Writing*. New York: Dutton, 1969.

Antin, Mary. *The Promised Land*. Boston: Houghton, 1912.

Anzaldua, Gloria. *Borderlands/La Frontera: The New Mestiza*. San Francisco: Aunt Lute Books, 1987.

Aristotle. *Poetics*. Trans. S. H. Butcher. New York: Hill & Wang, 1961.

Bakhtin, Mikhail. *The Dialogic Imagination: Four Essays*. Trans. Caryl Emerson and Michael Holquist. Austin: University of Texas Press, 1981.

Beaujour, Elizabeth Klosty. "Bilingualism." In *The Garland Companion to Vladimir Nabokov*, ed. Vladimir E. Alexandrov, 37–43. New York: Garland, 1995.

Benjamin, Walter. "The Storyteller." In *Illuminations*, trans. Harry Zohn. New York: Schocken, 1969.

Benveniste, Emile. *Problems in General Linguistics*. Trans. Mary Elizabeth Meek. Coral Gables: University of Miami Press, 1971.

Bergland, Betty. "Postmodernism and the Autobiographical Subject: Reconstructing the 'Other.'" In *Autobiography and Postmodernism,* ed. Kathleen Ashley, Leigh Gilmore, and Gerald Peters. Amherst: University of Massachusetts Press, 1994.

Berthoff, Ann E. *The Making of Meaning: Metaphors, Models, and Maxims for Writing Teachers.* Upper Montclair, N.J.: Boynton/Cook, 1981.

Beverly, John. "The Margin at the Center: On *Testimonio.*" In *De/colonizing the Subject: The Politics of Gender in Women's Autobiography,* ed. Sidonie Smith and Julia Watson. Minneapolis: University of Minnesota Press, 1992.

Boelhower, William. *Through a Glass Darkly: Ethnic Semiosis in American Literature.* New York: Oxford University Press, 1987.

Brontë, Charlotte. *Jane Eyre.* Ed. Jane Jack and Margaret Smith. London: Oxford University Press, 1969.

Brown, H. Douglas. *Principles of Language Learning and Teaching.* 2d ed. Englewood Cliffs, N.J.: Prentice-Hall, 1987.

Brown, James W. *Fictional Meals and Their Function in the French Novel, 1789–1848.* Toronto: University of Toronto Press, 1984.

Bruner, Jerome. *Actual Minds, Possible Worlds.* Cambridge: Harvard University Press, 1986.

———. "Life as Narrative." *Social Research* 54 (Spring 1987): 11–32.

———. "The Remembered Self." In *The Remembering Self: Construction and Accuracy in the Self-Narrative,* ed. Ulric Neisser and Robyn Fivush. Cambridge: Cambridge University Press, 1994.

Budick, Emily. *Blacks and Jews in Literary Conversation.* Cambridge: Cambridge University Press, 1998.

Burstein, Janet Handler. *Writing Mothers, Writing Daughters: Tracing the Maternal in Stories by American Jewish Women.* Urbana: University of Illinois Press, 1996.

Cahan, Abraham. *The Education of Abraham Cahan.* 1926. Trans. Leon Stein, Abraham P. Conan, and Lynn Davison. Philadelphia: Jewish Publication Society of America, 1969.

———. *The Rise of David Levinsky.* 1917. Reprint, New York: Penguin Books, 1993.

Chang, Joan Chiung-huei. *Transforming Chinese American Literature: A Study of History, Sexuality, and Ethnicity.* New York: Peter Lang, 2000.

Chang, Lan Samantha. *Hunger: A Novella and Stories.* New York: W. W. Norton, 1998.

Chernin, Kim. *The Flame Bearers.* New York: Random House, 1986.

————. *In My Father's Garden: A Daughter's Search for a Spiritual Life.* Chapel Hill: Algonquin Books, 1996.

————. *In My Mother's House: A Daughter's Story.* New York: Harper and Row, 1983.

————. *The Woman Who Gave Birth to Her Mother: Seven Stages of Change in Women's Lives.* New York: Viking, 1998.

Cheung, King-Kok. *Articulate Silences: Hisaye Yamamoto, Maxine Hong Kingston, Joy Kogawa.* Ithaca, N.Y.: Cornell University Press, 1993.

Chin, Frank. "Come All Ye Asian American Writers of the Real and the Fake." In *The Big Aiiieeeee! An Anthology of Chinese American and Japanese American Literature,* ed. Jeffery Paul Chan, Frank Chin, Lawson Fusao Inada, and Shawn Wong. New York: Meridian, 1991.

————. *Donald Duk.* Minneapolis: Coffee House Press, 1991.

Chiu, Lisa, Judith Oster, et al., eds. *The Immigrant Experience: Voices and Visions.* Cleveland: Case Western Reserve University, 1992.

Chodorow, Nancy. *The Reproduction of Mothering.* Berkeley: University of California Press, 1998.

Choy, Wayson. *The Jade Peony.* New York: St. Martin's Press, 1997.

Chu, Patricia P. *Assimilating Asians: Gendered Strategies of Authorship in Asian America.* Durham, N.C.: Duke University Press, 2000.

Cisneros, Sandra. *The House on Mango Street.* New York: Vintage, 1989.

Clayton, Jay. *The Pleasures of Babel: Contemporary American Literature and Theory.* New York: Oxford University Press, 1993.

Coates, Paul. *The Double and the Other: Identity as Ideology in Post-romantic Fiction.* Houndsmill and London: Macmillan, 1988.

Conway, Jill Ker. *When Memory Speaks.* New York: Alfred A. Knopf, 1998.

Cooper, Alan. *Philip Roth and the Jews.* Albany: SUNY Press, 1996.

Corder, S. P. "Language Learner Language." In *Understanding Second and Foreign Language Learning: Issues and Approaches,* ed. Jack C. Richards. Rowley, Mass.: Newbury, 1978.

Couser, G. Thomas. *Altered Egos: Authority in American Autobiography.* New York: Oxford University Press, 1989.

Diamant, Naomi. "Linguistic Universes in Henry Roth's *Call It Sleep.*" *Contemporary Literature* 27 (1986): 336–55.

Eakin, Paul John. *Fictions in Autobiography: Studies in the Art of Self-invention.* Princeton: Princeton University Press, 1985.

————. *How Our Lives Become Stories: Making Selves.* Ithaca, N.Y.: Cornell University Press, 1999.

Eco, Umberto. *The Role of the Reader: Explorations in the Semiotics of Texts.* Bloomington: Indiana University Press, 1979.

Ehrlich, Elizabeth. *Miriam's Kitchen: A Memoir*. New York: Penguin, 1998.

Eliot, T. S. "Four Quartets." In *The Complete Poems and Plays*. New York: Harcourt, Brace and Company, 1952.

Eng, Phoebe. *Warrior Lessons: An Asian American Woman's Journey into Power*. New York: Pocket Books, 1999.

Erikson, Erik H. *Identity: Youth and Crisis*. New York: Norton, 1968.

Ervin-Tripp, Susan M. "Interaction of Language, Topic, and Listener." *American Anthropologist* 66 (1964): 86–102.

Faigley, Lester. *Fragments of Rationality: Postmodernity and the Subject of Composition*. Pittsburgh: Pittsburgh University Press, 1992.

Far, Sui Sin. *Mrs. Spring Fragrance and Other Writings*. Urbana: University of Illinois Press, 1995.

Ferraro, Thomas J. *Ethnic Passages: Literary Immigrants in Twentieth-Century America*. Chicago: University of Chicago Press, 1993.

Fischer, Michael. "Ethnicity and the Post-modern Arts of Memory." In *Writing Culture: The Poetics and Politics of Ethnography*, ed. James Clifford and George Marcus, 194–233. Berkeley: University of California Press, 1986.

Fisher, Jerilyn. "Kim Chernin." In *Jewish American Women Writers: A Bio-Bibliographical and Critical Sourcebook*, ed. Ann R. Shapiro et al. Westport, Conn.: Greenwood Press, 1994.

Foer, Jonathan Safran. *Everything Is Illuminated*. Boston: Houghton Mifflin, 2002.

Folkenflik, Robert. "The Self as Other." In *The Culture of Autobiography: Constructions of Self-Representation*, ed. Robert Folkenflik. Stanford: Stanford University Press, 1993.

Foucault, Michel. "What Is an Author?" Trans. Josué Harari. In *The Critical Tradition: Classic Texts and Contemporary Trends*, ed. David A. Richter, 978–87. New York: Bedford/St. Martin's, 1989.

Freud, Sigmund. "The 'Uncanny.'" 1919. In *On Creativity and the Unconscious: Papers on the Psychology of Art, Literature, Love, and Religion*, ed. Benjamin Nelson. New York: Harper and Row, 1958.

Frost, Robert. "The Figure a Poem Makes." In *Collected Poems, Prose, and Plays*, ed. Richard Poirier and Mark Richardson. New York: Library of America, 1995.

———. "A Letter to *The Amherst Student*." In *Collected Poems, Prose, and Plays*, ed. Richard Poirier and Mark Richardson. New York: Library of America, 1995.

———. *Selected Letters of Robert Frost*. Ed. Lawrance Thompson. New York: Holt, Rinehart, and Winston, 1964.

Furman, Andrew. *Contemporary Jewish American Writers and the Multicultural Dilemma: Return of the Exiled.* Syracuse: Syracuse University Press, 2000.

———. "Immigrant Dreams and Civic Promises: Identity in Early Jewish American Literature and Gish Jen's *Mona in the Promised Land.*" *MELUS* 25 (Spring 2000): 209–26.

Gale, Xin Liu. *Teachers, Discourses, and Authority in the Postmodern Classroom.* Albany: SUNY Press, 1996.

Gardner, R. C., and W. E. Lambert. *Attitudes and Motivation in Second Language Learning.* Rowley, Mass.: Newbury, 1972.

Garner, Shirley Nelson. "Breaking Silence: *The Woman Warrior.*" In *The Intimate Critique: Autobiographical Literary Criticism,* ed. Diane Friedman, Olivia Fey, and Frances Murphy Zaubar. Durham, N.C.: Duke University Press, 1993.

Gergen, Kenneth J. "Mind, Text, Society: Self-Memory in Social Context." In *The Remembering Self: Construction and Accuracy in the Self-Narrative,* ed. Ulric Neisser and Robyn Fivush. Cambridge: Cambridge University Press, 1994.

Gilligan, Carol. *In a Different Voice: Psychological Theory and Women's Development.* Cambridge: Harvard University Press, 1982.

Gilman, Sander L. *Jewish Self-Hatred: Anti-Semitism and the Hidden Language of the Jews.* Baltimore: Johns Hopkins University Press, 1986.

Gilmore, Leigh. *Autobiographics: A Feminist Theory of Women's Self-Representation.* Ithaca, N.Y.: Cornell University Press, 1994.

Girgus, Sam. *The New Covenant: Jewish Writers and the American Idea.* Chapel Hill: University of North Carolina Press, 1984.

Gold, Herbert. *Family: A Novel in the Form of a Memoir.* New York: Arbor House, 1981.

———. *Fathers.* 1962. Reprint, New York: Primus/Donald I. Fine, 1966.

Goldberg, Myla. *Bee Season.* New York: Alfred A. Knopf, 2001.

Gornick, Vivian. *Fierce Attachments.* New York: Simon and Schuster, 1987.

———. Introduction to *How I Found America,* by Anzia Yezierska, ed. Vivian Gornick. New York: Persea Books, 1991.

Grierson, Bruce. "Spellbound." *New York Times Magazine,* September 1, 2002, pp. 48–51, 56–57.

Grinberg, Leon, and Rebeca Grinberg. *Psychoanalytic Perspectives on Migration and Exile.* Trans. Nancy Festinger. New Haven: Yale University Press, 1984.

Grosjean, François G. *Life with Two Languages: An Introduction to Bilingualism.* Cambridge: Harvard University Press, 1982.

———. "Living with Two Languages and Two Cultures." In *Cultural and Language Diversity and the Deaf Experience,* ed. Ila Parasnis. Cambridge: Cambridge University Press, 1996.

Guiora, Alexander Z., et al. "Language. Personality and Culture or the Whorfian Hypothesis Revisited." In *On TESOL '81,* ed. Mary Hines and William Rutherford. Washington: Teachers of English to Speakers of Other Languages, 1981.

Gusdorf, Georges. "Conditions and Limits of Autobiography." Trans. James Olney. In *Autobiography: Essays Theoretical and Critical,* ed. James Olney. Princeton: Princeton University Press, 1980.

Hall, Edward T. *The Silent Language.* New York: Anchor/Doubleday, 1973.

Hallam, Clifford. "The Double as Incomplete Self: Toward a Definition of Doppelganger." In *Fearful Symmetry: Doubles and Doubling in Literature and Film,* ed. Eugene J. Crook. Tallahassee: University of Florida Press, 1981.

Hamers, Josiane F. "Cognitive and Language Development of Bilingual Children." In *Cultural and Language Diversity and the Bilingual Experience,* ed. Ila Parasnis. Cambridge: Cambridge University Press, 1996.

Hampl, Patricia. *I Could Tell You Stories: Sojourns in the Land of Memory.* New York: W. W. Norton, 1999.

Harding, D. W. "Psychological Processes in the Reading of Fiction." *British Journal of Aesthetics* 2 (1962): 133–47.

Harper, Phillip Brian. *Framing the Margins: The Social Logic of Postmodern Culture.* New York: Oxford University Press, 1994.

Harshav, Benjamin. "The Semiotics of Yiddish Communication." In *What Is Jewish Literature?* ed. Hana Wirth-Nesher. Philadelphia: Jewish Publication Society, 1994.

Heller, Agnes. "Death of the Subject?" In *Constructions of the Self,* ed. George Levine. New Brunswick, N.J.: Rutgers University Press, 1992.

Henriksen, Louise Levitas. *Anzia Yezierska: A Writer's Life.* New Brunswick, N.J.: Rutgers University Press, 1988.

Hirsch, Marianne. *The Mother/Daughter Plot: Narrative, Psychoanalysis, Feminism.* Bloomington: Indiana University Press, 1989.

Ho, Wendy. *In Her Mother's House: The Politics of Asian American Mother-Daughter Writing.* Walnut Creek, Calif.: AltaMira Press, 1999.

Hoffman, Eva. *Lost in Translation: A Life in a New Language.* New York: E. P. Dutton, 1989.

Hokenson, Jan Welsh. "Intercultural Autobiography." *a/b: Auto/Biography Studies* 10 (1995): 92–113.

Holland, Norman N. *The Brain of Robert Frost: A Cognitive Approach to Literature*. New York: Routledge, 1988.

hooks, bell. *Talking Back: Thinking Feminist, Thinking Black*. Boston: South End Press, 1989.

Horowitz, Sara. "Jewish Studies as Oppositional? Gettin' Mighty Lonely Out Here." In *Styles of Cultural Opposition*, ed. Philip Goldstein, 152–64. Newark: University of Delaware Press, 1994.

———. "Portnoy's Sister—Who's Complaining? Contemporary Jewish-American Women's Writing on Judaism." *Jewish Book Annual* 51 (1994): 26–41.

Howe, Irving. "The Self in Literature." In *Constructions of the Self*, ed. George Levine. New Brunswick, N.J.: Rutgers University Press, 1992.

———. *World of Our Fathers: The Journey of the East European Jews to America and the Life They Made*. New York: Harcourt, Brace, Jovanovich, 1976.

———, ed. *Jewish-American Stories*. New York: New American Library, 1977.

Iser, Wolfgang. *The Act of Reading: A Theory of Aesthetic Response*. Baltimore: Johns Hopkins University Press, 1978.

JanMohamed, Abdul R., and David Lloyd, eds. *The Nature and Context of Minority Discourse*. New York: Oxford University Press, 1990.

Jen, Gish. Interview. In *Words Matter: Conversations with Asian American Writers*, ed. King-Kok Cheung. Honolulu: University of Hawaii Press, 2000.

———. *Mona in the Promised Land*. New York: Alfred A. Knopf, 1996.

———. *Typical American*. Boston: Houghton Mifflin, 1991.

Kang, Younghill. *East Goes West: The Making of an Oriental Yankee*. 1937. Reprint, New York: Kaya Production, 1997.

Kazin, Alfred. "The Self as History: Reflections on Autobiography." In *Telling Lives: The Biographer's Art*, ed. Marc Pachter. Washington: New Republic Books, 1979.

Kearns, Doris. "Angles of Vision." In *Telling Lives: The Biographer's Art*, ed. Marc Pachter. Washington: New Republic Books, 1979.

Keppler, C. F. *The Literature of the Second Self*. Tucson: University of Arizona Press, 1972.

Kessler-Harris, Alice. Foreword to *Bread Givers*, by Anzia Yezierska. New York: Persea, 1999.

Kim, Elaine. *Asian American Literature: An Introduction to the Writings and Their Social Context*. Philadelphia: Temple University Press, 1982.

———. "Defining Asian American Realities through Literature." In *The Nature and Context of Minority Discourse,* ed. Abdul R. JanMohamed and David Lloyd. New York: Oxford University Press, 1990.

Kim, Thomas W. "'For a paper son, paper is blood': Subjectivation and Authenticity in Fae Myenne Ng's *Bone.*" *MELUS* 24:4 (1999): 41–56.

Kingston, Maxine Hong. *China Men.* New York: Alfred A. Knopf, 1980.

———. *The Woman Warrior: Memoirs of a Girlhood among Ghosts.* New York: Alfred A. Knopf, 1976.

Krashen, Stephen D. *The Input Hypothesis: Issues and Implications.* London: Longman Group, 1995.

Kundera, Milan. "The Great Return." *New Yorker,* May 20, 2002, p. 96.

Lawrence, Karen R. "Roth's *Call It Sleep:* Modernism on the Lower East Side." In *New Essays on* Call It Sleep, ed. Hana Wirth-Nesher. Cambridge: Cambridge University Press, 1996.

Lee, Gus. *China Boy: A Novel.* New York: Dutton, 1991.

———. *Honor and Duty.* New York: Knopf, 1994.

Levine, George, ed. *Constructions of the Self.* New Brunswick, N.J.: Rutgers University Press, 1992.

Lim, Shirley Geok-lin. "The Tradition of Chinese American Women's Life Stories: Thematics of Race and Gender in Jade Snow Wong's *Fifth Chinese Daughter* and Maxine Hong Kingston's *Woman Warrior.*" In *American Women's Autobiography: Fea(s)ts of Memory,* ed. Margo Culley. Madison: University of Wisconsin Press, 1992.

Linde, Charlotte. *Life Stories: The Creation of Coherence.* New York: Oxford University Press, 1993.

Ling, Amy. *Between Worlds: Women Writers of Chinese Ancestry.* New York: Pergamon Press, 1990.

Lionnet, Françoise. *Autobiographical Voices: Race, Gender, Self-Portraiture.* Ithaca, N.Y.: Cornell University Press, 1989.

Lowe, Pardee. *Father and Glorious Descendant.* Boston: Little, Brown, and Co., 1943.

Lu, Min-zhan. "From Silence to Words: Writing as Struggle." *College English* 49 (1987): 437–48.

Lvovich, Natasha. *The Multilingual Self: An Inquiry into Language Learning.* Mahwah, N.J.: Lawrence Erlbaum, 1997.

Lyons, Bonnie. *Henry Roth: The Man and His Work.* New York: Cooper Square Publishers, 1976.

Ma, Sheng-mei. *Immigrant Subjectivities in Asian American and Asian Diaspora Literatures.* Albany: SUNY Press, 1998.

Mandel, Barrett J. "Full of Life Now." In *Autobiography: Essays Theoretical and Critical,* ed. James Olney. Princeton: Princeton University Press, 1980.

Mar, Elaine M. *Paper Daughter: A Memoir.* New York: HarperCollins, 1999.

Mark, Diane Lei Lin, and Ginger Chih. *A Place Called Chinese America.* Dubuque, Iowa: Kendall/Hunt, 1982.

Mason, Mary G. "The Other Voice: Autobiographies of Women Writers." In *Autobiography: Essays Theoretical and Critical,* ed. James Olney. Princeton: Princeton University Press, 1980.

Materassi, Mario. "Shifting Urbanscape: Roth's 'Private' New York." In *New Essays on* Call It Sleep, ed. Hana Wirth-Nesher. Cambridge: Cambridge University Press, 1996.

McHale, Brian. "Henry Roth in Nighttown, or, Containing *Ulysses.*" In *New Essays on* Call It Sleep, ed. Hana Wirth-Nesher. Cambridge: Cambridge University Press, 1996.

Miller, Arthur. *Salesman in Beijing.* New York: Viking, 1984.

Min, Pyong Gap, ed. *Asian Americans: Contemporary Issues and Trends.* Thousand Oaks, Calif.: Sage Press, 1995.

Mintz, Lawrence E. "Humor and Ethnic Stereotypes in Vaudeville and Burlesque." *MELUS* 21:4 (Winter 1996): 19–28.

Neisser, Ulric. "Self-narratives: True and False." In *The Remembering Self: Construction and Accuracy in the Self-narrative,* ed. Ulric Neisser and Robyn Fivush. Cambridge: Cambridge University Press, 1994.

Ng, Fae Myenne. *Bone.* New York: Hyperion, 1993.

Nowottny, Winifred. *The Language Poets Use.* London: Athlone Press, 1962.

Olney, James. *Memory and Narrative: The Weave of Life Writing.* Chicago: University of Chicago Press, 1998.

Olsen, Tillie. "Tell Me a Riddle." In *Tell Me a Riddle.* 1956. Reprint, New York: Delta/Seymour Lawrence, 1989.

Olshen, Barry N. "Subject, Persona, and Self in the Theory of Autobiography." In *a/b: Auto/Biography Studies* 10 (1995): 5–16.

Oster, Judith. "'God Loves Stories,' Jews Love Questions: I. B. Singer Questions God." *Journal of the Short Story in English* (Fall 1999): 11–24.

———. *Toward Robert Frost: The Reader and Poet.* Athens: University of Georgia Press, 1991.

Ozick, Cynthia. *The Cannibal Galaxy.* New York: E. P. Dutton, 1984.

———. *The Puttermesser Papers.* New York: Random House, 1997.

Palij, Michael, and Doris Aaronson. "The Role of Language Background in Cognitive Processing." In *Cognitive Processing in Bilinguals,* ed.

Richard Jackson Harris. New York: Elsevier Science Publishing, 1992.

Perry, William C. *Forms of Intellectual and Ethical Development in the College Years: A Scheme.* New York: Holt, Rinehart, and Winston, 1970.

Pinsker, Sanford. *The Comedy That "Hoits": An Essay on the Fiction of Philip Roth.* Columbia: University of Missouri Press, 1975.

———. *Jewish American Fiction, 1917–1987.* New York: Twayne, 1992.

Ragland-Sullivan, Ellie. *Jacques Lacan and the Philosophy of Psychoanalysis.* Urbana: University of Illinois Press, 1986.

Rapoport, Nessa. "Summoned to the Feast." In *Writing Our Way Home: Contemporary Stories by American Jewish Writers,* ed. Ted Solotaroff and Nessa Rapoport. New York: Schocken, 1992.

Richards, Jack C. "Models of Language Use and Language Learning." In *Understanding Second and Foreign Language Learning: Issues and Approaches,* ed. Jack C. Richards. Rowley, Mass.: Newbury House, 1978.

———. "Second Language Learning." In *A Survey of Applied Linguistics,* ed. Ronald Wardaugh and H. Douglas Brown. Ann Arbor: University of Michigan Press, 1982.

Richardson, Susan B. "The Lessons of *Donald Duk.*" *MELUS* 24 (Winter 1999): 57–76.

Rodriguez, Richard. "Aria: A Memoir of a Bilingual Childhood." In *American Voices: Multicultural Literacy and Critical Thinking,* 2d ed., ed. Dolores LaGuardia and Hans P. Guth. Mountain View, Calif.: Mayfield Publishing, 1996. Originally published in *American Scholar,* 1981.

———. *Hunger of Memory: The Education of Richard Rodriguez.* New York: Bantam Books, 1982.

Rogers, Robert. *A Psychoanalytic Study of the Double in Literature.* Detroit: Wayne State University Press, 1970.

Rogin, Gilbert. "What Happens Next?" In *What Happens Next?* New York: Random House, 1971.

Rölvaag, O. E. *Peder Victorious: A Tale of the Pioneers Twenty Years Later.* 1929. Reprint, trans. Nora O. Solam and O. E. Rölvaag, Lincoln: University of Nebraska Press, 1957.

Rosenbaum, Thane, et al. "The Jewish Literary Revival." *Tikkun* 12:6 (November–December 1997), 33–51.

Rosenblatt, Louise M. *The Reader, the Text, the Poem: The Transactional Theory of the Literary Work.* Carbondale: Southern Illinois University Press, 1978.

Rosten, Leo [Leonard Q. Ross, pseud.]. *The Education of H*Y*M*A*N*

K*A*P*L*A*N. 1937. Reprint, San Diego: Harcourt Brace Jovanovich, Harvest, 1964.

Roth, Henry. *Call It Sleep.* 1934. Reprint, New York: Avon Books, 1962.

———. *From Bondage.* Vol. 3 of *Mercy of a Rude Stream.* New York: St. Martin's Press, 1996.

———. *Shifting Landscape.* New York: St. Martin's Press, 1987.

Roth, Philip. *American Pastoral.* Boston: Houghton Mifflin, 1997.

———. *The Counterlife.* New York: Penguin, 1986.

———. *Deception.* New York: Simon and Schuster, 1990.

———. *The Facts: A Novelist's Autobiography.* New York: Farrar, Straus, and Giroux, 1988.

———. *Goodbye, Columbus, and Five Short Stories.* 1959. Reprint, New York: Bantam, 1969.

———. *Operation Shylock: A Confession.* New York: Simon and Schuster, 1993.

———. *Patrimony: A True Story.* New York: Simon and Schuster, 1991.

———. *Portnoy's Complaint.* 1969. Reprint, New York: Bantam, 1970.

———. *Reading Myself and Others.* New York: Farrar, Straus, and Giroux, 1975.

———. *Shop Talk: A Writer and His Colleagues and Their Work.* Boston: Houghton Mifflin, 2001.

———. *Zuckerman Bound: A Trilogy and Epilogue.* New York: Farrar, Straus, and Giroux, 1985.

Schechner, Mark. *After the Revolution: Studies in Contemporary Jewish American Imagination.* Bloomington: Indiana University Press, 1987.

Schenck, Celeste. "All of a Piece." In *Life/Lines: Theorizing Women's Autobiography,* ed. Bella Brodski and Celeste Schenck. Ithaca, N.Y.: Cornell University Press, 1988.

Schumann, John H. "Social and Psychological Factors in Second Language Acquisition." In *Understanding Second and Foreign Language Learning,* ed. Jack C. Richards. Rowley, Mass.: Newbury House, 1978.

Schwartz, Lynne Sharon. "The Opiate of the People." In *Acquainted with the Night and Other Stories.* New York: Harper and Row, 1984.

Searles, George J., ed. *Conversations with Philip Roth.* Jackson: University Press of Mississippi, 1992.

See, Lisa. *On Gold Mountain: The One-Hundred-Year Odyssey of My Chinese-American Family.* New York: St. Martin's Press, 1995.

Selinker, Larry, and John T. Lamendella. "Fossilization in Second Language Learning." In *Readings on English as a Second Language: For*

Teachers and Teacher Trainees, 2d ed., ed. Kenneth Croft. Boston: Little, Brown, 1980.

Shapiro, Gerald, ed. *American Jewish Fiction: A Century of Stories.* Lincoln: University of Nebraska Press, 1998.

Siebenschuh, William R. "The Image of the Child and the Plot of *Jane Eyre.*" *Studies in the Novel* 8 (1976): 304–17.

Singh, Amritjit, Joseph Skerrett Jr., and Robert E. Hogan, eds. *Memory, Narrative, and Identity: New Essays in Ethnic American Literatures.* Boston: Northeastern University Press, 1998.

Skenazy, Paul, and Tera Martin, eds. *Conversations with Maxine Hong Kingston.* Jackson: University of Mississippi Press, 1998.

Smith, Paul. *Discerning the Subject.* Theory and History of Literature, vol. 55. Minneapolis: University of Minnesota Press, 1988.

Smith, Sidonie. *A Poetics of Women's Autobiography: Marginality and the Fictions of Self-representation.* Bloomington: Indiana University Press, 1987.

Sokoloff, Naomi. *Imagining the Child in Modern Jewish Fiction.* Baltimore: Johns Hopkins University Press, 1992.

Sollors, Werner. *Beyond Ethnicity: Consent and Descent in American Culture.* New York: Oxford University Press, 1986.

———. "'A world somewhere, somewhere else': Language, Nostalgic Mournfulness, and Immigrant Family Romance in *Call It Sleep.*" In *New Essays on* Call It Sleep, ed. Hana Wirth-Nesher. Cambridge: Cambridge University Press, 1996.

Solotaroff, Ted. "The Open Community." In *Writing Our Way Home: Contemporary Stories by American Jewish Writers,* ed. Ted Solotaroff and Nessa Rapoport. New York: Schocken, 1992.

Spacks, Patricia Meyer. *Imagining a Self: Autobiography and Novel in Eighteenth-Century England.* Cambridge: Harvard University Press, 1976.

Spence, Jonathan. *The Search for Modern China.* New York: W. W. Norton, 1990.

Steiner, George. "Unsentimental Education." *New Yorker,* August 15, 1977, 85–89.

Sternberg, Meir. "Polylingualism as Reality and Translation as Mimesis." *Poetics Today* 2 (1981): 221–39.

Stubbs, Katherine. Introduction to *Arrogant Beggar,* by Anzia Yezierska. Durham, N.C.: Duke University Press, 1996.

Summerfield, Geoffrey, and Judith Summerfield. *Texts and Contexts: A*

Contribution to the Theory and Practice of Teaching Composition. New York: Random House, 1986.

Swain, Merrill. "Home-school Language Switching." In *Understanding Second and Foreign Language Learning: Issues and Approaches,* ed. Jack C. Richards. Rowley, Mass.: Newbury House, 1978.

Takaki, Ronald. *Strangers from a Different Shore: A History of Asian Americans.* New York: Penguin, 1990.

Talese, Gay. "The Italian-American Voice: Where Is It?" In *American Identities: Contemporary Multicultural Voices,* ed. Robert Pack and Jay Parini. Hanover, N.H.: University Press of New England, 1994.

Tan, Amy. *The Hundred Secret Senses.* New York: G. P. Putnam, 1995.

———. *The Joy Luck Club.* 1989. New York: G. P. Putnam, 1989.

———. *The Kitchen God's Wife.* New York: G. P. Putnam, 1991.

———. "Mother Tongue." In *One World, Many Cultures,* ed. Stuart Hirschberg. New York: Macmillan, 1992.

Taylor, Charles. *Sources of the Self: The Making of Modern Identity.* Cambridge: Harvard University Press, 1989.

Tuchman, Gaye, and Harry Gene Levine. "New York Jews and Chinese Food: The Social Construction of an Ethnic Pattern." In *A Reader on Regional and Ethnic Foods,* ed. Barbara G. Shortridge and James R. Shortridge. Lanham, Md.: Rowman and Littlefield, 1998.

TuSmith, Bonnie. *All My Relatives: Community in Contemporary Ethnic American Literatures.* Ann Arbor: University of Michigan Press, 1994.

Uba, Laura. *Asian Americans: Personality Patterns, Identity, and Mental Health.* New York: Guilford, 1994.

Walker, Alice. *In Search of Our Mothers' Gardens: Womanist Prose.* San Diego: Harcourt, Brace & Co., 1983.

Walker, Nancy. "No Laughing Matter." In *American Women's Autobiography: Fea(s)ts of Memory,* ed. Margo Culley. Madison: University of Wisconsin Press, 1992.

Weidman, Jerome. "My Father Sits in the Dark." In *My Father Sits in the Dark and Other Selected Stories.* New York: Random House, 1961.

Weinberg, Sydney Stahl. *World of Our Mothers: The Lives of Jewish Immigrant Women.* Chapel Hill: University of North Carolina Press, 1988.

Welty, Eudora. *One Writer's Beginnings.* New York: Warner Books, 1984.

Whitman, Pearl. "My Pearly Doesn't Get C's." *Cleveland Jewish News,* December 22, 1989.

Wiesel, Elie. *The Gates of the Forest.* Trans. Frances Frenaye. New York: Holt, Rinehart, and Winston, 1966.

Wimmers, Inge Crosman. *Poetics of Reading: Approaches to the Novel.* Princeton: Princeton University Press, 1988.

Wirth-Nesher, Hana. "Between Mother Tongue and Native Language: Multilingualism in Henry Roth's *Call It Sleep.*" *Prooftexts* 10 (1990): 297–312.

———. "'Passing' in the Promised Land." Paper presented at a conference of the Israel Association of American Studies, Jerusalem and Tel Aviv, May 1999.

———, ed. *New Essays on* Call It Sleep. Cambridge: Cambridge University Press, 1996.

———, ed. *What Is Jewish Literature?* Philadelphia: Jewish Publication Society, 1994.

Wong, Jade Snow. *Fifth Chinese Daughter.* 1945. Reprint, New York: Harper and Row, 1950.

Wong, Morrison G. "Chinese Americans." In *Asian Americans: Contemporary Issues and Trends,* ed. Pyong Gap Min. Thousand Oaks, Calif.: Sage Press, 1995.

Wong, Sau-ling Cynthia. "Immigrant Autobiography: Some Questions of Definition and Approach." In *American Autobiography: Retrospect and Prospect,* ed. Paul John Eakin. Madison: University of Wisconsin Press, 1991.

———. *Reading Asian American Literature: From Necessity to Extravagance.* Princeton: Princeton University Press, 1993.

Woodward, Kathleen. "The Mirror Stage of Old Age." In *Memory and Desire: Aging, Literature, Psychoanalysis,* ed. Kathleen Woodward and Murray M. Schwartz. Bloomington: Indiana University Press, 1986.

Xu Xin et al., eds. *Encyclopedia Judaica, Chinese Edition.* Shanghai: Shanghai People's Publishing House, 1993.

Yezierska, Anzia. *All I Could Never Be.* New York: Brewer, Warren, and Putnam, 1932.

———. *Bread Givers.* 1925. Reprint, New York: Persea, 1999.

———. *How I Found America: Collected Stories of Anzia Yezierska.* Ed. Vivian Gornick. New York: Persea, 1991.

———. *Hungry Hearts.* 1920. Reprint, New York: Signet, 1996.

———. *Red Ribbon on a White Horse.* 1950. Reprint, New York: Persea, 1981.

———. *Salome of the Tenements.* 1923. Reprint, Urbana: University of Illinois Press, 1995.

Yin, Xiao-huang. *Chinese American Literature since the 1850s.* Urbana: University of Illinois Press, 2000.

Zia, Helen. *Asian American Dreams: The Emergence of an American People.* New York: Farrar, Straus, and Giroux, 2000.

Index

Abrams, M. H., *30n19*

Absence: of family members, 234; in *Bone,* 239; and loss of family member, 246

Adolescents: and language ego, 66; and biculturality, 66–67; and dating in Hoffman, 78; in *Fathers,* 148, 150–51

Albright, Daniel, 230

Alger, Horatio, 21–22

Alienation: in postwar literature, 23; in Kingston, 152

American Dream, 21

Americanization: in schools, 169–70; in *Patrimony,* 219

American Pastoral (Philip Roth), 156–62; hungers, 156–57; desire to belong, 159–61; self-creation, 161–62

Antin, Mary, 171–72, 211; education of, 191

Anti-Semitism: in personal experience, 11–12; in *Fathers,* 151; in *The Cannibal Galaxy,* 174–75; in *The Counterlife,* 224–25; in Communist Russia, 247

Anzaldua, Gloria, 89

Aristotle: *Poetics,* 29

Audience: importance of, 56; importance of telling, 245, 248, 250–51; importance of to teller, 250; reader as, 254

Autobiography: as distinguished from self-portrait, 32; and self-construction in Hoffman, 41–42; relational,

208; relational as gendered or cultural, 208–9; as lived, 210–12; and genre blurring, 212–13; vs. fiction, 214–15, *215n19,* 217; vs. privacy, 219–20; as salvation, 221, *221n28;* and life, 229–30; and desire for reconciliation, 232–33; as establishing the self, 233; and importance of audience, 233–34, 254. *See also* Life writing; Relational writing

Bakhtin, Mikhail, *72n21, 78n24,* 85

Bellow, Saul, 23

Benjamin, Walter, 142–43

Benveniste, Emile, 55–56; on "I," ego, subjectivity, 44, *44nn14,15*

Bergland, Betty, 45

Biblical topoi, 211

Bicultural(s): definition of, 59–60; conflicts and difficulties of, 60; and new ideas, 66–67

Bilingualism: and identity, 58–59; research on, 61; and personality/behavior, 61–63; advantages of, 67–68, *68n14;* and class, 88–89

Bone (Ng), 237–39; absence, 234; family vs. blood ties, 237–38; identity through papers, 238; narrative structure, 239

Bruner, Jerome, 208, 212, 229, 256

Burstein, Janet Handler, 213, *248n52*

Cahan, Abraham, 175–76: education of, 192; on bicultural education,

278

Index

Cahan, Abraham (*cont.*)
193–94. See also *Rise of David Levinsky, The*
Call It Sleep (Henry Roth), 107–21; mirrors, 40; culture-bound language, 97–98; child as focalizer, 107, 107*n39;* languages, 107, 110; sounds, 108, 109–10; coal symbolism, 111; Isaiah's call to prophecy, 111; Passover seder, 111, 112*n43;* narrative technique, 111–15, 114*n44;* voices, 112; identity confusion, 113–14; unity, 115; voices, 115; religious symbolism, 116; fragmentation, 116–17, 114*n44;* education, 192
Chang, Joan Chiung-huei, 252*n58*
Chang, Lan Samantha: "The Unforgetting," 154–56
Chernin, Kim: *In My Mother's House,* 245–51; *In My Father's Garden,* 247*n50; The Flame Bearers,* 247*n50; The Woman Who Gave Birth to Her Mother,* 250
Chernin, Rose: Communist, 245–46
Cheung, King-Kok, 103, 244, 244–45*n46*
Chin, Frank, 260; and Jeffery Paul Chan, 46. See also *Donald Duk*
China: Jews in, 6; Judaic studies in, 7
China Boy (Lee), 234–37; language, 85–86; mothers, 234–35; father figures, 236–37
China Men (Kingston): scholar father, 182–83
Chinese (language), 100
Chinese Americans: similarities to Jews, 5–6
Chodorow, Nancy, 208, 208*n3*
Choy, Wayson. See *Jade Peony, The*
Chu, Patricia, 101*n28*
Cisneros, Sandra: *The House on Mango Street,* 206
Coates, Paul: on doubles, 49
Code-switching: in texts, 93, 96–101; among bilinguals, 95–96; and reader response, 96–97; vs. translation, 97
Cooper, Alan, 55*n35,* 216, 221, 226
Counterlife, The (Philip Roth), 222–27; writers, 220; importance of circum-

cision, 222; home, for Jews, 224; anti-Semitism, 224–25
Culture: Hoffman as observer of, 78

Discontinuity, Jewish, 151–52
Donald Duk (Chin), 162–68; Chinese and railroad, 162–63, 164–66; as "seder," 163, 167
Doubles: in *The Woman Warrior,* 46, 49–51; in "Eli, the Fanatic," 46, 52–55; aspects of, 48–51

Eakin, Paul John, 207–8, 245, 247*n51*
Education: desire for, 171–72; opportunity, 171–72; value to cultures, 172–74; in *China Men,* 173, 182–83; secular, value of, 174; conflicts in, 174, 191–92; Cahan's, 175–76; in *The Rise of David Levinsky,* 176, 184–88; in *Typical American,* 176–77; on Lower East Side, 178; importance of, to Chinese, 179–82; in *Mona in the Promised Land,* 181; parental pressure, 181, 189–90; Imperial Examination, 182; desire for, in Yezierska, 183–84; importance of, in Cahan, 185–87, 187*n29;* idealized, 188, 190–91; teachers, in Cahan, 192; bicultural, in Cahan, 193; and separation from family, 194–95; in *The Woman Warrior,* 195–96; in Yezierska, 196; and Chinese women, 197, 197*n39;* conflicts in Jade Snow Wong, 197–99; conflicts in philosophies of, 198–204; William Perry's studies of, 199–200, 200*nn41,42,* 202*n43;* student conflicts in philosophies of, 200–203
"Eli, the Fanatic" (Philip Roth): doubles in, 52–55
Eng, Phoebe, 20*n8,* 181–82, 253
Erikson, Erik: on identity, 44, 45*n16*
Ervin-Tripp, Susan: bilingual research, 16, 61
Ethnicity: defense of own, 16
Exoticism, 19

Facts, The (Philip Roth), 214–16; ethnic loyalty in, 15*n2*

Permissions

Chapter 2 appeared in slightly different form in *MELUS* 23:4 (Winter 1998): 59–85, and is reprinted here with permission.

Excerpts from "The Unforgetting," from *Hunger* by Lan Samantha Chang. Copyright © 1998 by Lan Samantha Chang. Used by permission of W. W. Norton & Company, Inc., and The Wylie Agency (UK) Ltd.

Excerpts from *Fathers* by Herbert Gold. Published by Arbor House. Reprinted by permission of Curtis Brown, Ltd. Copyright © 1962, 1964, 1965, 1966 by Herbert Gold.

Excerpts from *Lost in Translation* by Eva Hoffman, copyright © 1989 by Eva Hoffman. Used by permission of Dutton, a division of Penguin Putnam Inc.

Excerpts from *The Woman Warrior: Memoirs of a Girlhood among Ghosts* by Maxine Hong Kingston, copyright © 1975, 1976 by Maxine Hong Kingston. Used by permission of Alfred A. Knopf, a division of Random House, Inc., and A. M. Heath & Co. Ltd.

Excerpts from *Call It Sleep* by Henry Roth. Copyright © 1934, renewed © 1962 by Henry Roth. Reprinted by permission of Farrar, Straus and Giroux, LLC.

Excerpts from *American Pastoral* by Philip Roth. Copyright © 1987 by Philip Roth. Reprinted by permission of Houghton Mifflin Company. All rights reserved. In the United Kingdom, published by Jonathan Cape; excerpts reprinted by permission of The Random House Group Ltd.

Excerpts from "Eli, the Fanatic," from *Goodbye, Columbus* by Philip Roth. Copyright © 1959, renewed 1987 by Philip Roth. Reprinted by permission of Houghton Mifflin Company. All rights reserved.

Excerpt from "My Pearly Doesn't Get C's," by Pearl Whitman, reprinted from *Cleveland Jewish News,* December 22, 1989.